NOT FOR TOURISTS™ Guide to Manhattan

D1231021

Happy Mazza Media LLC New York

2002

published and designed by:

Happy Mazza Media LLC

NFT_{TM}- NOT FOR TOURISTS_{TM}- GUIDE TO MANHATTAN 2002

www.notfortourists.com

Concept by
Jane Pirone

Information Design
Jane Pirone
Rob Tallia

Editor
Jane Pirone

Managing Editor
Rob Tallia

Writing and Editing
Jane Pirone
Diana Pizzari
Rob Tallia

Database Design
Scot Covey

Graphic Design / Production
Sue Yuen Beh
Scot Covey
Ng Wing Yan
Aaron Rodriguez

Neighborhood Editors
Krikor Daglian
Bill Hahn
Lulu Lolo
Skipp Porteous
Steve Sonkin
Diana Wienbroer

Research / Data Entry
Jodie Ousley
Diana Pizzari

Very Special Thanks
Jodie Ousley
Diana Pizzari

Printed in China
ISBN# 0-9672303-4-9 $16.95

Every effort has been made to ensure that the information in this book is as up-to-date as possible at press time. However, many details are liable to change—as we have learned. The publishers can not accept responsibility for any consequences arising from use of this book.

Dear **NFT**™ User:

First of all, we'd like to thank all those folks who have purchased and commented on either the 2000 or 2001 editions of Not For Tourists-Guide to Manhattan. Your feedback has simply made **NFT**™ a better book.

Second, we love the idea that since we update **NFT**™'s listings every year, we have the chance (or the excuse) to fix and/or re-design things that have annoyed us. So, for 2002, we've worked on some of those things, including a newly-designed foldout map of the subway system. Additionally, we've added a 6-page detailed list of selected restaurants on pp. 202-207. This new listing gives much more information, including pricing and a description, of the restaurants that we've selected for each neighborhood. We've also added an alphabetical list of hotels, a two-page directory on Gay and Lesbian information, and (at the 11th hour), added the new subway line information to the back of the book (unfortunately, we didn't have enough time to add it in to the grid pages themselves...we'll do that in 2003).

On a happy note, we wanted to mention that **NFT**™ has won a *PRINT* Magazine design award. **NFT**™ will be highlighted in *PRINT*'s Regional Design Annual due out in September 2001. Needless to say, we're very excited about this prestigious award. We also wanted to thank WNYC, and especially Brian Lehrer and Abby Lovinger, for allowing us to take part in their February and June 2001 fund drives. We enjoyed our interviews with Brian during "On the Line," and we hope to continue to work with them in the future.

We'd also like to thank some of our new "neighborhood editors" for providing wonderful feedback—especially Krikor Daglian (grid 5), Steve Sonkin (grid 13), and Diane Wienbroer & Skipp Porteous (grid 14). These **NFT**™ users went above and beyond the call of duty to provide us with absolutely up-to-date and relevant information on their neighborhoods. If anyone else is interested in becoming a neighborhood editor, we're more than happy to hear from you—simply contact us at our website, www.notfortourists.com.

Finally, as always, the general plea—if something is not in **NFT**™ (that you think should be), or if we've claimed something exists that no longer does, we want to know about it. And while we've made the best possible effort to make sure that *x* store really is in *y* location, if we've placed it wrong this time around, tell us about it and we'll get it right next year. Check out the handy on-line comment form on our website, www.notfortourists.com, for submitting comments, suggestions, and corrections to us.

Here's hoping you find what you need,

Jane Pirone
Editor, NFT™**—Manhattan**
www.notfortourists.com

MANHATTAN NEIGHBORHOODS

Table of Contents

Financial District
Essentials

Financial District
Essentials

A thicket of skyscrapers mask an astounding amount of old, wonderful buildings in this area, such as Federal Hall, Trinity Church, the Cunard Building, and the Customs House. The American International Building, at 70 Pine Street, is the least-known great Art Deco building in the world.

$ ATMs

A • Apple • 88 Pine St.
At • Atlantic • 15 Maiden Lane
B • Bank of New York • 20 Broad St.
B • Bank of New York • 48 Wall St.
B • Bank of New York • 45 Wall St.
Bt • Bank of Tokyo • 100 Broadway
Ch • Chase • 4 New York Plaza
Ch • Chase • 14 Wall St.
Ch • Chase • 52 Broadway
Ch • Chase • 55 Water St.
Ch • Chase • 1 Chase Plaza
Ch • Chase • 5 WTC
Ch • Chase • 214 Broadway
Ch • Chase • 2 WTC
Ch • Chase • 20 Pine St.
Ci • Citibank • 120 Broadway
Ci • Citibank • 101 WTC Concourse
Ci • Citibank • 107 William St.
Ci • Citibank • 1 Broadway
Ci • Citibank • 111 Wall St.
Co • Commercial Bank • 183 Broadway
Ea • EAB • 120 Broadway
F • Fleet • 130 Liberty St.
F • Fleet • 150 Broadway
F • Fleet • 175 Water St.
Fu • Fuji • 2 WTC
G • Greenpoint • 55 Nassau St.
H • HSBC • 140 Broadway
H • HSBC • 70 Pine St.
H • HSBC • 5 WTC
H • HSBC • 212 Broadway
H • HSBC • 110 William St.
H • HSBC • 100 Maiden Lane
H • HSBC • World Trade Center
H • HSBC • 140 Broadway
R • Republic National • 26 Broadway

O Bagels

• Le Bagle Inc 2 • 25 John St.

H Hospital

• The Floating Hospital • Pier 11

★ Landmarks

• American International Building • 70 Pine St.
• Battery Maritime Building • 11 South St.
• Bowling Green • Broadway & State St.
• Cunard Building • 25 Broadway
• Customs House/Museum of the American Indian • 1 Bowling Green
• Federal Hall • 26 Wall St.
• New York Stock Exchange • 20 Broad St.
• South Street Seaport • South St.
• St. Paul's Chapel & Cemetery • B'way & Fulton St.
• The Federal Reserve Bank • 33 Liberty St.
• Trinity Church & Cemetery • B'way & Wall St.
• Vietnam Veterans Plz. • Coenties Slip & Water St.
• World Trade Center • World Trade Center

Marketplace

• Century 21 • 22 Cortlandt St.
• Jubilee Marketplace • 99 John St.
• South Street Seaport Marketplace, Pier 17 • 17 East River Pier

R 24 Hour Pharmacy

• Duane Reade • 7 WTC

Post Offices

• Bowling Green • 25 Broadway
• Church St. Station • 90 Church St.
• Peck Slip • 1 Peck Slip
• Wall Street • 73 Pine St.

S School

• Greater New York Chapter • 80 Maiden Lane

Financial District
Sundries / Entertainment

True to the mayor's prediction, downtown is becoming a more appealing place to live, thanks to places such as the 24-hour Jubilee market on John St. It's exciting to actually see some (a few, at least) people walking around past 7 p.m.

24-Hour Copy Centers

- Kinko's • 100 Wall St.
- National Reproductions • 130 Cedar St.

Bars

- North Star Pub • 93 South St.
- Paris Cafe • 119 South St.

Cafes

- Donna Lynn's Coffee & Expresso Bar • 30 Water St.
- New World Coffee • 1 New York Plaza
- New World Coffee • 100 Wall St.
- New World Coffee • 1 Broadway
- Pasqua • 1 Liberty Plaza
- Starbucks • 45 Wall St.
- Starbucks • 195 Broadway
- Starbucks • 55 Broad St.
- Starbucks • 24 Pearl St.

Farmer's Markets

- Greenmarket • Battery Park Pl. & Broadway
- Greenmarket • Church St. & Fulton St.

Gyms

- Bally Sports Club • 25 Broadway
- Cardio Fitness Center • 79 Maiden La.
- Dolphin Fitness Clubs • 156 William St.
- Dolphin Fitness Clubs • 110 Greenwich St.
- Executive Fitness Center • 3 WTC
- HRC Tennis & Yacht • Piers 13 & 14
- Lucille Roberts Health Club • 143 Fulton St.
- New York Health & Racquet Club • 39 Whitehall St.
- New York Sports Clubs • 30 Cliff St.
- New York Sports Clubs • 30 Wall St.
- Wall Street Boxing Fitness Inc. • 76 Beaver St.

Hardware Stores

- Apple Specialties • 19 Rector St.
- Dick's Hardware • 205 Pearl St.
- Fulton Supply & Hardware • 74 Fulton St.
- Wolff Hardware • 127 Fulton St.

Liquor Stores

- Arber Liquors • 28 John St.
- Famous Wines & Liquor • 27 William St.
- G's Wine & Spirits • 95 Trinity Place
- Maiden Lane Wine & Liquor • 6 Maiden Lane
- New York Wine Exchange • 9 Beaver St.
- Water Street Wine & Spirit • 79 Pine St.

Pet Store

- Petland Discounts • 132 Nassau St.

Restaurants

- Burritoville • 20 John St.
- Burritoville • 36 Water St.
- Cosi Sandwich Bar • 54 Pine St.
- Cosi Sandwich Bar • 55 Broad St.
- Daily Soup • 2 Rector St.
- Daily Soup • 41 John St.
- Daily Soup • 55 Broad St.
- Le Marais • 15 John St.
- Lemongrass Grill • 110 Liberty St.
- Quartino • 21 Peck Slip
- Red • 14 Fulton St.
- St. Maggie's Cafe • 120 Wall St.

Video Rental

- Ann St Entertainment • 21 Ann St.
- Thunder Video • 100 Greenwich St.

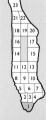

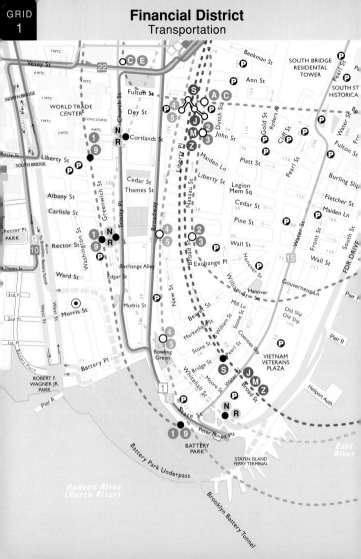

Financial District
Transportation

There is no such thing as street parking until after 7 p.m., and only then near the Fulton Fish Market. Fortunately, almost every subway line in the city has stops in this area. Be careful about driving on South Street before 9 a.m., since it is usually blocked off for fish market business.

Subways

1 **9** . . . . Rector St

1 **9** . . . . South Ferry

1 **9** . . . . Cortlandt St

2 **3** . . . . Wall St

4 **5** . . . . Bowling Green

4 **5** . . . . Wall St

A **C** **J** **M** **Z** **2** **3** **4** **5** . . . . Fulton St–
Broadway–Nassau St

C **E** . . . . World Trade Center

J **M** **Z** . . . . Broad St

N **R** . . . . Rector St

N **R** . . . . Whitehall St–South Ferry

N **R** . . . . Cortlandt St

Bus Lines

1 . . . . Fifth & Madison Aves. (at Madison Ave)

6 . . . . . . 7th Ave./B'way/Ave. of the Americas
(at ./B'way/Ave of the Americas)

9 . . . . Ave. B/E. B'way
(at East Broadway)

10 . . . . 7th/8th Aves./Douglas Blvd.
(at /8 Ave/Douglass Blvd)

15 . . . . First/Second Aves. (at 2 Ave)

22 . . . Madison/Chambers St. (at Chambers St.)

⊙ Car Rental

• Hertz • 20 Morris St.

🅿 Parking Garages

• 111 Washington St.
• 45 Wall St.
• 179 Broadway
• 56 Fulton St.
• 151 Maiden Lane
• 10 Peck Slip
• 288 Pearl St.
• 167 Front St.
• 7 Hanover Sq.
• 70 Greenwich St.
• 140 Liberty St.
• 57 Ann St.
• 90 John St.
• 251 Pearl St.
• 55 Water St.
• 19 Cliff St.
• 1 Water St.
• 80 Pine St.
• 199 Water St.
• 38 Broadway
• 80 Gold St.
• 299 Pearl St.
• 1 Battery Park Plaza

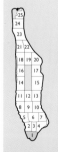

Watts St

Desbrosses St

Vestry St

Laight St

Washington St

Hubert St

Collister St

Beach St

Greenwich St

HUDSON
SQ

Ericsson Pl

North Moore St

Franklin St

Hudson St

Harrison St

Jay St

Staple St

Duane St

TRIBECA BRIDGE

Chambers St

Warren St

West St

Park Pl

BALL
FIELDS

Murray St

North End Ave

Pier 26

Pier 25

Thompson St

St Johns Lane

Varick St

W Broadway

Wooster St

Greene St

Mercer St

Grand St

Canal St

Lispenard St

Walker St

White St

Franklin St

Leonard St

Ave of The Americas

W. Broadway

Worth St

Thomas St

Duane St

Reade St

Chambers St

Warren St

Murray St

Park Pl

Barclay St

Church St

Franklin

Broadway

Cortlandt Alley

Cathern

Trimble

CIVIC
CENTER

CITY
HALL

CITY HALL
PARK

Park Row

7WTC

TriBeCa
Essentials

If anywhere in New York actually warrants insanely high real estate prices, it must be TriBeCa. Tons of gorgeous loft spaces and the surprising quietude of Duane Park make it highly desirable. Check out Bouley Bakery on West Broadway—it's one of the best bakeries in the city.

ATMs

B • Bank of New York • 233 Broadway
Ch • Chase • 281 Broadway
Ch • Chase • 423 Canal St.
Ch • Chase • 407 Broadway
Ci • Citibank • 108 Hudson St.
Ci • Citibank • 415 Broadway
Ci • Citibank • 250 Broadway
F • Fleet • 100 Church St.
H • HSBC • 110 W. Broadway
H • HSBC • 265 Broadway
H • HSBC • 253 Broadway
CU • Municipal Credit Union • 125 Barclay St.
CU • Skyline Federal Credit Union • 32 Ave. of the Americas

★ Landmarks

• City Hall • Park Row & Broadway
• Duane Park • Duane St.
• Harrison St. Houses •
  Harrison & Greenwich St.
• The Dream House • 275 Church St.
• Tweed Courthouse •
  Chambers St. & Broadway
• Walker's • 16 North Moore St.

Library

• New Amsterdam • 9 Murray St.

Marketplace

• Commodities • 117 Hudson St.
• Dr. Sound • 25 Mercer St.
• Pearl Paint • 308 Canal St.

Police Precinct

• 1st Precinct • 16 Ericsson Pl.

✉ Post Offices

• Canal Street • 350 Canal St.
• Church St. Station • 90 Church St.

Schools

• Audrey Cohen College • 75 Varick St.
• Chelsea Vocational High School •
  131 Ave. of the Americas
• College of Insurance • 101 Murray St.
• Drake Business School • 225 Broadway
• Manhattan Comm. College • 199 Chambers St.
• New York Academy of Art • 111 Franklin St.
• New York Law School • 57 Worth St.
• PS 234 Independence School •
  292 Greenwich St.
• Satellite Academy Program • 51 Chambers St.
• Stuyvesant High School • 345 Chambers St.

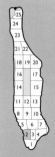

TriBeCa
Sundries / Entertainment

Watts St

Desbrosses St

Vestry St

Laight St

Hubert St

Collister St

Beach St

Washington St

HUDSON SQ

Ericsson Pl

North Moore St

Varick St

St Johns Lane

Ave of The Americas

Thompson St

W Broadway

Wooster St

Greene St

Mercer St

Grand St

Canal St

Lispenard St

Walker St

White St

Franklin St

Church St

Franklin

Broadway

Cat

Greenwich St

Harrison St

Jay St

Staple St

Hudson St

Franklin St

W. Broadway

Leonard St

Worth St

Thomas St

Trimble

Duane St

CIVIC CENTER

TRIBECA BRIDGE

Chambers St

Reade St

Warren St

West St

Park Pl

BALL FIELDS

Murray St

Chambers St

Warren St

CITY HALL

Park Pl

Barclay St

Murray St

CITY HALL PARK

Park Row

7 WTC

th End Ave

Pier 25

26

TriBeCa
Sundries / Entertainment

TriBeCa not only has one of Manhattan's great revival movie theaters, The Screening Room, but it also has the multi-use, ultra-hip Knitting Factory on Leonard Street to boast of.

 24-Hour Copy Centers

- Blumberg Excelsior Copy • 66 White St.
- Kinko's • 105 Duane St.

 Bars

- Bubble Lounge • 228 W. Broadway
- Ice • 528 Canal St.
- Lucky Strike • 59 Grand St.
- Nancy Whisky Pub • 1 Lispenard St.
- Racoon Lodge • 59 Warren St.
- Walker's • 16 North Moore St.

 Cafes

- Alice's Coffee Shop • 32 Avenue of the Americas
- Bassets Coffee & Tea Company • 123 W. Broadway
- Biblio's Cafe Book Store • 317 Church St.
- Downtown Delicious • 327 Greenwich St.
- Le Pain Quotidien • 100 Grand St.
- New Amsterdan Cafe • 291 Broadway
- Pasqua Coffee Bars • 100 Church St.

 Farmer's Markets

- Greenmarket • Chambers St. & Greenwich St.
- Greenmarket • Broadway & Thomas St.

 Gyms

- Eastern Athletic Clubs • 80 Leonard St.
- New York Sports Clubs • 151 Reade St.
- New York Sports Clubs • 217 Broadway
- Oishi Judo Club • 79 Leonard St.
- Tribeca Gym • 79 Worth St.

 Hardware Stores

- ACE Hardware • 160 W. Broadway
- CK & L Hardware • 307 Canal St.
- CNL • 378 Canal St.
- Tribeca Hardware • 154 Chambers St.

 Liquor Stores

- Brite Buy Wines & Spirits • 11 Ave. of the Americas
- City Hall Wines & Spirits • 108 Chambers St.
- Down Town Liquor Store • 90 Hudson St.
- Eighty Eight Wines & More Inc. • 57 Grand St.
- Hecht Liquors Inc. • 237 W. Broadway
- Ned Express.Com • 20 Harrison St.

 Movie Theatres

- Hudson River Park Conservancy • Pier 25 at North Moore St.
- Screening Room • 54 Varick St.
- Tribeca Performing Arts Center • 199 Chambers St.
- Void • 16 Mercer St.

Pet Stores

- Another Barking Zoo • 368 1/2 Greenwich St.
- Dog Essentials • 86 Franklin St.
- Dudley's Paw • 327 Greenwich St.

Restaurants

- Alison on Dominick Street • 38 Dominick St.
- Bouley Bakery • 120 W. Broadway
- Bubby's • 120 Hudson St.
- Burritoville • 144 Chambers St.
- Cafe Noir • 32 Grand St.
- Chanterelle • 2 Harrison St.
- Danube • 30 Hudson St.
- Il Giglio • 81 Warren St.
- Kitchenette • 80 W. Broadway
- Kori • 253 Church St.
- Le Pain Quotidien • 100 Grand St.
- Nobu • 105 Hudson St.
- Tiffin • 18 Murray St.
- Yaffa's • 353 Greenwich St.

Video Rental

- 323 Canal Video • 323 Canal St.

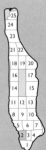

Parking and driving is usually quite decent here, except for a) Canal Street, and b) The Holland Tunnel. They're finally beginning to fix Greenwich Street, which makes us happy.

Subways

1 2 3 9 . . . . Chambers St

1 9 . . . . Canal St

1 9 . . . . Franklin St

2 3 . . . . Park Pl

A C . . . . Chambers St

A C E . . . . Canal St

C E . . . . World Trade Center

N R . . . . City Hall

N R . . . . Canal St

Bus Lines

1 . . . . Fifth & Madison Aves. (at Madison Ave)

6 . . . . . 7th Ave./B'way/Ave. of The Americas

9 . . . . Ave. B/E. Broadway (at East Broadway)

10 . . . . Abingdon Sq.

103 . 5th Ave./Ave. of the Americas/Riverside Dr.

15 . . . . 8th/9th St. Crosstown

22 . . . 7th Ave./Ave. of the Americas/Broadway

Ⓟ Parking Garages

- 280 Church St.
- 31 Vestry St.
- 75 Park Pl.
- 137 Hudson St.
- 370 Canal St.
- 411 Broadway
- 9 North Moore St.
- 84 White St.
- 15 Worth St.
- 343 Broadway
- 377 Greenwich St.
- 108 Leonard St.
- 308 Greenwich St.
- 86 Warren St.
- 56 North Moore St.
- 14 White St.
- 45 Dominick St.
- 51 Walker St.
- 35 Reade St.
- 75 Reade St.
- 48 Franklin St.
- 124 Hudson St.
- 61 Grand St.
- 9 Wooster St.
- 256 West St.
- 87 Murray St.
- 349 Canal St.

⦿ Car Rentals

- National • 138 Reade St.
- United Car Rental •
  74-76 Ave. of The Americas

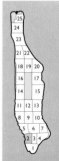

The library on East Broadway is newly refurbished! The post office on Doyers St. always has a hellish line—it's worth it to go somewhere else. There's a lot of great civic architecture, including the Municipal Building and the Surrogate Court. Also check out the reconstructed Foley Square and the beautiful City Hall Park.

ATMs

- Ab • Abacus • 181-183 Canal St.
- B • Bank of New York • 233 Broadway
- Ch • Chase • 281 Broadway
- Ch • Chase • 423 Canal St.
- Ch • Chase • 407 Broadway
- Ch • Chase • 180 Canal St.
- CT • Chinatrust Bank • 208 Canal St.
- CA • Chinese American Bank • 225 Park Row
- CA • Chinese American Bank • 77 Bowery
- Ci • Citibank • 415 Broadway
- Ci • Citibank • 250 Broadway
- Ci • Citibank • 164 Canal St.
- Ci • Citibank • 2 Mott St.
- D • Dime • 221 Canal St.
- F • Fleet • 260 Canal St.
- F • Fleet • 50 Bayard St.
- F • Fleet • 100 Church St.
- H • HSBC • 268 Canal St.
- H • HSBC • 265 Broadway
- H • HSBC • 254 Canal St.
- H • HSBC • 27 E. Broadway
- H • HSBC • 29 Bowery St.
- H • HSBC • 50 Bowery
- H • HSBC • 17 Chatham Sq.
- H • HSBC • 253 Broadway
- CU • Skyline Federal Credit Union • 32 Ave. of the Americas
- U • United Orient Bank • 185 Canal St.

Hospital

- NYU Downtown Hospital • 170 William St.

★ Landmarks

- Bridge Cafe • Corner of Dover & Water St.
- Chinatown Ice Cream Factory • Bayard St
- City Hall • Park Row & Broadway
- Doyers St. (Bloody Angle) • Doyers St.
- Hall of Records • Chambers and Park Row
- Happy Mazza Media • 2 E. Broadway
- Municipal Building • Chambers and Park Row
- The Dream House • 275 Church St.
- Tweed Courthouse • Chambers St. & Broadway

📖 Libraries

- Chatham Square • 33 E.Broadway
- New Amsterdam • 9 Murray St.

Ⓜ Marketplace

- Gourmet Garage • 451 Broome St.
- J&R Music & Computer World • 33 Park Row
- Pearl Paint • 308 Canal St.

🅿 Police Precinct

- 5th Precinct • 19 Elizabeth St.

✉ Post Offices

- Canal Street • 350 Canal St.
- Chinatown • 6 Doyers St.
- Church St. Station • 90 Church St.
- Peck Slip • 1 Peck Slip

Schools

- Drake Business School • 225 Broadway
- Murray Bergtraum High School • 411 Pearl St.
- New York Law School • 57 Worth St.
- Pace University • 1 Pace Plaza
- PS 124 • Confucius Plaza
- PS 126 Jacob Riis School • 80 Catherine St.
- PS 130 DeSoto School • 143 Baxter St.
- Satellite Academy Program • 51 Chambers St.
- Stenotype Academy • 15 Park Row

Community Gardens

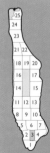

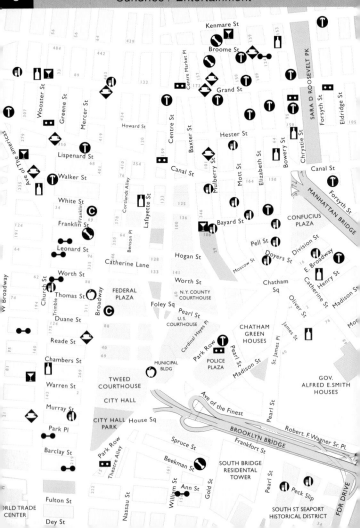

If you haven't had the crab soup dumplings at Joe's Shanghai on Pell Street, you should. Our favorite Vietnamese is Pho Viet Huong, our favorite Thai is Thailand Restaurant, and our favorite Malaysian is Baba. If you're not in the mood for Asian cuisine, you're in the wrong grid.

24-Hour Copy Centers

- Blumberg Excelsior Copy • 66 White St.
- Kinko's • 105 Duane St.

Bars

- Double Happiness • 173 Mott St.
- Lucky Strike • 59 Grand St.
- Metropolitan Improvement Company • 3 Madison St.
- Nancy Whisky Pub • 1 Lispenard St.
- Racoon Lodge • 59 Warren St.
- Winnie's • 104 Bayard St.

Cafes

- Alice's Coffee Shop • 32 Avenue of the Americas
- Biblio's Cafe Book Store • 317 Church St.
- Cafe Palermo • 148 Mulberry St.
- Le Pain Quotidien • 100 Grand St.
- Little Italy Coffee Shop • 151 Mulberry St.
- New Amsterdam Cafe • 291 Broadway
- Pasqua Coffee Bars • 100 Church St.
- Sambuca's Cafe & Desserts • 105 Mulberry St.
- The Beard • 125B Elizabeth St.

Farmer's Markets

- Greenmarket • Chambers St. & Centre St.
- Greenmarket • Broadway & Thomas St.

Gyms

- Dolphin Fitness Clubs • 156 William St.
- Eastern Athletic Clubs • 80 Leonard St.
- New York Sports Clubs • 217 Broadway
- Oishi Judo Club • 79 Leonard St.
- Tribeca Gym • 79 Worth St.
- Wu Mei Kung Fu • 21 Mott St.
- Xie He Jian Kang Center • 302 Broome St.

Hardware Stores

- Centre Plumbing & Hardware • 233 Centre St.
- Chinatown 25 Cents Store • 7 Elizabeth St.
- CK & L Hardware • 307 Canal St.
- CNL • 378 Canal St.
- Design Source • 115 Bowery
- East Broadway Appliance Hardware • 59 E. Broadway
- General Machinery • 358 Broome St.
- Grand Hardware • 99 Chrystie St.
- Kessler Hardware • 229 Grand St.
- Lendy Electric Equipment • 182 Grand St.
- Mott Hardware • 52 Kenmare St.
- Nelson Hardware • 88 Elizabeth St.
- OK Hardware • 438 Broome St.
- T&Y Hardware • 101 Chrystie St.
- Wei Qiang Zheng • 55 Chrystie St.
- Weinstein & Holtzman Inc • 29 Park Row
- World Construction Inc • 78 Forsyth St.

Liquor Stores

- Bowery Discount Wine & Liquors • 133 Bowery
- Brite Buy Wines & Spirits • 11 Ave. of the Americas
- Chez Choi Liquor & Wine • 49 Chrystie St.
- City Hall Wines & Spirits • 108 Chambers St.
- Eighty Eight Wines & More Inc. • 57 Grand St.
- Royal Wine & Liquor • 45 Madison St.
- Sam Wai Liquor Store • 17 E. Broadway
- Walker Liquors • 101 Lafayette St.
- Wine Wo Liquor Discount Ctr • 24 Bowery

Pet Stores

- Aqua Star Pet Shop • 172 Mulberry St.
- Dog Essentials • 86 Franklin St.
- Petplace • 5 Beekman St.
- Win Tropical Aquariums • 169 Mott St.

Restaurants

- Ba Ba Malaysian • 53 Bayard St.
- Bridge Cafe • 279 Water St.
- Cafe Noir • 32 Grand St.
- Joe's Shanghai • 9 Pell St.
- Kori • 253 Church St.
- Le Pain Quotidien • 100 Grand St.
- Mandarin Court • 61 Mott St.
- New York Noodle Town • 28 1/2 Bowery
- Pho Viet Huong • 73 Mulberry St.
- Ping's Seafood • 20 East Broadway
- Quartino • 21 Peck Slip
- Thailand Restaurant • 106 Bayard St.
- Tiffin • 18 Murray St.
- Vegetarian Paradise • 33 Mott St.
- Vietnam • 11-13 Doyers St.

Video Rentals

- 323 Canal Video • 323 Canal St.
- Charming Video • 200 Centre St.
- J & R Music World • 23 Park Row
- Laser Video Center • 97 Chrystie St.
- Terence Video • 282 Grand St.
- UE Enterprises Center • 153 Centre St.
- UE Enterprises • 118 Mott St.

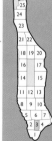

While the newly-reconstructed Chatham Square is visually more appealing, its design has not done much to improve the traffic flow. The Brooklyn Bridge is best approached from Pearl Street. Be careful about driving east on Canal Street—you have to make a right on Bowery or else you'll drive over the Manhattan Bridge (Canal Street is one-way going west between Bowery and Chrystie). Forget about parking during the day.

Subways

1 2 3 9 . . . . Chambers St

1 9 . . . . Cortlandt St

1 9 . . . . Franklin St

2 3 . . . . Park Pl

4 5 6 J M Z . . . Brooklyn Bridge–
City Hall–Chambers St

6 N R J M Z . . . . Canal St

2 3 4 5 A C J M Z . . . . Fulton St–
Broadway–Nassau St

A C E . . . . Canal St

B D Q . . . . Grand St

C E . . . . Cortlandt St

J M . . . . Bowery

N R . . . . City Hall

Bus Lines

1 . . . . . Broadway & Centre St. (at Centre St)

6 . . . Church St. and Broadway (at Broadway)

9 . . . . Park Row

10 . . . . W. Broadway

15 . . . E. Broadway & Park Row (at Park Row)

22 . . . Chambers & Madison St. (at Madison St)

103 . . . . . . Bowery & Park Row (at Park Row)

. . . . . . Lafayette & Canal Sts. (at Canal St)

Car Rentals

- Mirkin Alex • 298 Mulberry St.
- Park On Auto Service • 75 Kenmare St.

Parking Garages

- 320 Pearl St.
- 395 Broome St.
- 280 Church St.
- 169 William St.
- 370 Canal St.
- 411 Broadway
- 180 Park Row
- 61 Chrystie St.
- 84 White St.
- 343 Broadway
- 174 Centre St.
- 10 Peck Slip
- 142 Grand St.
- 204 Lafayette St.
- 288 Pearl St.
- 167 Front St.
- 332 Pearl St.
- 108 Leonard St.
- 86 Warren St.
- 15 Dover St.
- 14 White St.
- 51 Walker St.
- 89 Chrystie St.
- 62 Mulberry St.
- 196 Mulberry St.
- 35 Reade St.
- 44 Elizabeth St.
- 25 Beekman St.
- 75 Reade St.
- 103 Park Row.
- 80 Gold St.
- 299 Pearl St.
- 14 Kenmare St.
- 106 Mott St.
- 61 Grand St.
- 349 Canal St.

Lower East Side
Essentials

Rivington St

SAMUEL
GOMPERS
HOUSES

WILLIAMSBURG BRIDGE

Ped. B

Delancey St

CORLEAR
HOOKS

Broome St

HILLMAN HOUSES

Grand St

SEWARD
PARK
HOUSES

SEWARD
PARK
HOUSES

SAMUEL
DICKSTEIN
PLZ

VLADECK
HOUSES

Hester St

W.H.
SEWARD
PARK

CORLE
HO
PAR

Canal St

E. Broadway

Henry St

Madison St

Division St

Jefferson St

LA GUARDIA
HOUSES

Cherry St

Pike St

Rutgers St

RUTGERS
HOUSES

South St

FDR DRIVE

Pier 42

PATHMARK

MANHATTAN BRIDGE

Market St

Monroe St

KNICKER-
BOCKER
VILLAGE

Catherine St

Water St

GOV.
ALFRED E.SMITH
HOUSES

*East
River*

BROOKLYN BRIDGE

Rivington St
Suffolk St
Clinton St
Attorney St
Ridge St
Pitt St
Willett St
Abraham
Kazan St
Cannon St
Lewis St
Orchard St
Ludlow St
Essex St
Norfolk St
Allen St
Forsyth St
Eldridge St
Forsyth St
Gouverneur St
Montgomery St
Gouverneur St
Jackson St

Lower East Side
Essentials

The Lower East Side is the home of Kossar's Bialys on Grand Street between Essex and Norfolk—they make the best bialys ever, period. Check out Hong Kong Supermarket for Asian specialties. And the 24-hour Pathmark, believe it or not, has its own parking lot.

 ATMs

- BP • Banco Popular • 134 Delancey St.
- Ch • Chase • 108-109 Delancey St.
- Ch • Citibank • 411 Grand St.
- E • Emigrant • 465 Grand St.
- F • Fleet • 318 Grand St.
- F • Fleet • 126 Delancey St.

Bagels

- Kossar's Bagels and Bialys • 367 Grand St.
- Kossar's Bagels and Bialys • 39 Essex St.

 Hospital

- Gouverneur Hospital • 227 Madison St.

★ **Landmarks**

- Bialystoker Synagogue • 7-11 Willet St.
- Eldridge St. Synagogue • 12 Eldridge St.
- Lower East Side Tenement Museum • 90 Orchard St.

Library

- Seward Park • 192 E. Broadway

 Marketplace

- Gertel's Bake Shop • 53 Hester St.
- Guss' Pickles • 35 Essex St.
- Hong Kong Supermarket • 109 East Broadway
- Pathmark • 233 Cherry St.

 24 Hour Pharmacy

- Rite Aid • 408 Grand St.

✉ **Post Office**

- Knickerbocker • 130 E. Broadway

Schools

- IS 131 Dr. Sun Yat Sen School • 100 Hester St.
- JHS 056 Corlears School • 220 Henry St.
- Mesivta Tifereth Jerusalem • 141 E. Broadway
- PS 001 Alfred E. Smith School • 8 Henry St.
- PS 002 Meyer London School • 122 Henry St.
- PS 020 Anna Silver School • 166 Essex St.
- PS 042 Benjamin Altman School • 71 Hester St.
- PS 110 F. Nightingale School • 285 Delancey St.
- PS 124 Yung Wing School • 40 Division St.
- PS 126 Jacob Riis School • 80 Catherine St.
- PS 134 Henrietta Szold School • 293 E. Broadway
- PS 137 John L Bernstein School • 327 Cherry St.
- Seward Park High School • 350 Grand St.

 Community Gardens

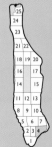

Lower East Side
Sundries / Entertainment

Rivington St

Suffolk St

Clinton St

Attorney St

Ridge St

SAMUEL
GOMPERS
HOUSES

WILLIAMSBURG BRIDGE

Delancey St

Broome St

Pitt St

Willett St

Abraham Kazan St

Cannon St

Lewis St

CORLEARS
HOOKS

HILLMAN HOUSES

Allen St

Orchard St

Ludlow St

Essex St

Norfolk St

Clinton St

Grand St

SEWARD
PARK
HOUSES

SEWARD
PARK
HOUSES

SAMUEL
DICKSTEIN
PLZ

VLADECK
HOUSES

Cherry St

Jackson St

CORLEARS
HOOK
PARK

Hester St

W.H.
SEWARD
PARK

E. Broadway

Jefferson St

Henry St

Madison St

Montgomery St

Gouverneur St

Gouverneur St

Eldridge St

Canal St

Division St

LA GUARDIA
HOUSES

Forsyth St

Pike St

Rutgers St

Cherry St

South St

FDR DRIVE

Pier 42

RUTGERS
HOUSES

RUTGERS
PARK

MANHATTAN BRIDGE

Market St

Monroe St

Catherine St

KNICKER-
BOCKER
VILLAGE

Water St

East
River

GOV.
ALFRED E. SMITH
HOUSES

BROOKLYN BRIDGE

Our favorite hangout place is Tonic on Norfolk Street—great music, great café, great vibe. Also check out the cool indie press in the same building. This area is not the culinary capital of Manhattan, unless you love fried chicken and McDonald's.

Bars

- Bar 169 • 169 East Broadway
- Good World Barber Shop • 3 Orchard Street
- Welcome to the Johnsons • 123 Rivington St.

Cafes

- Bluestockings • 172 Allen St.

Hardware Stores

- Fung Chung Hardware • 154A E. Broadway
- Grand Home Center • 71 Allen St.
- HH Hardware • 111 Rivington St.
- International Electrical • 77 Allen St.
- Karlee Hardware • 98 E. Broadway
- Weilgus & Sons • 158 E. Broadway

Liquor Stores

- Gary's Liquor Inc. • 141 Essex St.
- Good Time Liquor • 135 Division St.
- Ivory Wines & Liquors • 563 Grand St.
- Jade Fountain Liquor • 123 Delancey St.
- Loon Chun Liquor • 47 Pitt St.
- Schapiro Wine Co. • 124 Rivington St.
- Seward Park Liquors Inc • 393 Grand St.

Movie Theatre

- New Federal Theatre • 292 Henry

Pet Stores

- Pet Projects Unlimited • 75 Montgomery St.
- Petland • 85 Delancey St.
- Sammy Aquarium • 11 Essex St.

Restaurants

- Canton • 45 Division St.
- Cup & Saucer • 89 Canal St.
- El Castillo de Jaqua • 113 Rivington St.
- Essex Restaurant • 120 Essex St.
- Good World Bar & Grill • 3 Orchard St.
- Great Shanghai • 27 Division St.
- Ratners • 138 Delancey St.

Video Rentals

- City Video • 79 Allen St.
- Terence Video • 282 Grand St.
- The Video Store • 128 Rivington St.
- USA Shenchow Trading Corp • 125 Canal St.

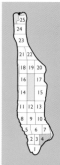

Lower East Side
Transportation

TOWERS

Rivington St

SAMUEL
GOMPERS
HOUSES

WILLIAMSBURG BRIDGE

Ped. BRID

Delancey St

J M Z

CORLEARS
HOOKS

Broome St

HILLMAN HOUSES

Grand St

14

SAMUEL
DICKSTEIN
PLZ

VLADECK
HOUSES

9

SEWARD
PARK
HOUSES

SEWARD
PARK
HOUSES

CORLEAR
HOOK
PARK

W.H.
SEWARD
PARK

Henry St

Madison St

Gouverneur St

Gouverneur St

East Broadway

Jefferson St

15

Canal St

LA GUARDIA
HOUSES

Montgomery St

Division St

Marginal

Pier 4

Forsyth St

22

15

Cherry St

FDR DRIVE

RUTGERS
HOUSES

Rutgers St

South St

Pier 42

Pike St

PATHMARK

Market St

MANHATTAN BRIDGE

**East
River**

Monroe St

Catherine St

Water St

GOV.
ALFRED E.SMITH
HOUSES

BROOKLYN BRIDGE

Rivington St
Suffolk St
Clinton St
Attorney St
Ridge St

Pitt St
Willett St
Abraham
kazan St
Cannon St
Lewis St

Norfolk St

Essex St

Orchard St
Ludlow St

Allen St

Eldridge St

Hester St

Clinton St

Jackson St

Cherr

If they ever finish working on the Williamsburg Bridge, it'll be great—four lanes in either direction and a reconstructed J/M/Z line. The work done already has improved things considerably. Take advantage of the reconstructed East River Esplanade off of South Street if you're biking, skating, or walking—it's got the best views of the bridges.

Subways

Ⓕ . . . . East Broadway

Ⓕ Ⓙ Ⓜ Ⓩ . . . . . Delancey St–Essex St

Bus Lines

9 . . . . E. Broadway & Essex St. (at Essex St)

14 . . . . Grand St.

15 . . . . Allen St.

22 . . . . Madison St.

8/39 . . . . Delancey St.

21 . . . . Forsyth St.

🅿 Gas Station

• Mobil • 2 Pike St.

🅿 Parking Garages

• 275 Delancey St.
• 135 Delancey St.
• 105 Essex St.
• Broome & Ludlow Sts.
• 40 Henry St.
• 2 Division St.
• 47-59 Henry St.
• 223 South St.

West Village
Essentials

W 15th St

W 14th St

W 13th St

Little W 12th St

Ninth Av

Gansevoort St

Horatio St

Jane St

W 12th St

Bethune St

Eighth Av

Bank St

W 11th St

Perry St

Charles St

W 10th St

Christopher St

Charles Ln

Weehawken St

West St

Barrow St

Morton St

Leroy St

Clarkson St

W Houston St

King St

Charlton St

Vandam St

Spring St

Greenwich Av

Waverly Pl

W 4th St

Bleecker St

Grove St

Commerce St

Bedford St

Carmine St

W 12th St

W 11th St

Avenue of The Americas (Sixth Av)

W 10th St

W 9th St

W 8th St

Waverly Pl

Sheridan Sq

Washington Pl

Jones St

Cornelia St

W 4th St

W 3rd St

Minetta La

Bleecker St

MacDougal St

Sullivan St

Prince St

Spring St

St. Luke's Pl

JAMES J.
WALKER PARK

Downing St

Hudson St

Greenwich St

Washington St

West Side Highway

Hudson
River

Renwick St

Holland
Tunnel

Varick St

Watts St

Broome St

Dominick St

Spring St

Canal St

Grand St

Seventh Av South

If you like quiet tree-lined streets (who doesn't?) then this is the neighborhood for you. The northwest and southwest parts are in the process of converting from manufacturing to residential and commercial areas, although services are still scant west of Hudson St. The Hudson River Greenway is fantastic—we can't wait for the entire west side to be done. It's got a wonderful vibe, both during the day and at night. The West Village also has one of New York's premier gourmet shops, Balducci's.

ATMs

- Ch • Chase • 158 W. 14th St.
- Ch • Chase • 302 W. 12th St.
- Ch • Chase • 345 Hudson St.
- Ci • Citibank • 75 Christopher St.
- D • Dime • 325 Bleecker St.
- D • Dime • 340 Ave. of the Americas
- E • Emigrant Savings Bank • 375 Hudson St.
- H • HSBC • 101 W. 14th St.
- H • HSBC • 225 Varick St.

Bagels

- Bagel Buffet • 406 Ave. of the Americas
- Bagelry • 200 14th St.
- Bagelry • 502 Hudson St.
- Bagels on the Square • 7 Carmine St.
- Dizzy Izzy's NY Bagels Inc. • 185 Varick St.
- Famous Bagel Buffet • 510 Ave. of the Americas
- Murray's Bagels • 500 Ave. of the Americas
- The Bagel Restaurant • 68-70 W. 4th St.

Hospitals

- St. Vincent's AIDS Center •
  412 Ave. of the Americas
- St. Vincent's Hospital & Medical Center •
  153 W. 11th St.

Landmarks

- Chumley's • 86 Bedford St.
- Jefferson Market Courthouse •
  425 Ave. of the Americas
- Stonewall • 53 Christopher St.
- The Ear Inn • Washington & Spring
- Westbeth Building • Washington & Bethune
- White Horse Tavern • 567 Hudson St.

Libraries

- Early Childhood Resource & Information • 66 Leroy St.
- Hudson Park • 66 Leroy St.
- Jefferson Market • 425 Ave. of the Americas

Marketplace

- Alphabets • 47 Greenwich Ave.
- Balducci's • 424 Sixth Ave.
- Fat Beats • 406 Sixth Ave.
- Porto Rico Importing Company • 201 Bleecker St.

24-Hour Pharmacy

- Duane Reade • 378 Ave. of the Americas

Police Precinct

- 6th Precinct • 233 W. 10th St.

Post Offices

- Village • 201 Varick St.
- West Village • 527 Hudson St.

Schools

- Chelsea Vocational High School • 131 Sixth Ave.
- Empire State College-State University of New York • 225 Varick St.
- Executive High School Internship Program • 16 Clarkson St.
- Joffrey Ballet School • 434 Ave. of the Americas
- Merce Cunningham Studio • 463 West St.
- PS 3 The Charette School • 490 Hudson St.
- PS 41 Greenwich Village School • 116 W. 11th St.
- PS 721 Manhattan Occupational Training School • 250 W. Houston St.
- St. Joseph's Washington Place School • 111 Washington Pl.
- St. Vincent's Hospital Medical School • 153 W. 11th St.
- St. Vincent's Hospital School of Nursing • 27 Christopher St.
- The Village Community School • 272 W. 10th St.

Community Garden

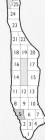

West Village
Sundries / Entertainment

West Village
Sundries / Entertainment

The Corner Bistro has the best burgers in Manhattan, and the Ear Inn is one of our all-time bars. Many gay and lesbian bars are in this neighborhood. The area below Houston Street is seeing more restaurants move in to accomodate new office workers, but many are closed nights and weekends.

Bars

- Art Bar • 52 8th Ave.
- Automatic Slims • 733 Washington St
- Blind Tiger Ale House • 518 Hudson St.
- Chumley's • 86 Bedford St.
- Duplex • 61 Christopher St.
- Ear Inn • 326 Spring St.
- Henrietta Hudson • 438 Hudson St
- Red Light Bistro • 50 Ninth Ave.
- Village Idiot • 355 W. 14th St.
- White Horse Tavern • 567 Hudson St.

Cafes

- Brewbar Coffee • 13 8th Ave.
- Brewbar Coffee • 327 W. 11th St.
- Cafe Sha Sha • 510 Hudson St.
- Caffe dell'Artista • 46 Greenwich Ave.
- Caffe Rafaella • 134 Seventh Ave. S
- Dalton Coffee Ltd. • 50 Grove St.
- Grey Dog's Coffee • 33 Carmine St.

Farmer's Markets

- Greenmarket • Eighth Ave & 12th St.
- Jefferson Market • 425 Ave. of Americas

Gyms

- Crunch Fitness • 152 Christopher St.
- Fitcare Com • 170 Varick St.
- Jeff's Gym • 224 W. 4th St.
- New York Sports Clubs • 125 7th Ave. S
- Printing House Fitness & Racquet Club • 421 Hudson St.
- Revolution Studios • 104 W. 13th St.
- Serge Gym • 451 West St.
- West Village Workout • 140 Charles St.
- Workout Partners Fitness • 30 Vandam St.

Hardware Stores

- Alternative Housewares & Hardware • 710 Greenwich St.
- Barney's Hardware • 467 Sixth Ave.
- Blaustein Paint & Hardware • 304 Bleecker St.
- Garber Hardware • 49 Eighth Ave.
- Hardware Mart • 151 W. 14th St.
- Jonathan's Decorative Hardware • 12 Perry St.
- Lock-It Hardware • 59 Carmine St.
- Nanz Custom Hardware • 20 Vandam St.
- The Lumber Store • 71 Eighth Ave.
- Village Supply • 306 W. 13th St.

Liquor Stores

- Burgundy Wine Co. • 323 W. 11th St.
- Casa Oliveira Wines & Liquors • 98 Seventh Ave. S.
- Castle Wines & Liquors • 168 Seventh Ave. S
- Christopher St. Liquor Shoppe • 45 Christopher St.
- Golden Rule Wine & Liquor • 457 Hudson St.
- Imperial Liquors • 579 Hudson St.
- Manley's Liquor Store • 35 Eighth Ave.
- North Village Wine & Liquor • 254 W. 14th St.
- Sea Grape Wine & Spirits • 512 Hudson St.
- Spirits Of Carmine • 52 Carmine St.
- Spring Street Wine Shop • 187 Spring St.
- Village Vintner • 448 Ave. of the Americas
- Village Wine & Spirits • 486 Ave. of the Americas
- Young's Liquor Store • 135 Waverly Pl.

Movie Theatres

- Clearview's Waverly Twin • 323 Sixth Ave.
- Film Forum • 209 W. Houston St.
- Hudson Park Conservancy • Pier 54 at 13th St.
- Reel Diner • 357 West Street

Pet Stores

- Beasty Feast • 237 Bleecker St.
- Beasty Feast • 680 Washington St.
- Beasty Feast • 630 Hudson St.
- Fetch • 43 Greenwich Ave.
- Groom-O-Rama • 496 Ave. of the Americas
- Parrots & Pups • 45 Christopher St.
- Pet Palace • 109 W. 10th St.
- Pet's Kitchen • 116 Christopher St.
- Petland Discounts • 389 Avenue of Americas
- Urban Bird • 19 Greenwich Ave.
- Urban Pets • 18 Christopher St.

Restaurants

- Aquagrill • 210 Spring St.
- Babbo • 110 Waverly Place
- Benny's Burritos • 13 Greenwich Ave.
- Corner Bistro • 331 W. 4th St.
- Cowgirl Hall of Fame • 519 Hudson St.
- El Cid • 322 W. 15th St.
- Florent • Gansevoort St.
- French Roast • 78 W. 11th St.
- Gray's Papaya • 63 W. 8th St.
- Home • 20 Cornelia St.
- Les Deux Gamins • 170 Waverly Place
- Lupe's East L.A. Kitchen • 110 Sixth Ave.
- Mary's Fish Camp • 246 W. 4th St.
- Moustache • 90 Bedford St.
- One If By Land, TIBS • 17 Barrow St.
- Po • 31 Cornelia St.
- Rio Mar • 7 Ninth Ave.
- Taste of India • 181 Bleecker St.
- Two Boots • 201 W. 11th St.
- Yama • 38-40 Carmine St.

Video Rentals

- Badlands Video • 388 West St.
- Crazy Fantasy Video • 333 Sixth Ave.
- Evergreen Video • 37 Carmine St.
- Kim's West • 350 Bleecker St.
- Mrs. Hudson's Video Take-Away • 573 Hudson St.
- Video Oyster • 137 W. 12th St.
- Vital Videos Inc • 119 Christopher St.
- Vivid Video • 100 Christopher St.
- World of Video • 51 Greenwich Ave.

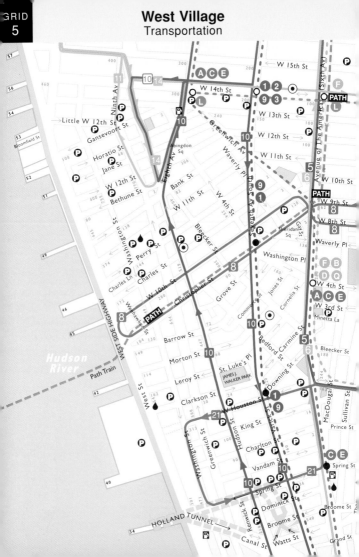

It's pretty tough to park anywhere east of Washington St. All approaches to the Holland Tunnel suck. Thankfully, there is a great bike lane on Hudson Street, though the one on Sixth Ave. doesn't start until 9th Street. The 1/9 subway stop on Christopher Street is quite nice—too bad they're not all like that.

Subways

1 **2** **3** **9** **F** **L** . . 14 St–6 Av (at 6 Ave)

1 **9** . . . . Christopher St–Sheridan Sq

1 **9** . . . . Houston St (at Varick St)

A **C** **E** **B** **D** **F** **Q** . . . . . . W 4 St

A **C** **E** **L** . . . . 14 St–8 Av (at 8 Ave)

C **E** . . . . Spring St

Bus Lines

5 . . . . 5th Ave./Ave. of the Americas/Riverside Dr.

6 . . . . . . 7th Ave./Ave. of the Americas/Broadway

8 . . . . 8th/9th St. Crosstown

10 . . . . 7th Ave./8th Ave./Central Park West

10 . . . . Abingdon Sq.

11 . . . . 9th Ave./10th Ave. (at ./10th Ave)

14 . . . . 14th St. Crosstown

21 . . . . Houston St. Crosstown

PATH Path Stations

• Christopher St.
• 9th St.
• 14th St.

● Car Rentals

• Dollar • 99 Charles St.
• Hertz • 18 Morton St.
• Zupa Brothers • 145 W. 14th St.

● Car Washes

• Apple Management • 332 W. 11th St.
• Carz-A-Poppin Carwash • 124 Ave. of the Americas
• Two Guys General Auto Repair • 359 West St.
• Village Car Wash & Lube • 359 West St.

 Gas Stations

• Getty • 63 Eighth Ave.
• Mobil • 140 Ave. of the Americas
• Mobil • 299 West St.

P Parking Garages

• 3 Sheridan Sq.
• 375 Hudson St.
• 396 Hudson St.
• 61 Jane St.
• 756 Washington St.
• 77 W. 15th St.
• 99 Jane St.
• 332 W. 11th St.
• 64 Charlton St.
• 520 Broome St.
• 40 North River Pier #100
• 47 Seventh Ave.
• 551 Greenwich St.
• 14 Charlton St.
• 2024 Varick St.
• 101 W. 12th St.
• 243 Hudson St.
• 534 Hudson St.
• 239 Hudson St.
• 274 Spring St.
• 738 Greenwich St.
• 107 W. 13th St.
• 41 Doninick St.
• 90 Gavsevoort St.
• 738 Greenwich St.
• 70-72 Eighth Ave.
• 140 Charles St.
• 222 W. 14th St.
• 161 Varick St.
• 10 Ninth Ave.
• 97 Charles St.
• 388 Hudson St.
• 160 W. 10th St.
• 122 W. 3rd St.
• 122 Varick St.
• 20 Morton St.
• 296 Hudson St.
• Pier 40
• 26 Little W. 12th St.
• 214 W. Houston St.
• 246 Spring St.
• 166 Perry St.
• 19 Ninth Ave.
• 1935 W. Houston St.
• 134 W. 10th St.
• 445 Washington St.
• 575 Washington St.

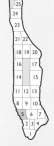

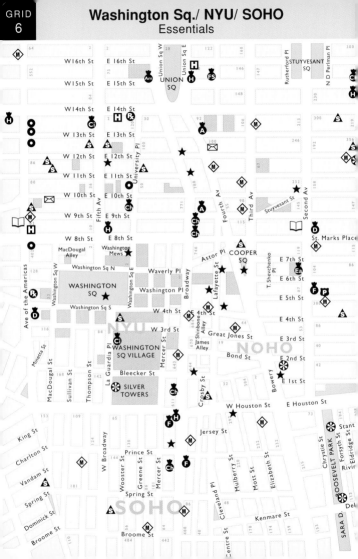

W 16th St   E 16th St

Union Sq W   Union Sq E

STUYVESANT SQ

Rutherford Pl

N D Perlman Pl

W 15th St   E 15th St

UNION SQ

Am

W 14th St   E 14th St

W 13th St   E 13th St

W 12th St   E 12th St

University Pl

W 11th St   E 11th St

W 10th St   E 10th St

Fifth Av

Fourth Av

Third Av

Second Av

Stuyvesant St

W 9th St   E 9th St

W 8th St   E 8th St

St. Marks Place

MacDougal Alley

Washington Mews

Washington Sq N

Waverly Pl

Astor Pl   COOPER SQ

E 7th St

T. Shevchenko Pl

E 6th St

Ave of the Americas

Washington Sq W

WASHINGTON SQ

Washington Sq E

Washington Pl

Broadway

Lafayette St

E 5th St

Washington Sq S

W 4th St

E 4th St

NYU

W 3rd St

Shinbone Alley

Great Jones St

E 3rd St

NOHO

Minetta St

La Guardia Pl

Mercer St

WASHINGTON SQ VILLAGE

James Alley

Bond St

E 2nd St

E 1st St

Bleecker St

Bowery

MacDougal St

Sullivan St

Thompson St

SILVER TOWERS

Crosby St

W Houston St   E Houston St

Chrystie St

Forsyth St

Eldridge St

ROOSEVELT PARK

King St

W Broadway

Wooster St

Greene St

Mercer St

Prince St

Jersey St

Charlton St

Vandam St

Spring St

Dominick St

Broome St

SOHO

Spring St

Broome St

Cleveland Pl

Mulberry St

Mott St

Elizabeth St

Centre St

Kenmare St

SARA D.

Washington Sq./ NYU/ SOHO
Essentials

This area seems like it's being taken over by NYU—they're building new dorms at an astonishing rate. However, many great shops and galleries still abound in Soho and on Broadway. Also an architectural "greatest hits."

 ATMs

- Am • Amalgamated • 11-15 Union Sq. W.
- A • Apple • 145 Fourth Ave.
- Ch • Chase • 158 W. 14th St.
- Ch • Chase • 32 University Pl.
- Ch • Chase • 756 Broadway
- Ch • Chase • 766 Broadway
- Ch • Chase • 255 First Ave.
- Ch • Chase • 525 Broadway
- Ch • Chase • 623 Broadway
- Ci • Citibank • 555 LaGuardia Pl.
- Ci • Citibank • 72 Fifth Ave.
- Ci • Citibank • 262 First Ave.
- D • Dime • 340 Ave. of the Americas
- D • Dime • 130 Second Ave.
- Ea • EAB • 105 Second Ave.
- F • Fleet • 72 Second Ave.
- F • Fleet • 528 Broadway
- F • Fleet • 589 Broadway
- H • HSBC • 101 W. 14th St.
- H • HSBC • 245 First Ave.
- H • HSBC • 1 E. 8th St.
- H • HSBC • 10 Union Sq. East
- H • HSBC • 599 Broadway

Bagels

- Bagel Bob's Campus • 51 University Pl.
- Bagel Buffet • 406 Ave. of the Americas
- David's Bagels • 220 First Ave.
- Famous Bagel Buffet • 510 Ave. of the Americas
- La Bagel • 263 First Ave.
- Murray's Bagels • 500 Ave. of the Americas

 Hospitals

- Beth Israel Medical Center • 10 Union Sq. E.
- New York Eye & Ear Infirmary • 310 E. 14th St.
- St.Vincent's AIDS Center • 412 Ave. of the Americas

★ Landmarks

- Bayard-Condict Building • 65 Bleecker St.
- CBGB & OMFUG • Bowery & Bleecker Sts.
- Colonnade Row • 428 Lafayette St.
- Con Edison Building • 145 E. 14th St.
- Cooper Union • 30 Cooper Sq.
- Grace Church • 802 Broadway
- Great Jones Fire House • Great Jones & Bowery
- Jefferson Market Courthouse • 425 Ave. of the Americas
- Milano's • W. Houston & Mott Sts.
- Old Merchant's House • 29 E. 4th St.
- Salmagundi Club • 47 Fifth Ave.
- Singer Building • 561 Broadway
- St. Mark's-in-the-Bowery Church • 131 E.10th St.
- The Public Theater • 425 Lafayette St.
- The Strand Bookstore • Broadway & 12th St.
- Washington Mews • University Pl. (entrance)
- Washington Square Park • Washington Square

Libraries

- Jefferson Market • 425 Ave. of the Americas
- Ottendorfer • 135 Second Ave.

 Marketplace

- Balducci's • 424 Sixth Ave.
- Blades Downtown • 659 Broadway
- Canal Jean • 504 Broadway
- Computers • 7 Great Jones St.
- Daily 235 • 235 Elizabeth St.
- Dean & DeLuca • 560 Broadway
- East Village Cheese • 40 Third Ave.
- Fat Beats • 406 Sixth Ave.
- Gourmet Garage • 451 Broome St.
- Kate's Paperie • 561 Broadway
- Kiehl's • 109 Third Ave.
- Mondo Kim's • 6 St. Mark's Place
- New York Central • 62 Third Ave.
- Other Music • 15 E. 4th St.
- Porto Rico Importing Company • 40 St. Mark's Place
- Porto Rico Importing Company • 107 Thompson St.
- Tower Records • 692 Broadway
- Utrecht Art and Drafting Supplies • 111 Fourth Ave.
- Veniero's • 342 E. 11th St.
- White Trash • 304 E. 5th St.

 24-Hour Pharmacies

- Duane Reade • 378 Ave. of the Americas
- Duane Reade • 24 E. 14th St.

 Police Precinct

- 9th Precinct • 321 E. 5th St.

✉ Post Offices

- Cooper • 93 Fourth Ave.
- Patchin • 70 W. 10th St.

 Schools

- Allied Health Program in Orthopedics • 310 E. 14th St.
- Chelsea Vocational High School • 131 Sixth Ave.
- Cooper Union • 30 Cooper Sq.
- Eugene Lang College • 65 W. 11th St.
- Institute of Audio Research • 64 University Pl.
- Joffrey Ballet School • 434 Ave. of the Americas
- Manhattan Night Comprehensive High School • 240 Second Ave.
- New Museum • 65 Fifth Ave.
- New School For Social Research • 66 W. 12th St.
- New York University • 70 Washington Sq. S.
- Nikolais And Louis Dance Lab • 375 W. Broadway
- Parson's School of Design • 66 Fifth Ave.
- Pratt Institute • 295 Lafayette St.
- PS 019 Asher Levy School •185 First Ave.
- PS 751 Career Development Ctr •113 E. 4th St.

 Community Gardens

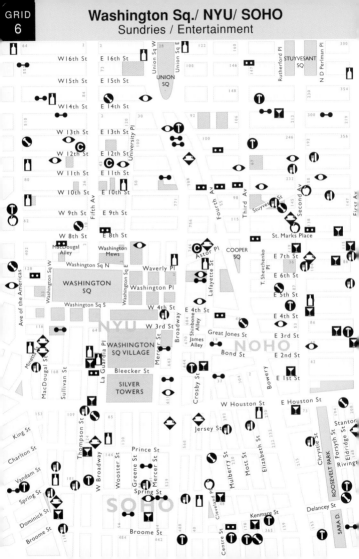

Bored? What's not here? There's a hundred cafes, a hundred bars, art stores, hardware stores—everything. If you need to get anything at all, it's probably somewhere in this grid. Milano's is the classic NYC dive bar, and Blue Ribbon (open 'til 4 a.m.) is one of our favorite restaurants.

24-Hour Copy Centers
- Kinko's • 24 E. 12th St.
- Kinko's • 13-25 Astor Pl.
- The Village Copier • 20 W. 13th St.

Bars
- Bar 89 • 89 Mercer St.
- Beauty Bar • 231 E. 14th St.
- Blue & Gold • 74 E. 7th St.
- Burp Castle • 41 E. 7th St.
- D.B.A. • 41 First Ave.
- Double Happiness • 173 Mott St.
- Edge • 95 E. 3rd St.
- Fanelli's • 94 Prince St.
- Fez • 380 Lafayette St.
- Holiday Lounge • 75 St. Mark's Pl.
- International Bar • 120 1/2 First Ave.
- KGB • 85 E. 4th St.
- Madame X • 94 W. Houston St.
- Mars Bar • 25 E. 1st St.
- Milano's • 51 E. Houston St.
- Peculier Pub • 145 Bleecker St.
- Red Bench • 107 Sullivan St.
- Spring Lounge • 48 Spring St.
- WCOU Radio Bar • 115 First Ave.

Cafes
- Bluestockings • 172 Allen St.
- Caffe Della Pace • 48 E. 7th St.
- Caffe Reggio • 119 MacDougal St.
- Cloister Cafe • 238 E. 9th St.
- Day Break • 47 E. 12th St.
- Dean & Deluca Cafe • 121 Prince St.
- Housing Works Used Book Cafe • 126 Crosby St.
- Juice & Java Station • 581 Broadway
- La Laterna di Vittorio • 129 MacDougal St
- Once Upon A Tart • 135 Sullivan St.
- Starbucks • 21 Astor Place

Farmer's Markets
- Greenmarket • Lafayette St. & Spring St.
- Greenmarket • Second Ave. & 10th St.
- Jefferson Market • 425 Ave. of the Americas
- Ottendorfer • 135 Second Ave.

Gyms
- Adolphus Fitness • 47 W. 14th St.
- Crunch Fitness • 404 Lafayette St.
- Crunch Fitness • 54 E. 13th St.
- David Barton Gym • 623 Broadway
- David Barton Gym • 552 Ave. of the Americas
- Dolphin Fitness East • 242 E. 14th St.
- One-On-One Training • 63 Greene St.
- Jeff's Gym • 224 W. 4th St.
- Lucille Roberts Health Club • 80 Fifth Av
- New York Health & Racquet Club • 24 E. 13th St.
- New York Sports Clubs • 34 W. 14th St.
- New York Sports Clubs • 503-511 Broadway
- One-on-One Training • 826 Broadway
- Plus One Fitness Clinic • 113 Mercer St.
- Printing House Fitness • 106 Crosby St.
- RE:AB • 33 Bleecker St.
- Revolution Studios • 104 W. 14th St.
- Sage Fitness • 80 E. 11th St.
- Sol Goldman YM-YWHA of Educational Alliance • 344 E. 14th St.
- Workout Partners Fitness • 30 Vandam
- World Gym • 232 Mercer St.
- Xie He Jian Kang Center • 302 Broome

Hardware Stores
- 14th St. Hardware • 211 E. 14th St.
- Ace Hardware • 130 Fourth Ave.
- Allied Hardware • 59 Second Ave.
- Barney's Hardware • 467 Sixth Ave.
- Brickman and Sons • 55 First Ave.
- Centre Plumbing & Hardware • 233 Centre St.
- Circa 2000 • 225 Lafayette St.
- East Hardware • 79 Third Ave.
- General Machinery • 358 Broome St.
- H & W Hardware • 220 First Ave.
- Hardware Mart • 151 W. 14th St.
- Metropolitan Hardware • 175 Spring St.
- Mott Hardware • 52 Kenmare St.
- Nanz Custom Hardware • 20 Vandam St.
- OK Hardware • 438 Broome St.
- Saifee Hardware • 114 First Ave.
- Shapiro Hardware • 63 Bleecker St.
- T&Y Hardware • 101 Chrystie St.

Liquor Stores
- Anthony Liquors • 52 Spring St.
- Astor Wines & Spirits • 12 Astor Pl.
- Casa Liquor & Wine • 258 Sixth Ave.
- Crossroads Wine & Liquor • 55 W. 14th St.
- East Village Vines • 138 First Ave.
- Elizabeth & Vine • 253 Elizabeth St.
- Franks Liquor Shop • 46 Union Sq. E
- S & P Liquor & Wine • 300 E. 5th St.
- Soho Wine & Spirits Inc. • 461 W. Broadway
- Spring Street Wine Shop • 187 Spring St.
- Thompson Wine & Spirits • 222 Thompson St.
- Union Square Wine & Spirits • 33 Union Sq W
- Village Vintner • 448 Ave. of the Americas
- Village Wine & Spirits • 486 Ave. of the Americas
- Warehouse Wines & Spirits • 735 Broadway
- Washington Sq. Wine & Liquor • 545 La Guardia Pl.
- Wine Gallery • 576 Ave. of the Americas
- Wines On 1st • 224 First Ave.
- Zeekman B&S • 47 University Pl.
- Zeichner Wine & Liquor • 279 First Ave.

Movie Theatres
- Angelika Film Center • 18 W. Houston St.
- Anthology Film Archives • 32 Second Ave
- Astor Place Theatre • 434 Lafayette St.
- Cinema Classics • 332 E. 11th St.
- Cinema Village • 22 E. 12th St.
- City Cinemas: Village East Cinemas • 189 Second Ave.
- Clearview's Waverly Twin • 323 Sixth Ave
- Fez • 380 Lafayette St.
- Loews Village • 66 Third Ave.
- Manhattan Ensemble Theatre Inc. • 55 Mercer
- Millennium • 66 E. 4th St.
- New School • 66 W. 12th St.
- NYU Cantor Film Center • 36 E. 8th St.
- Quad Cinema • 34 W. 13th St.
- St. Mark's-in-the-Bowery Archives • 131 E. 10th St.
- United Artists: Union Square • 850 Broadway at 13th St.

Pet Stores
- Animal Cracker • 26 First Ave.
- Aqua Star Pet Shop • 172 Mulberry St.
- Creature Features • 3 Great Jones St.
- Groom-O-Rama • 496 Ave. of Americas
- JBJ Discount Pet Shop • 151 E. Houston St.
- New World Aquarium • 5 W. 8th St.
- Pacific Aquarium & Plant Inc. • 46 Delancey St.
- Pet Bar • 132 Thompson St.
- Pet's Garden • 239 E. 5th St.
- Petland Discounts • 7 E. 14th St.
- Petland Discounts • 389 Ave. of Americas
- Whiskers • 235 E. 9th St.
- Win Tropical Aquariums • 169 Mott St.

Restaurants
- Aquagrill • 210 Spring St.
- Around The Clock • 8 Stuyvesant St.
- Arturo's • 106 W. Houston St.
- Balthazar • 80 Spring St.
- Baluchi's • 104 Second Ave.
- Ben's Pizza • 177 Spring St.
- Blue Ribbon • 97 Sullivan St.
- Bluie Ribbon Sushi • 119 Sullivan St.
- Boca Chica • 13 First Ave.
- Coffee Shop • Union Sq.W.
- Corner Bistro • 331 W. 4th St.
- Dojo • 14 W. 4th St.
- Dok Suni's • 119 First Ave.
- First • 87 First Ave.
- French Roast • 78 W. 11th St.
- Ghenet • 284 Mulberry St.
- Iso • 175 Second Ave.
- John's of 12th Street • 302 E. 12th St.
- Lupe's East L.A. Kitchen • 110 Sixth Ave.
- M & R Bar • 264 Elizabeth St.
- Penang • 109 Spring St.
- Sammy's Roumanian • 157 Chrystie St.
- Shabu-Tatsu • 216 E. 10th St.
- Taste of India • 181 Bleecker St.
- Zen Palate • 34 Union Sq. E

Video Rental
- Blockbuster Video • 780 Broadway
- Blockbuster Video • 151 Third Ave.
- Couch Potato Video • 9 E. 8th St.
- Crazy Fantasy Video • 333 Sixth Ave.
- Hollywood Video • 46 Third Ave.
- Kim's Video • 6 St. Mark's Pl.
- Kim's Video III • 144 Bleecker St.
- NYC Video & CD • 61 4th Ave.
- Tla Video • 54 W. 8th St.
- Tower Video • 383 Lafayette St.

Washington Sq./ NYU/ SOHO
Transportation

Considering how exciting and vibrant this section of the city is, parking should be way worse than it is. Contains one of the subway system's weirdest anomalies—you can only transfer to the B, D, F, Q from the 6 train's downtown track—there is no free transfer from the uptown side. For biking, use Lafayette Street to go north and either Fifth Ave. or Second Ave. to go south.

Subways

④ ⑤ ⑥ ⓡ ⓡ ⓛ	14 St–Union Square
⑥	Astor Place
⑥	Bleecker St
⑥	Spring St
Ⓐ Ⓒ Ⓔ Ⓑ Ⓓ Ⓕ Ⓠ	W 4 St
Ⓑ Ⓓ Ⓕ Ⓠ ⑥	Broadway–Lafayette St
Ⓒ Ⓔ	Spring St
Ⓕ	2 Avenue
Ⓛ	3 Avenue (at 14 St)
Ⓛ	1 Avenue (at 14 St)
Ⓝ Ⓡ	8 St–NYU
Ⓝ Ⓡ	Prince St

Bus Lines

1	Fifth and Madison Aves.
2	Fifth and Madison Aves./Powell Blvd.
3	Fifth and Madison Aves./St. Nicholas Ave.
5	Fifth Ave./Ave. of the Americas/Riverside Dr.
6	7th Ave./Broadway/Ave. of the Americas
7	Columbus Ave./Amsterdam Ave./Lenox Ave./6th/7th Aves./Broadway
8	8th/9th Sts. Crosstown
9	Avenue B/E. Broadway
14	14th St. Crosstown
15	First/Second Aves. (at 2 Ave)
21	Houston St./Avenue C
102	Third Ave./Lexington Ave./Amsterdam Ave.
101	Third Ave./Lexington Ave./Malcolm X
103	Third Ave./Lexington Ave.

⦿ Car Rentals

- Autorent Car Rental • 307 E. 11th St.
- Avis • 68 E. 11th St.
- Big Apple Car Rental • 220 E. 9th St.
- Enterprise • 221 Thompson St.
- Exotic Rentals • 19 E. 12th St.
- Mirkin Alex • 298 Mulberry St.
- National • 21 E. 12th St.
- Nationwide • 60 E. 9th St.
- NY On-The-Go Rent A Car • 741 Broadway

◆ Car Washes

- Broadway-Houston Car Wash • 614 Broadway
- Carz-A-Poppin Carwash • 124 Ave. of the Americas

Ⓟ Gas Stations

- Amoco • 610 Broadway
- Downtown Automotive • 326 Bowery
- Gaseteria • Lafayette & Houston St.
- Mobil • 140 Ave. of the Americas
- Mobil • 24 Second Ave.
- Park On Auto Service • 75 Kenmare St.
- Sunoco • Bowery & E. 3rd St.

Ⓟ Parking

- 395 Broome St.
- 44 W. 15th St.
- 501 Broadway
- 503 Broadway
- 60 E. 12th St.
- 77 W. 15th St.
- 137 Wooster St.
- 101 E. 13th St.
- 97 E. Houston St.
- 321 Bowery
- 372 W. Broadway
- 20 E. 9th St.
- 520 Broome St.
- 220 E. 9th St.
- 20 W. 13th St.
- 60 E. 8th St.
- 3 Washington Sq. Village
- 101 W. 12th St.
- 61 Chrystie St.
- 146 Third Ave.
- 92 Greene St.
- 174 Centre St.
- 204 Lafayette St.
- 375 Lafayette St.
- 11 Fifth Ave.
- 48 W. 15th St.
- 122 W. 3rd St.
- 21 E. 12th St.
- 2 Fifth Ave.
- 60 E. 10th St.
- 557 Broadway
- 310 E. 11th St.
- 224 Mulberry St.
- 303 Elizabeth St.
- 73-84 Third Ave.
- 74 Third Ave.
- 64 Cooper Sq.
- 303 E. 6th St.
- 165 Mercer St.
- 196 Mulberry St.
- 12 Cooper Sq.
- 76 E. 13th St.
- 85 Fourth Ave.
- 25 W. 13th St.
- 360 W. Broadway
- 12 E. 13th St.
- 403 Lafayette St.
- 14 Kenmare St.
- 70 E. 10th St.
- 221 Thompson St.
- 7 W. 14th St.
- 10 W. 15th St.
- 36 Delancey St.

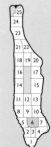

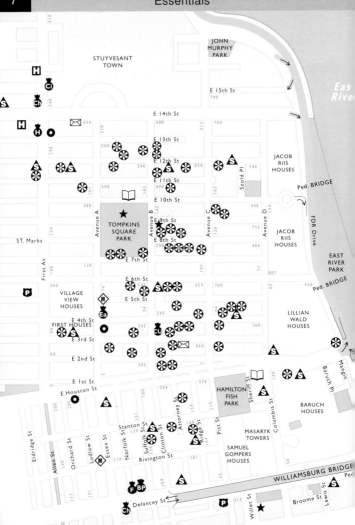

We think David's Bagels on First Avenue rocks. A Citibank on 7th Street and Avenue B would be nice.

 ATMs

BP • Banco Popular • 134 Delancey St.
Ch • Chase • 108-109 Delancey St.
Ch • Chase • 255 First Ave.
Ci • Citibank • 262 First Ave.
Ea • EAB • 50 Ave. A
F • Fleet • 126 Delancey St.
H • HSBC • 245 First Ave.
CU • Lower East Side People's Federal Credit Union • 37 Ave. B

Bagels

• 535 Self Corp. • 203 E. Houston St.
• David's Bagels • 220 First Ave.
• La Bagel • 263 First Ave.
• The Bagel Zone • Ave. A between 3rd & 4th Sts.

Hospital

• Beth Israel Medical Center • 281 First Ave.

★ Landmarks

• Bialystoker Synagogue • 7-11 Willet St.
• Charlie Parker House • Ave. B at Tompkins Sq Pk
• Tompkins Square Park • Ave. A and 9th St.

Libraries

• Hamilton Fish Park • 415 E. Houston St.
• Tompkins Square • 331 E. 10th St.

Ⓜ Marketplace

• Economy Candy • 108 Rivington St.
• Etherea • 66 Ave. A

Police Precincts

• 7th Precinct • 19 1/2 Pitt St.
• 9th Precinct • 321 E. 5th St.

✉ Post Offices

• Peter Stuyvesant • 432 E. 14th St.
• Tompkins Square • 244 E. 3rd St.

Ⓢ Schools

• JHS 022 G. Straubenmuller School • 111 Columbia St.
• JHS 025 Marta Valle School • 145 Stanton St.
• JHS 060 Ottilia M. Beha School • 420 E. 12th St.
• Lower East Side Prep School • 145 Stanton St.
• PS 015 Roberto Clemente School • 333 E. 4th St.
• PS 019 Asher Levy School • 185 First Ave.
• PS 034 F. D. Roosevelt School • 730 E. 12th St.
• PS 061 Anna Howard Shaw School • 610 E. 12th St.
• PS 063 William McKinley School • 121 E. 3rd St.
• PS 064 Robert Simon School • 600 E. 6th St.
• PS 094 • 442 E. Houston St.
• PS 097 Mangin School • 525 E. Houston St.
• PS 110 F. Nightingale School • 285 Delancey St.
• PS 140 Nathan Straus School • 123 Ridge St.
• PS 142 Amalia Castro School • 100 Attorney St.
• PS 188 John Burroughs School • 442 E. Houston St.

❋ Community Gardens

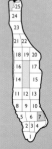

Kim's Video and Two Boots Video have the best selection of movies in Manhattan. There're more bars on Avenue A than you can shake a swizzle stick at. Some favorites, though: 2A, 7B, Bouche Bar, Mona's, and Parkside. Joe's Bar is our absolute favorite.

Bars

- 2A • 25 Ave. A
- 7B • 108 Ave. B
- 9C • 700 E. 9th St.
- Barmacy • 538 E. 14th St.
- Barramundi • 147 Ludlow St.
- Bouche Bar • 530 E. 5th St.
- D.B.A. • 41 First Ave.
- International Bar •
  120 1/2 First Ave.
- Joe's Bar • 520 E. 6th St.
- Lakeside Lounge • 162 Ave. B
- Lansky Lounge • 104 Norfolk St.
- Liquids • 266 E. 10th St.
- Max Fish • 178 Ludlow St.
- Mona's • 224 Ave. B
- Motor City • 127 Ludlow St.
- Parkside Lounge •
  317 E. Houston St.
- Sophie's • 507 E. 5th St.
- WCOU Radio Bar •
  115 First Ave.
- Welcome to the Johnsons •
  123 Rivington St.

Cafes

- Alt Coffee Inc. • 139 Avenue A
- Bluestockings • 172 Allen St.
- C K Coffee Shop •
  536 E. 14th St.
- Cafe Gigi • 417 E. 9th St.
- Cafe Pick Me Up • 145 Ave. A
- Des Moines • 41 Ave. A
- Hugh Grande Cafe •
  32 Avenue C
- Pink Pony Cafe • 176 Ludlow St.
- Yaffa Café • 97 St. Mark's Place

Farmer's Market

- Tompkins Square Park •
  Ave. A and 7th St.

Gyms

- Dolphin Fitness Clubs •
  155 E. 3rd St.
- Gladiator's Gym • 503 E. 6th St.

Hardware Stores

- Brickman and Sons •
  55 First Ave.
- CHP Hardware • 96 Ave. C
- East Side Lumber •
  421 E. 13th St.
- H & W Hardware •
  220 First Ave.
- HH Hardware •
  111 Ludlow St.
- I. Rothstein • 56 Clinton St.
- JR Hardware • 129 Ave. C
- Rosa Hardware • 85 Pitt St.
- Saifee Hardware • 114 First Ave.

Liquor Stores

- Ave. A Wine & Liquor •
  196 Ave. A
- Ave. C Liquor • 193 Ave. C
- Bee Liquors • 225 Ave. B
- East Village Wines •
  138 First Ave.
- Jade Fountain Liquor •
  123 Delancey St.
- Loon Chun Liquor • 47 Pitt St.
- Marty's Liquors • 133 Avenue D
- Nizga Liquors • 58 Ave. A
- Sale Price Liquor • 24 Ave. C
- Schapiro Wine Co. •
  124 Rivington St.
- Wines On 1st • 224 First Ave.
- Zeichner Wine & Liquor • 279
  First Ave.

Movie Theatres

- Nyurican Poets Café •
  236 E. 3rd St.
- Tonic • 107 Norfolk St.
- Two Boots Pioneer Theater •
  155 E. 3rd St.

Pet Stores

- Animal Cracker • 26 First Ave.
- Petland Discounts •
  530 E. Houston St.
- Mikey's Pet Shop • 130 E. 7th St.
- Petland • 85 Delancey St.

Restaurants

- 7A • 7th St. & Ave. A
- Benny's Burritos • 93 Ave. A
- Boca Chica • 13 First Ave.
- Cafe Margaux • 175 Ave. B
- Dojo • 24-26 St. Mark's Place
- Dok Suni's • 119 First Ave.
- El Castillo de Jaqua •
  113 Rivington St.
- Essex Restaurant • 120 Essex St.
- First • 87 First Ave.
- Il Bagatto • 192 E. 2nd St.
- Katz's Delicatessen •
  205 E. Houston St.
- Khyber Pass • 34 St. Mark's Place
- Mama's Food Shop •
  200 E. 3rd St.
- Moustache • 265 E. 10th St.
- Odessa • 119 Ave. A
- Old Devil Moon • 511 E. 12th St.
- Ratners • 138 Delancey St.
- Takahachi • 85 Ave. A
- The Hat (Sombrero) •
  108 Stanton St.
- Two Boots • 42 Ave. A

Video Rentals

- Alpha Video • 134 Ave. C
- Blockbuster Video •
  250 E. Houston St.
- Bus Stop Video Shop • 3 Ave. D
- Kim's Video • 85 Ave. A
- The Video Store •
  128 Rivington St.
- Two Boots Video • 44 Ave. A b/w
  Third & Fourth Sts.

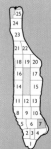

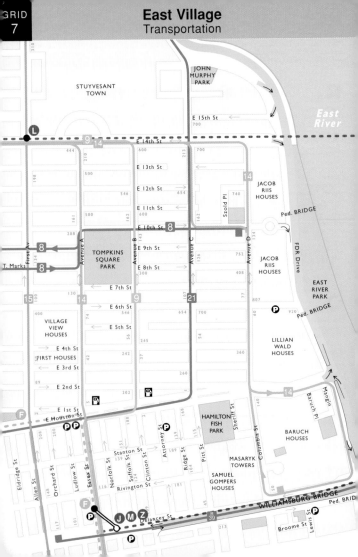

East Village
Transportation

Parking is usually pretty good except for Friday and Saturday night when the Bridge & Tunnel crowd invades. The East Village badly needs a subway line that has a Tompkins Square Park stop, but it will never happen, no matter how gentrified the neighborhood gets, so you can just forget it.

Subways

Ⓕ . . . . 2 Avenue

Ⓕ Ⓙ Ⓜ Ⓩ . . . . . Delancey St–Essex St
(at Essex St)

Ⓛ . . . . 1 Avenue (at 14 St)

Bus Lines

🚌8 . . . . 9th and 10th St (at 10 St)

🚌9 . . . . 14th St and Ave. B (at Ave B)

🚌14 . . . 14th St and Ave. A/D (at Ave A/Ave D)

🚌15 . . . . First Ave.

🚌21 . . . . 1st St and Ave. C (at Ave C)

🚌⁹⁄₃₉ . . . . Delancey St.

🅿 Gas Stations

• Gaseteria • Ave. B/Houston St
• Mobil • 253 E. 2nd St.

Ⓟ Parking

• 275 Delancey St.
• 135 Delancey St.
• 215 E. Houston St.
• 207 E. Houston St.
• 105 Essex St.
• 151 Attorney St.
• 990 E. 6th St.
• 54 Suffolk St.

W 37th St

W 36th St

W 35th St

W 34th St

W 33rd St

Post Office

W 31st St

W 30th St

W 29th St

W 28th St

Chelsea Park

W 27th St

W 26th St

W 25th St

W 24th St

W 23rd St

W 22nd St

W 21st St

W 20th St

W 19th St

W 18th St

W 17th St

W 16th St

W 15th St

W 14th St

Jacob K. Javits
Convention
Center

Twelfth Av

WEST SIDE HIGHWAY

Eleventh Av

Tenth Av

Ninth Av

Eighth Av

Penn

Station

South

Houses

Chelsea Piers

Hudson
River

PK

78

76

73

72

67

62

61

60

59

57

More services are desperately needed, especially by the Javits Center area (unless you count the services of transvestite prostitutes as "essential"). However, Chelsea Piers (p.225) will shortly be joined by several other interesting waterfront projects.

ATMs

CF • Carver Federal Savings • 261 Eighth Ave.
Ch • Chase • 475 W. 23rd St.
Ch • Chase • 238 Eighth Ave.
Ci • Citibank • 322 W. 23rd St.
Ci • Citibank • 111 Eighth Ave.

Bagels

• Chelsea Bagels • 300 W. 23rd St.
• Unbagelievable • 75 Ninth Ave.

Hospital

• St.Vincent's Senior Health at Penn South • 275 Eighth Ave.

Landmarks

• J.A. Farley Post Office •
30th St. and Eighth Ave.
• Jacob K. Javits Convention Center •
36th St. and Eleventh Ave.

Marketplace

• B&H Photo • 420 Ninth Ave.
• Chelsea Wholesale Flower Market •
75 Ninth Ave.

24-Hour Pharmacy

• Rite Aid • 282 Eighth Ave.

Police Precinct

• Mid-Town South • 357 W. 35th St.

Post Offices

• Central Parcel Post • 325 W. 15th St.
• JA Farley General • 421 Eighth Ave.
• Morgan General • 341 Ninth Ave.

Schools

• General Theological Seminary • 175 Ninth Ave.
• IS 70 O'Henry School • 333 W. 17th St.
• PS 11 William T Harris School •
320 W. 21st St.
• PS 33 Chelsea School • 281 Ninth Ave.
• Tech Career Institutes • 320 W. 31st St.
• Technical Career Institute • 500 Eighth Ave.

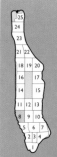

Chelsea
Sundries / Entertainment

Even though this area has several of New York's most happening dance clubs and has seen an amazing increase in the number of art galleries, it's time for Blockbuster to head west towards Eleventh Avenue!

 Bars

- Gavin Brown's Enterprise • 436 W. 15th St.
- Rebar Lounge • 127 Eighth Ave.
- Red Rock West • 457 W. 17th St.
- Village Idiot • 355 W. 14th St.

 Cafes

- Big Cup Tea & Coffee House • 228 8th Ave.
- Dalton Coffee Ltd. • 300 W. 23rd St.
- Java Works • 309 W. 17th St.

 Gyms

- American Fitness Centers • 128 Eighth Ave.
- Basketball City Inc • Pier 63
- Gleason's Gym • Chelsea Piers-Pier 62
- Midtown Tennis Club • 341 8th Ave.
- New York Sports Clubs • 270 8th Ave.
- Origins Feel Good Health Spa • Chelsea Piers-Pier 62
- Sports Center at Chelsea Piers • Chelsea Piers-Pier 60

 Hardware Stores

- Diener Park • 194 Eighth Ave.
- Greenspan Simon Hardware • 261 W. 35th St.
- London True Value Hardware • 191 Ninth Ave.
- Mercer Sq. Hardware • 286 Eighth Ave.
- MJ Hardware & Electric • 520 Eighth Ave.
- NF Hardware • 219 Ninth Ave.
- SGS Hardware • 157 Eighth Ave.
- United Equipment and Supply • 419 Ninth Ave.
- Young Hardware • 399 Eighth Ave.

Liquor Stores

- 34th Street Winery • 460 W. 34th St.
- 9th Ave. Wine & Liquor • 474 Ninth Ave.
- Brian's Liquor • 336 Ninth Ave.
- Chelsea Liquor • 114 Ninth Ave.
- Chelsea Wine Vault • 75 Ninth Ave.
- Delauren Wines & Liquors • 332 Eighth Ave.
- House of Cheers • 261 W. 18th St.
- London Terrace Liquor • 221 9th Ave.
- Philippe Wine & Liquor • 312 W. 23rd St.

 Movie Theatres

- Clearview's Chelsea West • 333 W. 23rd St.
- Clearview's Chelsea • 260 W. 23rd St.
- Gavin Brown's Enterprise • 436 W. 15th St.
- The Kitchen • 512 W. 19th St.

Pet Stores

- Barking Zoo • 172 Ninth Ave.
- Petland Discounts • 312 W. 23rd St.

Restaurants

- Bendix Diner • 219 Eighth Ave.
- Bottino • 246 Tenth Ave.
- Chelsea Bistro & Bar • 358 W. 23rd St.
- El Cid • 322 W. 15th St.
- Empire Diner • 210 Tenth Ave.
- Frank's Restaurant • 85 Tenth Ave.
- Grand Sichuan Int'l • 229 Ninth Ave.
- Havana Chelsea • 190 Eighth Ave.
- La Lunchonette • 130 Tenth Ave.
- Moonstruck Diner • 400 W. 23rd St.
- Pacific East • 318 W. 23rd St.
- Skylight Diner • 402 W. 34th St.
- Tick Tock Diner • 481 Eighth Ave.
- Woo Chon • 8-10 W. 36th St.

Video Rental

- Alan's Alley Video • 207A Ninth Ave.
- Blockbuster Video • 128 Eighth Ave.
- E4 Entertainment • 447 W. 36th St.
- Rina Inc. • 364 W. 23rd St.
- Video Blitz • 267 W. 17th St.
- Video Blitz • 144 Eighth Ave.

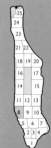

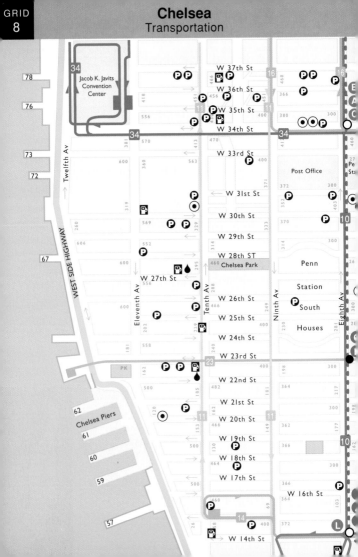

Parking and driving in this area is quite bad during the day and quite good at night, although there just aren't many spots at all above 30th Street. Tragically, there are no subway lines west of Eighth Avenue.

Subways

Ⓐ Ⓒ Ⓔ . . . . 34 St–Penn Station (at 8 Ave)

Ⓐ Ⓒ Ⓔ Ⓛ . . . . . . 14 St–8 Av (at 8 Ave)

Ⓒ Ⓔ . . . . 23rd St (at 8 Ave)

Bus Lines

10 . . . . . . 7th Ave./8th Ave./Central Park West

11 . . . . 9th Ave./10th Ave.

14 . . . . 14th St. Crosstown

18 . . . . 34th St. Crosstown

23 . . . . 23rd St. Crosstown

34 . . . . 34th St. Crosstown

⊙ Car Rentals

- Allstar Rent-A-Car • 325 W. 34th St.
- Berma Limousine • 537 W. 20th St.
- Nationwide • 241 W. 26th St.
- New York Rent-A-Car • 325 W. 34th St.
- New York Rent-A-Car • 230 W. 31st St.
- U-Save Auto Rental • 333 Tenth Ave.

⬤ Car Washes

- 235 10th Ave. Car Wash • 235 Tenth Ave.
- Steve's Detailing & Tires • 516 W. 27th St.

⒢ Gas Stations

- Amoco • 436 Tenth Ave.
- Citigas • Tenth Ave. & 27th St.
- Exxon • 165 Tenth Ave.
- Gaseteria • Tenth Ave. & 36th St.
- Getty • 63 Eighth Ave.
- Getty • 239 Tenth Ave.
- Mobil • 56 Tenth Ave.

Ⓟ Parking

- 422 W. 15th St.
- 320 W. 30th St.
- 349 W. 37th St.
- 519 W. 37th St.
- 510-515 W. 37th St.
- 509 W. 34th St.
- 514 W. 23rd St.
- 521 W. 21st St.
- 346 W. 37th St.
- 451 Tenth Ave.
- 444 Tenth Ave.
- 445 W. 35th St.
- 360 W. 31st St.
- 430 W. 37th St.
- 429 W. 36th St.
- 524 W. 23rd St.
- 451 Ninth Ave.
- 420 W. 33rd St.
- 520 Eighth Ave.
- 545 W. 25th St.
- 333 W. 26th St.
- 282 Eleventh Ave.
- 85 Eighth Ave.
- 325 W. 34th St.
- 111 Eighth Ave.
- 343 Tenth Ave.
- 516 W. 30th St.
- 530 W. 30th St.
- 438 W. 18th St.
- 438 W. 19th St.
- 300 W. 31st St.
- 249 Tenth Ave.
- 279 Tenth Ave.
- 320 W. 36th St.

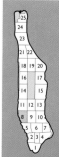

If you stand in the middle of traffic at the junction of Broadway, Fifth Avenue, and 24th Street and turn slowly around, you'll see the Flatiron Building, the Met Life Building, the New York Life Building, and the Empire State Building. It's perhaps the single most awe-inspiring spot in all of Manhattan, if you don't get run over.

💰 ATMs

- Am • Amalgamated • 11-15 Union Sq. W.
- At • Atlantic • 100 W. 32nd St.
- At • Atlantic • 960 Sixth Ave.
- At • Atlantic • 620 Sixth Ave.
- BL • Bank Leumi • 1400 Broadway
- B • Bank of New York • 162 Fifth Ave.
- B • Bank of New York • 350 Fifth Ave.
- BN • Broadway National • 250 Fifth Ave.
- CF • Carver Federal Savings • 261 Eighth Ave.
- Ch • Chase • 158 W. 14th St.
- Ch • Chase • 238 Eighth Ave.
- Ch • Chase • 305 Seventh Ave.
- Ch • Chase • 399 Seventh Ave.
- Ch • Chase • 33 E. 23rd St.
- Ch • Chase • 71 W. 23rd St.
- Ch • Chase • 5 W. 19th St.
- Ch • Chase • 245 Fifth Ave.
- Ch • Chase • 349 Fifth Ave.
- Ch • Chase • 86 Fifth Ave.
- Ch • Chase • Penn Station
- Ch • Chase • 2 Penn Plaza
- Ch • Chase • 221 Park Ave. S.
- Ch • Chase • 386 Park Ave. S.
- Ch • Chase • 390 Park Ave. S.
- Ch • Chase • 1411 Broadway
- Ch • Chase • 98 Madison Ave.
- CH • Cho Hung • 241 Fifth Ave.
- Ci • Citibank • 72 Fifth Ave.
- Ci • Citibank • 322 W. 23rd St.
- Ci • Citibank • 111 Eighth Ave.
- Ci • Citibank • 201 W. 34th St.
- Ci • Citibank • 717 Ave. of the Americas
- Ci • Citibank • 411 Fifth Ave.
- Ci • Citibank • 326 Fifth Ave.
- Ci • Citibank • 1 Park Ave.
- Co • Commercial Bank • 1407 Broadway
- Co • Commercial Bank • 404 Fifth Ave.
- Co • Commercial Bank • 2 Park Ave. at 33rd St.
- Ea • EAB • 1107 Broadway
- Ea • EAB • 5 Penn Plaza
- Ea • EAB • 475 Park Ave. S.
- F • Fleet • 116 Fifth Ave.
- F • Fleet • 350 Fifth Ave.
- F • Fleet • 4 Penn Plaza
- F • Fleet • 515 Seventh Ave.
- F • Fleet • Penn Plz. 33rd St. & 2nd Ave.
- FS • Fourth Federal Savings • 242 W. 23rd St.
- G • Greenpoint • 358 Fifth Ave.
- G • Greenpoint • 1 Penn Plaza
- HA • Hanvit America Bank • 1250 Broadway
- H • HSBC • 101 W. 14th St.
- H • HSBC • 10 Union Sq. East
- H • HSBC • 1330 Broadway
- MT • Manufacturers and Traders Trust Co. • 95 Madison Ave.
- N • North Fork Bank • 1001 Ave. of the Americas
- N • North Fork Bank • 120 W. 23rd St.

🥯 Bagels

- 23rd St Bagel • 170 W. 23rd St.
- Bagel Maven • 362 Seventh Ave.
- Chelsea Bagels • 300 W. 23rd St.
- Hot Bagels • 688 Ave. of the Americas
- Le Bon Bagel • 980 Ave. of the Americas
- Nathan Cafe & Deli • 319 Fifth Ave.
- Pick A Bagel On Sixth • 601 Ave. of the Americas

🏥 Hospitals

- American Association For Bikur Cholim Hospital • 156 Fifth Ave.
- Beth Israel Medical Center • 10 Union Sq. E.
- National Jewish Center For Immunology • 450 Seventh Ave.
- New York Foundling Hospital • 590 Ave. of the Americas
- St.Vincent's Senior Health at Penn South • 275 Eighth Ave.

★ Landmarks

- Chelsea Hotel • 23rd St. btwn. 7th and 8th Aves.
- Empire State Building • 34th St. & Fifth Ave.
- Flatiron Building • 175 Fifth Ave.
- Flower District • 28th St. btwn. 6th and 7th Aves.
- Garment District • West 30's south of Herald Square
- Macy's Herald Square • 151 W. 34th St.
- Madison Square Garden • 4 Penn Plz.
- Madison Square Park • 23rd St.
- Metropolitan Life Insurance Co. • 1 Madison Ave.
- Penn Station • 31th St. and Eighth Ave.
- Theodore Roosevelt Birthplace • 28 E. 20th St.
- Union Square • 14th St.-Union Sq.

📖 Libraries

- Andrew Heiskell Library for The Blind • 40 W. 20th St.
- Muhlenberg • 209 W. 20th St.
- Science, Industry, and Business Library • 188 Madison Av

Ⓜ Marketplace

- Bed Bath & Beyond • 620 Sixth Ave.
- Different Spokes • 240 Seventh Ave.
- Fishs Eddy • 889 Broadway
- Loehmann's • 101 Seventh Ave.
- Macy's • 151 W. 34th St.
- Paragon Sporting Goods • 867 Broadway
- Sam Flax, Inc. • 12 W. 20th St.
- Stern's • 899 Sixth Ave.
- The Sports Authority • 401 Seventh Ave.

℞ 24-Hour Pharmacies

- Duane Reade • 300 Park Ave. S
- Rite Aid • 282 Eighth Ave.

Ⓟ Police Precinct

- 10th Precinct • 230 W. 20th St.

✉ Post Offices

- Empire State • 19 W. 33rd St.
- Greeley Square • 40 W. 32nd St.
- JA Farley General • 421 Eighth Ave.
- Old Chelsea • 217 W. 18th St.

🎓 Schools

- American Academy Of Dramatic Arts • 120 Madison Ave.
- Bourel Technical • 50 W. 32nd St.
- Empire State College-SUNY • 229 W. 28th St.
- Fashion Institute of Technology • 227 W. 27th St.
- High School of Fashion Industries • 225 W. 24th St.
- Liberty High School • 250 W.18th St.
- New Museum • 65 Fifth Ave.
- New York College Of Optometry • 100 E. 24th St.
- New York School Of Astrology • 545 Eighth Ave.
- Norman Thomas • 111 E. 33rd St.
- NY Institute of Credit • 71 W. 23rd St.
- Parson's School of Design • 66 Fifth Ave.
- PS 723 Manhattan Trans Ctr • 22 E. 28th St.
- Studio Semester • 229 W. 28th St.
- Technical Career Institute • 500 Eighth Ave.
- Touro College • 27 W. 23rd St.

Flatiron/Lower Midtown
Sundries / Entertainment

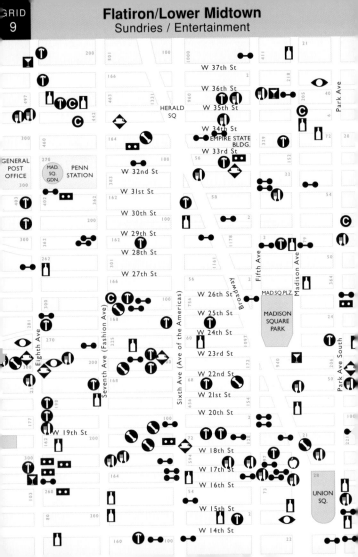

The Flatiron/Lower Midtown area contains two of New York's most famous business districts, the Garment District (in the west 30s south of Herald Square) and the Flower District (28th Street between 6th and 7th Avenues). For great burgers, check out Old Town Bar. Kang Suh is one of several great Korean restaurants—they're all worth trying.

24-Hour Copy Centers

- Kinko's • 191 Madison Ave.
- Kinko's • 245 Seventh Ave.
- On-Site Sourcing, Inc. • 443 Park Ave. S
- Sir Speedy • 225 W. 34th St.
- Sir Speedy • 234 W. 35th St.

Bars

- Community Bar and Grill • 216 Seventh Ave.
- Ginger Man • 11 E. 36th St.
- Live Bait • 14 E. 23rd St.
- Rebar Lounge • 127 Eighth Ave.
- Wakamba • 543 Eighth Ave.

Cafes

- Big Cup Tea & Coffee House • 228 8th Ave.
- Cafe Beyond • 620 Avenue of the Americas
- Dalton Coffee Ltd. • 300 W. 23rd St.
- Emack & Bolio's • 151 W. 34th St. , 4th Floor
- Milan Coffee & Coffee Bar • 120 W. 23rd St.
- West Front Store • 28 W. 32nd St.
- Xando Coffee & Bar • 257 Park Ave. S

Farmer's Market

- Greenmarket • Broadway & 17th St.

Gyms

- 19th St. Gym • 22 W. 19th St.
- Adolphus Fitness • 47 W. 14th St.
- American Fitness Centers • 128 Eighth Ave.
- Anderson's Martial Arts • 42 W. 30th St.
- Athletic Complex • 3 Park Ave.
- Bally Sports Club • 139 W. 32nd St.
- Bally Total Fitness • 641 Ave. Americas
- Body Sculpture • 50 W. 34th St.
- Cardio Fitness Center • 79 Madison Ave.
- Chau's Wu Mui Kung Fu • 159 W. 25th St.
- David Barton Gym • 552 Ave. of the Americas
- Definitions • 139 Fifth Ave.
- Equinox Fitness Club • 897 Broadway & 19th St.
- Fitness Results • 137 Fifth Ave.
- Johnny Lats Gym • 7 E. 17th St.
- Kingsway International Boxing • 1 W. 28th St.
- Kodokan Judo & Self Defense • 152 W. 26th St.
- Kyokushin USA • 284 Fifth Ave.
- Lucille Roberts Health Club • 80 Fifth Ave.
- Middletown Health Club • 290 Fifth Ave.
- Midtown Tennis Club • 341 8th Ave.
- New York Sports Clubs • 50 W. 34th St.
- New York Sports Clubs • 200 Madison Ave.
- New York Sports Clubs • 303 Park Ave. S.
- New York Sports Clubs • 1372 Broadway
- New York Sports Clubs • 270 8th Ave.
- New York Sports Clubs • 34 W. 14th St.
- New York Sports Clubs • 404 5th Ave.
- Park Ave. Athletic Complex • 3 Park Ave.
- Pierre Romain • 208 W. 29th St.
- Revolution Studios • 104 W. 14th St.
- Steel Gym • 146 W. 23rd St.
- Synergy Fitness Clubs • 4 Park Ave.
- Workout Partners • 208 W. 29th St.
- YMCA of Greater NY: McBurney • 215 W. 23rd St.
- Zone Studios 121 • 31 E. 31st St.

Hardware Stores

- 727 Hardware • 727 Ave. of the Americas
- A&M 28th St. Hardware • 15 E. 28th St.
- Adco Hardware • 23 W. 35th St.
- Admore Hardware & Lock • 11 E. 33rd St.
- B&N Hardware • 12 W. 19th St.
- Diener Bars • 194 Eighth Ave.
- Elm Electric & Hardware • 884 Sixth Ave.
- Greenspan Simon Hardware • 261 W 35th St.
- Halmor Hardware and Supply • 48 W. 22nd St.
- Hardware Mart • 151 W. 14th St.
- Harris Hardware • 17 W. 18th St.
- J&M Hardware & Locksmiths • 238 Park Ave. S.
- Jamali Hardware & Garden Supplies • 149 W. 28th St.
- KDM Hardware • 150 W. 26th St.
- Kove Brothers Hardware • 189 Seventh Ave.
- Mercer Sq. Hardware • 286 Eighth Ave.
- Midcity Hardware • 130 W. 25th St.
- MJ Hardware & Electric • 520 Eighth Ave.
- Scherman & Grant • 545 Eighth Ave.
- SGS Hardware • 157 Eighth Ave.
- Spacesaver Hardware • 132 W. 23rd St.
- Whitey's Hardware • 37 W. 32nd St.
- Young Hardware • 399 Eighth Ave.

Liquor Stores

- Bombay Spirits • 224 W. 35th St.
- Chelsea Wine Cellar • 200 W. 21st St.
- Crossroads Wine & Liquor • 55 W. 14th St.
- Delauren Wines & Liquors • 332 Eighth Ave.
- Franks Liquor Shop • 46 Union Sq. E.
- Harry's Liquors • 270 W. 36th St.
- Honig's Wines and Liquors • 61 W. 23rd St.
- House of Cheers • 261 W. 18th St.
- J L Wine & Liquors • 60 E. 34th St.
- Kessler Liquors • 23 E. 28th St.
- Landmark Wine & Spirit • 167 W. 23rd St.
- Madison Ave. Liquors • 244 Madison Ave.
- North Village Wine & Liquor • 254 W. 14th St.
- Old Chelsea Wine & Liquor Store • 86 Seventh Ave.
- Philippe Wine & Liquor • 312 W. 23rd St.
- Quality House • 2 Park Ave.
- Royal Wine & Liquor Store • 45 Madison Ave.
- Sonest Liquors • 878 Sixth Ave.
- Union Square Wine & Spirits • 33 Union Sq W
- Wine Gallery • 576 Ave. of Americas
- Yuk Cheun Liquor • 195 Madison Ave.

Movie Theatres

- Clearview's Chelsea • 260 W. 23rd St.
- Clearview's Chelsea West • 333 W. 23rd St.
- Loews 19th St. East • 890 Broadway
- Morgan Library • 29 E. 36th St.

Pet Stores

- Blue Ribbon Dog Company • 20 W. 22nd St.
- Doggone Purrrty • 151 W. 25th St.
- New York Pet Spa and Hotel • 145 W. 18th St.
- Outsect • 147 W. 22nd St.
- Pet Parade • 144 W. 19th St.
- Petco • 860 Broadway
- Petland Discounts • 312 W. 23rd St.

Restaurants

- Basta Pasta • 37 W. 17th St.
- Bendix Diner • 219 Eighth Ave.
- Burritoville • 264 W. 23rd St.
- Cafeteria • 119 Seventh Ave.
- Coffee Shop • Union Sq. W.
- Cosi Sandwich Bar • 3 E. 17th St.
- Francisco's Centro Vasco • 159 W. 23rd St.
- Hangawi • 12 E. 32nd St.
- Havana Chelsea • 190 Eighth Ave.
- Kang Suh • 1250 Broadway
- Kum Gang San • 49 W. 32nd St.
- L'Express • 249 Park Ave. S
- Le Madri • 168 W. 18th St.
- Mesa Grill • 102 Fifth Ave.
- Old Town Bar • 45 E. 18th St.
- Pacific East • 34 W. 23rd St.
- Park Avenue Country Club • 381 Park Ave. S
- Patria • 250 Park Ave. S
- Periyali • 35 W. 20th St.
- Tick Tock Diner • 481 Eighth Ave.
- Toledo • 6 E. 36th St.
- Union Square Cafe • 21 E. 16th St.
- Zen Palate • 34 Union Sq.

Video Rentals

- 155 Video Center • 155 W. 33rd St.
- 603 Video Store • 603 Ave. of the Americas
- Blockbuster Video • 128 Eighth Ave.
- International Express Video • 219 Madison Ave.
- Koryo Video • 7 W. 32nd St.
- Penn Visual • 252 W. 31st St.
- Video Blitz • 144 Eighth Ave.
- Video Blitz • 267 W. 17th St.
- Westcoast Video • 295 Park Ave. S.

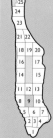

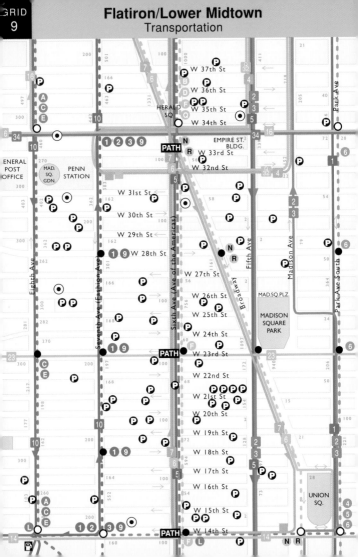

Parking during the day and on weekends is extremely difficult in this area, due to the number of business districts and commercial enterprises that are here. Driving isn't much better, since Lincoln Tunnel traffic has far-ranging repercussions.

Subways

1 2 3 9 . . 34 St (at 7th Av–Penn Station)

1 2 3 9 F L . . . 14 St–6 Av (at 6 Ave)

1 9 . . . . 28 St (at 7 Av)

1 9 . . . . 23 St (at 7 Av)

1 9 . . . . 18 St (at 7 Av)

4 5 6 N R L . . . . 14 St–Union Square

6 . . . . 33rd St (at Park Av)

6 . . . . 28rd St (at Park Av)

6 . . . . 23rd St (at Park Av)

A C E . . . . . . 34 St–Penn Station (at 8 Av)

A C E L . . . . 14 St–8 Av (at 8 Ave)

B D F Q N R 34 St–Herald Sq (at 6 Av)

C E . . . . 23rd St (at 8 Av)

F . . . . 23rd St (at 6 Av)

N R . . . . 28 St (at Broadway)

N R . . . . 23 St (at Broadway)

Bus Lines

1 2 3 . . . . 5th Ave./Madison Ave.

4 . . . . 5th Ave./Madison Ave./Broadway

5 . 5th Ave./Ave. of the Americas/Riverdale Dr.

6 . . . 7th Ave./Broadway/Ave. of the Americas

7 . . . Columbus Ave./Amsterdam Ave./Lenox/
6th Ave./7th Ave./Broadway

10 . . . . . 7th Ave./8th Ave. (Central ParkWest)/
Frederick Douglass Blvd.

14 . . . . 14th St. Crosstown

16 . . . . 34th St. Crosstown

23 . . . . 23rd St. Crosstown

32 . . . . Penn Station–Jackson Heights, Queens

PATH Path Stations

• 14 St—Hoboken & Journal Square
• 23 St.—Hoboken & Journal Square
• 33 St.—Hoboken & Journal Square

Gas Station

• Getty • 63 Eighth Ave.

Car Rentals

• Atlas Auto • 839 Ave. of the Americas
• Eldan Rent-A-Car • 350 Fifth Ave.
• Hertz • 250 W. 34th St.
• Nationwide • 241 W. 26th St.
• New York Rent-A-Car • 230 W. 31st St.
• Zupa Brothers • 145 W. 14th St.

Parking (72 locations)

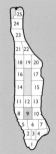

Murray Hill/Stuyvesant Town/Gramercy
Essentials

E 37th St

E 36th St

Sniffen Ct

Queens-
Midtown Tunnel

E 35th St

Avenue C

E 16th St

E 15th St

E 34th St

E 33rd St

KIPS BAY
PLAZA

E 32nd St

East
River

E 31st St

Lexington Av

Third Av

Second Av

First Av

E 30th St

NYU
MEDICAL
CENTER

E 29th St

E 28th St

Park Av South

E 27th St

BELLEVUE
HOSPITAL
CENTER

E 26th St

Broadway Alley

E 25th St

WATERSIDE
PLAZA

E 24th St

VET. ADM.
MEDICAL
CENTER

E 23rd St

Asser Levy Pl

MARINA &
SKYPORT

E 22nd St

Franklin D Roosevelt Drive

Marginal St

E 21st St

GRAMERCY
PARK

PETER COOPER VILLAGE

E 20th St

Irving Place

E 19th St

E 18th St

E 17th St

STUYVESANT
TOWN

Union Sq E

E 16th St

Rutherford Pl

Stuyvesant Square

Nathan D Perlman Pl

E 15th St

Avenue C

E 14th St

This area is home to one of Manhattan's most pastoral and beautiful settings, Gramercy Park, and one of the city's biggest hospitals, NYU. It also contains two humongous and drab residential communities, Stuyvesant Town and Peter Cooper Village.

ATMs

Am • Amalgamated • 301 Third Ave.
Ch • Chase • 255 First Ave.
Ch • Chase • 221 Park Ave. S.
Ch • Chase • 386 Park Ave. S.
Ch • Chase • 390 Park Ave. S.
Ch • Chase • 400 E. 23rd St.
Ch • Chase • 400 Second Ave.
Ch • Chase • 450 Third Ave.
Ci • Citibank • 1 Park Ave.
Ci • Citibank • 481 First Ave.
Ci • Citibank • 262 First Ave.
Ci • Citibank • 25 Waterside Plaza
Co • Commercial Bank • 2 Park Ave. at 33rd St
Ea • EAB • Park Ave. S.
FS • Flushing Savings Bank • 33 Irving Pl.
G • Greenpoint • 254 E. 34th St.
H • HSBC • 245 First Ave.
H • HSBC • 10 Union Sq. East
I • Independence Community • 250 Lexington A

Bagels

• Bagel De Juer • 478 Third Ave.
• Bagel & Schmear • 116 E. 28th St.
• Bagelry • 425 Third Ave.
• Bagels Around the Clock • 637 Second Ave.
• Daniel's Bagel Corp. • 569 Third Ave.
• David's Bagels • 331 First Ave.
• Eastbridge Bagels • 587 First Ave.
• Ess-A-Bagel • 359 First Ave.
• La Bagel • 263 First Ave.
• Pick A Bagel On Third • 297 Third Ave.
• Shaun's Bagel Café Inc. • 178 Lexington Ave.

Hospitals

• Bellevue Hospital Center • 462 First Ave.
• Beth Israel Medical Center • 281 First Ave.
• Beth Israel Medical Center • 10 Union Sq. E.
• Cabrini Medical Center • 227 E. 19th St.
• Hospital For Joint Diseases • 301 E. 17th St.
• New York Eye & Ear Infirmary • 310 E. 14th St.
• NYU Medical Center: Tisch Hospital • 560 First Ave.
• V.A. Hospital • 408 First Ave.

★ Landmarks

• Con Edison Building • 145 E. 14th St.
• Gramercy Park • Irving Place at 20th St.
• National Arts Club • 15 Gramercy Park South
• Pete's Tavern • 129 E. 18th St.
• Sniffen Court • 36th St. at Third Ave.
• The Players • 16 Gramercy Park South

Libraries

• Epiphany • 228 E. 23rd St.
• Kips Bay • 446 Third Ave.

24-Hour Pharmacies

• CVS Pharmacy • 342 E. 23rd St.
• Duane Reade • 300 Park Ave. S
• Duane Reade • 155 E. 34th St.
• Duane Reade • 24 E. 14th St.
• Rite Aid • 542 Second Ave.

Police Precinct

• 13th Precinct • 230 E. 21st St.

✉ Post Offices

• Madison Square • 149 E. 23rd St.
• Murray Hill • 205 E. 36th St.
• Murray Hill • 115 E. 34th St.
• Peter Stuyvesant • 432 E. 14th St.
• Station 138 (Macy's) • 151 34th St

Schools

• Allied Health Program in Orthopedics • 310 E. 14th St.
• Baruch College • 151 E. 25th St.
• Beth Israel Medical Center • 307 First Ave.
• Mabel Dean Bacon Vocational HS • 127 E. 22 St.
• Manhattan Night Comprehensive High School • 240 Second Ave.
• New York College Of Optometry • 100 E. 24th St.
• NY City • 135 E. 22nd St.
• NYU Dental School • First Ave. and 24th St.
• NYU Medical Center • 30th St. and First Ave.
• Phillips-Beth Israel School of Nursing • 310 E. 22nd St.
• PS 040 Augustus St. Gaudens • 319 E. 19th St.
• PS 106 Bellevue Hospital • 27th St. & First Ave.
• PS 116 Mary L. Murray School • 210 E. 33rd St.
• PS 226 • 345 E. 15th St.
• PS-JHS 047 School for the Deaf • 225 E. 23rd St.
• School Of Visual Arts • 209 E. 23rd St.
• Washington Irving High • 40 Irving Pl.

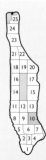

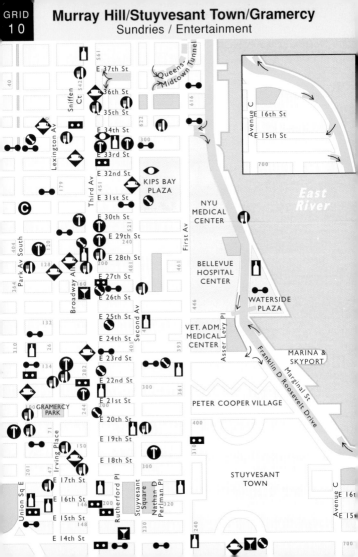

E 37th St

Queens-Midtown Tunnel

E 36th St

E 35th St

E 34th St

E 33rd St

E 32nd St

KIPS BAY PLAZA

E 31st St

E 30th St

E 29th St

E 28th St

E 27th St

E 26th St

E 25th St

E 24th St

E 23rd St

E 22nd St

E 21st St

E 20th St

E 19th St

E 18th St

E 17th St

E 16th St

E 15th St

E 14th St

Sniffen Ct

Lexington Av

Third Av

Broadway Alley

Park Av South

Second Av

First Av

Irving Place

Rutherford Pl

Stuyvesant Square

Nathan D Perlman Pl

Union Sq E

GRAMERCY PARK

NYU MEDICAL CENTER

BELLEVUE HOSPITAL CENTER

VET. ADM. MEDICAL CENTER

Asser Levy Pl

WATERSIDE PLAZA

PETER COOPER VILLAGE

STUYVESANT TOWN

Franklin D Roosevelt Drive

Marginal St

MARINA & SKYPORT

East River

Avenue C

E 16th St

E 15th St

Avenue C

E 16t

E 15

Check out the new Kips Bay Plaza, which has a great movie theatre and a Borders. El Parador is an excellent Mexican restaurant; Little India, on Lexington Ave. in the upper 20s, has several good restaurants, including Pongal and the aptly-named Curry in a Hurry (every ten meals, you get one free!)

24-Hour Copy Center
• On-Site Sourcing, Inc. • 443 Park Ave. S.

Bars
• Abbey Tavern • 354 Third Ave.
• Barmacy • 538 E. 14th St.
• Beauty Bar • 231 E. 14th St.

Cafes
• C K Coffee Shop • 536 E. 14th St.
• Cafe Aubette • 119 E. 27th St.
• Coffee Craze NY • 166 E. 33rd St.
• Expresso Coffee Roaster Corp. • 157 E. 18th St.
• Guy & Gallard • 230 Lexington Ave.
• Little Peace • 23A Lexington Ave.
• Starbucks • 585 Second Ave.
• Sufi Restaurant • 130 E. 28th St.
• Uncommon Grounds • 533 3rd Ave.
• Xando Coffee & Bar • 257 Park Ave. S
• Zido's Coffee Expresso Bar • 294 3rd Ave.

Gyms
• Athletic Complex • 3 Park Ave.
• Bally Sports Club • 554 2nd Ave.
• Club 29 • 155 E. 29th St.
• Dolphin Fitness East • 242 E. 14th St.
• Dolphin Fitness Clubs • 201 E. 23rd St.
• Duomo • 11-13 E. 26th St.
• Luye Aquafit • 310 E. 23rd St.
• Manhattan Place Condominium Health Club •
630 First Ave.
• New York Budo • 350 Third Ave.
• New York Sports Clubs • 303 Park Ave. S.
• New York Sports Clubs • 614 Second Ave.
• New York Sports Clubs • 131 E. 31st St.
• Park Ave. Athletic Complex • 3 Park Ave.
• Peak Performance Sport & Fitness Center •
106 E. 19th St.
• Rivergate Fitness Center • 401 E. 34th St.
• Sol Goldman YM-YWHA • 344 E. 14th St.
• Synergy Fitness Clubs • 4 Park Ave.
• Waterside Swim & Health Club •
35 Waterside Plaza at FDR Dr.

Hardware Stores
• 14th St. Hardware • 211 E. 14th St.
• Gurell Hardware • 132 E. 28th St.
• Homefront Hardware & Lumber •
202 E. 29th St.
• J&M Hardware & Locksmiths • 238 Park Ave. S.
• Kips Bay Hardware Co. • 601 Second Ave.
• Lumber Boys • 698 Second Ave.
• Lumberland Hardware • 400 Third Ave.
• Render of 72nd • 485 Third Ave.
• Simon's Hardware & Bath • 421 Third Ave.
• Town & Village Hardware • 345 E. 18th St.
• Vercesi Hardware • 152 E. 23rd St.
• Warshaw Hardware & Electrical • 248 Third Ave.

Liquor Stores
• Elman's Liquors • 279 Third Ave.
• First Ave. Wine & Spirits Supermarket • 383 First Ave.
• Flynn Winfield Liquor Ltd. • 558 Third Ave.
• Franks Liquor Shop • 46 Union Sq. E.
• Gramercy Park Wines & Spirits • 121 E. 23rd St.
• House of Wine & Liquor • 250 E. 34th St.
• Italian Wine Merchants • 108 E. 16th St.
• Kwon Tain Liquor Inc. • 161 Third Ave.
• McAdam Buy Rite • 398 Third Ave.
• Quality House • 2 Park Ave.
• Royal Wine Merchants Ltd. • 25 Waterside Plaza
• Stuyvesant Sq Liquors • 333 Second Ave.
• Welcome Wine & Spirits • 424 Second Ave.
• Zeichner Wine & Liquor • 279 First Ave.

Movie Theatres
• City Cinemas: Murray Hill • 160 E. 34th St.
• Loews Kips Bay • Second Ave. & 32nd St.

Pet Stores
• Furry Paws • 120 E. 34th St.
• Furry Paws 5 • 310 E. 23rd St.
• Natural Pet • 238 Third Ave.
• Petco • 550 Second Ave.
• Petland Discounts • 404 Third Ave.
• Petland Discounts • 7 E. 14th St.
• Petland Discounts • 530 E. 14th St.

Restaurants
• El Parador Cafe • 325 E. 34th St.
• Gemini Restaurant • 641 Second Ave.
• Gramercy Restaurant • 184 Third Ave.
• I Trulli • 122 E. 27th St.
• Jackson Hole • 521 Third Ave.
• Jai Ya Thai • 396 Third Ave.
• L'Express • 249 Park Ave. S.
• Old San Juan • 462 Second Ave.
• Park Avenue Country Club • 381 Park
Ave. S.
• Patria • 250 Park Ave. S
• Pete's Tavern • 129 E. 18th St.
• Pongal • 110 Lexington Ave.
• Pongsri Thai • 311 Second Ave.
• Sarge's Deli • 548 Third Ave.
• Sonia Rose • 150 E. 34th St.
• Tatany • 380 Third Ave.
• Union Pacific • 111 E. 22nd St.
• Verbena • 54 Irving Place
• Water Club • 500 E. 30th St.
• Yama • 122 E. 17th St.
• Zen Palate • 34 Union Sq. E.

Video Rentals
• Blockbuster Video • 78 Third Ave.
• Blockbuster Video • 312 First Ave.
• Blockbuster Video • 151 Third Ave.
• Blockbuster Video • 155 E. 34th St.
• Video Stop Inc • 367 Third Ave.
• Westcoast Video • 295 Park Ave. S.

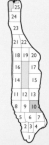

Murray Hill/Stuyvesant Town/Gramercy
Transportation

E 38th St

E 37th St

E 36th St

Queens-
Midtown Tunnel

E 35th St

34

E 34th St

Sniffen Ct.

16

E 33rd St

E 32nd St

KIPS BAY
PLAZA

E 31st St

NYU
MEDICAL
CENTER

E 30th St

E 29th St

Lexington Av

Third Av

Second Av

First Av

E 28th St

21 BELLEVUE
HOSPITAL
CENTER

E 27th St

Broadway Alley

E 26th St

WATERSIDE
PLAZA

E 25th St

Asser Levy Pl

VET. ADM.
MEDICAL
CENTER

E 24th St

MARINA &
SKYPORT

6 23 E 23rd St

Franklin D Roosevelt Drive

Marginal St

E 22nd St

Park Av South

15 15

E 21st St

PETER COOPER VILLAGE

101
214
102
103

E 20th St

GRAMERCY
PARK

E 19th St

Irving Place

E 18th St

STUYVESANT
TOWN

E 17th St

Rutherford Pl

Stuyvesant
Square

Nathan D
Perlman Pl

4
5
6

E 16th St

Union Sq E

E 15th St

E 16th St

E 15th St

N
R

L

L

9 14

L

E 14th St

East
River

Avenue

E 16th St

E 15th St

Avenue

E 16th St

E 15th St

Overnight parking is difficult, but there are many meter spots to be had, especially on the avenues. The Gulf gas station at the marina on 23rd Street doesn't service automobiles anymore. The reconstruction of Union Square is still not done, and we're still waiting for that Second Avenue subway line.

Subviews

4 5 6 N R L . 14 St–Union Square

6 . . . . 33rd St (at Park Av)

6 . . . . 28th St (at Park Av)

6 . . . . 23rd St (at Park Av)

L . . . . 3 Avenue (at 14 St)

L . . . . 1 Avenue (at 14 St)

Bus Lines

1 2 3 . . . . 5th Ave./Madison Ave.

9 . . . . Ave. B/East Broadway

14 . . . . 14th St. Crosstown

15 . . . . 1st/2nd Aves. (at 2 Ave)

16 . . . . 34th St. Crosstown

21 . . . . Houston St. Crosstown

23 . . . . 23rd St. Crosstown

98 . . . . 3rd Ave./Lexington Ave.

101 . . . . 3rd Ave./Lexington Ave.

102 . . . . 3rd Ave./Lexington Ave.

103 . . . . 3rd Ave./Lexington Ave.

⦿ Car Rentals

- Dollar • 329 E. 22nd St.
- Hertz • 150 E. 24th St.
- National • 142 E. 31rd St.

🅿 Parking

- 110 E. 16th St.
- 155 E. 34th St.
- 211 E. 18th St.

- 230 Lexington Ave.
- 57-59 Irving Place
- 57 Irving Pl.
- 350 E. 30th St.
- 500 E. 34th St.
- 222 Lexington Ave.
- 4 Park Ave.
- 530 First Ave.
- 200 E. 27th St.
- 146 Third Ave.
- 345 E. 37th St.
- 398 Park Ave. S.
- 155 E. 29th St.
- 171 Lexington Ave.
- 300 E. 34th St.
- 142 E. 31st St.
- 144 E. 17th St.
- 151 E. 31st St.
- 415 E. 37th St.
- 329 E. 22nd St.
- 488 Third Ave.
- 202 E. 18th St.
- 329 E. 21st St.
- 340 E. 34th St.
- 320 E. 23rd St.
- 200 E. 32nd St.
- 333 E. 34th St.
- 245 E. 19th St.
- 300 E. 25th St.
- 240 E. 27th St.
- 420 E. 20th St.
- 50 Park Ave.
- 200 E. 24th St.
- 242 E. 25th St.
- 150 E. 18th St.
- 401 E. 23rd St.
- 575 First Ave.
- 148 E. 33rd St.
- 145 E. 34th St.
- 201 E. 28th St.
- FDR Drive & E. 34th St.
- 400 E. 34th St.
- 130 E. 18th St.
- 214 E. 24th St.
- 132 E. 35th St.

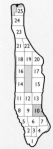

W 60th St

Columbus
Circle

99

W 59th St

98

W 58th St

Broadway

W 57th

97

96

W 56th St

95

W 55th St

94

W 54th St

92

DEWITT
CLINTON
PARK

W 53rd St

Hudson
River

West Side Hwy

Twelfth Av

Eleventh Av

W 52nd St

W 51st St

90

W 50th St

Tenth Av

W 49th St

Ninth Av

Eighth Av

88

W 48th St

W 47th St

86

W 46th St

W 45th St

W 44th St

84

W 43rd St

83

W 42nd St

81

W 41st St

Dyer Ave

PORT AUTHORITY
BUS TERMINAL

W 40th St

Lincoln Tunnel

W 39th ST

Jacob K. Javits
Convention
Center

W 38th ST

W 37th ST

The continuing gentrification of Hell's Kitchen (and name change to "Clinton") will doubtlessly increase the number of essential services, for instance the number of banks. The area around the Port Authority Bus Terminal is still one of the most authentically seedy places in Manhattan.

ATMs

Ch • Chase • 524 W. 57th St.
Ch • Chase • 821 Eighth Ave.
Ch • Chase • 969 Eighth Ave.
Ch • Chase • 124 W. 60th St.
Ci • Citibank • 401 W. 42nd St.
Ci • Citibank • 1748 Broadway
F • Fleet • 428 W. 59th St.
F • Fleet • Port Authority Bus Terminal
H • HSBC • 661 Eighth Ave.
H • HSBC • 1790 Broadway

Bagels

• Bagel Baron of 57th • 315 W. 57th St.
• Bagel House • 308 W. 50th St.
• H & H Bagels • 639 W. 46th St.

Hospitals

• Roosevelt Hospital Center • 1000 Tenth Ave.
• St. Clare's Family Health Center • 350 W. 51st St.
• St. Clare's Hospital & Health Center • 415 W. 51st St.

★ Landmarks

• Intrepid Sea, Air, and Space Museum • 12th Ave. /45th St.
• Theater Row • 42nd St. / 9th and 10th Aves.

Library

• Columbus • 742 Tenth Ave.

Marketplace

• CompUSA • 1775 Broadway

24-Hour Pharmacies

• CVS Pharmacy • 1 Columbus Pl. (58th St. & Ninth Ave.)
• Duane Reade • 224 W. 57th St.
• Rite Aid • 303 W. 50th St.

Police Precinct

• Mid-Town North • 324 W. 54th St.

✉ Post Offices

• Columbus Circle • 27 W. 60th St.
• Radio City • 322 W. 52nd St.
• Times Square • 340 W. 42nd St.

Ⓢ Schools

• Alfred Adler Institute • 1780 Broadway
• American Academy McAllister Institute • 450 W. 56th St.
• Creative Writing Center • 439 W. 49th St.
• Fordham University • 113 W. 60th St.
• HS Of Graphic Communication Arts • 439 W. 49th St.
• Interboro Institute • 450 W. 56th St.
• John Jay College • 899 Tenth Ave.
• New York School Of Astrology • 545 Eighth Ave.
• Park West High School • 525 W. 50th St.
• PS 017 Hudson River • 328 W. 48th St.
• PS 051 Elias Howe School • 520 W. 45th St.
• PS 058 Manhattan School • 317 W. 52nd St.
• PS 111 Adolph S. Ochs School • 440 W. 53rd St.

✿ Community Gardens

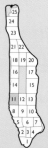

Hell's Kitchen
Sundries / Entertainment

W 60th St
W 59th St
W 58th St
W 57th St
W 56th St
W 55th St
W 54th St
W 53rd St
W 52nd St
W 51st St
W 50th St
W 49th St
W 48th St
W 47th St
W 46th St
W 45th St
W 44th St
W 43rd St
W 42nd St
W 41st St
W 40th St
W 39th ST
W 38th ST
W 37th ST

Columbus Circle

Broadway

DEWITT CLINTON PARK

Hudson River

West Side Hwy

Twelfth Av

Eleventh Av

Tenth Ave

Ninth Av

Eighth Av

Dyer Ave

PORT AUTHORITY BUS TERMINAL

Lincoln Tunnel

Jacob K. Javits Convention Center

99
98
97
96
95
94
92
90
88
86
84
83
81

500
400
890
300
798
780
824
742
636
610
570
520
502
258
600
870
724

Again, as more money pours into Hell's Kitchen, more services should start to crop up along 10th and 11th Avenues.

 Bars

- Rudy's Bar & Grill • 627 Ninth Ave.
- Russian Vodka Room • 265 W. 52nd St.
- Wakamba • 543 Eighth Ave.

 Cafes

- Cupcake Cafe • 522 Ninth Ave.
- Cyber Cafe • 250 W. 49th St.
- Starbucks • 322 W. 57th St.
- Starbucks • 682 Ninth Ave.
- Starbucks • 600 Eighth Ave.
- The Coffee Pot • 350 W. 49th St.

 Farmer's Market

- Greenmarket • Ninth Ave. & 57th St.

 Gyms

- A Body Sculpt Fitness • 300 W. 40th St.
- Bally Sports Club • 350 W. 50th St.
- Crunch Fitness • 560 W. 43rd St.
- Iowa Sports Management • 456 W. 43rd St.
- Manhattan Plaza Health Club • 482 W. 43rd St.
- Mid-City Gym • 244 W. 49th St.
- New York School of Tai Chi • 308 W. 38th St.
- New York Underground Fitness • 440 W. 57th St.
- The Strand Health Club • 500 W. 43rd St.

 Hardware Stores

- Columbus Hardware Inc. • 852 Ninth Ave.
- Garden Hardware & Supply Co. • 785 Eighth Ave.
- HT Sales Co. True Value • 718 Tenth Ave.
- Lopez Sentry Hardware • 691 Ninth Ave.
- Metropolitan Lumber & Hardware • 617 Eleventh Ave.
- New Era Industrial Hardware Inc. • 359 W. 54th St.
- Scherman & Grant • 545 Eighth Ave.
- Straight Hardware & Supply Co. • 613 Ninth Ave.

Liquor Stores

- 9th Ave. Wine & Liquor • 474 Ninth Ave.
- Athens Wine & Liquor • 302 W. 40th St.
- B & G Wine & Liquor Store • 507 W. 42nd St.
- Cambridge Wine & Liquors Inc. • 594 Eighth Ave.
- Columbus Circle Liquor Store Inc. • 1780 Broadway
- Fifty-Fifth Street Liquor Store • 410 W. 55th St.
- First Liquor Store • 840 Ninth Ave.
- Ninth Avenue Vintner • 669 Ninth Ave.
- Ninth Avenue Wine & Liquors • 860 Ninth Ave.
- Shon 45 Liquors • 840 Eighth Ave.
- Vintage Wine Warehouse • 665 Eleventh Ave.
- West 57th St. Wine & Spirit • 340 W. 57th St.

 Movie Theatres

- Cineplex Odeon: Encore Worldwide • 340 W. 50th St.
- Common Basis Theater • 750 Eighth Ave.
- Show World • 675 Eighth Ave.

 Pet Stores

- Canine Castle Ltd. • 410 W. 56th St.
- Petland Discounts • 734 Ninth Ave.
- Spoiled Brats • 340 W. 49th St.

Restaurants

- Afghan Kebab House • 764 Ninth Ave.
- Baluchi's • 240 W. 56th St.
- Burritoville • 352 W. 39th St.
- Burritoville • 625 Ninth Ave.
- Churruscaria Plataforma • 316 W. 49th St.
- Hallo Berlin • 402 W. 51st St.
- Island Burgers & Shakes • 766 Ninth Ave.
- Jezebel • 630 Ninth Ave.
- Joe Allen • 326 W. 46th St.
- Les Sans Culottes • 347 W. 46th St.
- Meskerem • 468 W. 47th St.
- Old San Juan • 765 Ninth Ave.
- Orso • 322 W. 46th St.
- Pongsri Thai • 244 W. 48th St.
- Sandwich Planet • 534 Ninth Ave.
- Soul Cafe • 444 W. 42nd St.
- Zen Palate • 663 Ninth Ave.

Video Rentals

- 57th St. Video & Photo • 332 W. 57th St.
- 691 Video Center Corp • 691 Eighth Ave.
- 763 Video Store • 763 Eighth Ave.
- Blockbuster Video • 829 Eighth Ave.
- Blockbuster Video • 588 Ninth Ave.
- DVDS Palace • 733 8th Ave.
- Liman Video Rentals • 614 W. 49th St.
- Rec Video • 301 W. 46th St.

Hell's Kitchen
Transportation

W 60th St

W 59th St

W 58th St

W 57th St

W 56th St

W 55th St

W 54th St

W 53rd St

W 52nd St

W 51st St

W 50th St

W 49th St

W 48th St

W 47th St

W 46th St

W 45th St

W 44th St

W 43rd St

W 42nd St

W 41st St

W 40th St

W 39th ST

W 38th ST

W 37th St

Columbus Circle

Broadway

DEWITT CLINTON PARK

Hudson River

West Side Hwy

Twelfth Av

Eleventh Av

Tenth Av

Ninth Av

Eighth Av

Dyer Ave

PORT AUTHORITY BUS TERMINAL

Lincoln Tunnel

Jacob K. Javits Convention Center

99
98
97
96
95
94
92
90
88
86
84
83
81

57
31
11
11
31
104
50
50
42
42
42
34
27
104
16
10
16

500
400
890
800
798
824
636
702
610
576
600
258
502
300
224

The Lincoln Tunnel jams this area up during the day (if you're coming from downtown, try taking the 10th Avenue approach. If you're coming from uptown, you're screwed). The mishmash of Columbus Circle also doesn't help matters. Parking is usually terrible because of the Theater District and the Javits Convention Center. This is also where the West Side "Highway" begins to have traffic lights and becomes a parking lot for most of the day (try taking 11th Avenue downtown if you can).

Subways

① ⑨ Ⓐ Ⓒ Ⓑ Ⓓ Ⓒ Ⓔ 59 St–Columbus Circle

Ⓐ Ⓒ Ⓔ . . . . . 42 St–Port Authority (at 8 Av)

Ⓒ Ⓔ . . . . 50 St (at 8 Av)

Bus Lines

10 . . . . . . 7th Ave./8th Ave./Central Park West

11 . . . . 9th Ave./10th Ave.

16 . . . . 34th St. Crosstown

16 . . . . 49/50th St. Crosstown

23 . . . . 23rd St. Crosstown

34 . . . . 34th St. Crosstown

42 . . . . 42nd St. Crosstown

50 . . . . 49/50th St. Crosstown

57 . . . . 57th St. Crosstown

104 . . . . Broadway

◉ Car Rentals

• AAA Access Auto Rental • 542 W. 49th St.
• All State Auto Rental • 541 W. 43rd St.
• Arrow-U-Drive Inc. • 505 W. 57th St.
• Autorent Car Rental • 415 W. 45th St.
• Avis • 460 W. 42nd St. (also Dockside Service)
• Budget • 304 W. 49th St.
• Courier Car Rental • 537 Tenth Ave.
• Enterprise • 653-659 Eleventh Ave.
• Manhattan Auto Group • 787 Eleventh Ave.
• Martin's Manhattan • 677 Eleventh Ave.
• United Car Rental • 501 W. 55th St.
• United Rent A Car • 330 W. 58th St.

◆ Car Washes

• Kenny Car Wash System • 625 Eleventh Ave.
• Westside Highway Car Wash • 638 W. 47th St.

ⓟ Gas Stations

• Gaseteria • 59th St. & Eleventh Ave.
• Mobil • 718 Eleventh Ave.
• Sunoco • 639 Eleventh Ave.

Ⓟ Parking

• 304 W. 49th St.
• 328 W. 39th St.
• 333 W. 46th St.
• 641 W. 59th St.
• 888 Eighth Ave.
• 346 W. 37th St.
• 425 W. 59th St.
• 300 W. 55th St.
• 408 W. 57th St.
• 515 W. 43rd St.
• 305 W. 48th St.
• 380 W. 50th St.
• 350 W. 50th St.
• 235 W. 56th St.
• 326 W. 40th St.
• 555 W. 57th St.
• 301 W. 53rd St.
• 361 W. 42nd St.
• 754 Eighth Ave.
• 350 W. 40th St.
• 841 Tenth Ave.
• 640 W. 42nd St.
• 713 Tenth Ave.
• 435 W. 57th St.
• 405 W. 38th St.
• 622 W. 57th St.
• 257 W. 47th St.
• 747 Tenth Ave.
• 343 W. 42nd St.
• 430 W. 41st St.
• 325 W. 58th St.
• 500 Tenth Ave.
• 345 W. 58th St.
• 264 W. 42nd St.
• 541 W. 38th St.
• 639 W. 55th St.
• 415 W. 45th St.

• 540 W. 59th St.
• 527 W. 58th St.
• 605 W. 45th St.
• 303 W. 46th St.
• 320 W. 57th St.
• 411 W. 55th St.
• 900 Eighth Ave.
• 423 W. 53rd St.
• 322 W. 44th St.
• 427 W. 42nd St.
• 306 W. 44th St.
• 332 W. 44th St.
• 618 W. 49th St.
• 541 W. 43rd St.
• 311 W. 50th St.
• 301 W. 51st St.

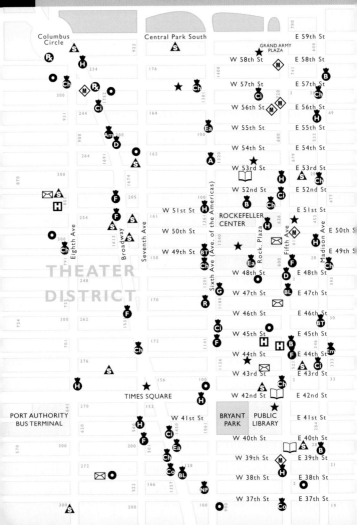

Columbus
Circle

Central Park South

GRAND ARMY
PLAZA

E 59th St

W 58th St

E 58th St

W 57th St

E 57th St

W 56th St

E 56th St

W 55th St

E 55th St

W 54th St

E 54th St

W 53rd St

E 53rd St

W 52nd St

E 52nd St

W 51st St

E 51st St

ROCKEFELLER
CENTER

W 50th St

E 50th St

W 49th St

E 49th St

THEATER

W 48th St

E 48th St

DISTRICT

W 47th St

E 47th St

W 46th St

E 46th St

W 45th St

E 45th St

W 44th St

E 44th St

W 43rd St

E 43rd St

W 42nd St

E 42nd St

TIMES SQUARE

PORT AUTHORITY
BUS TERMINAL

W 41st St

BRYANT
PARK

PUBLIC
LIBRARY

E 41st St

W 40th St

W 39th St

E 39th St

W 38th St

E 38th St

W 37th St

E 37th St

Eighth Ave

Broadway

Seventh Ave

Sixth Ave (Ave. of the Americas)

Rock. Plaza

Fifth Ave

Madison Ave

For all intents and purposes, this is the heart of New York. However, Times Square, the Theater District, and Rockefeller Center are all areas that many New Yorkers avoid. Instead, try the beautifully reconstructed Bryant Park, the classy Oak Bar at the Plaza Hotel, and Phillipe Starck's utterly cool Royalton Hotel.

💰 ATMs

Am • Amalgamated • 1710 Broadway
A • Apple • 1320 Ave. of the Americas
BL • Bank Leumi • 1400 Broadway
BL • Bank Leumi • 579 Fifth Ave.
B • Bank of New York • 51 W. 51st St.
B • Bank of New York • 530 Fifth Ave.
B • Bank of New York • 260 Madison Ave.
B • Bank of New York • 575 Madison Ave.
BT • Bank of Tokyo • 360 Madison Ave.
BT • Bank of Tokyo • 1251 Ave. of the Americas
Ch • Chase • 821 Eighth Ave.
Ch • Chase • 969 Eighth Ave.
Ch • Chase • 1411 Broadway
Ch • Chase • 100 W. 57th Street
Ch • Chase • 11 W. 51st Street
Ch • Chase • 1251 Ave. of the Americas
Ch • Chase • 1501 Broadway
Ch • Chase • 510 Fifth Avenue
Ch • Chase • 401 Madison Ave.
Ch • Chase • 488 Madison Ave.
Ch • Chase • 600 Madison Ave.
Ci • Citibank • 1748 Broadway
Ci • Citibank • 1430 Broadway
Ci • Citibank • 40 W. 57th St.
Ci • Citibank • 640 Fifth Ave.
Ci • Citibank • 1155 Ave. of the Americas
Ci • Citibank • 330 Madison Ave.
Co • Commercial Bank • 1407 Broadway
Co • Commercial Bank • 404 Fifth Ave.
D • Dime • 589 Fifth Avenue
D • Dime • 1700 Broadway
Ea • EAB • 1440 Broadway
Ea • EAB • 1 Rockefeller Plaza
Ea • EAB • 1345 Ave. of the Americas
Em • Emigrant • 335 Madison Ave.
F • Fleet • 515 Seventh Ave.
F • Fleet • Port Authority Bus Terminal
F • Fleet • 1633 Broadway
F • Fleet • 1675 Broadway
F • Fleet • 592 Fifth Ave.
F • Fleet • 1140 Ave. of the Americas
F • Fleet • 1535 Broadway
F • Fleet • 529 5th Ave.
G • Greenpoint • 1200 Ave. of The Americas
H • HSBC • 661 Eighth Ave.
H • HSBC • 1790 Broadway
H • HSBC • 550 Seventh Ave.
H • HSBC • 1271 Ave. of the Americas
H • HSBC • 41 Rockefeller Plaza
H • HSBC • 1095 Ave. of the Americas
H • HSBC • 666 Fifth Ave.
H • HSBC • 437 Madison Ave.
H • HSBC • 452 Fifth Ave.
H • HSBC • 555 Madison Ave.
N • North Fork Bank • 1001 Ave. of the Americas
R • Republic National • 1185 Sixth Ave.

🥯 Bagels

• B & Y Edibles Inc. • 36 W. 48 St.
• Bagel Baron of 57th • 315 W. 57th St.
• Bagel House • 308 W. 50th St.
• Bagel-N-Bean • 828 Seventh Ave.
• Bagels & Co. • 243 W. 38th St.
• Bagels Off Fifth • 4 E. 38th St.
• Bruegger's Bagels • 1115 Ave. of the Americas
• Le Bon Bagel • 980 Ave. of the Americas
• Moms Bagels • 15 W. 45th St.
• Pick A Bagel On 57th • 200 W. 57th St.

🏥 Hospitals

• American Friends of Laniado Hospital • 18 W. 45th St.
• National Jewish Center for Immunology & Respiratory
  Medicine • 535 Fifth Ave.
• St. Clare's Family Health Center • 350 W. 51st St.

★ Landmarks

• Carnegie Hall • 154 W. 57th St.
• Museum of Modern Art (MoMA) • 11 W. 53rd St.
• New York Public Library • Fifth Ave. and 42nd St.
• Plaza Hotel • 768 Fifth Ave.
• Rockefeller Center • 600 Fifth Ave.
• Royalton Hotel • 44th St. between Fifth and Sixth Aves.
• St. Patrick's Cathedral • Fifth Ave. and 50th St.
• Times Square • 42nd St-Times Sq.

📖 Libraries

• Donnell Library Center • 20 W. 53rd St.
• Humanities and Social Science Library • 42nd St. and Fifth Ave.
• Mid-Manhattan Library • 455 Fifth Ave.

Ⓜ Marketplace

• Bergdorf Goodman • 754 Fifth Ave.
• CompUSA • 420 Fifth Ave.
• CompUSA • 1775 Broadway
• Felissimo • 10 W. 56th St.
• Henri Bendel • 712 Fifth Ave.
• Lord & Taylor • 424 Fifth Ave.
• Saks Fifth Avenue • 611 Fifth Ave.

℞ 24-Hour Pharmacies

• CVS Pharmacy • 1 Columbus Pl. (58th St. & Ninth Ave.)
• Duane Reade • 224 W. 57th St.
• Duane Reade • 1633 Broadway
• Rite Aid • 303 W. 50th St.

Ⓟ Police Precinct

• Mid-Town North • 324 W. 54th St.

✉ Post Offices

• Appraisers Stores • 580 Fifth Ave. Suite 407
• Bryant • 23 W. 43rd St.
• Midtown • 223 38th St.
• Radio City • 322 W. 52nd St.
• Rockefeller Center • 610 Fifth Ave.

Ⓢ Schools

• Alfred Adler Institute • 1780 Broadway
• Berkeley College • 3 E. 43rd St.
• Circle In The Square Theater School •
  1633 Broadway
• City University Of New York •
  33 W. 42nd St.
• Institute Of Allied Medical Professionals
  • 23D 106 Central Park South
• Laboratory Institute Of Merchandising •
  12 E. 53rd St.
• New York Academy of Comedic Arts •
  1626 Broadway
• New York School Of Astrology •
  545 Eighth Ave.
• Practicing Law Institute • 810 Seventh Ave.
• PS 058 Manhattan School • 317 W. 52nd St.
• Spanish American Institute • 215 W. 43rd St.
• Wood Tobe-Coburn School • 8 E. 40th St.

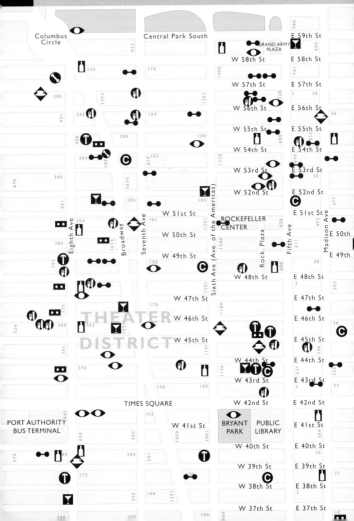

Columbus Circle

Central Park South

E 59th St

GRAND ARMY PLAZA

W 58th St   E 58th St

W 57th St   E 57th St

W 56th St   E 56th St

W 55th St   E 55th St

W 54th St   E 54th St

W 53rd St   E 53rd St

W 52nd St   E 52nd St

W 51st St   E 51st St

ROCKEFELLER CENTER

W 50th St   E 50th St

Rock. Plaza

W 49th St   E 49th

Eighth Ave

Broadway

Seventh Ave

Sixth Ave (Ave. of the Americas)

Fifth Ave

Madison Ave

W 48th St   E 48th St

W 47th St   E 47th St

THEATER

W 46th St   E 46th St

DISTRICT

W 45th St   E 45th St

W 44th St   E 44th St

W 43rd St   E 43rd St

W 42nd St   E 42nd St

TIMES SQUARE

W 41st St   E 41st St

PORT AUTHORITY BUS TERMINAL

BRYANT PARK   PUBLIC LIBRARY

W 40th St   E 40th St

W 39th St   E 39th St

W 38th St   E 38th St

W 37th St   E 37th St

Midtown has three of the best places to see a movie in town—the huge Ziegfeld, the classy Paris, and outdoors at Bryant Park. Oh, and don't forget Show World.

24-Hour Copy Centers

- ADS Copying • 29 W. 38th St
- Kinko's • 16 E. 52nd St
- Kinko's • 1211 Ave. of the Americas
- Kinko's • 233 W. 54th St
- National Reproductions • 25 W. 45th St.
- The Village Copier • 25 W. 43rd St.

Bars

- Heartland Brewery • 1285 Sixth Ave.
- Howard Johnson's • 1551 Broadway
- Oak Bar • 768 Fifth Ave.
- Russian Vodka Room • 265 W. 52nd St.
- The Royalton • 44 W. 44th St.
- Wakamba • 543 Eighth Ave.
- Whiskey Bar • 235 W. 46th St.

Cafes

- Bean Bar Inc. • 24 W. 45th St.
- Starbucks • 1166 Avenue of the Americas
- Starbucks • 750 Seventh Ave.
- Starbucks • 550 Madison Ave.
- Starbucks • 322 W. 57th St.
- Starbucks • 600 Eighth Ave.

Gyms

- A Body Sculpt Fitness • 300 W. 40th St.
- Art Of Fitness • 39 W. 56th St.
- Athletic and Swim Club at Equitable Center • 787 Seventh Ave.
- Bally Sports Club • 350 W. 50th St.
- Bally Sports Club • 335 Madison Ave.
- Bally Total Fitness • E. 53rd St. & Fifth Ave.
- Bally Total Fitness • 667 Fifth Ave.
- Callanetics Studios of Manh. • 154 W. 57th St.
- Cardio Fitness Center • Rockefeller Center
- Definitions • 712 Fifth Ave.
- Drago's Gymnasium, Inc. • 50 W. 57th St.
- Fitness By Design • 41 W. 57th St.
- Fitness Center at the New York Palace • 455 Madison Ave.
- Gravity • 118 W. 57th St.
- New York Health & Racquet Club • 110 W. 56th St.
- New York Health & Racquet Club • 20 E. 50th St.
- New York Sports Clubs • 1601 Broadway
- New York Sports Clubs • 380 Madison Ave.
- New York Sports Clubs • 1372 Broadway
- New York Sports Clubs • 1657 Broadway
- New York Sports Clubs • 19 W. 44th St.
- New York Sports Clubs • 404 5th Ave.
- Prescriptive Fitness • 250 W. 54th St.
- Radu's Physical Culture Studio • 24 W. 57th St.
- Ritz Plaza Health Club • 235 W. 48th St.
- Russian Bear Health & Fitness • 853 7th Ave.
- Sheraton New York & Manhattan Health Clubs • 811 Seventh Ave.
- Sports Club/LA • 45 Rockefeller Plaza
- Town Sports International • 888 Seventh Ave.
- U.S. Athletic Training Center • 515 Madison Ave.
- Ultimate Training Center • 532 Madison Ave.

Hardware Stores

- A A A Locksmiths • 44 W. 46th St.
- Barson Hardware Co., Inc. • 35 W. 44th St.
- Central Hardware & Elec. Corp. • 1055 Ave. of the Americas
- Friedlander Enterprises, Inc. • 250 W. 54th St.
- Garden Hardware & Supply Co. • 785 Eighth Ave.
- New Era Industrial Hardware Inc. • 359 W. 54th St.
- New Hippodrome Hardware, Inc. • 23 W. 45th St.
- Scherman & Grant • 545 Eighth Ave.

Liquor Stores

- Acorn Wine & Liquor Co. • 268 W. 46th St.
- Athens Wine & Liquor • 302 W. 40th St.
- Cambridge Wine & Liquors Inc. • 594 Eighth Ave.
- Columbus Circle Liquor Store Inc. • 1780 Broadway
- Fifty-Fifth Street Liquor Store • 40 W. 55th St.
- Madison Ave. Liquors • 244 Madison Ave.
- Midtown Wine & Liquor Shop • 44 E. 50th St.
- Morrell & Co. Wine & Spirits • 1 Rockefeller Plaza
- Morrell & Co. Wine & Spirits Merchants • 535 Madison Ave.
- Morrell & Company • 14 W. 49th St.
- O'Ryan Package Store, Inc. • 1424 Ave. of the Americas
- Park Av Liquor Shop • 292 Madison Ave.
- Royal Bee, Inc. • 1119 Ave. of the Americas
- Schumer's Wine & Liquors • 59 E. 54th St.
- Shon 45 Liquors • 840 Eighth Ave.
- West 57th St. Wine & Spirit • 340 W. 57th St.

Movie Theatres

- AMC Empire 25 • 234 W. 42nd St.
- Bryant Park Summer Film Festival (outdoors) • Bryant Park, between 40th and 42nd Sts.
- Cine One & Two • 711 7th Ave.
- Cineplex Odeon: Encore Worldwide • 340 W. 50th St.
- Cineplex Odeon: Ziegfeld • 141 W. 54th St.
- Common Basis Theater • 750 Eighth Ave.
- Crown Theatres • 712 Fifth Ave.
- Loews 42nd Street E. Walk • 42nd St. & 8th Ave. in Times Square
- Loews Astor Plaza • 44th St. between Broadway & Eighth Ave.
- Loews State • 1540 Broadway
- Museum of Modern Art • 11 W. 53rd St.
- Museum of TV and Radio • 25 W. 52nd St.
- New Manhattan Repertory, Inc. • 1650 Broadway
- New York Public Library-Donnell Library Center • 20 W. 53rd St
- Paris Theatre • 4 W. 58th St.
- Show World • 675 Eighth Ave.

Pet Store

- Animal Acts • 233 W. 54th St.

Restaurants

- '21' Club • 21 W. 52nd St.
- Aquavit • 13 W. 54th St.
- Baluchi's • 240 W. 56th St.
- Carnegie Deli • 854 Seventh Ave.
- Cosi Sandwich Bar • 11 W. 42nd St.
- Cosi Sandwich Bar • 1633 Broadway
- Cosi Sandwich Bar • 38 E. 45th St.
- Cosi Sandwich Bar • 61 W. 48th St.
- Joe Allen • 326 W. 46th St.
- Les Sans Culottes • 347 W. 46th St.
- Nation Restaurant & Bar • 12 W. 45th St.
- Orso • 322 W. 46th St.
- Pongsri Thai • 244 W. 48th St.
- Redeye Grill • 890 Seventh Ave.
- Virgil's Real BBQ • 152 W. 44th St.

Video Rentals

- 57th St. Video & Photo • 330 W. 57th St.
- 691 Video Center Corp • 691 Eighth Ave.
- 763 Video Store • 763 Eighth Ave.
- Blockbuster Video • 829 Eighth Ave.
- DVDS Palace • 468 8th Ave.
- High Quality Video, Inc. • 21 W. 45th, 2nd fl.
- International Express Video • 219 Madison Ave.
- Rec Video • 301 W. 46th St.
- Video 54th Street • 231 W. 54th St.

Midtown
Transportation

Columbus
Circle

W 59th St — E 59th St

GRAND ARMY
PLAZA

W 58th St — E 58th St

W 57th St

W 56th St

W 55th St

W 54th St

W 53rd St — E 53rd St

W 52nd St — E 52nd St

W 51st St

ROCKEFELLER
CENTER

W 50th St

W 49th St

THEATER

DISTRICT

W 48th St — E 48th St

W 47th St — E 47th St

W 46th St

W 45th St — E 45th St

W 44th St — E 44th St

W 43rd St — E 43rd St

TIMES SQUARE

W 42nd St — E 42nd St

PORT AUTHORITY
BUS TERMINAL

W 41st St — E 41st St

BRYANT   PUBLIC
PARK   LIBRARY

W 40th St — E 40th St

W 39th St — E 39th St

W 38th St — E 38th St

W 37th St — E 37th St

Midtown
Transportation

During the day, forget driving, forget parking. At night, however, 57th Street is one of the quickest cross-town routes in Manhattan. Times Square is a mess 24 hours a day.

Subways

1 9 . . . . 50 St (at Broadway)

1 9 A C B D . 59 St–Columbus Circle

1 2 3 9 N R 7 S . . . Times Square–42 St (at Broadway)

A C E . . . . . 42 St–Port Authority (at 8 Av)

B D E . . . . 7 Av (at 53 St)

B D F Q 47-50 Sts–Rockefeller Ctr (at 6 Av)

B D F Q . . . . 42 St–5 Av

B D . . . . 57 St (at 6 Av)

C E . . . . 50 St (at 8 Av)

E F . . . . 5 Av (at 53 St)

N R . . . . 57 St (at 7 Av)

N R . . . . 49 St (at 7 Av)

N R . . . . 5 Av (at 59 St)

Car Rentals

- Avis • 153 W. 54th St.
- Budget • 1330 Ave. of the Americas
- Dollar • 156 W. 54th St.
- Dollar • 235 W. 56th St.
- Europe By Car • 1 Rockefeller Plz., Conc. 4
- Hertz • 126 W. 55th St.
- Hertz Truck & Van Rental • 126 W. 55th St.
- Manhattan Rent-A-Car • 1330 Ave. of the Americas
- National • 252 W. 40th St.
- Nations • 241 W. 40th St.
- NRC Rent-A-Car • 251 W. 40th St.

P Parking (91 locations)

Bus Lines

1 2 3 4 . . . . 5th Ave./Madison Ave.

5 . 5th Ave./Ave. of the Americas/Riverside Dr.

6 . . . 7th Ave./Broadway/Ave. of the Americas

7 . . . Columbus Ave./Amsterdam Ave./Lenox/
6th Ave./7th Ave./Broadway

10 . . . . 7th Ave./8th Ave. (Central Park West)/
Frederick Douglass Blvd.

16 . . . . 34th St. Crosstown

27 . . . . 49th St./50th St. Crosstown

30 . . . . 57th St./72nd St. Crosstown

42 . . . . 42nd St. Crosstown

33 . . . . . Penn Station-Jackson Heights, Queens

57 . . . . 57th St. Crosstown

104 . . . . Broadway/42nd St. (at 42 St)

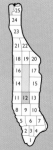

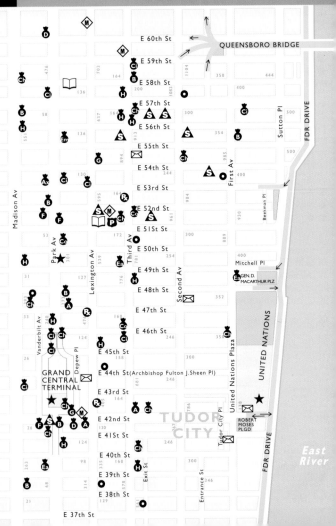

E 60th St

QUEENSBORO BRIDGE

E 59th St

E 58th St

E 57th St

E 56th St

E 55th St

E 54th St

Sutton Pl

FDR DRIVE

E 53rd St

First Av

E 52nd St

E 51St St

E 50th St

Madison Av

Beekman Pl

Mitchell Pl

E 49th St

GEN. D.
MACARTHUR PLZ

E 48th St

Park Av

Lexington Av

Third Av

Second Av

E 47th St

E 46th St

E 45th St

UNITED NATIONS

United Nations Plaza

E 44th St (Archbishop Fulton J.Sheen Pl)

Vanderbilt Av

Depew Pl

E 43rd St

E 42nd St

TUDOR
CITY

GRAND
CENTRAL
TERMINAL

ROBERT
MOSES
PLGD

E 41St St

Tudor City Pl

FDR DRIVE

East
River

E 40th St

Exit St

Entrance St

E 39th St

E 38th St

E 37th St

East Midtown
Essentials

This is a busy and diverse part of town, packed with consulates, hotels, Grand Central Terminal, the United Nations, the Queensboro Bridge, and two exclusive housing enclaves—Tudor City and Sutton Place. Park Avenue between 40th and 60th Streets contains some of the finest examples, if not the finest example, of every major architectural style from the past 100 years.

💰 ATMs

- Ax • AmEx Travel Related Services • 375 Park Ave.
- A • Apple • 666 Third Ave.
- A • Apple • 277 Park Ave.
- A • Apple • 122 East 42nd St.
- B • Bank of New York • 260 Madison Ave.
- B • Bank of New York • 575 Madison Ave.
- B • Bank of New York • 100 E. 42nd St.
- B • Bank of New York • 1006 First Ave.
- B • Bank of New York • 360 Park Ave.
- B • Bank of New York • 277 Park Ave.
- B • Bank of New York • 979 Third Ave.
- B • Bank of New York • 207 E. 58th St.
- Ch • Chase • First Ave. and 55th St.
- Ch • Chase • 401 Madison Ave.
- Ch • Chase • 221 Park Ave.
- Ch • Chase • Grand Central Lobby
- Ch • Chase • 1 Dag Ham. Plaza
- Ch • Chase • 241 E. 42nd St.
- Ch • Chase • 60 E. 42nd St.
- Ch • Chase • 633 Third Ave.
- Ch • Chase • 825 UN Plaza
- Ch • Chase • 200 E. 57th St.
- Ch • Chase • 410 Park Ave.
- Ch • Chase • 850 Third Ave.
- Ch • Chase • 770 Lexington Ave.
- Ch • Chase • 600 Madison Ave.
- Ci • Citibank • 399 Park Ave.
- Ci • Citibank • 330 Madison Ave.
- Ci • Citibank • 734 Third Ave.
- Ci • Citibank • 460 Park Ave.
- Ci • Citibank • 135 E. 53rd St.
- Ci • Citibank • 200 Park Ave.
- Ci • Citibank • 320 Park Ave.
- Ci • Citibank • 985 Third Ave.
- Co • Commercial Bank • 750 Third Ave.
- Co • Commercial Bank • 845 Third Ave.
- Co • Commercial Bank • 320 Park Ave.
- D • Dime • 510 Park Ave.
- D • Dime • 110 E. 42nd St.
- Ea • EAB • 90 Park Ave.
- Ea • EAB • 866 UN Plaza
- Ea • EAB • 800 Third Ave.
- E • Emigrant • 115 E. 56th St.
- F • Fleet • 345 Park Ave.
- F • Fleet • 56 E. 42nd St.
- G • Greenpoint • 109 E. 42nd St.
- G • Greenpoint • 643 Lexington Ave.
- H • HSBC • 1010 Third Ave.
- H • HSBC • 250 Park Ave.
- H • HSBC • 415 Madison Ave.
- H • HSBC • 441 Lexington Ave.
- H • HSBC • 777 Third Ave.
- H • HSBC • 919 Third Ave.
- H • HSBC • 555 Madison Ave.
- H • HSBC • 605 Third Ave.
- H • HSBC • 950 Third Ave.
- H • HSBC • 101 Park Ave.

⭕ Bagels

- Bagels Around the Clock • 637 Second Ave.
- Daniel's Bagel Corp. • 569 Third Ave.
- Ess-A-Bagel • 831 Third Ave.
- Jumbo Bagels & Bialys • 1070 Second Ave.
- Tal Bagels Inc. • 979 First Ave.
- TE Bagels • 141 E. 44th St.

★ Landmarks

- Chrysler Building • 405 Lexington Ave.
- Citicorp Center • 153 E. 53rd St.
- Grand Central Station • 42nd St.
- Seagram Building • 375 Park Ave.
- The United Nations • First Ave.
- The Waldorf-Astoria • 301 Park Ave.

📖 Libraries

- 58th St. • 127 E. 58th St.
- Terence Cardinal Cooke-Cathedral • 560 Lexington

Ⓜ Marketplace

- Bloomingdales • 1000 Third Ave.
- Diesel • 770 Lexington Ave.
- Rand McNally Map & Travel Center • 150 E. 52nd St.
- Zaro's Bread Basket • 89 E. 42nd St.

℞ 24-Hour Pharmacies

- Duane Reade • 485 Lexington Ave.
- Duane Reade • 866 Third Ave.
- Duane Reade • 405 Lexington Ave.

🅿 Police Precinct

- 17th Precinct • 167 E. 51st St.

✉ Post Offices

- Dag Hammarskold • 884 Second Ave.
- Franklin D. Roosevelt • 909 Third Ave.
- Grand Central Station • 450 Lexington Ave.
- Tudor City • 5 Tudor City Pl.
- United Nations • 405 E. 42nd St.

🅂 Schools

- 59 Beekman Hill School • 228 E. 57th St.
- Cathedral High School • Second Ave. & 56th St.
- High School of Art & Des • 1075 Second Ave.
- Katharine Gibbs School• 200 Park Ave.
- Neighborhood Playhouse School • 340 E. 54th St.
- SCS Business & Tech School • 575 Lexington Ave.
- The Sonia Moore Studio • 900 Third Ave.
- Turtle Bay Music School • 244 E. 52nd St.

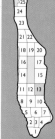

East Midtown
Sundries / Entertainment

Some of New York's top eateries are in this grid—including Vong, Smith & Wollensky, Dawat, March, and Lutece. Check the cool new stores under the Queensboro Bridge—including the Food Emporium and the Terence Conran Shop. If you want to go slumming, the Subway Inn is the place.

 ## 24-Hour Copy Centers

- Copycats • 216 E. 45th St.
- Kinko's • 305 E. 46th St.
- Kinko's • 600 Third Ave.
- Kinko's • 153 E. 53rd St.
- Kinko's • 747 Third Ave.
- Metro Copy • 222 E. 45th St.

 ## Bars

- Campbell Apartment • Grand Central Terminal
- P.J. Clarke's • 915 Third Ave.
- Subway Inn • 143 E. 60th St.

Cafes

- Columbus Bakery • 957 First Ave.
- New World Coffee • 830 3rd Ave.
- New World Coffee • 135 E. 57th St.
- Pasqua Inc. • 909 3rd Ave.
- Sandella's Cafe • 150 E. 52nd St.
- Serendipity 3 • 225 E. 60th St.
- Starbucks • 639 3rd Ave.
- Starbucks • 550 Madison Ave.
- Starbucks • 280 Park Ave.
- Starbucks • 757 Third Ave.
- Starbucks • 685 Third Ave.
- The Coffee Beanery Ltd. • 569 Lexington Ave.
- Uncommon Grounds • 533 3rd Ave.

Farmer's Market

- Greenmarket • Second Ave. & 47th St.

Gyms

- Absolute Fitness • 343 Lexington Ave.
- Away Spa-Gym • 541 Lexington Ave.
- Bally Sports Club • 335 Madison Ave.
- Body Perfection • 123 E. 54th St.
- Cardio Fitness Center • 52nd St. & Park Ave.
- Cardio Fitness Center • Grand Central
- Crunch Fitness • 1109 Second Ave.
- Dag Hammarskjold Tower • 240 E. 47th St.
- Dolphin Fitness Clubs • 330 E. 59th St.
- Doral Fitness • 90 Park Ave.
- Equinox Fitness • 521 E. 43rd St.
- Equinox Fitness Club • 250 E. 54th St.
- Excelsior Athletic Club • 301 E. 57th St.
- Fitness Center at the New York Palace • 455 Madison Ave.
- Guest Passes • 301 E. 38th St.
- Huma Sports Training Center Inc • 400 E. 51st St.
- Inform Fitness • 201 E. 56th St.
- Lift Gym Inc • 139 E. 57th St.
- Manhattan Place Condominium Health Club • 630 First Ave.
- Metamorphosis Absolute Fitness Club • 50 E. 42nd St.

- Midtown Karate Dojo Inc • 465 Lexington Ave.
- Millennium NY UN Health Club • United Nations Plaza
- New York Health & Racquet Club • 132 E. 45th St.
- New York Health & Racquet Club • 20 E. 50th St.
- New York Health & Racquet Club (Spa) • 115 E. 57th St.
- New York Sports Clubs • 502 E. 59th St.
- New York Sports Clubs • 575 Lexington Ave.
- New York Sports Clubs • 614 Second Ave.
- New York Sports Clubs • 380 Madison Ave.
- New York Sports Clubs • 633 Third Ave.
- New York Sports Clubs • 502 Park Ave.
- Plus One Fitness Clinic • 301 Park Ave.
- Spa 227 • 227 E. 56th St.
- Sparta Strength and Conditioning • 133 E. 55th St.
- U.S. Athletic Training Center • 515 Madison Ave.
- Ultimate Training Center • 532 Madison Ave.
- Vanderbilt Health Club • 240 E. 41st St.
- YMCA • 224 E. 47th St.
- YWCA • 610 Lexington Ave.

 ## Hardware Stores

- 55th St. Hardware • 155 E. 55th St.
- Gasnick Supply Company True Value • 992 Second Ave.
- Kramer's • 952 Second Ave.
- Lumber Boys • 698 Second Ave.
- Midtown Hardware • 155 E. 45th St.

Liquor Stores

- Ambassador Wines & Spirits • 1020 Second Ave.
- American First Liquors • 1059 First Ave.
- Beekman Liquors • 500 Lexington Ave.
- D'Vine Wines • 764 Third Ave.
- Diplomat Wine & Spirits • 939 Second Ave.
- Flynn Winfield Liquor Ltd. • 558 Third Ave.
- Grand Harvest Wines • 107 E. 42nd St.
- Jeffrey Wine & Liquors • 939 First Ave.
- Madison Ave. Liquors • 244 Madison Ave.
- Midtown Wine & Liquor Shop • 44 E. 50th St.
- Morrell & Co. • 535 Madison Ave.
- Park Av Liquor Shop • 292 Madison Ave.
- Schumer's Wine & Liquors • 59 E. 54th St.
- Sussex Liquor Store • 300 E. 41st St.
- Sutton Wine Shop • 403 E. 57th St.
- Turtle Bay Liquors • 857 2nd Ave.
- Wine Shop • 345 Lexington Ave.
- Worl Wines and Spirits • 857 Second Ave.

Movie Theatres

- Cineplex Odeon: Coronet Cinemas • 993 Third Ave.
- City Cinemas 1, 2, 3 • 1001 Third Ave.
- City Cinemas: Eastside Playhouse • 919 Third Ave.

- City Cinemas: Sutton 1 & 2 • 205 E. 57th St.
- Clearview's 59th St. East • 239 E. 59th Ave.
- Crown Gotham Cinema • 969 Third Ave.
- Crown Theatres • 375 Park Ave.
- French Institute • Florence Gould Hall, 55 E. 59th St.
- Instituto Cervantes • 122 E. 42nd St.
- Japan Society • 333 E. 47th St.
- Reading Entertainment • 950 Third Ave.
- YWCA • 610 Lexington Ave.

Pet Stores

- Beekman Pet Emporium • 900 First Ave.
- Furry Paws • 1039 Second Ave.
- International Kennel Club • 1032 Second Ave.
- Not Just Dogs • 244 E. 60th St.
- Petland Discounts • 976 Second Ave.
- Sutton Dog Parlour Kennel & Daycare Center • 311 E. 60th St.
- Video Couch & Pet Supplies • 715 Second Ave.

 ## Restaurants

- An American Place • 565 Lexington Ave.
- Chianti • 1043 Second Ave.
- Clarke's P.J. • 915 Third Ave.
- Cosi Sandwich Bar • 165 E. 52nd St.
- Cosi Sandwich Bar • 60 E. 56th St.
- Dawat • 210 E. 58th St.
- Docks Oyster Bar • 633 Third Ave.
- Felidia • 243 E. 58th St.
- Four Seasons • 99 E. 52nd St.
- Lutece • 249 E. 50th St.
- March • 405 E. 58th St.
- Menchanko-tei • 131 E. 45th St.
- Oyster Bar • Grand Central Terminal
- Palm • 837 Second Ave.
- Rosa Mexicano • 1063 First Ave.
- Sarge's Deli • 548 Third Ave.
- Shun Lee Palace • 155 E. 55th St.
- Smith & Wollensky • 797 Third Ave.
- Sono • 106 E. 57th St.
- Sparks Steak House • 210 E. 46th St.
- Vong • 200 E. 54th St.

Video Rentals

- Flick's Video To Go Eastside • 1093 2nd Ave.
- Intl. Film & Video Center • 989 First Ave.
- New York Video • 949 First Ave.
- Quick Photo • 962 Second Ave.
- Video Couch & Pet Supplies • 715 Second Ave.

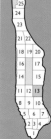

QUEENSBORO BRIDGE

N R
to Queens

FDR DRIVE

E 60th St

N R
59th St   Lexington Av   E 59th St

E 58th St

E 57th St

E 56th St

E 55th St

E 54th St

Lexington Av   E 53rd St

F E
to Queens

E 52nd St

E 51 St St

E 50th St
Mitchell Pl

GEN. D.
MACARTHUR PLZ

E 49th St

E 48th St

E 47th St

E 46th St

E 45th St

UNITED NATIONS

United Nations Plaza

FDR DRIVE

Park Av

Vanderbilt Ave

Madison Av

Lexington Av

Third Av

Second Av

First Av

Beekman Pl

Sutton Pl

Depew Pl

E 44th St (Archbishop Fulton J.Sheen Pl)

E 43rd St

7
to Queens
Shea Stadium
Tennis Center

E 42nd St

E 41st St

TUDOR
CITY

E 40th St

E 39th St

E 38th St

E 37th St

Tudor City Pl

Exit St

Entrance St

East
River

East Midtown
Transportation

Other than the quirky ramps running around Grand Central and the snarl around the Queensboro Bridge, traffic in this area could be far worse than it is. For instance, Park Avenue is a surprisingly excellent way to head downtown at rush hour. The best route to the Queensboro from downtown is First Avenue to 57th Street. However, it's always wise to pay attention for when the President or some other major dignitary is at the U.N., because you'll want to use mass transit that day. Street parking will always remain a dream.

Subways

4 5 6 N R . . . . . Lexington Av–59 St.

4 5 6 7 S . . . Grand Central–42 St.

E F 6 . . . . 51 St–Lexington Ave.

Bus Lines

1 2 3 . . . . 5th Ave./Madison Ave.

15 . . . . 1st Ave./2nd Ave. (at 2 Ave)

27 50 . . . . 49th St./50th St. Crosstown

30 . . . . 72nd St./57th St. Crosstown

32 . . . . Queens-to-Midtown

31 . . . . York Ave./57th St. (at 57 St)

42 . . . . 42nd St. Crosstown

57 . . . . 57th St. Crosstown

57 . . . . Heights/Midtown Limited

98 101 102 103 . . . . 3rd Ave./Lexington Ave.

104 . . . . Broadway

⊙ Car Rentals

• Avis • 217 E. 43rd St.
• Avis • 240 E. 54th St.
• Budget • 225 E. 43rd St.
• Enterprise • 135 E. 47th St.
• Enterprise • 213 E. 43rd St.
• Hertz • 222 E. 40th St.
• Hertz • 310 E. 48th St.
• National • 138 E. 50th St.
• New York Rent-A-Car • 151 E. 51st St.
• Renault USA • 650 First Ave.

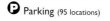 Gas Station

• East 53rd St. Garage • 411 E. 53rd St.

P Parking (95 locations)

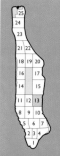

Upper West Side (Lower)
Essentials

RIVERSIDE
PARK

Riverside Drive

BOAT
BASIN

79th St
Marina

HENRY HUDSON PKWY

West End Av

Broadway

Amsterdam Av

Columbus Av

Central Park west

WEST DRIVE

MUSEUM OF
NATURAL
HISTORY ★

79 St

65 S

W 85th St
W 84th St
W 83rd St
W 82nd St
W 81st St
W 80th St
W 79th St
W 78th St
W 77th St
W 76th St
W 75th St
W 74th St
W 73rd St
W 72nd St
W 71st St
W 70th St
W 69th St
W 68th St
W 67th St
W 66th St
W 65th St
W 64th St
Lincoln Plaza
W 63rd St
W 62nd St
W 61st St
W 60th St

Hudson
River

PIER

HENRY HUDSON PKWY

Riverside Blvd

Freedom Pl

LINCOLN
TOWERS

LINCOLN
CENTER

AMSTERDAM
HOUSES

FORDHAM
UNIVERSITY

The presence of Lincoln Center and the Museum of Natural History gives the southern half of the Upper West Side more than its share of the major cultural hotspots in Manhattan. And you can stop by several truly remarkable apartment buildings (the Ansonia, the Apthorp, the Dorilton, the Dakota, the Majestic, and the San Remo) on your way to Strawberry Fields to pay respect to Mr. Lennon.

ATMs

- CU • ABC Employees Federal • 30 W. 66th St., 1st Fl.
- CU • ABC Employees Federal • 77 W. 66th St., Lobby
- A • Apple • 2100 Broadway
- B • Bank of New York • 47 W. 62nd St.
- Ch • Chase • 1934 Broadway
- Ch • Chase • 2099 Broadway
- Ch • Chase • 260 Columbus Ave.
- Ch • Chase • 2219 Broadway
- Ch • Chase • 124 W. 60th St.
- Ch • Chase • 1 Lincoln Plaza
- Ci • Citibank • 162 Amsterdam Ave.
- Ci • Citibank • 175 W. 72nd St.
- Co • Commercial Bank • 2025 Broadway
- F • Fleet • 192 Columbus Ave.
- H • HSBC • 301 Columbus Ave.
- J • Jamaica Savings • 1995 Broadway
- N • North Fork Bank • 175 W. 72nd St.

Bagels

- B-J's Bagels • 130 W. 72nd St.
- Bagel Talk • 368 Amsterdam Ave.
- H & H Bagels • 2239 Broadway
- New York City Bagels • 164 Amsterdam Ave.

★ Landmarks

- Ansonia Hotel • Broadway at 73rd St.
- Lincoln Center • Broadway at 64th St.
- Museum of Natural History • Central Park West at 79th St.
- The Dakota • Central Park West at 72nd St.
- The Dorilton • Broadway at 71st St.
- The Majestic • Broadway at 71st St.
- The San Remo • Central Park West at 74th St.

📖 Libraries

- New York Public Library for the Performing Arts • 40 Lincoln Center Plaza
- Riverside • 127 Amsterdam Ave.
- St. Agnes • 444 Amsterdam Ave.

Marketplace

- Fishs Eddy • 2176 Broadway
- Gryphon Record Shop • 233 W. 72nd St.
- Lincoln Stationers • 1889 Broadway
- Zabar's • 2245 Broadway

24-Hour Pharmacies

- Duane Reade • 2025 Broadway
- Rite Aid • 210 Amsterdam Ave.

P Police Precinct

- 20th Precinct • 120 W. 82nd St.

✉ Post Offices

- Ansonia • 178 Columbus
- Columbus Circle • 27 W. 60th St.
- Planetarium • 131 W. 83rd St.

S Schools

- Alvin Ailey American Dance Center • 211 W. 61st St.
- American Musical and Drama Academy • 2109 Broadway
- Beacon High School • 227 W. 61st St.
- Fiorello H. LaGuardia High School • 108 Amsterdam Ave.
- Fordham University • 113 W. 60th St.
- IS 044 William J O'Shea School • 100 W. 77th St.
- Louis D. Brandeis High School • 145 W. 84th St.
- Mannes College Of Music • 150 W. 85th St.
- Metropolitan Center • 1855 Broadway
- New York Institute of Tech • 1855 Broadway
- PS 009 Renaissance School • 100 W. 84th St.
- PS 087 William Sherman • 160 W. 78th St.
- PS 191 Amsterdam School • 210 W. 61st St.
- PS 199 Jesse Straus School • 270 W. 70th St.
- PS 252 • 20 West End Ave.
- The Calhoun School • 81st St. & West End Ave.

✳ Community Garden

Upper West Side (Lower)
Sundries / Entertainment

W 85th St
W 84th St
W 83rd St
W 82nd St
W 81st St
W 80th St
W 79th St
W 78th St
W 77th St
W 76th St
W 75th St
W 74th St
W 73rd St
W 72nd St
W 71st St
W 70th St
W 69th St
W 68th St
W 67th St
W 66th St
W 65th St
W 64th St
W 63rd St
W 62nd St
W 61st St
W 60th St

RIVERSIDE
PARK

BOAT
BASIN

79th St
Marina

PIER

Hudson
River

RIVERSIDE
PARK

Riverside Drive

HENRY HUDSON PKWY

West End Av

Broadway

Amsterdam Av

Columbus Av

Central Park West

MUSEUM OF
NATURAL
HISTORY

LINCOLN
TOWERS

Riverside Blvd

Freedom Pl

HENRY HUDSON PKWY

AMSTERDAM
HOUSES

LINCOLN
CENTER

Lincoln Plaza

FORDHAM
UNIVERSITY

Upper West Side (Lower)
Sundries / Entertainment

Home to the famous Zabar's, several quality watering holes (such as the Dublin House and the All-State Café), and the viciously tasty and unhealthy Big Nick's Burger Joint (at 2175 Broadway), this part of the Upper West Side has more character than people suspect at first glance.

 Bars

- Dublin House • 225 W. 79th St.
- P & G • 279 Amsterdam Ave.
- Racoon Lodge • 480 Amsterdam Ave.

 Cafes

- Columbus Bakery • 474 Columbus Ave.
- Coopers Coffee Ltd. III • 2315 Broadway
- Drip • 489 Amsterdam Ave.
- Emack & Bolio's • 389 Amsterdam Ave.
- New World Coffee • 416 Columbus Ave.
- New World Coffee Inc. • 159 Columbus Ave.
- Peter's • 184 Columbus Ave.
- Starbucks • 1841 Broadway
- Timothy's Coffees of the World • 261 Columbus Ave.
- Xando Coffee & Bar • 2160 Broadway

 Farmer's Markets

- 77th St. & Columbus Ave.
- 73rd St. & Broadway

 Gyms

- Alfred Condominium Health Club • 161 W. 61st St.
- All Star Fitness Center • 75 West End Ave.
- BodyHeat Fitness • 49 W. 73rd St.
- Club 30 • 30 W. 63rd St.
- Crunch Fitness • 160 W. 83rd St.
- Equinox Fitness Club • 344 Amsterdam Ave.
- Extravertical Climbing Center • 61 W. 62nd St.
- New York Sports • 2162 Broadway
- New York Sports Clubs • 23 W. 73rd St.
- New York Sports Clubs • 248 W. 80th St.
- New York Sports Clubs • 61 W. 72nd St.
- Reebok Sports Club NY • 160 Columbus Ave.
- Sports Club/LA • 160 Columbus Ave.
- Top Of The One Club • 1 Lincoln Plz
- West River Racquet Ball • 424 West End Ave.
- World Gym • 1926 Broadway
- YMCA of Greater NY: Westside • 5 W. 63rd St.

Hardware Stores

- A & I Hardware • 207 Columbus Ave.
- Amsterdam Hardware • 147 Amsterdam Ave.
- Beacon Paint & Wallpaper Co. Inc. • 371 Amsterdam Ave.
- Ben Franklin Paints • 2193 Broadway
- Gartner's Hardware Inc. • 134 W. 72nd St.
- Klosty Hardware • 471 Amsterdam Ave.
- Riverside Houseware Inc. • 2315 Broadway
- Ronnie's Hardware • 208 Columbus Ave.
- Roxy Hardware and Paint Co. • 469 Columbus Ave.
- Supreme Hardware & Supply Co. Inc. • 65 W. 73rd St.
- True Value Hardware • 466 Columbus Ave.

Liquor Stores

- 67 Wine & Spirits Inc. • 179 Columbus Ave.
- 79th Street Wine & Spirits Corp. • 230 W. 79th St.
- Acker Merrall • 160 W. 72nd St.
- Beacon Wines & Spirits • 2120 Broadway
- Central Wine & Liquor Store • 227 Columbus Ave.
- Nancy's Wines • 313 Columbus Ave.
- New Erlich Wines & Spirits Inc. • 222 Amsterdam Ave.
- Rose Wine & Liquor Corp • 449 Columbus Ave.
- West End Wine Inc. • 204 West End Ave.
- West Side Wine & Spirits Shop • 481 Columbus Ave.

Movie Theatres

- American Museum of Natural History • Central Park West at 79th St.
- Clearview's 62nd & Broadway • 1871 Broadway
- Lincoln Plaza Cinemas • 30 Lincoln Plaza at Broadway & 62nd St.
- Loew's 84th St. • 2310 Broadway
- Makor • 35 W. 67th St.
- Sony Lincoln Square & IMAX Theatre • 1992 Broadway
- Walter Reade Theater • 70 Lincoln Center Plaza

 Pet Stores

- Furry Paws 4 • 141 Amsterdam Ave.
- Pet Bowl • 440 Amsterdam Ave.
- Petland Discounts • 137 W. 72nd St.
- The Pet Market • 210 W. 72nd St.

Restaurants

- All State Cafe • 250 W. 72nd St.
- Balducci's • 155 W. 66th St.
- Baluchi's • 283 Columbus Ave.
- Big Nick's • 2175 Broadway
- Cafe Des Artistes • 1 W. 67th St.
- Caprice • 199 Columbus Ave.
- China Fun • 246 Columbus Ave.
- Citarella • 2135 Broadway
- D & S Place • 169 Amsterdam Ave.
- EJ'S Luncheonette • 447 Amsterdam Ave.
- Fairway Cafe • 2127 Broadway
- French Roast • 2340 Broadway
- Gray's Papaya • 2090 Broadway
- Harry's Burrito Junction • 241 Columbus Ave.
- Jean Georges • 1 Central Park West
- John's Pizzeria • 48 W. 65th St.
- Josie's • 300 Amsterdam Ave.
- La Caridad 78 • 2197 Broadway
- La Fenice • 2014 Broadway
- Lenge • 200 Columbus Ave.
- Manhattan Diner • 2180 Broadway
- Penang • 240 Columbus Ave.
- Picholine • 35 W. 64th St.
- Rose Mexicano • 51 Columbus Ave.
- Saloon, The • 1920 Broadway
- Santa Fe • 72 W. 69th St.
- Sarabeth's • 423 Amsterdam Ave.
- Taco Grill • 146 W. 72nd St.
- Van West • 247 W. 72nd St.
- Vince and Eddie's • 70 W. 68th St.
- Vinnie's Pizza • 285 Amsterdam Ave.

 Video Rentals

- Blockbuster Video • 199 Amsterdam Ave.
- Channel Video • 472 Columbus Ave.
- Flik's Video 2 Go • 175 W. 72nd St.
- Tower Records-Video-Books • 1961 Broadway

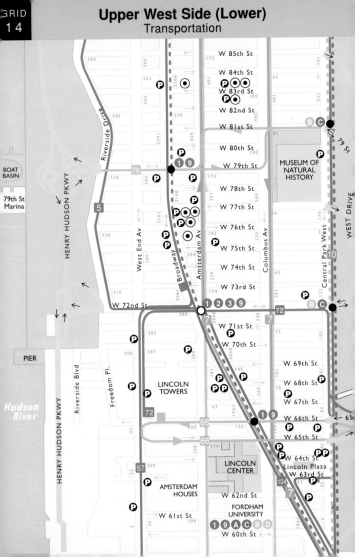

Upper West Side (Lower)
Transportation

Parking and driving are both actually doable in this area, with most of the available spots on or near Riverside Drive. We recommend the 79th Street Transverse for crossing Central Park to go to the east side. The Lincoln Center area is by far the messiest traffic problem here—you can avoid it by taking West End Avenue.

Subways

1 2 3 9 . . . . 72nd St at Broadway
1 9 . . . . 79th St at Broadway
1 9 . . . . 66th St Lincoln Center
B C . . . . . . 72nd St at Central Park West
B C . . 81st St- Museum of Natural History

Bus Lines

5 . 5th Ave./Ave. of the Americas/Riverside Dr.
7 . . . . Columbus Ave./Amsterdam Ave./
Lenox Ave./6th Ave./Broadway
10 . . . . 7th Ave./8th Ave./Douglass Blvd.
11 . . . . 9th Ave./10th Ave. (at 10th Ave)
57 . . . . 57th St. Crosstown
66 . . . . 66th St./67th St. Crosstown
72 . . . . 72nd St. Crosstown
79 . . . . 79th St. Crosstown
104 . . . . Broadway/42nd St. (at 42 St)

Car Rentals

• Avis • 216 W. 76th St.
• Budget • 207 W. 76th St.
• Enterprise • 147 W. 83rd St.
• Hertz • 210 W. 77th St.
• Hertz Truck & Van Rental • 210 W. 77th St.
• Manhattan Rent- A-Car • 143 W. 83rd St.
• National • 219 W. 77th St.
• New York Rent-A-Car • 146 W. 83rd St.

Parking

• 110 West End Ave.
• 200 W. 79th St.
• 80 Central Park West
• 350 Amsterdam Ave.
• 155 W. 70th St.
• 210 W. 76th St.
• 254 W. 79th St.
• 201 W. 75th St.
• 44 W. 62nd St.
• 10 W. 66th St.
• 1916 Broadway
• 214 W. 80th St.
• 30 W. 63rd St.
• 2000 Broadway
• 165 West End Ave.
• 1 Lincoln Plaza
• 200 W. 71st St.
• 147 W. 83rd St.
• 150 W. 83rd St.
• 150 West End Ave.
• 60 W. 66th St.
• 225 W. 83rd St.
• 150 W. 68th St.
• 65 W. 66th St.
• 155 W. 68th St.
• 143 W. 68th St.
• 3 Lincoln Plaza
• 15 W. 72nd St.
• 207 W. 76th St.
• 15 West End Ave.
• 2109 Broadway
• 75 West End Ave.
• 203 W. 77th St.

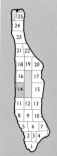

Upper East Side (Lower)
Essentials

E 86th St

E 85th St

E 84th St

E 83rd St

E 82nd St

E 81st St

E 80th St

E 79th St

E 78th St

E 77th St

E 76th St

E 75th St

E 74th St

E 73rd St

E 72nd St

E 71st St

E 70th St

E 69th St

E 68th St

E 67th St

E 66th St

E 65th St

E 64th St

E 63rd St

E 62nd St

E 61st St

E 60th St

Fifth Ave

Madison Ave

Park Ave

Lexington Ave

Third Ave

Second Ave

First Ave

York Ave

East End Ave

CARL SCHURZ PARK

JOHN JAY PARK

ROCKEFELLER UNIVERSITY

FDR Drive

East River

ROOSEVELT I TRAMW

QUEENSBORO B

The southern half of the Upper East Side is a hotbed of culture, research, and education, containing one of the world's top museums (the Metropolitan Museum of Art); several top schools, including Cornell University Medical Center and Rockefeller University; and perhaps the foremost cancer hospital in the world, Memorial Sloan-Kettering Cancer Center.

ATMs

- A • Apple • 1555 First Ave.
- B • Bank of New York • 1100 Third Ave.
- B • Bank of New York • 706 Madison Ave.
- Ch • Chase • 770 Lexington Ave.
- Ch • Chase • 1003 Lexington Ave.
- Ch • Chase • 1025 Madison Ave.
- Ch • Chase • 201 E. 79th St.
- Ch • Chase • 300 E. 64th St.
- Ch • Chase • 360 E. 72nd St.
- Ch • Chase • 501 E. 79th St.
- Ch • Chase • 515 E. 72nd St.
- Ch • Chase • 940 Madison Ave.
- Ch • Chase • 1121 Madison Ave.
- Ch • Chase • 600 Madison Ave.
- Ci • Citibank • 1078 Third Ave.
- Ci • Citibank • 1266 First Ave.
- Ci • Citibank • 1285 First Ave.
- Ci • Citibank • 1510-12 First Ave.
- Ci • Citibank • 171 E. 72nd St.
- Ci • Citibank • 757 Madison Ave.
- Ci • Citibank • 976 Madison Ave.
- Co • Commercial Bank • 1180 Third Ave.
- Co • Commercial Bank • 1258 Second Ave.
- Co • Commercial Bank • 300 E. 79th St.
- D • Dime • 510 Park Ave.
- D • Dime • 1520 York Ave.
- E • Emigrant • 1270 Lexington Ave.
- E • Emigrant • 812-814 Lexington Ave.
- F • Fleet • 1143 Lexington Ave.
- FF • Fourth Federal Savings • 1355 First Ave.
- G • Greenpoint • 1010 Third Ave.
- H • HSBC • 1165 Third Ave.
- H • HSBC • 1340 Third Ave.
- H • HSBC • 1002 Madison Ave.

Bagels

- 1101 Bagel Corp • 1101 Lexington Ave.
- Bagelry • 1228 Lexington Ave.
- Bagelworks • 1229 First Ave.
- Café Group of New York • 1228 Second Ave.
- Eastside Bagel • 1496 First Ave.
- Einstein Bros. Bagels • 1336 First Ave.
- Elaine's Bagel Ltd. • 941 Park Ave.
- H & H Bagels East • 1551 Second Ave.
- Hot & Tasty Bagels • 1323 Second Ave.
- NYC Bagels • 1228 Second Ave.
- Pick A Bagel On Second • 1473 Second Ave.
- The Bagel Shoppe • 1421 Second Ave.
- The Bread Factory Cafe • 785 Lexington Ave.

Hospitals

- Gracie Square Hospital • 420 E. 76th St.
- Hospital For Special Surgery • 535 E. 70th St.
- Lenox Hill Hospital • 100 E. 77th St.
- Manhattan Eye, Ear & Throat Hospital • 210 E. 64th St.
- Memorial Sloan-Kettering Cancer Center • 1275 York Ave.
- New York Presbyterian/Weill Cornell Medical Center • 525 E. 68th St.

Landmarks

- Abigail Adams Smith Museum • 421 E. 61st St.
- Asia Society • 725 Park Ave.
- Frick Collection • 1 E. 70th St.
- Metropolitan Museum of Art • 1000 Fifth Ave.
- Temple Emanu-El • 1 E. 65th St.
- Whitney Museum of American Art • 945 Madison Ave.

Libraries

- 67th Street • 328 E. 67th St.
- Webster • 1465 York Ave.
- Yorkville • 222 E. 79th St.

M Marketplace

- Barneys New York • 660 Madison Ave.
- Bloomingdales • 1000 Third Ave.
- Diesel • 770 Lexington Ave.
- Gourmet Garage • 301 E. 64th St.

24-Hour Pharmacies

- CVS Pharmacy • 1400 Second Ave.
- CVS Pharmacy • 1223 Second Ave.
- Duane Reade • 1279 Third Ave.
- Eckerd • 1299 Second Ave.

P Police Precinct

- 19th Precinct • 153 W. 67th St.

Post Offices

- Cherokee • 1539 First Ave.
- Gracie • 229 E. 85th St.
- Lenox Hill • 221 E. 70th St.

Schools

- Brandeis University • 12 E. 77th St.
- City University of New York • 535 E. 80th St.
- Cornell University Medical College• 445 E. 69th St.
- Evening School • 317 E. 67th St.
- Hunter College • 695 Park Ave.
- JHS 167 Robert F. Wagner School • 220 E. 76th St.
- Julia Richman High School • Second Ave. & 67th St.
- Manhattan International High School • 317 E. 67th St.
- Martha Graham School • 316 E. 63rd St.
- Marymount Manhattan College • 221 E. 71st St.
- New York School Of Interior Design • 170 E. 70th St.
- PS 006 Lillie D. Blake School • 45 E. 81st St.
- PS 158 Bayard Taylor School • 1458 York Ave.
- PS 183 R. L. Stevenson School • 419 E. 66th St.
- PS 190 New School • 311 E. 82nd St.
- Rockefeller University • 1230 York Ave.
- Sotheby's Educational Studies • 1334 York Ave.
- Vanguard High School • 317 E. 67th St.

CARL
SCHURZ
PARK

E 86th St
E 85th St
E 84th St
E 83rd St
E 82nd St
E 81st St
E 80th St
E 79th St
E 78th St
E 77th St
E 76th St
E 75th St
E 74th St
E 73rd St
E 72nd St
E 71st St
E 70th St
E 69th St
E 68th St
E 67th St
E 66th St
E 65th St
E 64th St
E 63rd St
E 62nd St
E 61st St
E 60th St
F 59th St

Fifth Ave
Madison Ave
Park Ave
Lexington Ave
Third Ave
Second Ave
First Ave
York Ave
East End Ave

JOHN
JAY
PARK

ROCKEFELLER
UNIVERSITY

FDR Drive

East
River

ROOSEVELT ISLA
TRAMWAY

QUEENSBORO BRID

The Upper East Side has itself covered pretty well here, and it also has another of New York's classic movie theaters, the Beekman.

24-Hour Copy Centers

- Copycats • 968 Lexington Ave.
- Kinko's • 1122 Lexington Ave.

Bars

- Finnegan's Wake • 1361 First Ave.
- Hi-Life • 1340 First Ave.
- Oak Bar • 768 Fifth Ave.
- Racoon Lodge • 1439 York Ave.
- Subway Inn • 143 E. 60th St.

Cafes

- Cafe Plus Inc. • 1269 First Ave.
- Cafe Word of Mouth • 1012 Lexington Ave
- DT ° UT • 1626 Second Ave.
- Java Girl • 348 E. 66th St.
- La Fleur Dejour Cafe • 348 E. 62nd St.
- Le Pain Quotidien • 1131 Madison Ave.
- New World Coffee • 1046 3rd Ave.
- Rohrs M • 303 E. 85th St.
- Serendipity 3 • 225 E. 60th St.
- Starbucks • 1445 First Ave.

Gyms

- Body Sculpt • 242 E. 79th St.
- Belaire Health Club • 524 E. 72nd St.
- Casa Fitness Club • 48 E. 73rd St.
- Casa at the Regency • 540 Park Ave.
- Definitions • 39 E. 78th St.
- Eastside Sports Physical Therapy 244 E. 84th St.
- Elissa's Personal Best Gym •334 E. 79th St.
- Equinox Fitness • 205 E. 85th St.
- Equinox Fitness Club • 140 E. 63rd St. & Lexington Ave.
- Hampton House Health Club • 404 E. 79th St.
- Lenox Hill Neighborhood House • 331 E. 70th St.
- Liberty Fitness Center • 244 E. 84th St.
- New York Health & Racquet Club • 1433 York Ave.
- New York Sports Clubs • 502 E. 59th St.
- New York Sports Clubs • 349 E. 76th St.
- New York Sports Clubs • 502 Park Ave.
- New York Sports Clubs • 1470 1st Ave.
- Pavilion Personal Fitness Center • 500 E. 77th St.
- Promenade Health Club • 530 E. 76th St.
- River Terrace Health Club • 515 E. 72nd St.
- Savoy Spa • 200 E. 61st St.
- Sports Club/LA • 328 E. 61st St.
- Strathmore Swim & Health Club • 400 E. 84th St.
- Synergy USA Inc • 1438 Third Ave.
- The Training Floor • 428 E. 75th St.
- Trainers Place • 1421 3rd Ave.

Hardware Stores

- 72nd Street Hardware • 1398 Second Ave.
- ATB Locksmith & Hardware Inc •
- Gotham City Hardware • 310 E. 75th St.
- Gracious Home • 1220 Third Ave.

- Kraft Hardware Inc. • 306 E. 61st St.
- Lexington Hardware & Electric Co. • 797 Lexington Ave.
- New York Paint & Hardware • 1593 Second Ave.
- Queensboro Hardware Co. • 1157 Second Ave.
- Rainbow Ace Hardware • 1449 First Ave.
- S & V General Supply Co. • 1450 First Ave.
- Sutton Hardware & Home Center • 1153 First Ave.
- Third Ave. Supply Co. • 1301 Third Ave.

Liquor Stores

- 76 Liquors • 1473 First Ave.
- Carlyle Wines Ltd. • 997 Madison Ave.
- Cork and Bottle Liquor Store • 1158 First Ave.
- East River Liquors • 1364 York Ave.
- Embassy Liquors Inc. • 796 Lexington Ave.
- Garnet Wines & Liquors Inc. • 929 Lexington Ave.
- Headington Wine & Liquors • 1135 Lexington Ave.
- In Vino Veritas • 1375 First Ave.
- Kris & Bill Wine & Liquor • 1587 Second Ave.
- Lumers Fine Wines & Spirits • 1479 Third Ave.
- McCabe's Liquor Store • 1347 Third Ave.
- Milli Liquors Inc • 300 E. 78th St.
- Monro Wines & Liquors Inc. • 68 East End Ave.
- Rosenthal Wine Merchant • 318 E. 84th St.
- Sherry-Lehman Co. Inc. • 679 Madison Ave
- Stuart's Wines & Spirits • 1043 Third Ave.
- The Wine Cart • 235 E. 69th St.
- The Wine Shop Inc. • 1585 First Ave.
- Viski Wines Inc. • 1347 Third Ave.
- Waldorf Liquor Shop • 1495 York Ave.
- Windsor Wine Shop • 1114 First Ave.
- York Wines & Spirits • 1291 First Ave.
- Yorkshire Wines & Spirits • 1646 First Ave.

Movie Theatres

- Asia Society • 725 Park Ave.
- Cineplex Odeon: Beekman 1254 Second Ave.
- Cineplex Odeon: Coronet Cinemas 993 Third Ave.
- City Cinemas 1, 2, 3 • 1001 Third Ave.
- Clearview's 59th St. East • 239 E. 59th St.
- Clearview's First & 62nd St. • 400 E. 62nd St.
- Czech Center • 1109 Madison Ave.
- French Institute / Florence Gould Hall, 55 E. 59th St.
- Goethe Institute • 1014 Fifth Ave.
- Loews New York Twin • 1271 Second Ave.
- Loews Tower East • 1230 Third Ave.
- Metropolitan Museum of Art • 1000 Fifth Ave.
- New York Youth Theater • 593 Park Ave.
- United Artists: 64th and 2nd Ave. • 1210 Second Ave.
- United Artists: E. 85th St. • 1629 First Ave.
- Whitney Museum • 945 Madison Ave.

Pet Stores

- American Kennels • 798 Lexington Ave.
- Animal Attractions • 343 E. 66th St.
- Calling All Pets • 301 E. 76th St.

- Calling All Pets • 1590 York Ave.
- Canine Styles • 830 Lexington Ave.
- Grooming All Pets • 1590 York Ave.
- Karen's For People Plus Pets • 1195 Lexington Ave.
- Le Chien Pet Salon • 1044 Third Ave.
- Lolly's Pet Salon • 228 E. 80th St.
- Not Just Dogs • 244 E. 60th St.
- Pet Market • 1570 1st Ave.
- Pet Necessities • 236 E. 75th St.
- Pet Party • 1431A York Ave.
- Peters Emporium For Pets • 1449 Second Ave.
- Pets on Lex • 1271 Lexington Ave.
- Sutton Dog Parlour Kennel & Daycare Center • 311 E. 60th St.
- Z Spot • 965 Madison Ave.

Restaurants

- Afghan Kebab House • 1345 Second Ave.
- Atlantic Grill • 1341 Third Ave.
- Aureole • 34 E. 61st St.
- Baluchi's • 1149 First Ave.
- Baluchi's • 1565 Second Ave.
- Brunelli's • 1409 York Ave.
- Canyon Road • 1470 First Ave.
- Daniel • 60 E. 65th St.
- EJ'S Luncheonette • 1271 Third Ave.
- Haru • 1329 Third Ave.
- J.G. Melon • 1291 Third Ave.
- Jackson Hole • 232 E. 64th St.
- Jo Jo • 160 E. 64th St.
- John's Pizzeria • 408 E. 64th St.
- Mary Ann's • 1503 Second Ave.
- Maya • 1191 First Ave.
- Our Place • 1444 Third Ave.
- Park Avenue Cafe • 100 E. 63rd St.
- Penang • 1596 Second Ave.
- Post House • 28 E. 63rd St.
- Rain • 1059 Third Ave.
- Rughetta • 347 E. 85th St.
- Serafina Fabulous Grill • 29 E. 61st St.
- Totonno Pizzeria Napolitano • 1544 Second Ave.
- Viand • 1011 Madison Ave.
- Viand • 673 Madison Ave.

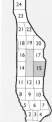 Video Rentals

- Blockbuster Video • 1251 Lexington Ave.
- Blockbuster Video • 1646 1st Ave.
- Blockbuster Video • 1530 Second Ave.
- Blockbuster Video • 1270 First Ave.
- Champagne Video • 1416 First Ave.
- Filmfest Video • 1594 York Ave.
- Couch Potato Video • 1456 Second Ave.
- Express Video • 421 E. 72nd St.
- Fifth Dimension Video Corp • 1427 York Ave.
- Video Vogue • 976 Lexington Ave.
- Videoroom • 1487 Third Ave.
- York Video Inc • 1472 York Ave.
- Zitomer Department Store & Electronics • 969 Madison Ave.

Upper East Side (Lower)
Transportation

Upper East Side (Lower)
Transportation

Parking is extremely difficult during the day due to the number of schools in this area. It gets a bit better (but not much) at night, especially in the upper seventies and lower eighties near the FDR (you'll never find legal street parking near Bloomingdale's, however). Park Ave. is the best street to travel downtown during rush hour.

Subways

4 5 6 . . . . 86th St at Lexington Ave.

6 . . . . 77th St at Lexington Ave.

6 . . . . 68th St at Lexington Ave.

4 5 6 N R . . . 60th St at Lexington Ave.

N R . . . . 5th Ave. at 60th St.

Bus Lines

1 2 3 . . . . 5th Ave./Madison Ave.

4 . . . . 5th Ave./Madison Ave./Broadway

14 . . . . 14th St. Crosstown

15 . . . . 1st/2nd Aves. (at 2 Ave)

30 . . . . 72nd St./57th St. Crosstown

31 . . . . York Ave./57th St. Crosstown

66 . . . . 67th St./68th St Crosstown

72 . . . . 72nd St. Crosstown

79 . . . . 79th St. Crosstown

98 . . . . Washington Heights/Midtown

101 102 103 98 . . . . 3rd Ave./Lexington Ave

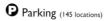 Car Rentals

- Avis • 310 E. 64th St.
- Budget • 234 E. 85th St.
- Dollar • 157 E. 84th St.
- Enterprise • 425 E. 61st St.
- Hertz • 327 E. 64th St.
- Hertz • 355 E. 76th St.
- National • 305 E. 80th St.

P Gas Station

- Mobil • York Ave. and 61st St.

P Parking (145 locations)

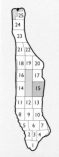

Upper West Side (Upper)
Essentials

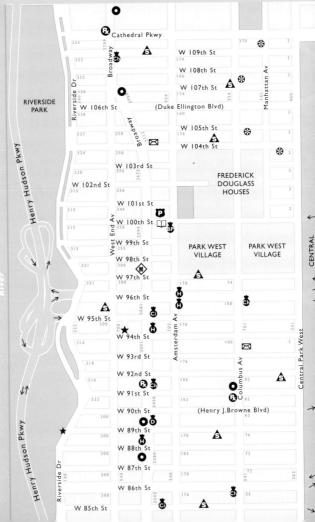

This part of the Upper West Side is extremely residential. Riverside Drive, West End Avenue, and Central Park West are all highly desirable addresses—if you can afford it. Check out Riverside Park for all sorts of amusements.

💰 ATMs

BP • Banco Popular • 799 Amsterdam Ave.
Ch • Chase • 59 W. 86th St.
Ch • Chase • 2460 Broadway
Ch • Chase • 2760 Broadway
Ch • Chase • 90 W. 96th St.
Ci • Citibank • 2350 Broadway
Ci • Citibank • 2560 Broadway
D • Dime • 2438 Broadway
H • HSBC • 2401 Broadway
H • HSBC • 739 Amsterdam Ave.
H • HSBC • 2520 Broadway
H • HSBC • 743 Amsterdam Ave.

⭕ Bagels

• Absolute Bagels • 2788 Broadway
• Columbia Bagels • 2836 Broadway
• Columbus Star Bagels • 618 Columbus Ave.
• Cooper's Bagels • 2415 Broadway
• Hot & Crusty Bagel Café • 2387 Broadway

⭐ Landmarks

• Pomander Walk • 261-7 W. 94th St.
• Soldiers and Sailors Monument •
  Riverside Drive and 89th St.

📖 Library

• Bloomingdale • 150 W. 100th St.

Ⓜ Marketplace

• Gourmet Garage • 2567 Broadway

℞ 24-Hour Pharmacies

• CVS Pharmacy • 606 Columbus Ave.
• Duane Reade • 2465 Broadway
• Rite Aid • 2833 Broadway

🅿 Police Precinct

• 24th Precinct • 151 W. 100th St.

✉ Post Offices

• Cathedral • 215 W.104th St.
• Park West • 693 Columbus Ave.

🅢 Schools

• JHS 054 B. Washington School •
  103 W. 107th St.
• Mannes College Of Music • 150 W. 85th St.
• PS 075 Emily Dickinson School •
  735 West End Ave.
• PS 084 Lillian Weber School • 32 W. 92nd St.
• PS 145 Bloomingdale School • 150 W. 105th St.
• PS 163 Alfred E. Smith School • 163 W. 97th St.
• PS 165 Robert E. Simon School •
  234 W. 109th St.
• PS 166 Arts & Sciences School •
  132 W. 89th St.

�֍ Community Gardens

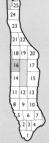

Upper West Side (Upper)
Sundries / Entertainment

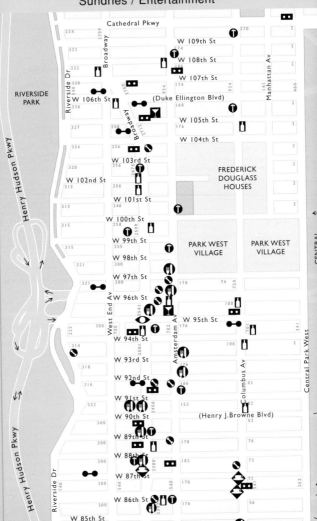

Cathedral Pkwy
Broadway
W 109th St
W 108th St
W 107th St
(Duke Ellington Blvd)
W 106th St
W 105th St
W 104th St
W 103rd St
W 102nd St
W 101st St
W 100th St
W 99th St
W 98th St
W 97th St
W 96th St
W 95th St
W 94th St
W 93rd St
W 92nd St
W 91st St
W 90th St
W 89th St
W 88th St
W 87th St
W 86th St
W 85th St

RIVERSIDE PARK

Riverside Dr

Henry Hudson Pkwy

Hudson River

Henry Hudson Pkwy

Riverside Dr

West End Av

Amsterdam Av

Columbus Av

(Henry J. Browne Blvd)

FREDERICK DOUGLASS HOUSES

PARK WEST VILLAGE

PARK WEST VILLAGE

Manhattan Av

Central Park West

CENTRAL

Broadway is the place to go for all your sundries needs—especially north of 90th Street.

 Bars
- Abbey Pub • 207 W. 105th St.
- Dive Bar • 732 Amsterdam Ave.

 Cafes
- Lite Delights • 532 Columbus Ave.
- Starbucks • 540 Columbus Ave.
- Starbucks • 2379 Broadway

 Farmer's Markets
- Greenmarket • Amsterdam Ave. & Columbus Ave.

 Gyms
- Aquatic Recreational Management Inc. • 341 W. 87th St.
- Body Strength Fitness • 250 W. 106th St.
- Dolphin Fitness Clubs • 700 Columbus Ave.
- Equinox Fitness Club • 2465 Broadway & 92nd St.
- Lucille Roberts Health Club • 2700 Broadway
- Paris Health Club • 752 West End Ave.
- The Episode • 929 West End Ave.

 Hardware Stores
- AJO Lumber & Woodworking Co Inc. • 817 Amsterdam Ave.
- Altman Hardware Inc. • 641 Amsterdam Ave.
- Aquarius Hardware & Houseware • 601 Amsterdam Ave.
- Broadway Home Center Inc. • 2672 Broadway
- C&S Hardware • 788 Amsterdam Ave.
- Cohen B & Son • 969 Amsterdam Ave.
- Garcia Hardware Store • 995 Columbus Ave.
- Grand Metro Home Centers Inc. • 2524 Broadway
- Jimmy's Hardware • 914 Columbus Ave.
- Mike's Lumber Store Inc. • 224 Amsterdam Ave.
- Mike's Lumber Store Inc. • 254 W. 88th St.
- Quintessentials • 532 Amsterdam Ave.
- World Houseware • 2617 Broadway

 Liquor Stores
- Academy Liquor Store • 2648 Broadway
- Adel Wine & Liquor • 925 Columbus Ave.
- Columbus Ave Wine & Spirits • 730 Columbus Ave.
- Gotham Wines And Liquors • 2519 Broadway
- H & H Broadway Wine Center Ltd. • 2669 Broadway
- Hong Liquor Store Inc • 2616 Broadway
- Martin Brothers Liquor Store • 2781 Broadway
- Mitchell's Wine & Liquor Store • 200 W. 86th St.
- Polanco Liquor Store • 948 Amsterdam Ave.
- Riverside Liquor Co • 2746 Broadway
- Roma Discount Wine & Liquor • Amsterdam Ave. at 96th St.
- The Wine Place • 2406 Broadway
- Turin Wines & Liquors Inc. • 609 Columbus Ave.
- Westlane Wines & Liquor • 689 Columbus Ave.

 Movie Theatres
- Clearview's Metro Twin • 2626 Broadway
- Clearview's Olympia Twin • 2770 Broadway
- Symphony Space • 2537 Broadway

 Pet Stores
- Amazing Pet Products • 564 Columbus Ave.
- Amsterdam Aquarium & Pet Shop • 652 Amsterdam Ave.
- Amsterdog Groomers • 586 Amsterdam Ave.
- Aquarius Aquarium Installation • 214 Riverside Dr.
- Little Creatures • 770 Amsterdam Ave.
- NY Aquatics and Pet Wherehouse • 209 W. 96th St.
- Pet Stop • 564 Columbus Ave.
- Petland Discounts • 2708 Broadway
- Sporn Pet Products Inc • 274 W. 86th St.

 Restaurants
- Cafe Con Leche • 726 Amsterdam Ave.
- Carmine's • 2450 Broadway
- Docks Oyster Bar • 2427 Broadway
- Flor de Mayo • 2651 Broadway
- Gabriela's • 685 Amsterdam Ave.
- Gennaro • 665 Amsterdam Ave.
- Jackson Hole • 517 Columbus Ave.
- Lemongrass Grill • 2534 Broadway
- Mary Ann's • 2452 Broadway
- Pampa • 768 Amsterdam Ave.
- Saigon Grill • 2381 Broadway

Video Rentals
- Arthfoto Corp. • 2474 Broadway
- Blockbuster Video • 552 Amsterdam Ave.
- Blockbuster Video • 2689 Broadway
- Blockbuster Video • 726 Amsterdam Ave.
- Books, Videos, & More • 580 Amsterdam Ave.
- Bus Stop Video • 9 W. 110th St.
- Hollywood Video • 535 Columbus Ave.
- Khan Entertainment Center Inc. • 2768 Broadway
- Movie Place • 237 W. 105th St.
- Solis's Video • 965 Amsterdam Ave.

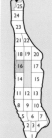

Upper West Side (Upper)
Transportation

RIVERSIDE PARK

Henry Hudson Pkwy

Hudson River

Riverside Dr.

West End Av

Amsterdam Av

Columbus Av

Central Park West

CENTRAL

Cathedral Pkwy

W 109th St
W 108th St
W 107th St

(Duke Ellington Blvd)

W 106th St

W 105th St

W 104th St

W 103rd St
W 102nd St
W 101st St
W 100th St
W 99th St
W 98th St
W 97th St
W 96th St
W 95th St
W 94th St
W 93rd St
W 92nd St
W 91st St

(Henry J. Browne Blvd)

W 90th St
W 89th St
W 88th St
W 87th St
W 86th St
W 85th St

FREDERICK DOUGLASS HOUSES

PARK WEST VILLAGE

PARK WEST VILLAGE

Manhattan Av

Henry Hudson Pkwy

The 96th Street Transverse is by far the best way to cross Central Park. And isn't it nice that the Upper West Side has two separate subway lines?

Subways

1 **9** . . . . 86th St at Broadway

1 **2** **3** **9** . . . . 96th St at Broadway

1 **9** . . . . 103th St at Broadway

1 **9** . . . . 110th St at Broadway

B **C** . . . . 86th St at Central Park West

B **C** . . . . 96th St at Central Park West

B **C** . . . . 103th St at Central Park West

B **C** . . . . 110th St at Central Park West

Bus Lines

4 . . . 5th Ave./Madison Ave. (at Madison Ave)

5 . . . . 5th Ave./6th Ave./Riverside Dr.

7 . . . . Columbus Ave./Amsterdam Ave.

10 . . . . 7th Ave./Central Park West

11 . . . . Columbus Ave./Amsterdam Ave.

60 . . . . LaGuardia Airport

86 . . . . 86th St. Crosstown

96 . . . . 96th St. Crosstown

104 . . . . Broadway

106 . . . . 106th St. Crosstown

116 . . . . 116th St. Crosstown

⊙ Car Rentals

• A A AMCAR • 303 W. 96th St.
• Aamcar • 315 W. 96th St.
• New York Rent A Car • 963 Columbus Ave.

🅿 Gas Station

• Exxon • 303 W. 96th St.

🅿 Parking

• 175 W. 90th St.
• 70 W. 95th St.
• 103 W. 108th St.
• 120 W. 97th St.
• 205 W. 89th St.
• 711 West End Ave.
• 50 W. 93rd St.
• 101 W. 90th St.
• 276 W. 97th St.
• 215 W. 95th St.
• 137 W. 108th St.
• 271 W. 87th St.
• 175 W. 87th St.
• 601 Amsterdam Ave.
• 50 W. 97th St.
• 100 W. 92nd St. #1
• 137 W. 89th St.
• 102 W. 107th St.
• 214 W. 95th St.
• 600 Columbus Ave.
• 204 W. 101st St.
• 204 W. 102nd St.
• 323 W. 96th St.
• 234 W. 108th St.
• 151 W. 108th St.
• 1056 Fifth Ave.

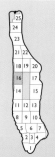

If you were unsure as to whether or not New York had enough cultural institutions, Museum Mile should convince you. The Guggenheim is one of the greatest architectural tours de force in Manhattan, notwithstanding its rapaciously high admission fees. Note the strange icon dispersal between everything north of 96th Street and everything south of 96th Street.

ATMs

- Ch • Chase • 126 E. 86th St.
- Ch • Chase • 255 E. 86th St.
- Ch • Chase • 453 E. 86th St.
- Ch • Chase • 2065 Second Ave.
- Ch • Chase • 1121 Madison Ave.
- Ci • Citibank • 123 E. 86th St.
- Ci • Citibank • 1275 Madison Ave.
- Ci • Citibank • 446 E. 86th St.
- Ci • Citibank • 1625-31 York Ave.
- CS • City and Suburban FSB • 345 E. 86th St.
- D • Dime • 1221 Madison Ave.
- E • Emigrant • 1270 Lexington Ave.
- FF • Fourth Federal Savings • 1751 Second Ave.
- H • HSBC • 1220 Madison Ave.
- H • HSBC • 186 E. 86th St.
- H • HSBC • 45 E. 89th St.

Bagels

- Amir Ram Bagels • 333 E. 86th St.
- Bagelry • 1324 Lexington Ave.
- Bagelry, Inc. • 1380 Madison Ave.
- Bagels Bob's On York • 1638 York Ave.
- Bagels Express of 2nd Ave. • 1804 Second Ave.
- David Bagel • 1651 Second Ave.
- Fanbro Bagel • 1700 First Ave.

Hospitals

- Beth Israel Medical Center: North Division • 170 East End Ave.
- Metropolitan Hospital • 1901 First Ave.
- Mt. Sinai Hospital • Fifth Ave. at 100th St.

Landmarks

- Cooper-Hewitt Museum • 2 E. 91st St.
- Gracie Mansion • Carl Schulz Park at 88th St.
- Guggenheim Museum • 1071 Fifth Ave.
- International Center of Photography • 1130 Fifth Ave.
- Jewish Museum • 1109 Fifth Ave.
- Museo Del Barrio • Fifth Ave. and 104th St.
- Museum of the City of New York • Fifth Ave. and 103rd St.
- St. Nicholas Russian Orthodox Cathedral • 15 E. 97th St.

Libraries

- 96th Street • 112 E. 96th St.
- Aguilar • 174 E. 110th St.

 Marketplace

- Modell's • 1535 Third Ave.

24-Hour Pharmacies

- Duane Reade • 401 E. 86th St.
- Duane Reade • 1231 Madison Ave.
- Rite Aid • 144 E. 86th St.

Police Precinct

- 23rd Precinct • 162 E. 102nd St.

Post Offices

- Gracie • 229 E. 85th St.
- Hell Gate • 153 E. 110th St.
- Yorkville • 1619 Third Ave.

Schools

- Central Park East Secondary School• 1573 Madison Ave.
- JHS 099 Julio De Burgos School • 410 E. 100th St.
- JHS 117 Jefferson Park School • 240 E. 109th St.
- National Academy School of Fine Arts • 5 E. 89th St.
- Park East High School • 234 E. 105th St.
- PS 050 Vito Marcantonio School • 433 E. 100th St.
- PS 072 • 131 E. 104th St.
- PS 083 Luis Munoz Rivera School • 219 E. 109th St.
- PS 108 Peter Minuit School • 1615 Madison Ave.
- PS 109 Century School • 215 E. 99th St.
- PS 121 Galileo School • 232 E. 103rd St.
- PS 146 Anna M. Short School • 421 E. 106th St.
- PS 151 Eleanore Roosevelt School • 1763 First Ave.
- PS 169 Robert F. Kennedy School• 110 E. 88th St.
- PS 171 Patrick Henry School • 19 E. 103rd St.
- PS 198 Isidor-Ida Straus School • 1700 Third Ave.
- Richard Green High School • 421 E. 88th St.
- School Of Cooperative Technical Education • 321 E. 96th St.

 Community Gardens

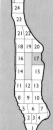

Upper East Side/East Harlem
Sundries / Entertainment

Duke
Ellington
Circle

RANDALL'S
ISLAND

EAST
RIVER
PROJECT

EAST
RIVER
HOUSING

FOOT BRIDGE

CARVER
HOUSES

CARVER
HOUSES

CARVER
HOUSES

GEORGE
WASHINGTON
HOUSES

GEORGE
WASHINGTON
HOUSES

GEORGE
WASHINGTON
HOUSES

Harlem
River

FDR Drive

CARL SCHURZ
PARK

E 111th St
E 110th St
E 109th St
E 108th St
E 107th St
E 106th St
E 105th St
E 104th St
E 103rd St
E 102nd St
E 101st St
E 100th St
E 99th St
E 98th St
E 97th St
E 96th St
E 95th St
E 94th St
E 93rd St
E 92nd St
E 91st St
E 90th St
E 89th St
E 88th St
E 87th St
E 86th St
E 85th St

Fifth Ave
Madison Ave
Park Ave
Lexington Ave
Third Ave
Second Ave
First Ave
York Ave
East End Ave

There's a dramatic change in the number of services north of 96th Street, much of which is due to several large housing projects. However, a few new building projects on 97th and 98th Streets illustrate the creep of gentrification north of 96th Street.

 ## 24-Hour Copy Center
• Copycats • 1646 Second Ave.

 ## Bars
• Kinsale Tavern • 1672 Third Ave.

 ## Cafes
• Le Pain Quotidien • 1131 Madison Ave.
• New World Coffee • 1595 3rd Ave.
• Rohrs M • 303 E. 85th St.
• Starbucks • 1642 3rd Ave.
• Starbucks • 120 E. 87th St.
• Timothy's Coffees of the World • 200 E. 94th St.

 ## Gyms
• Asphalt Green, Inc. • 555 E. 90th St.
• Bally Total Fitness • 144 E. 86th St.
• Carnegie Park Swim & Health Club • 200 E. 94th St.
• Dolphin Fitness Clubs • 1781 Second Ave.
• Eastside Body Builders/Pumping Iron Gym •
  403 E. 91st St.
• Equinox Fitness • 205 E. 85th St.
• Medfitness • 12 E. 86th St.
• Monterey Sports Club • 175 E. 96th St.
• New York Sports Clubs • 151 E. 86th St.
• New York Sports Clubs • 1635 3rd Ave.
• Pumping Iron Gym • 403 E. 91st St.
• YM-YWHA 92nd St.Y • 1395 Lexington Ave.

Hardware Stores
• 86th St. Locksmith • 201 E. 86th St.
• ATB Locksmith & Hardware Inc • 1603 York Ave.
• Bean Housewares, Inc. • 1190 Madison Ave.
• El Barrio Hardware • 1876 Third Ave.
• Johnny's Hardware • 151 E. 106th St.
• K & G Hardware & Supply • 401 E. 90th St.
• M & E Madison Hardware, Inc. • 1396 Madison Ave.
• Morales Brothers Hardware, Inc. • 1959 Third Ave.
• S Feldman Housewares • 1304 Madison Ave.
• Service Hardware Corp. • 1338 Lexington Ave.
• Wankel's Hardware & Paint • 1573 Third Ave.

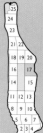

Liquor Stores
• 86th St. Wine & Liquor • 306 E. 86th St.
• Best Cellars • 1291 Lexington Ave.
• Edwin's Wines & Liquors • 176 E. 103rd St.
• K & D Wines & Spirits • 1366 Madison Ave.
• Park East Liquors • 1657 York Ave.
• Uptown Wine Shop Inc. • 1361 Lexington Ave.
• Van Keith Liquors • 1743 First Ave.
• West Coast Wine & Liquor, Inc. • 1440 Lexington Av.
• Wine Traders • 1693 Second Ave.
• Yorkshire Wines & Spirits • 1646 First Ave.

 ## Movie Theatres
• 92nd St.Y • Lexington Ave. at 92nd St.
• City Cinemas: East 86th St. • 210 E. 86th St.
• Clearview's Park & 86th St. Twin • 125 E. 86th St.
• Guggenheim Museum • 1071 Fifth Ave.
• Loews Orpheum • 1538 Third Ave.
• United Artists: E. 85th St. • 1629 First Ave.

 ## Pet Stores
• Calling All Pets • 1590 York Ave.
• Furry Paws • 1705 3rd Ave.
• Grooming All Pets • 1590 York Ave.
• PETCO • 147 E. 86th St.
• Petland Discounts • 304 E. 86th St.
• Pets on Lex • 1271 Lexington Ave.
• Shaggy Dog • 400 E. 88th St.
• Urban Pets • 1661 1st Ave.

Restaurants
• Barking Dog Luncheonette • 1678 Third Ave.
• Burritoville • 1606 Third Ave.
• Elaine's • 1703 Second Ave.
• Jackson Hole • 1270 Madison Ave.
• Rughetta • 347 E. 85th St.
• Saigon Grill • 1700 Second Ave.
• Viand • 300 E. 86th St.

Video Rental
• Blockbuster Video •
  1251 Lexington Ave.
• Blockbuster Video • 1646 First Ave.
• Blockbuster Video • 205 E. 95th St.
• Encore Entertainment •
  175 E. 96th St.
• Express Video • 1577 Third Ave.
• Filmfest Video • 1594 York Ave.
• We Deliver Videos • 1716 1st Ave.

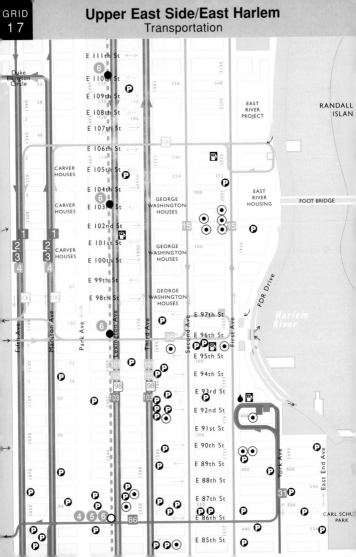

E 111th St →

E 110th St →

E 109th St →

E 108th St →

E 107th St →

E 106th St →

E 105th St →

E 104th St →

E 103rd St

E 102nd St →

E 101st St →

E 100th St →

E 99th St ←

E 98th St →

E 97th St →

E 96th St →

E 95th St →

E 94th St →

E 93rd St →

E 92nd St →

E 91st St →

E 90th St →

E 89th St →

E 88th St →

E 87th St →

E 86th St →

E 85th St →

Duke
Ellington
Circle

CARVER
HOUSES

CARVER
HOUSES

CARVER
HOUSES

GEORGE
WASHINGTON
HOUSES

GEORGE
WASHINGTON
HOUSES

GEORGE
WASHINGTON
HOUSES

EAST
RIVER
PROJECT

RANDALL
ISLAND

EAST
RIVER
HOUSING

FOOT BRIDGE

FDR DRIVE

Harlem
River

CARL SCHURZ
PARK

Fifth Ave

Madison Ave

Park Ave

Lexington Ave

Third Ave

Second Ave

First Ave

York Ave

East End Ave

Upper East Side/East Harlem
Transportation

How anyone ever thought that one subway was enough for the Upper East Side is beyond us. It isn't. However, parking is about the best here as it's going to ever get in Manhattan. The 96th Street entrance to the FDR is jammed most of the day, usually with really, really bad drivers. A popular portal for the bridge and tunnel crowd?

Subways

4 5 6 . . . . . E. 86th St at Lexington Ave.
6 . . . . E. 96th St at Lexington Ave.
6 . . . . E. 103rd St at Lexington Ave.
6 . . . . E. 110th St at Lexington Ave.

Bus Lines

1 2 3 . . . . 5th Ave./Madison Ave.
4 . . . . 5th Ave./Madison Ave./Broadway
15 . . . . 1st Ave./2nd Ave. (at 2 Ave)
31 . . . . York Ave./57th Ave. (at 57 St)
86 . . . . 86th St. Crosstown
96 . . . . 96th St. Crosstown
98 . . . . Washington Heights/Midtown
101 . . . . 3rd Ave./Lexington Ave.
102 . . . . 3rd Ave./Lexington Ave.
103 . . . . 3rd Ave./Lexington Ave.
2X . . . . . . 96th St./106th St. Crosstown

⊙ Car Rentals

- 1995 First Avenue Station • 1995 First Ave.
- A-Value Rent- A-Car, Inc. • 1989 First Ave.
- Apollo Auto Rental, Inc. • 335 E. 102nd St.
- Avis • 424 E. 90th St.
- Budget • 234 E. 85th St.
- Enterprise • 1833 First Ave.
- Farrell's Limousine Service • 428 E. 92nd St.
- Hertz • 412 E. 90th St.
- Manhattan Rent- A-Car • 165 E. 87th St.
- Marquis Auto Rental • 337 E. 102nd St.
- New York Rent A Car • 154 E. 87th St.
- New York Rent A Car • 215 E. 95th St.
- New York Rent-A-Car • 240 E. 92nd St.
- U-Drive • 1995 First Ave.

◆ Car Wash

- Eastside Car Wash • 1770 First Ave.

⛽ Gas Stations

- Amoco • 96th St. & First Ave.
- Amoco • 1599 Lexington Ave.
- BP • 1770 First Ave.
- Getty • 348 E. 106th St.

P Parking

- 1065 Park Ave.
- 110 East End Ave.
- 200 E. 90th St.
- 305 E. 86th St.
- 401 E. 86th St.
- 1623 Third Ave.
- 1832 Second Ave.
- 177 E. 109th St.
- 1675 York Ave.
- 245 E. 93rd St.
- 35 E. 85th St.
- 200 E. 94th St.
- 201 E. 87th St.
- 200 E. 89th St.
- 55 E. 87th St.
- 535 E. 86th St.
- 12 E. 86th St.
- 12 E. 85th St.
- 444 E. 86th St.
- 501 E. 87th St.
- 185 E. 85th St.
- 182 E. 95th St.
- 40 E. 94th St.
- 231 E. 94th St.
- 340 E. 93rd St.
- 50 E. 89th St.
- 118 E. 86th St.
- 1651 Third Ave.
- 115 E. 87th St.
- 234 E. 85th St.
- 1601 Third Ave.
- 156 E. 105th St.
- 401 E. 89th St.
- 400 E. 85th St.
- 440 E. 102nd St.
- 2019 First Ave.
- 249 E. 86th St.
- 250 E. 87th St.
- 120 E. 87th St.
- 200 East End Ave.
- 240 E. 92nd St.
- 302 E. 96th St.
- 169 E. 87th St.
- 345 E. 86th St.
- 222 E. 97th St.
- 160 E. 88th St.

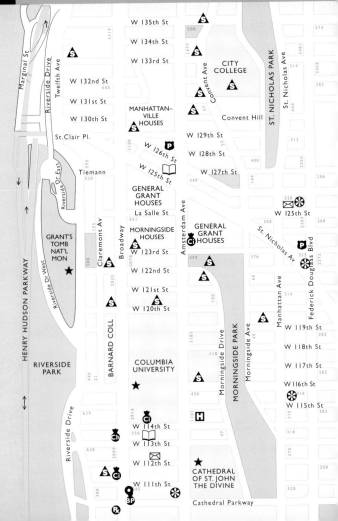

Marginal St

Riverside Drive

Twelfth Ave

W 135th St

W 134th St

W 133rd St

W 132nd St

W 131st St

W 130th St

St. Clair Pl.

MANHATTAN-VILLE HOUSES

CITY COLLEGE

Convent Ave

ST. NICHOLAS PARK

St. Nicholas Ave

Convent Hill

W 129th St

W 128th St

W 127th St

Tiemann

Riverside Dr East

Riverside Dr West

GRANT'S TOMB NAT'L MON

Broadway

Claremont Ave

W 126th St

W 125th St

GENERAL GRANT HOUSES

La Salle St

MORNINGSIDE HOUSES

W 123rd St

W 122nd St

W 121st St

W 120th St

Amsterdam Ave

GENERAL GRANT HOUSES

W 125th St

St. Nicholas Av

Frederick Douglass Blvd

Manhattan Ave

W 119th St

W 118th St

W 117th St

W 116th St

W 115th St

HENRY HUDSON PARKWAY

RIVERSIDE PARK

BARNARD COLL

COLUMBIA UNIVERSITY

Morningside Drive

MORNINGSIDE PARK

Morningside Ave

Riverside Drive

W 114th St

W 113th St

W 112th St

W 111th St

CATHEDRAL OF ST. JOHN THE DIVINE

Cathedral Parkway

Columbia/Morningside Heights
Essentials

This is perhaps one of the most truly economically diverse parts of the city, with tons of Columbia students mixing with high-, middle-, and low-income professionals and families. The Cathedral of St. John the Divine is the most eclectic and astounding building in Manhattan, which is no easy thing to accomplish (the vertical tour is highly recommended). Grant's Tomb is the least visited tourist attraction in Manhattan, which is a shame because it's totally cool.

💲 ATMs

BP • Banco Popular • 2852 Broadway
Ch • Chase • 2900 Broadway
Ci • Citibank • 2861 Broadway
Ci • Citibank • 1310 Amsterdam Ave.
Ci • Citibank • 545 W. 114th St. Columbia U.

⭕ Bagels

• Columbia Bagels • 2836 Broadway

🅷 Hospital

• St. Luke's Hospital Center •
  1111 Amsterdam Ave.

★ Landmarks

• Cathedral of St. John the Divine •
  112th St. and Amsterdam Ave.
• Columbia University • 116th St. and Broadway
• Grant's Tomb • 122nd St. and Riverside Drive.

📖 Libraries

• Columbia • 514 W. 113th St.
• George Bruce • 518 W. 125th St.

℞ 24-Hour Pharmacy

• Rite Aid • 2833 Broadway

🅿 Police Precincts

• 26th Precinct • 520 W. 126th St.
• 28th Precinct • 2271 Eighth Ave. (Frederick
  Douglass Blvd.)

✉ Post Offices

• Columbus University • 1123 Amsterdam Ave.
• Manhattanville • 365 W. 125th St.

🅂 Schools

• A. Philip Randolph Campus High School •
  Convent Ave. and W. 135th St.
• Bank Street College Of Education •
  610 W. 112th St.
• Barnard College • 3009 Broadway
• Columbia University • 435 W. 116th St.
• CUNY-City College • W. 131st St. -
  W. 140th St.
• IS 195 Roberto Clemente School •
  625 W. 133rd St.
• Jewish Theological Seminary of America •
  3080 Broadway
• JHS 043 Adam C. Powell School •
  509 W. 129th St.
• Manhattan School Of Music •
  120 Claremont Ave.
• PS 036 Margaret Douglas School •
  123 Morningside Dr.
• PS 125 Ralph Bunche School •
  425 W. 123rd St.
• PS 129 John H. Finley School •
  425 W. 130th St.
• PS 161 Pedro A. Campos School •
  499 W. 133rd St.
• PS 180 Hugo Newman School •
  370 W. 120th St.
• PS-IS 223 Mott Hall School •
  W. 131st St. and Convent Ave.
• Teachers College, Columbia
  University • 525 W. 120th St.
• Union Theologic Seminary •
  3041 Broadway at 121st St.

✳ Community Gardens

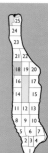

Columbia/Morningside Heights
Sundries / Entertainment

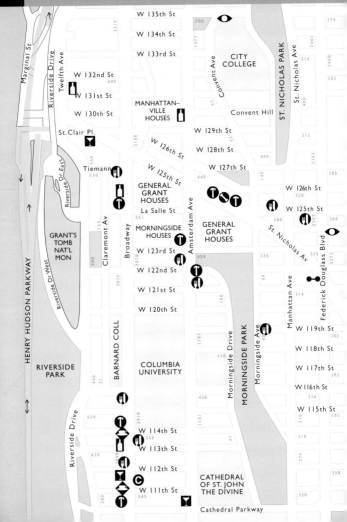

Columbia/Morningside Heights
Sundries / Entertainment

The new Magic Johnson Multiplex on 124th St. is a great thing for the neighborhood. Many services can be found near Columbia University on Broadway.

24-Hour Copy Center

- Kinko's • 2872 Broadway

Bars

- 1020 Amsterdam Corp. •1020 Amsterdam Ave.
- Cotton Club • 656 W. 125th St.
- Heights Bar & Grill • 2867 Broadway

Cafes

- New World Coffee • 2929 Broadway
- Starbucks • 2851 Broadway

Gym

- New York Sports Clubs • 300 W. 125th St.

Hardware Stores

- Academy Hardware & Supply Co. Inc. • 2869 Broadway
- Clinton Supply Co. • 1256 Amsterdam Ave.
- Columbia Hardware Co. • 2905 Broadway
- Glick Philip Supply Co. • 421 W. 125th St.
- Scotty Boys Hardware • 3147 Broadway
- TriBoro Hardware Co. • 433 W. 125th St.

Liquor Stores

- Amsterdam Liquor Mart • 1356 Amsterdam Ave.
- Campos Ernest F • 831 W. 131st St.
- International Wines and Spirits • 2903 Broadway
- Jimenez Ramon • 3139 Broadway

Movie Theatres

- Aaron Davis Hall • W. 135th St. and Convent Ave.
- Magic Johnson Harlem USA • 124th St. & Frederick Douglass Blvd.

Pet Stores

- Pet Place • 431 W. 125th St.

Restaurants

- Le Monde • 2885 Broadway
- M & G Soul Food Diner • 383 W. 125th St.
- Massawa • 1239 Amsterdam Ave.
- Ollie's • 2957 Broadway
- Terrace in the Sky • 400 W. 119th St.
- Zula • 1260 Amsterdam Ave.

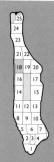

Columbia/Morningside Heights
Transportation

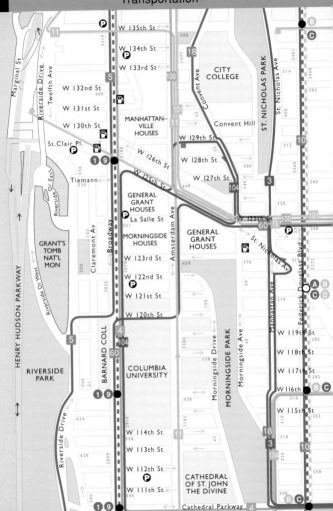

Columbia/Morningside Heights
Transportation

Driving and parking are both pretty decent around here, and the area is also served well by subway. We wish we could say that about the rest of the city.

Subways

1 **9** . . . . 125th St at Broadway

1 **9** . . . . 116th St at Broadway
(Columbia Univ.)

1 **9** . . . . 110th St at Broadway
(Cathedral Pkwy)

A **C** **B** **D** . 125th St at St. Nicholas Ave.

B **C** . . . . 135th St at St. Nicholas Ave.

B **C** . . . . 116th St at St. Nicholas Ave.

B **C** . . . . 110th St at St. Nicholas Ave.

Bus Lines

3 . . . . 5th Ave./Madison Ave.

4 . . . . 5th Ave./6th Ave./Riverside Dr.

5 . . . . Columbus Ave./Amsterdam Ave.

10 . . . . 7th Ave./Central Park West

11 . . . . Columbus Ave./Amsterdam Ave.

7/16 . . . . 116th St. Crosstown

18 . . . . LaGuardia Airport

60 . . . . Broadway

100 . . . . 86th St. Crosstown

101 . . . . 96th St. Crosstown

104 . . . . 106th St. Crosstown

 Car Wash

• Interchange Services • 663 W. 125th St.

 Gas Stations

• Amoco • 3233 Broadway
• Amoco • 355 W. 124th St.
• BP • 125th St. & Broadway
• Mobil • 3260 Broadway

P Parking

• 532 W. 122nd St.
• 325 W. 124th St.
• 3100 Broadway
• 627 W. 129th St.
• 526 W. 134th St.

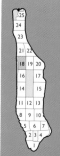

Harlem (Lower)
Essentials

W 135th St

LENOX
TERRACE

W 134th St

W 133rd St

W 132nd St

W 131st St

CITY
COLLEGE

Convent Hill

ST.
NICHOLAS
HOUSES

St. Nicholas Ave

ST. NICHOLAS PARK

W 130th St

W 129th St

W 128th St

W 127th St

W 126th St

W 125th St

W 124th St

Adam Clayton Powell Jr. Blvd

W 123rd St

W 122nd St

W 121st St

W 120th St

W 119th St

W 118th St

W 117th St

W 116th St

W 115th St

W 114th St

W 113th St

W 112th St

W 111th St

Frederick Douglass Blvd

St. Nicholas Ave

Manhattan Ave

Morningside Ave

Morningside Drive

MORNINGSIDE PARK

Lenox Ave (Malcolm X Blvd)

Mt. Morris Pk. W.

MARCUS
GARVEY
PARK

Fifth Ave

MARTIN
LUTHER
KING JR
TOWERS

Duke
Ellington

CATHEDRAL
ST. JOHN
THE DIVINE

This neighborhood revolves around all the shops and services on 125th Street—also the location of the famous Apollo Theater.

💲 ATMs

BP • Banco Popular • 231 W. 125th St.
CF • Carver Federal Savings • 75 W. 125th St.
Ch • Chase • 55 W. 125th St.
Ch • Chase • 2218 Fifth Ave.
Ch • Chase • 135th St. & Frederick
 Douglass Blvd.

⭕ Bagels

• Bagel Shop Teresa • 249 Lenox Ave.

🏥 Hospitals

• Renaissance Health Care Network •
 215 W. 125th St.
• The Paul Robeson Family Medical Center •
 140 W. 125th St.

⭐ Landmarks

• Apollo Theater • 253 W. 125th St.
• Duke Ellington Circle • 110th St. and Fifth Ave.
• Harlem YMCA • 180 W. 135th St.
• Sylvia's • 328 Lenox Ave.

📖 Libraries

• 115th St. • 203 W. 115th St.
• Harlem • 9 W. 124th St.

🅿️ Police Precincts

• 28th Precinct • 2271 Eighth Ave. (Frederick
 Douglass Blvd.)
• 32nd Precinct • 250 W. 135th St.

✉️ Post Offices

• Manhattanville • 365 W. 125th St.
• Morningside • 232 W. 116th St.

🅂 Schools

• CUNY-City College • W. 131st St. -
 W. 140th St.
• PS 036 Margaret Douglas School •
 123 Morningside Dr.
• PS 076 A. Philip Randolph School •
 220 W. 121st St.
• PS 092 Mary M. Bethune School •
 222 W. 134th St.
• PS 113 Whitehead Whaley School •
 240 W.113th St.
• PS 133 Fred R. Moore School • 2121 Fifth Ave.
• PS 144 Hans C. Anderson School •
 134 W. 122nd St.
• PS 149 Sojourner Truth School •
 34 W. 118th St.
• PS 175-IS Henry Highland • 175 W. 134th St.
• PS 185 John M. Langston School •
 20 W. 112th St.
• PS 207 Norbert Rillieux School •
 41 W. 117th St.
• PS 208 Alain L. Locke School • 21 W. 111th St.
• PS-IS 223 Mott Hall School •
 W. 131st St. and Convent Ave.
• Wadleigh High School • 215 W. 114th St.

❀ Community Gardens

Harlem (Lower)
Sundries / Entertainment

Sylvia's really is as good as everyone says it is.

 Bar

• Mr. B Cocktail Lounge • 2297 Seventh Ave.

 Cafe

• Home Sweet Harlem Cafe • 270 W. 135th St.

 Gyms

• New York Sports Clubs • 300 W. 125th St.
• YMCA • 180 W. 135th St.

![icon] Hardware Stores

• Bill's Hardware & Paints Inc • 1 W. 125th St.
• Citi General Hardware • 100 St. Nicholas Ave.
• Concordia Electrical & Plumbing •
  2297 Seventh Ave. (Adam Clayton Powell)
• Glick Philip Supply Co. • 421 W. 125th St.
• Harlem Locksmith • 1846 Seventh Ave.
  (Adam Clayton Powell Jr. Blvd.)
• Manhattan Paint Fair Inc. • 17 W. 125th St.
• StaLoc Lock & Hardware Ltd • 1958 Seventh
  Ave. (Adam Clayton Powell Jr. Blvd.)
• TriBoro Hardware Co. • 433 W. 125th St.
• Virgo Houseware & Hardware •
  188 Lenox Ave.

![icon] Liquor Stores

• 115th St. Liquor Store Inc. • 5 E. 115th St.
• 312 Lenox Liquors • 312 Lenox Ave.
• 458 Lenox Liquors Inc. • 458 Lenox Ave.
• A&D Liquor • 23 Lenox Ave.
• Conrad Spirits Ltd. • 178 Lenox Ave.
• Fred's Wine & Liquors • 77 Lenox Ave.
• Grand Liquors • 2049 Eighth Ave.
• Harlem USA Wine & Liquor Store •
  101 W. 132nd St.
• Just In Liquors • 2178 Fifth Ave.
• Olympic Liquor • 2341 Eighth Ave.

 Movie Theatre

• Magic Johnson Harlem USA •
  124th St. & Frederick Douglass Blvd.

![icon] Pet Store

• Pet Place • 431 W. 125th St.

![icon] Restaurants

• Amy Ruth's • 113 W. 116th St.
• Emily's • 1325 Fifth Ave.
• M & G Soul Food Diner • 383 W. 125th St.
• Sylvia's • 328 Lenox Ave.

![icon] Video Rentals

• Blockbuster Video • 121 W. 125th St.
• Films & Games • 243 W. 125th St.
• Ndyndory Video • 365 Lenox Ave.
• TK Video Store • 135 W. 116th St.
• Video World • 46 St. Nicholas Ave.

Harlem (Lower)
Transportation

Driving across 110th Street should be good, but it's usually a pain. 116th Street is much better. Parking is pretty good, even on the major avenues. There's a bike lane on St. Nicholas Avenue.

Subways

2 **3** . . . . 135th St. at Malcolm Blvd.

2 **3** . . . . . 125th St. at Malcolm X Blvd.

2 **3** . . . . . 116th St. at Malcolm X Blvd.

2 **3** . . . . . 110th St. at Malcolm X Blvd.
(Central Park North)

B **C** . . . . . 135th St. at St. Nicholas Ave.

A **B** **C** **D** . . 125th St. at St. Nicholas Ave.

B **C** . . . . . 116th St. at St. Nicholas Ave

B **C** . . . . 110th St. at St. Nicholas Ave.
(Cathedral Parkway)

Bus Lines

1 . . . . 5th Ave./Madison Ave.

2 . . . . . . 5th Ave./Madison Ave./Powell Blvd.

3 . . 5th Ave./Madison Ave./St. Nicholas Blvd.

4 . . . . 5th Ave./Madison Ave./Broadway

7 . . . . Columbus Ave./Amsterdam Ave./Lenox
Ave./6th Ave./7th Ave./Broadway

10 . . . 7th Ave./8th Ave./Fred. Douglass Blvd.

15 . . . . 125th St. Crosstown

35 . . . . 35th St. Crosstown

18 . . . . Convent Ave.

60 . . . . LaGuardia Airport via 125th St.

100 . . . . . . Amsterdam Ave./Broadway/125th St.

101 . . 3rd Ave./Lexington Ave./Amsterdam Ave.

102 . . 3rd Ave./Lexington Ave./Malcolm X Blvd.

104 . . . . Broadway

116 . . . . 116th St. Crosstown

Car Rentals

• Price King Rent A Car • 1 St. Nicholas Ave.

Gas Stations

• Amoco • 355 W. 124th St.
• Amoco • 2040 Frederick Douglass Blvd.
• Exxon • 2040 Frederick Douglass Blvd.

Parking

• 7 St. Nicholas Ave.
• 1330 Fifth Ave.
• 1325 Fifth Ave.
• 161 W. 132nd St.
• 325 W. 124th St.
• 121 W. 125th St.
• 506 Lenox Ave.
• 260 W. 126th St.
• 316 W. 118th St.

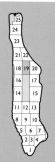

El Barrio
Essentials

THE
BRONX

E 135th St

ABRAHAM LINCOLN

HOUSING

E 132nd St

Harlem River

THIRD AVE BRIDGE

Harlem
River

E 131st St

E 130th St

E 129th St

Drive

E 128th St

E 127th St

WILLIS AVE BRIDGE

E 126th St

E 125th St (Dr. Martin Luther King Jr Blvd)

TRIBOROUGH BRIDGE

MARCUS
GARVEY
PARK

E 124th St

E 123rd St

Ronald McNair Pl

E 122nd St

SEN. R. WAGNER. SR. HOUSES

Paladino Ave

E 121st St

Sylvan Pl

E 120th St

E 119th St

P

E 118th St

Fifth Ave

Madison Ave

Park Ave

Lexington Ave

Third Ave

E 117th St

Second Ave

First Ave

Pleasant Ave

E 116th St

E 115th St

BP

SEN R.
TAFT
HOUSES

J.W.
JOHNSON
HOUSING

JEFFERSON
HOUSES

JEFFERSON
HOUSES

E 114th St

FDR Drive

JEFFERSON
PARK

E 112nd St

E 111st St

Duke
Ellington
Circle

E 110th St

El Barrio
Essentials

Rich and vibrant in history and culture, exploring El Barrio is highly recommended. Both Marcus Garvey and Jefferson Parks are excellent places to take a break, too.

ATMs

- A • Apple • 124 E. 125th St.
- BP • Banco Popular • 164 East 116th St.
- Ch • Chase • 2218 Fifth Ave.
- Ch • Chase • Lexington Ave. & 125th St.
- Ci • Citibank • 2261 First Ave.
- F • Fleet • Third Ave. & 122nd St.
- F • Fleet • 2250 3rd Ave.

Hospitals

- Manhattan Eye, Ear & Throat Hospital • 55 E. 124th St.
- North General Hospital • 1879 Madison Ave.

Landmarks

- Church of Our Lady of Mt. Carmel • 448 E. 115th St.
- Harlem Courthouse • 170 E. 127th St.
- Keith Haring "Crack is Wack" Mural • Second Ave. & 127th St.
- International Salsa Museum • 2127 Third Ave.
- Langston Hughes House • 20 E. 127th St.
- Marcus Garvey Park • E. 120-124th Sts. at Madison Ave.
- Watch Tower • Marcus Garvey Park

Libraries

- 125th St. • 224 E. 125th St.
- Aguilar • 174 E. 110th St.

Marketplace

- Butler Lumber Co. • 2311 Third Ave.
- Casa Latina Music Store • 151 E. 116th St.
- Lore Upholstery • 2201 Third Ave.
- Numero Uno Dept. Store • 179 E. 116th St.
- The Demolition Depot • 216 E. 125th St.
- Pathmark • 160 E. 125th St.

Police Precinct

- 25th Precinct • 120 E. 119th St.

Post Offices

- Hell Gate • 153 E. 110th St.
- Triborough • 167 E. 124th St.

Schools

- Helene Fuld School of Nursing North • 1879 Madison Ave.
- JHS 045 J. S. Roberts School • 2351 First Ave.
- JHS 101 Bridge School • 141 E. 111th St.
- Manhattan Center for Science & Math • Pleasant Ave. & 116th St.
- NY College of Podiatric Medicine • 53 E. 124th St.
- PS 007 Samuel Stern School • 160 E. 120th St.
- PS 030 Hernandez-Hughes School • 144 E. 128th St.
- PS 057 James W. Johnson School • 176 E. 115th St.
- PS 079 Horan School • 55 E. 120th St.
- PS 096 Joseph Lanzetta School • 216 E. 120th St.
- PS 101 Draper School • 141 E. 111th St.
- PS 102 Cartier School • 315 E. 113th St.
- PS 108 Peter Minuit School • 1615 Madison Ave.
- PS 112 Jose Celso Barbasa School • 535 E. 119th St.
- PS 133 Fred R. Moore School • 2121 Fifth Ave.
- PS 138 • 144 E. 128th Ave.
- PS 155 William Paca School • 319 E. 117th St.
- PS 206 Barbosa School • 508 E. 120th St.

Community Gardens

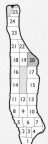

El Barrio
Sundries / Entertainment

THE
BRONX

E 135th St

ABRAHAM LINCOLN

HOUSING

E 132nd St

Harlem River

THIRD AVE BRIDGE

Harlem River

E 131st St

E 130th St

Drive

E 129th St

E 128th St

WILLIS AVE BRIDGE

E 127th St

E 126th St

E 125th St (Dr. Martin Luther King Jr Blvd)

TRIBOROUGH BRIDGE

MARCUS GARVEY PARK

E 124th St

E 123rd St

E 122nd St

SEN. R. WAGNER. SR. HOUSES

Paladino Ave

Ronald McNair Pl

E 121st St

Sylvan Pl

E 120th St

E 119th St

E 118th St

Fifth Ave

Madison Ave

Park Ave

Lexington Ave

Third Ave

E 117th St

Second Ave

First Ave

Pleasant Ave

E 116th St

E 115th St

E 114th St

SEN R. TAFT HOUSES

J.W. JOHNSON HOUSING

JEFFERSON HOUSES

JEFFERSON HOUSES

JEFFERSON PARK

FDR Drive

E 112nd St

E 111th St

Duke Ellington Circle

E 110th St

El Barrio
Sundries / Entertainment

Patsy's Pizza really is the "original" New York thin-crust pizza, and Rao's is another New York landmark restaurant.

Farmer's Market

- La Marqueta • E. 112-116th Sts. at Park Ave.

Hardware Stores

- B & B Supply & Hardware • 2338 Second Ave.
- Johnny's Hardware • 151 E. 106th St.
- N & J Locksmith & Hardware Inc. • 1637 Park Ave.
- Novelle • 218 E. 125th St.
- SM Hardware • 2139 Third Ave.

Liquor Stores

- 115th St. Liquor Store Inc. • 5 E. 115th St.
- 249 E. 115th Liquor • 249 E. 115th St.
- JM Liquor • 1861 Lexington Ave.
- Just In Liquors • 2178 Fifth Ave.
- Lexington Wine & Liquor • 2010 Lexington Ave.
- New York Beverage • 207 E. 123rd St.
- R A Landrau • 2334 Second Ave.
- Ramos Liquor Store • 1814 Madison Ave.
- Two Islands Wine & Liquor Store • 2255 First Ave.

Pet Stores

- Elbario Pet Shop • 122 E. 116th St.
- Harlem Pet Gallery • 1931 Madison Ave.
- Ideal Pet Warehouse, Ltd. • 356 E. 116th St.
- JB Pets • 111 E. 125th St.

Restaurants

- Andy's Colonial • 2257 First Ave.
- Emily's • 1325 Fifth Ave.
- Patsys Pizza • 2287-91 First Ave.
- Rao's • 455 E. 114th St.

Video Rental

- First Run Video • 1147 1/2 Second Ave.

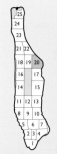

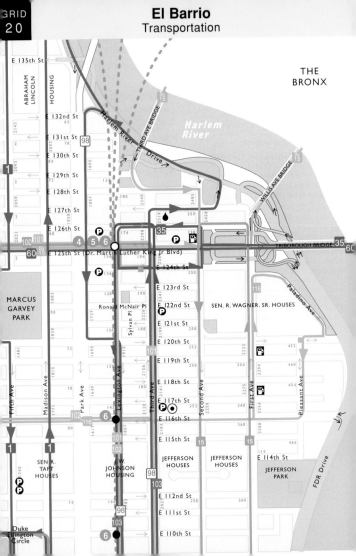

El Barrio
Transportation

The best route to the Triborough is to go up Third Avenue and make a right on 124th Street, especially when the FDR is jammed. We feel for the folks who live over on Pleasant Ave and have to hike five miles to the nearest subway (or worse yet, wait for the bus).

Subways

4 5 6 . . . . . . 125th St. & Lexington Ave.
6 . . . . 116th St. & Lexington Ave.
6 . . . . 110th St. & Lexington Ave.

Bus Lines

1 . . . . 5th and Madison Aves.
15 . . . . 1st/2nd Aves. (at 2 Ave)
35 . . . . Randall's Island/Ward Island
60 . . . . LaGuardia Airport
98 . . . . Washington Heights/Midtown
16/19 . . . . 125th St. Crosstown
101 . . . . 3rd/Lexington/Amsterdam Aves.
102 . . . . . 3rd/Lexington Aves./Malcolm X. Blvd.
104 . . . . 3rd/Lexington Aves.
116 . . . . 116th St. Crosstown

Car Rental

• Alpha Auto Rental Inc • 220 E. 117th St.

Car Wash

• JRP Carwash • 247 E. 127th St.

Gas Stations

• Amoco • 2276 First Ave.
• Amoco • 125th St. and Second Ave.
• Gaseteria • 119th St. & First Ave.

Parking

• 227 E. 125th St.
• 1330 Fifth Ave.
• 1325 Fifth Ave.
• 221 E. 122nd St.
• 228 E. 117th St.
• 124 E. 124th St.
• 128 E. 126th St.

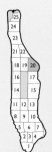

Manhattanville/Hamilton Heights
Essentials

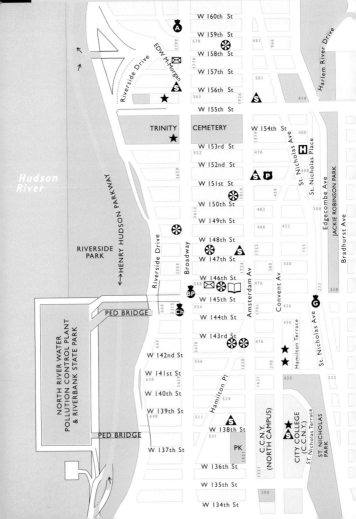

Manhattanville/Hamilton Heights
Essentials

Riverbank State Park should be the dictionary definition of the phrase "only in New York"—a park built over a sewage treatment plant. Trinity Cemetery and Audubon Terrace are two completely overlooked Manhattan landmarks, and Hamilton Terrace is one of the prettiest streets in the city. We await gentrification.

 ## ATMs

A • Apple • 3815 Broadway
BP • Banco Popular • 3540 Broadway
Ch • Chase • 3515 Broadway
G • Greenpoint • 700 St. Nicholas Ave.

Hospital

• New York Foundling Hospital-Project Basement • 546 W. 153rd St.

★ Landmarks

• Audubon Terrace, including: - American Academy and Institute of Arts and Letters - American Numismatic Museum -Hispanic Society of America • W. 155th St.
• City College • W. 135th St. & Convent Ave.
• Hamilton Grange National Memorial • 287Convent Ave.
• Hamilton Heights Historic District • W. 141st- W. 145th Sts. and Convent Ave.
• Trinity Church Cemetery's Graveyard of Heroes • 3699 Broadway

Library

• Hamilton Grange • 503 W. 145th St.

 ## Police Precinct

• 30th Precinct • 451 W. 151st St.

✉ Post Office

• Hamilton Grange • 521 W. 146th St.

 ## Schools

• Boricua College • 3755 Broadway
• CUNY-City College • W. 131st St. - W. 140th St.
• Dance Theatre Of Harlem Inc. • 466 W. 152nd St.
• PS 028 Wright Brothers School • 475 W. 155th St.
• PS 153 Adam C. Powell School • 1750 Amsterdam Ave.
• PS 192 Jacob H. Schiff School • 500 W. 138th St.

❀ Community Gardens

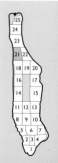

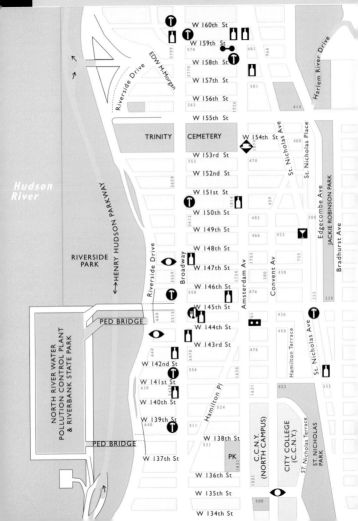

Bar

- St. Nick's Pub • 773 St. Nicholas Ave.

Cafe

- Fernando Coffee Shop • 1875 Amsterdam Ave.

Gym

- Elmo's Gym Co., Inc. • 552 W. 158th St.

Hardware Stores

- 3841 Hardware • 3841 Broadway
- All Star Hardware Distributors Inc. • 3547 Broadway
- Cohen & Cohen, Inc. • 1982 Amsterdam Ave.
- Felix Supply • 3650 Broadway
- Frame Hardware • 3806 Broadway
- Fred's Locksmith and Hardware • 708 St. Nicholas Ave.
- O&J Hardware Co. • 3405 Broadway
- Westside Home Center • 3447 Broadway

Liquor Stores

- Almanzar Liquor Store • 1806 Amsterdam Ave.
- Augustine Wines & Liquor Inc. • 550 W. 145th St.
- Duran Liquor Store • 2001 Amsterdam Ave.
- H L K Liquors Inc. • 3375 Broadway
- In Good Spirits Corp. • 3819 Broadway
- JOCL Liquor Store • 561 W. 147th St.
- Jumasol Liquors Inc. • 1963 Amsterdam Ave.
- La Alta Gracia Liquor Store • 3435 Broadway
- New York Minority Beverages Inc. • 501 W. 145th St.
- South North • 3490 Broadway
- Unity Liquors Inc. • 708 St. Nicholas Ave.

Movie Theatres

- Aaron Davis Hall • W. 135th St. and Convent Ave.
- Africa Arts Theatre Co. Inc • 660 Riverside Dr.
- Nova Cinema • 3589 Broadway

Restaurant

- Copeland's • 547 W. 145th St.

Video Rental

- Video Box • 1706 Amsterdam Ave.

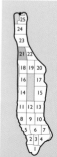

Manhattanville/Hamilton Heights
Transportation

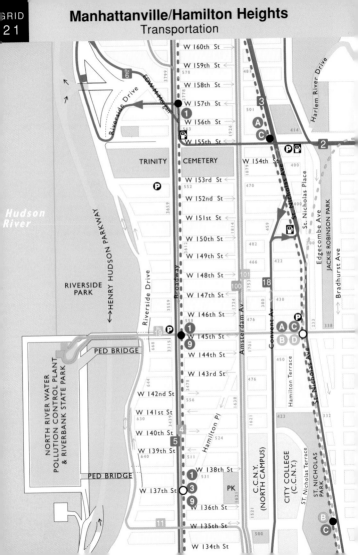

W 160th St
W 159th St
W 158th St
W 157th St
W 156th St
W 155th St
W 154th St
W 153rd St
W 152nd St
W 151st St
W 150th St
W 149th St
W 148th St
W 147th St
W 146th St
W 145th St
W 144th St
W 143rd St
W 142nd St
W 141st St
W 140th St
W 139th St
W 138th St
W 137th St
W 136th St
W 135th St
W 134th St

Harlem River Drive
Edgecombe Ave
St. Nicholas Place
St. Nicholas Ave
Jackie Robinson Park
Bradhurst Ave
Nicholas Ave
Convent Ave
Amsterdam Av
Hamilton Terrace
Hamilton Pl
Broadway
Riverside Drive
HENRY HUDSON PARKWAY
Riverside Drive
Edgar Allan

TRINITY CEMETERY

Hudson River

RIVERSIDE PARK

NORTH RIVER WATER POLLUTION CONTROL PLANT & RIVERBANK STATE PARK

PED BRIDGE

PED BRIDGE

C.C.N.Y. (NORTH CAMPUS)

CITY COLLEGE (C.C.N.Y.)

ST. NICHOLAS PARK

St. Nicholas Terrace

PK

Riverside Drive can be an intriguing alternative to traffic on the Henry Hudson, which begins to get serious during rush hour as one moves closer to the George Washington Bridge. A great way to get to the Bronx (and Yankee Stadium) from the Upper West Side is to take Broadway up to 155th Street and cross the Harlem River at the Macombs Dam Bridge. You heard it here first.

Subways

1 **9** . . . . Broadway at 157th St.

1 **9** . . . . Broadway at 145th St.

1 **3** **9** . . . . 137th St. at Broadway
(City College)

A **B** **C** **D** . 145th St. at St. Nicholas Ave.

B **C** . . . . 155th St. at St. Nicholas Ave.

A **C** . . . . 135th St. at St. Nicholas Ave

Gas Stations

- Mobil • 3740 Broadway
- Mobil • 150th St. & St. Nicholas Ave.

Parking

- 404 W. 155th St.
- 673 St. Nicholas Ave.
- 614 W. 153rd St.

Bus Lines

2 . . . . . . Fifth Ave./Madison Ave./Powell Blvd.

3 . . Fifth Ave./Madison Ave./St. Nicholas Blvd.

4 . . . . Fifth Ave./Madison Ave./Broadway

5 . . . . Fifth Ave./Ave. of the Americas/
Riverside Dr.

⁵⁄₆ . . . . E. 161st St./E 163rd St.

11 . . . . Ninth (Columbus Ave.)/Tenth
(Amsterdam Ave)/Convent Ave.

¹⁸⁄₁₉ . . . . 145th St. Crosstown

18 . . . . Convent Ave.

100 . . . . . . Amsterdam Ave./Broadway/125th St.

101 . . . . Third Ave./Lexington Ave./
Broadway/125th St.

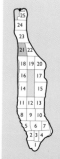

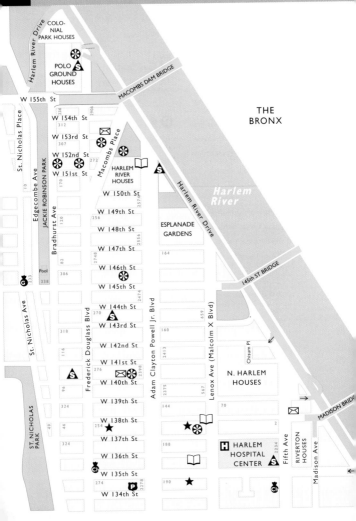

COLONIAL PARK HOUSES

Harlem River Drive

POLO GROUND HOUSES

MACOMBS DAM BRIDGE

W 155th St

THE BRONX

St. Nicholas Place

W 154th St

Edgecombe Ave

W 153rd St

W 152nd St

JACKIE ROBINSON PARK

Macombs Place

W 151st St

HARLEM RIVER HOUSES

Bradhurst Ave

W 150th St

Harlem River Drive

Harlem River

W 149th St

W 148th St

ESPLANADE GARDENS

W 147th St

W 146th St

145th ST BRIDGE

W 145th St

St. Nicholas Ave

Pool

W 144th St

Frederick Douglass Blvd

W 143rd St

Adam Clayton Powell Jr. Blvd

W 142nd St

Lenox Ave (Malcolm X Blvd)

W 141st St

Chisum Pl

W 140th St

N. HARLEM HOUSES

W 139th St

ST. NICHOLAS PARK

W 138th St

MADISON BRIDGE

W 137th St

W 136th St

Fifth Ave

H HARLEM HOSPITAL CENTER

RIVERTON HOUSES

W 135th St

Madison Ave

W 134th St

As much as people who live in the Polo Grounds Houses need housing, we really wish the Polo Grounds itself was still there.

 ATMs

- Ch • Chase • 2218 Fifth Ave.
- Ch • Chase • 135th St. & Frederick Douglass Blvd.
- G • Greenpoint • 700 St. Nicholas Ave.

H Hospital

- Harlem Hospital Center • 506 Lenox Ave.

★ Landmarks

- Abyssinian Baptist Church • 132 W. 138th St.
- Harlem YMCA • 180 W. 135th St.
- St. Nicholas Historic District • 202-250 W. 138th St. & W. 139th St.

Libraries

- Countee Cullen • 104 W. 136th St .
- Macomb's Bridge • 2650 Adam Clayton Powell Jr. Blvd.
- Schomburg Center for Research in Black Culture • 515 Malcolm X Blvd.

 Police Precinct

- 32nd Precinct • 250 W. 135th St.

✉ Post Offices

- College Station • 217 W. 140th St.
- Colonial Park • 99 Macombs Pl.
- Lincolnton • 2266 Fifth Ave.

Schools

- CUNY-City College • W. 131st St. -W. 140th St.
- PS 046 Tappan School • 2987 Frederick Douglass Blvd.
- PS 123 Mahalia Jackson School • 301 W. 140th St.
- PS 194 Countee Cullen School • 242 W. 144th St.
- PS 197 John Russwurm School • 2230 Fifth Ave.
- PS 200 James Smith School • 2589 Adam Clayton Powell Jr. Blvd.

❀ Community Gardens

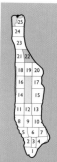

COLONIAL PARK HOUSES

Harlem River Drive

POLO GROUND HOUSES

MACOMBS DAM BRIDGE

W 155th St

THE BRONX

St. Nicholas Place

W 154th St   336   2906

W 153rd St   312

W 152nd St   307

Macombs Place

W 151st St   272

170

HARLEM RIVER HOUSES

Edgecombe Ave

JACKIE ROBINSON PARK

W 150th St   2574

Bradhurst Ave

W 149th St   256   120

Harlem River Drive

Harlem River

W 148th St

ESPLANADE GARDENS

W 147th St   164   2748

W 146th St   82

145th ST BRIDGE

W 145th St   306   2474

W 144th St   270

Adam Clayton Powell Jr. Blvd

659

St. Nicholas Ave

W 143rd St   318   2667

160

W 142nd St   116

Lenox Ave (Malcolm X Blvd)

2413

Chisum Pl

Frederick Douglass Blvd

W 141st St   2375   1398

567

N. HARLEM HOUSES

W 140th St   600   96

2775

W 139th St   324

70

144

ST. NICHOLAS PARK

W 138th St   254   46

2

W 137th St   324   496   188

2234

Fifth Ave

RIVERTON HOUSES

on Ave

HARLEM HOSPITAL CENTER

W 136th St

Bars

- Lickety Split Lounge & Restaurant • 2361 Seventh Ave.
- Mr. B Cocktail Lounge • 2297 Seventh Ave.
- St. Nick's Pub • 773 St. Nicholas Ave.

Cafe

- Home Sweet Harlem Cafe • 270 W. 135th St.

Farmer's Market

- Greenmarket • Lenox Ave. & W. 144th St.

Gyms

- Diamond Gym • 104 W. 145th St.
- YMCA • 180 W. 135th St.

Hardware Stores

- 615 Lenox Ave. Hardware • 615 Lenox Ave.
- B&E Hardware & Lockshop • 2647 Eighth Ave. (Frederick Douglass)
- B&J's Hardware • 2477 Seventh Ave. (Adam Clayton Powell)
- Concordia Electrical & Plumbing • 2297 Seventh Ave. (Adam Clayton Powell)
- Fred's Locksmith and Hardware • 708 St. Nicholas Ave.

Liquor Stores

- All-Rite Liquors • 2651 Eighth Ave.
- Dorden Liquors Inc. • 555 Lenox Ave.
- Friedland Wine & Liquor Store • 605 Lenox Ave.
- Luis Liquor Corp • 108 W. 145th St.
- Oz Liquors • 2610 Eighth Ave. (Frederick Douglass Blvd.)
- Stop One Wine & Liquor • 272 W. 154th St.
- Unity Liquors Inc. • 708 St. Nicholas Ave.

Movie Theatres

- New Heritage Theatre Group • 646 Lenox Ave.
- Schomburg Center for Research in Black Culture • 515 Malcolm X Blvd.

Restaurants

- Charles's Southern-Style Chicken • 2841 Eighth Ave.
- Londel's Supper Club • 2620 Frederick Douglass Blvd.

Video Rental

- Mad Videos • 318 W. 142nd St.

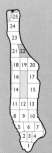

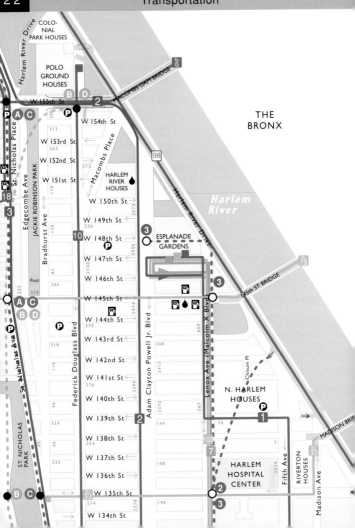

COLONIAL PARK HOUSES

Harlem River Drive

POLO GROUND HOUSES

B D 2

W 155th St

Macombs Dam Bridge

BX 6

THE BRONX

W 154th St
312

W 153rd St
307

W 152nd St
272

W 151st St
170

HARLEM RIVER HOUSES

St. Nicholas Place

Edgecombe Ave

JACKIE ROBINSON PARK

Macombs Place

Bradhurst Ave

18

3

98

Harlem River Drive

Harlem River

W 150th St
2574

W 149th St
256

2556

3

ESPLANADE GARDENS

W 148th St
10
2748

W 147th St
82

W 146th St
306

Pool
233
338

19

3

145th ST BRIDGE

A C
B D

W 145th St
2474

W 144th St
270

2396

2413

2398

2375

144

70

567

659

N. HARLEM HOUSES

Federick Douglass Blvd

Adam Clayton Powell Jr. Blvd

Lenox Ave (Malcolm X) Blvd

W 143rd St
318

W 142nd St
116

W 141st St
276

W 140th St
96

W 139th St
2

St. NICHOLAS PARK

W 138th St
254

W 137th St
324

W 136th St
188

Chisum Pl

103
7

MADISON BRID

1

33

Fifth Ave

RIVERTON HOUSES

Madison Ave

A C
B

W 135th St
2278
2276

38

B C

W 134th St
274
190

2

2234

HARLEM HOSPITAL CENTER

2
3

Subways

Ⓐ Ⓒ . . . . . St. Nicholas Ave. at 155th St.

Ⓐ Ⓑ Ⓒ Ⓓ . St. Nicholas Ave. at 145th St.

Ⓑ Ⓒ . . . . . 135th St. at St. Nicholas Ave.

Ⓑ Ⓓ . 155th St. at Frederick Douglass Blvd.

❷ ❸ . . . . . Malcolm X Blvd. at 135th St.

❸ . . . . Adam Clayton Powell Jr. Blvd.
at 148th St.

❸ . . . . Malcolm X Blvd. at 145th St.

Bus Lines

❶ . . . . 5th Ave./Madison Ave.

❷ . . . . 5th Ave./Madison Ave./Powell Blvd.

❸ . . . . 5th Ave./Madison Ave./St. Nicholas Ave.

⁶/₆ . . . . E. 161st St./E 163rd St.

❼ . . . . Columbus Ave./Amsterdam Ave./
6th Ave./7th Ave./Broadway

❿ . . . . 7th Ave./8th Ave. (Central Park West)/
Frederick Douglass Blvd.

18 . . . . Convent Ave.

116 . . . . 145th St. Crosstown

33 . . . . 145th St. Crosstown

98 . . . . Washington Heights/Midtown

100 . . . . 3rd Ave./Lexington Ave./
Malcolm X Blvd.

Car Washes

- Harlem Hand Car Wash • 2600 Seventh Ave.
  (Adam Clayton Powell Jr. Blvd.)
- Los Amigos • 119 W. 145th St.

Gas Stations

- Amoco • 232 W. 145th St.
- Getty • 119 W. 145th St.
- Getty • 89 St. Nicholas Pl.
- Merit Gasoline Stations • 128 W. 145th St.
- Mobil • 126 W. 145th St.

Parking

- 17 W. 139th St.
- 404 W. 155th St.
- 673 St. Nicholas Ave.
- 310 W. 144th St.
- 240 W. 148th St.
- 280 W. 155th St.
- 506 Lenox Ave.

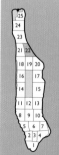

Washington Heights
Essentials

Riverside Drive

Cabrini Blvd

W 183rd St

Bennett Ave

Col. R. Magaw Pl

W 183rd St

Pinehurst Ave

W 182nd St

W 181st St

PLAZA
LAFAYETTE

W 180th St

W 179th St

W 178th St

BUS
TERMINAL

WASHINGTON BRIDGE

ALEXANDER HAMILTON BRIDGE

GEORGE WASHINGTON BRIDGE

The Little
Red Lighthouse

Fort Washington Ave

Wadsworth Ave

W 177th St

W 176th St

W 175th St

Harlem
River

J.N. WRIGHT
PARK

W 174th St

HIGH BRIDGE (PED

W 173rd St

W 172nd St

Haven Ave

St. Nicholas Ave

W 171st St

Audubon Ave

Pool

HIGH BRIDGE
PARK

W 170th St

W 169th St

Amsterdam Ave

Jumel Pl

W 168th St

Riverside Drive

COLUMBIA
PRESBYTERIAN
MEDICAL
CENTER

Harlem River Drive

N.Y.S.
PSYCHIATRIC
INSTITUTE

W 167th St

W 166th St

McKenna
Sq

W 165th St

Edgecombe Ave

WASHINGTON PARK

HENRY HUDSON PKWY

W 164th St

Broadway

W 163rd St

Fort Washington Ave

St. Nicholas Ave

W 162nd St

Jumel Terr

Hudson
River

W 161st St

Sylvan Terrace

ROGER
MORRIS
PARK

W 160th St

W 159th St

COLO
PAR
HOU

Washington Heights
Essentials

Sylvan Terrace is the most un-Manhattan-looking place in Manhattan. It's way cool.

$ ATMs

A • Apple • 4251 Broadway
BP • Banco Popular • 615 W. 181st St.
Ch • Chase • 3940 Broadway
Ci • Citibank • 4058 Broadway
Ci • Citibank • 4249 Broadway

Bagels

• Bagel City • 720 W. 181st St.

H Hospitals

• Babies & Children's Hospital Of New York •
  3959 Broadway
• Columbia-Presbyterian • 622 W. 168th St.

★ Landmarks

• George Washington Bridge • W. 178st St.
• Morris-Jumel Mansion • Edgecombe Ave. and
  161st St.
• Sylvan Terrace • between Jumel Terrace &
  St. Nicholas Ave.
• The Little Red Lighthouse • under the George
  Washington Bridge

Libraries

• Fort Washington • 535 W. 179th St.
• Washington Heights • 1000 St.Nicholas Ave.

P Police Precinct

• 33rd Precinct • 2120 Amsterdam Ave.

✉ Post Offices

• Audubon • 515 W. 165th St.
• Washington Bridge • 555 W. 180th St.

S Schools

• I S 164 Edward W Stitt School •
  401 W. 164th St.
• I S 90 • 21 Jumel Pl.
• IS 143 Eleanor Roosevelt School •
  511 W. 182nd St.
• P S 115 Humboldt School • 586 W. 177th St.
• P S 128 Audubon School • 560 W. 169th St.
• P S 173 • 306 Fort Washington Ave.
• P S 528 Bea Fuller Rodgers School •
  180 Wadsworth Ave.
• P S 8 • 168th St. & Amsterdam Ave.
• PS 132 Juan Pablo Duarte School •
  185 Wadsworth
• PS 528 Bea Fuller Rodgers School •
  180 Wadsworth

✸ Community Gardens

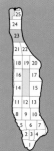

Washington Heights
Sundries / Entertainment

W 183rd St

W 183rd St

Cabrini Blvd

Bennett Ave

Col. R. Magraw Pl

W 182nd St

W 181st St

WASHINGTON BRIDGE

Pinehurst Ave

W 180th St

PLAZA
LAFAYETTE

W 179th St

ALEXANDER HAMILTON BRIDGE

BUS
TERMINAL

GEORGE WASHINGTON BRIDGE

W 178th St

Harlem
River

Fort Washington Ave

W 177th St

Broadway

Wadsworth Ave

W 176th St

W 175th St

HIGH BRIDGE (PED)

J.N. WRIGHT
PARK

W 174th St

W 173rd St

Pool

W 172nd St

St. Nicholas Ave

HIGH BRIDGE
PARK

Haven Ave

W 171st St

W 170th St

Audubon Ave

Harlem River Drive

W 169th St

Riverside Drive

W 168th St

Amsterdam Ave

COLUMBIA
PRESBYTERIAN
MEDICAL
CENTER

WASHINGTON
PARK

W 167th St

Jumel Pl

N.Y.S.
PSYCHIATRIC
INSTITUTE

HENRY HUDSON PKWY

W 166th St

McKenna
Sq

W 165th St

Broadway

St. Nicholas Ave

Edgecombe Ave

W 164th St

W 163rd St

Hudson
River

Fort Washington Ave

W 162nd St

Jumel Terr

ROGER
MORRIS
PARK

W 161st St

Sylvan Terr

W 160th St

W 159th St

COLO-
NIAL
PARK
HOUSES

Bar

- END Cocktail Lounge • 3865 Broadway

 Cafe

- El Primo Coffee Shop • 2153 Amsterdam Ave.

 Farmer's Market

- Greenmarket • Broadway & 175th St.

 Gyms

- Frank's Fitness Inc. • 4271 Broadway
- Urban Total Fitness Inc. •
  1387 St Nicholas Ave.

Hardware Stores

- 3841 Hardware • 3841 Broadway
- 756 Hardware Inc. • 756 W. 181st St.
- AHS Hardware • 2416 Amsterdam Ave.
- Blue Bell Lumber • 2360 Amsterdam Ave.
- Chavin Hardware, Inc. • 1348 St. Nicholas Ave.
- Cibao Hardware • 1041 St. Nicholas Ave.
- Cora Children Ware, Inc. • 4189 Broadway
- Ernesto's Hardware Store •
  2180 Amsterdam Ave.
- Fort Washington Hardware • 3918 Broadway
- Martinez Hardware • 1269 St. Nicholas Ave.
- Nunez Hardware • 4147 Broadway
- Nunez Mini Hardware • 1388 St. Nicholas Ave.
- Washington Heights Hardware •
  736 W. 181st St.

Liquor Stores

- All-Star Spirits, Ltd. • 4189 Broadway
- Campos Ernest F • 831 W. 181st St.
- Duran Liquor Store • 2001 Amsterdam Ave.
- Galicia Liquors, Inc. • 3906 Broadway
- Guadalupe Barbara • 4084 Broadway
- Heights Liquor Supermarket • 547 W. 181st St.
- In Good Spirits Corp. • 3819 Broadway
- Mc Liquor Store Inc. • 2208 Amsterdam Ave.
- Puma Wine & Liquor • 182 Audubon Ave.
- Vargas Liquor Store • 114 Audubon Ave.

 Movie Theatre

- Coliseum Theatre • Broadway at 181st St.

 Pet Stores

- Pet Place • 518 W. 181st St.

Restaurant

- Empire Szechuan • 4041 Broadway
- Kismat • 187 Fort Washington Ave.

Video Rental

- Blockbuster Video •
  4211 Broadway

Washington Heights
Transportation

Cabrini Blvd

W 183rd St

W 183rd St

Col. R Magaw Pl

Bennett Ave

W 182nd St

W 181st St

WASHINGTON BRIDGE

W 180th St

Pinehurst Ave

BUS TERMINAL

W 179th St

ALEXANDER HAMILTON BRIDGE

GEORGE WASHINGTON BRIDGE

W 178th St

W 177th St

Wadsworth Ave

Harlem River

Fort Washington Ave

W 176th St

W 175th St

HIGH BRIDGE (PED)

J.N. WRIGHT PARK

W 174th St

W 173rd St

Haven Ave

W 172nd St

Broadway

St Nicholas Ave

Audubon Ave

Amsterdam Ave

Pool

HIGH BRIDGE PARK

W 171st St

W 170th St

Riverside Drive

W 169th St

HENRY HUDSON PKWY

WASHINGTON PARK

W 168th St

COLUMBIA PRESBYTERIAN MEDICAL CENTER

Harlem River Drive

N.Y.S. PSYCHIATRIC INSTITUTE

W 167th St

Jumel Pl

McKenna Sq

W 166th St

W 165th St

Edgecombe Ave

Hudson River

W 164th St

W 163rd St

W 162nd St

ROGER MORRIS PARK

W 161st St

Jumel Terr

Sylvan Terr

W 160th St

W 159th St

COLON PARK HOUSE

The George Washington Bridge is slightly less of a nightmare than the other two Hudson River crossings, mainly because it can be reached independently from both the west and east sides and because it has several more lanes. If you have a choice, take the lower level going outbound, and always take the Harlem River Drive instead of the West Side Highway.

Subways

Ⓐ . . . . . Fort Washington Ave. & 175th St.

Ⓐ . . . . . Fort. Washington Ave. & 181st St.

Ⓐ Ⓒ . . . . Broadway & 168th St.

Ⓐ Ⓒ ❶ ❾ . Amsterdam Ave. & 163rd St.

❶ ❾ . . . . . St. Nicholas Ave. & 181st St.

Bus Lines

2 . . . . 5th and Madison Aves./
Adam Clayton Powell Jr. Blvd.

3 . . . 5th and Madison Aves./St. Nicholas Ave.

Bx7 . . . . to Riverdale, 238th St.-Broadway

4 . . . . 5th and Madison Aves./Broadway

5 . . . . 5th Ave./Ave. of the Americas/
Riverside Dr.

Bx7 . . . . Riverdale Ave./Broadway

Bx11 . . . . to Southern Blvd. via 170th St.

Bx13 . . . . to Yankee Stadium via Ogden Ave.

18 . . . . Convent Ave

Bx35 . . . . to West Farms Rd. via 167th St.

Bx36 . . . . to Olmstead Ave./Randall Ave.
via 180th St.

98 . . . . Washington Heights/Midtown

100 . . . . . . Amsterdam Ave./Broadway/125th St.

101 . . . . . . 3rd/Lexington Aves./Malcolm X Blvd.

⊙ Car Rental

- Aamcar: Uptown Car Rental • 506 181st St.

🅿 Gas Stations

- Raamco Service Station • 4275 Broadway
- Shell • 2420 Amsterdam Ave.
- Shell • 2149 Amsterdam Ave.

🅿 Parking

- 284 Audubon Ave.
- 1150 St. Nicholas Ave.
- 528 W. 162nd St.
- 554 W. 174th St.
- 506 W. 181st St.

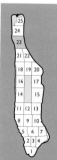

Fort George/Fort Tryon
Essentials

W 204th St
W 203rd St
W 202nd St
W 201st St

Ninth Ave
Tenth Ave

Dyckman St
Post Ave
Thayer St
Arden St
Dongan Pl
Sherman Ave
Sickles St
Ellwood St
W 196th St
Nagle Ave
Bogardus Pl
Hillside Ave
Broadway

DYCKMAN
HOUSES

Academy St

Harlem River

Margaret Corbin Dr.

THE
CLOISTERS

FORT
TRYON
PARK

Ft. George Hill
Ft. George Ave

Margaret
Corbin Plaza

W 193rd St
W 192nd St
W 193rd St
W 192nd St
W 191st St
W 190th St
W 190th St
W 189th St
W 188th St

Wadsworth Terr
Audubon Ave
Amsterdam Ave

HIGH
BRIDGE
PARK

GORMAN
PARK

Harlem River Drive

Hudson River

Cabrini Boulevard
Ft. Washington Ave
Overlook Terr
Bennett Ave

W 187th St
W 186th St
W 185th St

W 187th St
W 186th St
W 185th St
W 184th St
W 183rd St
W 182nd St
W 181st St

Wash Terr
St. Nicholas Ave
Wadsworth Ave

YESHIVA
UNIVERSITY

Laurel Hill Terr

HENRY HUDSON PARKWAY
HENRY HUDSON PARKWAY
Chittenden Ave

BENNETT
PARK

W 183rd St
Col. R.
Magaw Place

Broadway

P

W 180th St

WASHINGTON BRIDGE

PLAZA
LAFAYETTE

The Cloisters and Fort Tryon Park are absolutely two of the quietest and most beautiful places in Manhattan.

💰 ATMs

A • Apple • 4251 Broadway
BP • Banco Popular • 615 W. 181st St.
BP • Banco Popular • 175 Dyckman St.
Ch • Chase • 1421 St. Nicholas Ave.
Ch • Chase • 596 Fort Washington Ave.
Ch • Chase • 161 Dyckman St.
Ci • Citibank • 4249 Broadway

⬤ Bagels

• Bagel City • 720 W. 181st St.

★ Landmark

• The Cloisters • Fort Tryon Park

📖 Libraries

• Fort Washington • 535 W. 179th St.
• Washington Heights • 1000 St.Nicholas Ave.

🅿 Police Precinct

• 34th Precinct • 4295 Broadway

✉ Post Office

• Fort George • 4558 Broadway

🅂 Schools

• Beth Medrash Jeshurun • 220 Bennett Ave.
• George Washington High School •
  549 Audubon Ave.
• IS 143 Eleanor Roosevelt School •
  511 W. 182nd St.
• IS 218 Salome Urena School • 4600 Broadway
• P S 528 Bea Fuller Rodgers School •
  180 Wadsworth Ave.
• PS 005 Ellen Lurie School • 3703 Tenth Ave.
• PS 048 Officer Buczek School •
  4360 Broadway
• PS 132 Juan Pablo Duarte School •
  185 Wadsworth
• PS 152 Dyckman Valley School • 93 Nagle Ave.
• PS 189 • 2580 Amsterdam Ave.
• PS 528 Bea Fuller Rodgers School •
  180 Wadsworth
• PS/IS 187 Hudson Cliffs School •
  349 Cabrini Blvd.
• Yeshiva University • 500 W. 185th St.

✤ Community Gardens

Fort George/Fort Tryon
Sundries / Entertainment

THE CLOISTERS

Margaret Corbin Dr

DYCKMAN HOUSES

Dyckman St
Post Ave
Thayer St
Dongan Pl
Arden St
Sherman Ave
Sickles St
Ellwood St
Nagle Ave
W 196th St
Broadway
Bogardus Pl
Hillside Ave

W 204th St
W 203rd
W 202nd
W 201st
Ninth Ave
Tenth Ave
Academy St

Ft. George Hill
Ft. George Ave

FORT TRYON PARK

Harlem

Margaret Corbin Plaza

W 193rd St
W 192nd St
W 191st St
W 190th St
W 189th St
W 188th St
W 187th St
W 186th St
W 185th St
W 184th St
W 183rd St
W 182nd St
W 181st St
W 180th St

Wadsworth Terr
Bennett Ave
Ft. Washington Ave
Cabrini Boulevard
Overlook Terr
Chittenden Ave

GORMAN PARK

Audubon Ave
Amsterdam Ave
St. Nicholas Ave
Wadsworth Ave
Broadway
Col. R. Magaw Place

HIGH BRIDGE PARK

HENRY HUDSON PARKWAY
HENRY HUDSON PARKWAY

Hudson River

YESHIVA UNIVERSITY
Laurel Hill Terr
Wash Terr

BENNETT PARK

PLAZA LAFAYETTE

WASHINGTON BRI

●━● Gyms

- Frank's Fitness Inc. • 4271 Broadway
- Multi Fitness • 104 Sherman Ave.
- Urban Total Fitness Inc. •
  1387 St Nicholas Ave.

ⓣ Hardware Stores

- 756 Hardware Inc. • 756 W. 181st St.
- AHS Hardware • 2416 Amsterdam Ave.
- Apex Supply Co. • 4580 Broadway
- Century Hardware • 4309 Broadway
- Castillo Hardware • 1449 St. Nicholas Ave.
- Geomart Hardware •
  607 Fort Washington Ave.
- Nagle Hardware Store • 145 Nagle Ave.
- Papelin Hardware • 1488 St. Nicholas Ave.
- VNJ Hardware • 4476 Broadway
- Washington Heights Hardware •
  736 W. 181st St.
- Win Mar Enterprises • 602 W. 184th St.

🍾 Liquor Stores

- 949 Liquor Store Inc. • 4329 Broadway
- Campos Ernest F • 831 W. 181st St.
- Dyckman Liquors,Inc. • 121 Dyckman St.
- Heights Liquor Supermarket • 547 W. 181st St.
- Hou & Hou Liquors • 1492 St. Nicholas Ave.
- Nunez Alex • 1598 St Nicholas Ave.
- Sanchez Liquors • 4500 Broadway
- Sherman Liquor Corp • 25 Sherman Ave.

Movie Theatre

- Coliseum Theatre • Broadway at 181st St.

🖊 Pet Stores

- Pet Place • 518 W. 181st St.

🍴 Restaurant

- Bleu Evolution • 808 W. 187th St.

●● Video Rentals

- Blockbuster Video • 4211 Broadway
- Blockbuster Video • 161 Dyckman St.

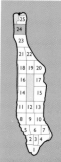

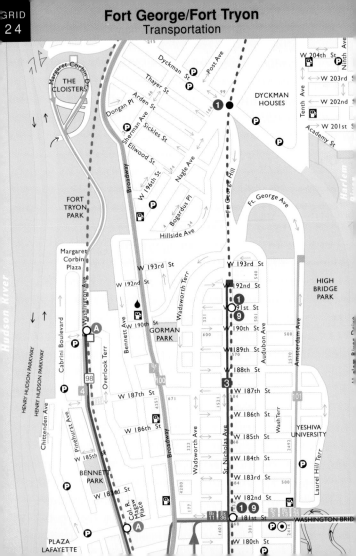

Pay close attention when you cross over into Manhattan from New Jersey on the George Washington Bridge, because if you miss the "Harlem River Drive–Last Exit in Manhattan" exit, you'll be crossing over into the Bronx and sitting in traffic on what is categorically the most miserable highway in all the world, the Cross Bronx Expressway.

Subways

Ⓐ . . . . Fort Washington Ave.
Ⓐ . . . . 190th St.
❶ . . . . Dyckman St.
❶ ❾ . . . . 181st St.
❶ ❾ . . . . 191st St.

Bus Lines

3 . . . . St. Nicholas Ave.
Bx3 . . . . 181st St
4 . . . . Ft. Washington Ave.
Bx7 . . . . Broadway
Bx11 . . . . 181st St
Bx13 . . . . 181st St
Bx35 . . . . 181st St
Bx36 . . . . 181st St
98 . . . . Ft. Washington Ave.
100 . . . . Broadway
101 . . . . Amsterdam Ave.

◉ Car Rental

- Aamcar: Uptown Car Rental • 506 W. 181st St
- Executive Business Service • 124 Fort George Ave.

◆ Car Wash

- Sunoco Ultra Car Wash • 4469 Broadway

🅿 Gas Stations

- Amoco • 4355 Broadway
- Gaseteria • 4519 Broadway
- Gaseteria • 204th St. & Tenth Ave.
- Getty • Dyckman St. & Seaman Ave.
- Raamco Service Station • 4275 Broadway
- Shell • 2420 Amsterdam Ave.
- Sunoco • 4469 Broadway

🅿 Parking

- 284 Audubon Ave.
- 200 Cabrini Blvd.
- 133 Dyckman St.
- 164 Dyckman St.
- 2479 Amsterdam Ave.
- 120-200 Cabrini Blvd.
- 120 Cabrini Blvd.
- 900 W. 190th St.
- 31 Nagle Ave.
- 400 W. 204th St.
- 141 Dyckman St.
- 140 Dyckman.
- 506 W. 181st St.
- 2 Sherman Ave.

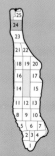

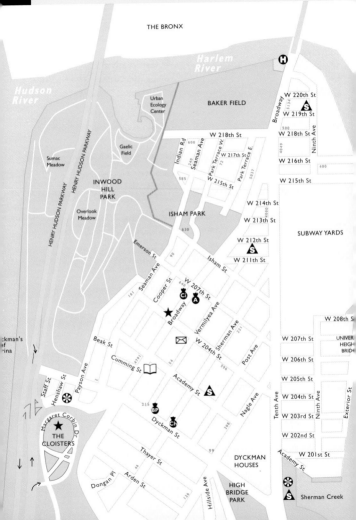

Inwood
Essentials

THE BRONX

Harlem River

Hudson River

Urban Ecology Center

BAKER FIELD

H

W 220th St

Broadway

S

W 219th St

Sumac Meadow

HENRY HUDSON PARKWAY

HENRY HUDSON PARKWAY

Gaelic Field

W 218th St

W 218th St

Indian Rd

Seaman Ave

Park Terrace W.

W 217th St

Park Terrace E.

W 216th St

INWOOD HILL PARK

W 215th St

W 215th St

Overlook Meadow

ISHAM PARK

W 214th St

W 213th St

SUBWAY YARDS

Emerson St

W 212th St

W 211th St

Seaman Ave

Isham St

Cooper St

W 207th St

C A

Broadway

Vermilyea Ave

Sherman Ave

W 208th St

UNIVER HEIGH BRID

Beak St

W 204th St

Post Ave

W 207th St

Cumming St

Academy St

S

W 206th St

W 205th St

Nagle Ave

Payson Ave

W 204th St

Tenth Ave

Ninth Ave

Exterior St

Staff St

Henshaw St

BP

W 203rd St

Margaret Corbin Dr.

Dyckman St

ch

W 202nd St

THE CLOISTERS

Thayer St

DYCKMAN HOUSES

Academy St

W 201st St

Dongan Pl

Arden St

Hillside Ave

HIGH BRIDGE PARK

S

Sherman Creek

ckman's f rina

Inwood
Essentials

Inwood is definitely Manhattan's best-kept housing secret—the houses along Payson Avenue and Seaman Avenue are very nice. Inwood Hill Park is a shady, overgrown, semi-wild park with a killer view of The Cloisters and Fort Tryon Park. Inwood also contains Manhattan's oldest building, the Dyckman House (it looks it!)

ATMs

A • Apple • 4950 Broadway
BP • Banco Popular • 175 Dyckman St.
Ch • Chase • 161 Dyckman St.
Ci • Citibank • 4949 Broadway

Hospital

- Columbia-Presbyterian Allen Pavilion • 5141 Broadway

Landmarks

- Dyckman House • 204th St. and Broadway
- The Cloisters • Fort Tryon Park

Library

- Inwood • 4790 Broadway at Academy

Post Office

- Inwood Post Office • 90 Vermilyea Ave.

Schools

- IS 052 Inwood School • 650 Academy St.
- PS 005 Ellen Lurie School • 3703 Tenth Ave.
- PS 018 • Ninth Ave. & 220th St.
- PS 098 Shorackappock School • 512 W. 212th St.

Community Gardens

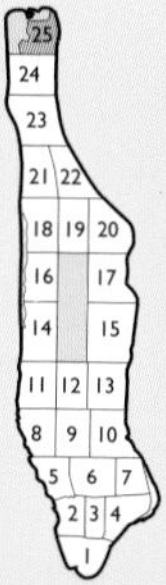

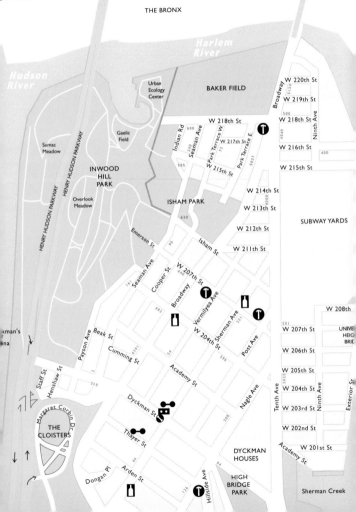

THE BRONX

Harlem River

Hudson River

Urban Ecology Center

BAKER FIELD

W 220th St

W 219th St

Broadway

W 218th St

Ninth Ave

Sumac Meadow

Gaelic Field

Indian Rd

Seaman Ave

Park Terrace W

W 218th St

Park Terrace E

W 217th St

W 216th St

W 215th St

INWOOD HILL PARK

Overlook Meadow

ISHAM PARK

W 214th St

W 213th St

SUBWAY YARDS

Emerson St

Isham St

W 212th St

W 211th St

Seaman Ave

Cooper St

W 207th St

Broadway

Vermilyea Ave

Sherman Ave

W 208th

Payson Ave

Beak St

Cumming St

W 204th St

Post Ave

W 207th St

UNIVE HEIG BRID

W 206th St

Academy St

Nagle Ave

W 205th St

Tenth Ave

W 204th St

Ninth Ave

Exterior St

Staff St

Henshaw St

Dyckman St

W 203rd St

W 202nd St

THE CLOISTERS

Margaret Corbin Dr.

Thayer St

DYCKMAN HOUSES

Academy St

W 201st St

Dongan Pl

Arden St

Hillside Ave

HIGH BRIDGE PARK

Sherman Creek

Gyms

- Inwood Martial Arts Academy • 95 Thayer St.
- Multi Fitness • 104 Sherman Ave.

 Hardware Stores

- Burton Supply Co., Inc. • 519 W. 207th St.
- Inwood Paint & Hardware • 5085 Broadway
- J&A Hardware • 132 Vermilyea Ave.
- Nagle Hardware Store • 145 Nagle Ave.

Pet Stores

- New York's Original Best Pets • 205 Dyckman St.

Liquor Stores

- Dyckman Liquors,Inc. • 121 Dyckman St.
- PJ Liquor Warehouse • 4898 Broadway
- Q Royal, Inc. • 517 W. 207th St.
- Sherman Liquor Corp • 25 Sherman Ave.

Video Rental

- Blockbuster Video • 161 Dyckman St.

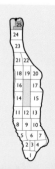

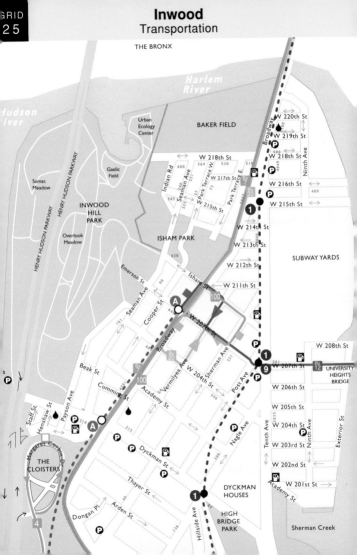

Inwood
Transportation

THE BRONX

Harlem River

Hudson River

Urban Ecology Center

BAKER FIELD

Sumac Meadow

Gaelic Field

INWOOD HILL PARK

Overlook Meadow

ISHAM PARK

SUBWAY YARDS

HENRY HUDSON PARKWAY

Indian Rd

Seaman Ave

Park Terrace W

Park Terrace E

Ninth Ave

W 220th St

W 219th St

W 218th St

W 217th St

W 216th St

W 215th St

W 214th St

W 213th St

W 212th St

W 211th St

Emerson St

Isham St

Cooper St

Seaman Ave

Broadway

W 207th St

Vermilyea Ave

W 204th St

Sherman Ave

Post Ave

W 208th St

W 207th St

UNIVERSITY HEIGHTS BRIDGE

Beak St

Cummings St

Academy St

W 206th St

W 205th St

Tenth Ave

Nagle Ave

Ninth Ave

W 204th St

W 203rd St

W 202nd St

W 201st St

Exterior St

Sherman Creek

Staff St

Henshaw St

Payson Ave

Margaret Corbin Dr

THE CLOISTERS

Dyckman St

Thayer St

Dongan Pl

Arden St

Hillside Ave

Academy St

DYCKMAN HOUSES

HIGH BRIDGE PARK

Inwood
Transportation

The stupid toll plaza at the tip of the Henry Hudson is only one of many reasons why driving in New York is nothing short of a nightmare. You might as well be getting your car washed at one of Inwood's many fine establishments. Parking is usually not too much of a problem, even close to Inwood Hill Park.

Subways

Ⓐ . . . . 207th St.
Ⓐ . . . . Dyckman St. & Broadway
❶ . . . . 215th St.
❶ ❾ . . . . 207th St.
❶ . . . . Dyckman St.

Bus Lines

④ . . . . 5th and Madison Aves./Broadway
⑦ . . . . Riverdale Ave./Broadway
⑫ . . . . Riverdale/263rd St. via Riverdale Ave.
⑳ . . . . Riverdale/246th St. via Henry
Hudson Parkway
⑩⓪ . . . . Amsterdam Ave./Broadway/125th St.

🌢 Car Washes

• Broadway Bridge Car Wash • 5134 Broadway
• Broadway Hand Car Wash • 4778 Broadway
• J&S Management Property • 284 Dyckman St.

🅿 Gas Stations

• Amoco • Tenth Ave. & Sherman Ave.
• Gaseteria • 204th St. & Tenth Ave.
• Getty • Dyckman St. & Seaman Ave.
• Getty • 4880 Broadway
• Merit • 401 W. 207th St. & Ninth Ave.
• Shell • 201st St. and Tenth Ave.
• Sunoco • 3936 Tenth Ave.

🅿 Parking

• 3976 Tenth Ave.
• 3966 Tenth Ave.
• 5060 Broadway
• 228 Nagle Ave.
• 133 Dyckman St.
• 164 Dyckman St.
• 3896 Tenth Ave.
• 270 Dyckman St.
• 4055 Tenth Ave.
• 400 W. 204th St.
• 141 Dyckman St.
• 140 Dyckman.
• 2 Sherman Ave.
• 512 W. 112th St.

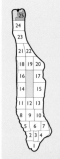

Brooklyn

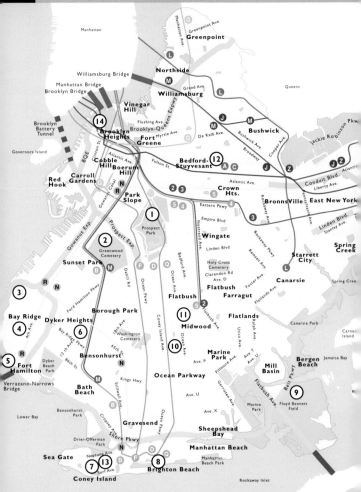

Until 1898, Brooklyn was its own city. Looking at it objectively today, it could still be a damn fine city all on its own. Of course, with glittering Manhattan just across the water, Brooklyn gets second billing, if not ignored altogether. This, of course, makes Brooklynites seethe with justifiable anger, for they believe their borough is just as beautiful and interesting as Manhattan. But since Manhattan rents are skyrocketing, more and more hipsters, yuppies, and just plain folks are moving to Brooklyn—which might make long-time residents start wishing they hadn't been bragging so much for the last 100 years. C'est la vie.

Communities

Brooklyn has 2.3 million people, which would make it one of the largest cities in the US. It has every single type of community you could wish for, and, of course, some you really wouldn't wish for. And many of these communities are in transition, including—but not limited to—Park Slope, Boerum Hill, Carroll Gardens, Red Hook, Williamsburg, Greenpoint, and Fort Greene (the communities all closest to Manhattan!)

However, if you've never explored further out into Brooklyn (other than the obligatory trip to Coney Island), you're missing some very interesting, and very different, neighborhoods. For instance, Bay Ridge ④ has beautiful single-family homes along its western edge, a killer view of the Verrazano Bridge, and excellent shops and restaurants. Dyker Heights ⑥ is almost all single-family homes, many of which go all-out with Christmas light displays during the holiday season. Brighton Beach ⑧ is continuing to be a haven to many Russian expatriates. And both Ocean Parkway ⑩ and Midwood ⑪ have quiet, tree-lined streets that can make one forget all about the hustle and bustle of downtown Brooklyn, or downtown anywhere else for that matter. Finally, while Bedford-Stuyvesant ⑫ does have its problems, it also has a host of cool public buildings, fun eateries, and beautiful brownstones.

Sports

Brooklyn can't wait for the San Andreas Fault Line to give its final heave, and toss all of California into the Pacific Ocean. Why? Because deep down, its residents know that it's the only way the Dodgers will ever come back to Brooklyn. But in the interim, you can check out the Brooklyn Cyclones, the Mets' Class A affiliate, at 1904 Surf Avenue in Coney Island.

Attractions

There are many reasons to dislike Coney Island ⑦, but they're simply not good enough when you stack it up against The Cyclone, the ferris wheel, Nathan's, Totonno's, the beach, the freaks, and The Warriors. Close by is the Aquarium ⑬. Nature trails, parked blimps, views of the water, and scenic marinas, all combine to make historical Floyd Bennet Field ⑨ a very interesting trip. For more beautiful views, you can check out Owl's Point Park ③ in Bay Ridge, or the parking lot ⑤ underneath the Verrazano-Narrows Bridge (located right off the Shore Parkway). It might not be New York's most beautiful bridge, but the Verrazano is hands-down the most awe-inspiring. Both Greenwood Cemetery ② and Prospect Park ① can provide enough greenery to keep you happy until you can get to Yosemite. Finally, Brooklyn Heights ⑭ is the most beautiful residential neighborhood in all of New York. Don't believe us? Go stand on the corner of Willow & Orange Streets.

Food

Here are some restaurants in some of the outlying areas of Brooklyn:
Bay Ridge: Tuscany Grill, 8620 Third Ave. The gorgonzola steak is a must.
Coney Island: Totonno Pizzeria Napolitano, 1524 Neptune Ave. Killer pizza, paper-thin. Bizarre hours.
Sunset Park: Nyonya, 5223 Eighth Ave. Good quality Malaysian.

① Prospect Park	⑥ Dyker Heights	⑪ Midwood
② Greenwood Cemetery	⑦ Coney Island	⑫ Bedford-Stuyvesant
③ Owl's Point Park	⑧ Brighton Beach	⑬ New York Aquarium
④ Bay Ridge	⑨ Floyd Bennett Field	⑭ Brooklyn Heights
⑤ Verrazano-Narrows Bridge	⑩ Ocean Parkway	

Manhattan

Manhattan Bridge

Dumbo

Brooklyn Bridge

Jay St.

Vinegar Hill

Flushing Ave.

Brooklyn-Queens Expwy.

Myrtle Ave.

Pratt Institute

Fort Greene

Fort Greene Park

De Kalb Ave.

Lafayette St.

Bedford Stuyvesa

Bedfor

Brooklyn Heights

Adams St.

Fulton Mall St.

Fulton St.

Carlton Ave.

Carroll Ave.

Atlantic Ave.

Washington

Joralemon St.

Cobble Hill

Henry St.

Clinton St.

Court St.

Smith St.

Boerum Hill

Atlantic Ave.

Flatbush Ave.

N R B M

Carroll St.

Park Slope

BQE

Carroll Gardens

Brooklyn Battery Tunnel

Van Brunt St.

3rd Ave.

5th Ave.

7th Ave.

Prospe Pa

Gowanus Canal

9th St.

Gowanus Exp.

Prospect Exp.

Red Hook

Port Auth Grain Terminal

20St.
21St.
23St.

Erie Basin

Greenw Cemeter

To do this area of Brooklyn real justice requires many more pages than we have to spare, but we thought that even an overview would be better than nothing. So apologies in advance for not going into more detail...

The Communities

Brooklyn Heights proper is roughly the area north of Atlantic Avenue and west of Court Street, and it's possibly the most beautiful of all New York neighborhoods. Cobble Hill, which is south of Atlantic Avenue, is almost as nice. Carroll Gardens, a long-standing middle-income Italian community, and Boerum Hill, a mixed community of Hispanics, African-Americans, and whites, are both being infiltrated by former Manhattanites who can no longer afford the rents. The result: mainly positive, including tons of new restaurants, bars, shops, etc. The downside? Rents, naturally have shot up. Park Slope is also experiencing infiltration, with many long-standing hippie residents still holding out. Fort Greene, while getting some of the aforementioned influx, is still a rough & tumble neighborhood to some extent. However, as Pratt Institute begins to get more and more recognition and money, this will undoubtedly change for the better. Finally, the bizarre and quirky outposts of Vinegar Hill ①, Dumbo ⑤, Red Hook, and Gowanus are all worth exploration.

Attractions

The beauty of walking around Brooklyn Heights—including the streets themselves, the Promenade ③, and Brooklyn Landing ②—is balanced by an equally powerful industrial landscape, beginning with the Brooklyn Bridge Anchorage ④ space (open as an art gallery and performance space in the summer), continuing with the waterfront ⑦ and abandoned grain elevator in Red Hook ⑧, the entire length of the Gowanus Canal ⑨, and ending with various rotting buildings at the Brooklyn Navy Yard ⑮. For more conventional sights, try the interior of the Grand Army Plaza Arch ⑩, the massive Brooklyn Museum ⑫, the Brooklyn Botanical Garden ⑪, and the ever-interesting shows at the Brooklyn Academy of Music ⑭. If this isn't enough, check out the sculpture littered all throughout the campus of Pratt Institute ⑬, and, finally, Ferdinando's Focacceria ⑥, on 151 Union Street in Carroll Gardens, west of the BQE. Ferdinando's has been there since 1904 and has the best cheap Sicilian food east of Palermo.

Food

Brooklyn Heights:
Grimaldi's, 19 Old Fulton St.
Henry's End, 44 Henry St.
Noodle Pudding, 38 Henry St.
The River Café, 1 Water St.

Boerum Hill:
Victory Kitchen, 116 Smith St.
Banania Café, 241 Smith St.
El Nueva Portal, 217 Smith St.
Ytournel, 299 Warren St.

Carroll Gardens:
Smith St. Kitchen, 174 Smith St.
Ferdinando's, 151 Union St.

Park Slope:
Taqueria, 719 5th Ave.
Max & Moritz, 426A Seventh Ave.
Olive Vine Café, 362 15th St.
Beso, 210 Fifth Ave.
Two Boots, 554 Second St.

Bars

Brooklyn Heights:
Waterfront Ale House,155 Atlantic Ave.

Boerum Hill:
The Brooklyn Inn, corner of Hoyt & Bergen Sts.
Quench, 284 Smith St.
The Boat, 175 Smith St.

Park Slope:
12th St. Bar & Grill, 1123 Eighth Ave.

Marketplace

Brooklyn Heights:
Peter's Ice Cream, 185 Atlantic Ave.
Sahadi, 187 Atlantic Ave.

Carroll Gardens:
Community Bookstore, 212 Court St.
American Beer Distributors, 256 Court St.
Caputo's Imported Foods, 460 Court St

Park Slope:
Bird, 430 7th Ave.

Movie Theaters

Brooklyn Heights:
Brooklyn Heights Cinema, 70 Henry St.
Regal Court Street 12, 108 Court St.

Cobble Hill:
Clearview's Cobble Hill Cinemas, 265 Court St.

Downtown Brooklyn:
BAM Rose Cinemas, 30 Lafayette Ave.

Park Slope:
Pavillion, 188 Prospect Park W.
Plaza Twin Cinemas, 314 Flatbush Ave.

Queens
Newtown Creek

Greenpoint

McGuines Blvd. Greenpoint Ave.

Kingsland Ave.

Manhattan Ave.

Humboldt St.

Franklin St.

BQE

Metropolitan

East Williamsbur

Ave

Northside

N. 9th St

McCarren Park

Bushwick Ave.

Southside

Grand Ave.

Manhattan Ave.

East River

Kent Ave.

Berry St.

Bedford Ave

Broadway

Union Ave.

J M Z

Williamsburg Bridge

Wallabout Channel

Williamsburg

Flushing Ave.

Manhattan

Myrtle Ave.

Navy Yard Basin

Navy Yard

VinegarHill

Flushing Ave.

Brooklyn-Queens Expwy

Lafayette Ave.

For many years, the word "Williamsburg" was synonymous with a large Hasidic Jewish community. Now, however, it's just as likely to conjure up the image of a hipster paradise (with, admittedly, high rents). And while Greenpoint is still predominantly Polish & Eastern European, more Manhattanites are beginning to flood into it as well-especially as space in Williamsburg becomes more scarce.

The Communities

Williamsburg has at least three distinct areas to it: the predominantly Jewish community centered around the Williamsburg Bridge and the J/M/Z subway line; the working-class-cum-hipster Northside/Southside area (which uses the L subway line, especially the Bedford St. stop); and the more mixed community of East Williamsburg. Greenpoint is more homogenously Polish, with several large industrial and/or artistic complexes around its northern and eastern edges. Both Williamsburg and Greenpoint are extremely interesting, vibrant, and constantly changing communities, and are worth serious exploration and frequent visits.

The downside is that it's very tough to even find a place for rent within a seven-block radius of the Bedford St. L stop, let alone be able to afford it. Since Williamsburg is mainly industrial buildings, this is due to a simple lack of space. So if all this wonderful Williamsburg talk sounds good enough to move in, be prepared for long walks to the L train, or interminable waits for the G train (there is a free transfer to the L in Williamsburg), or discovering the wonders of the J/M/Z line. If all else fails, you can go for the 30-foot Cris Craft and commute by boat every day to South Street Seaport.

Attractions

One major reason to go to Williamsburg is to eat steak. Located right off the Williamsburg Bridge on the corner of Broadway and Driggs Ave. is the 113-year-old Peter Luger Steakhouse, which is expensive, crowded, cash-only, and has the best damned steak you'll ever eat. Just down the block from Peter Luger's is Williamsburg's extensive waterfront, right off Kent Avenue. Kent has interesting bars, shops, crumbling buildings, radioactive waste facilities (try locating the controversial Radiac building), and stunning water and bridge views. Can you say "condominium complex?" Be prepared, Williamsburg-it's coming.

Food
Williamsburg:
Joe's Busy Corner, N. 7th and Driggs Ave.
Relish, 225 Wythe Ave.
Oznot's Dish, 79 Berry St.
Miss Williamsburg Diner, 206 Kent Ave.
Diner, 85 Broadway.
Planet Thailand, 141 N. 7th St.
Bliss, 191 Bedford Ave.

Greenpoint:
Thai Café, 923 Manhattan Ave.

East Williamsburg:
Phoebe's, 323 Graham Ave.

Bars
Williamsburg:
Black Betty, 366 Metropolitan Ave.
The Charleston, 174 Bedford Ave.,
Pete's Candy Store, 709 Lorimer St.
Café Right Bank, Kent St. at Broadway

Marketplace
Williamsburg:
Earwax Records, 218 Bedford Ave.
Beacon's Closet, 110 Bedford Ave.
Domsey's Warehouse, 431 Kent Ave.
Pop's Popular Clothing, Kent St. at Meserole St.
Williamsburg Greenmarket, Havemeyer St. & Broadway.

Queens

Queens has everything you'd expect of a big city—great art, great food, ethnic diversity, beautiful parks, sporting events, etc. However, since Queens is New York's largest borough, this is all spread out over 100 square miles. And as Mets fans have discovered long ago, it's more than a hop, skip, and a jump to Flushing-and then there's another 5 miles of Queens east of Flushing that's not even serviced by subway. But if you've got wheels or large, unfinished Thomas Pynchon novels for the subway, exploring Queens can be a blast.

Communities

Queens has almost 2 million people, and they are far from similar to each other. Astoria ① has the largest concentration of Greek people outside of Greece, Jackson Heights ⑥ has a vibrant Indian and Pakistani community, and that's just for starters. Mix in the relatively upscale communities of Whitestone ⑪ and Forest Hills, working class Howard Beach, industrial Maspeth, sprawling Jamaica, and sleepy Broad Channel ⑫ and you've got endless diversity.

Culture

We can't say enough about how cool Socrates Sculpture Park ② is. Located on the waterfront (next to founder Mark Di Suvero's sculpture studio) at the end of Broadway (take the N train to the Broadway stop and walk west), this park has had some of New York's best outdoor sculpture for the last ten years. Right down the street is the excellent Noguchi Museum ③. Astoria is also home to the American Museum of the Moving Image ⑤, located in the Kaufman-Astoria Studios district. In Hunter's Point, the expanded and brilliant P.S. 1 Art Museum ④ is a must-see. In Flushing Meadows-Corona Park, check out the gigantic Hall of Science ⑧. Finally, if you've never seen the scale model of New York City at the Queens Museum ⑨ in Corona Park, you should.

Sports

Home to the lovable New York Mets, Shea Stadium ⑩ is right off the 7 train and the Port Washington branch of the LIRR. Aqueduct Racetrack ⑭ has its own A train stop (open 11a.m.-7p.m. on racing days). Rockaway Beach ⑬ is great for swimming (especially mid-week!), and, if there doesn't happen to be anything you want to do at 3 a.m. in Manhattan, drive out to Whitestone Lanes ⑱, off the Linden Place exit of the Whitestone Expressway, for your 24-hour bowling pleasure. Every Labor Day, the popular U.S. Open is held at the National Tennis Center ⑦.

Nature

Queens is home to the vast Gateway National Recreation Area, which has some excellent trails at its Jamaica Bay Wildlife Refuge ⑮ facility. Alley Pond Park ⑯ also has several sections of interest, including the quiet "Upper Alley" area. Finally, the 165 wooded acres of Forest Park ⑰ provide excellent walks, ponds, and stands of trees.

Food

Below is an insanely short list of Queens eateries, but at least we can say that what's listed is great:
Astoria: Stamatis, 29-12 23rd Ave. Really great, unpretentious Greek food.
Corona: Park Side, 107-01 Corona Ave. Great neighborhood Italian.
Forest Hills: Nick's Pizza, 108-26 Ascan Ave. Queens' best pizza.
Jackson Heights: Jackson Diner, 37-47 74th St. Excellent, cheap Indian in a busy neighborhood.
Whitestone: Cooking With Jazz, 1201 154th St. Good Cajun food, many miles from Louisiana.

① Astoria
② Socrates Sculpture Park
③ Noguchi Museum
④ P.S. 1 Art Center
⑤ American Museum of the Moving Image
⑥ Jackson Heights
⑦ U.S. Open
⑧ Hall of Science
⑨ Queens Museum

⑩ Shea Stadium
⑪ Whitestone
⑫ Broad Channel
⑬ Rockaway Beach
⑭ Aqueduct Racetrack
⑮ Jamaica Bay Wildlife Refuge
⑯ Alley Pond Park
⑰ Forest Park
⑱ Whitestone Lanes

The Bronx

The Bronx gets probably the worst rap of any of the five boroughs, but it's really not deserved. And since part of The Bronx's problems were caused by Robert Moses, you really can't blame it. However, while there are many nice sections of The Bronx, it still feels as though they're the exceptions and not the rule.

Communities

The Bronx has perhaps the largest dichotomy between communities-the private, wooded mansions of Riverdale ④ versus the problematic South Bronx, a general name for the area near Yankee Stadium. The Bronx also contains a huge Co-Op complex (named "Co-Op City"), quiet streets around Pelham Parkway, several waterfront communities including City Island ⑫ (one of those rare, interesting places that feel totally un-New York), and one of New York's major universities, Fordham ⑨. Finally, although the community of Marble Hill ③ is physically in The Bronx, it's actually part of New York County.

Culture

Some of The Bronx's most interesting cultural spots are actually vestiges of long-gone institutions (or people). For instance, beautiful Woodlawn Cemetery ⑦ has the remains of Mayor Fiorello LaGuardia, Duke Ellington, and Herman Melville. The bizarre and interesting "Hall of Fame" at Bronx Community College ② is actually leftover from New York University's dismantled University Heights campus. And Wave Hill ⑤, formerly a private estate, is now a wonderful park and occasional concert venue.

Sports

Yankee Stadium ①, perhaps The Bronx's best-known landmark, has been a fixture on the Harlem River for over seventy years. Since opening, it's seen over 20 Yankee World Series championships. Another major Bronx sports institution is one of America's oldest golf courses, Van Cortlandt Golf Course ⑥, or "Vanny" to regulars. You walk past a beautiful lily pond with ducks before dealing with dry, brown fairways and garbage-strewn roughs. Ah, New York.

Nature

Besides an excellent and underrated system of parks-including Pelham Bay Park, Soundview Park, Van Cortlandt Park, and Ferry Point Park—The Bronx has its well-known Botanical Gardens ⑧ and zoo, now called the International Wildlife Conservation Park ⑩. It also has the extremely popular Orchard Beach ⑪.

Food

Belmont: Dominick's, 2335 Arthur Ave. Quintessential Italian eatery.
City Island: The Lobster Box, 34 City Island Ave. When in Rome, eat seafood.
Riverdale: Bellavista, 554 W. 235th St. Good, standard Italian food.
University Heights: Jimmy's Bronx Café, 281 W. Fordham Rd. A Bronx institution.

① Yankee Stadium
② The Hall of Fame
③ Marble Hill
④ Riverdale
⑤ Wave Hill
⑥ Van Cortlandt Golf Course
⑦ Woodlawn Cemetery
⑧ Botanical Garden
⑨ Fordham University
⑩ Int'l Wildlife Conservation Park
⑪ Orchard Beach
⑫ City Island

Staten Island

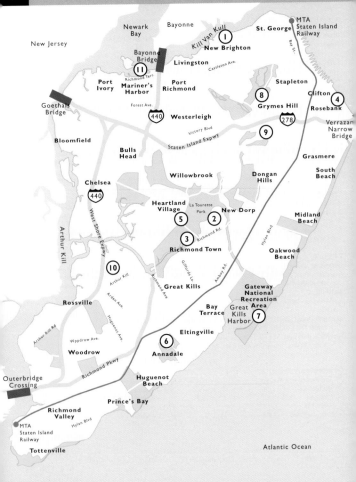

Staten Island. Night. The moon rises over the Fresh Kills Landfill. A dog howls in the distance. You take the last bite of your Philly Cheese Steak and wait for your quarry to emerge from the bushes. A rustle of leaves, and-well, okay, maybe it's not that exciting. But Staten Island, like bagels, MOMA, and Sonic Youth, is a New York institution. And even though many of its residents would like to secede from NYC, and many other NYC residents would like them to, everyone has to admit that it just wouldn't be the same. And anyway, who would take over the management of the Verrazano-Narrows Bridge?

But Staten Island, while perhaps not the most terribly exciting place, has its share of excellent cultural institutions, history, parks, quirks, and (of course) jerks. Here are some high(low)lights:

Culture

① Snug Harbor Cultural Center, 1000 Richmond Terrace. Staten Island's premiere cultural hotspot. This interesting complex of buildings was once a maritime hospital and home for retired sailors. Now it hosts excellent art exhibits and concerts, as well as providing gardens, a children's museum, Greek Revival architecture, and walking paths in its 83-acre setting.

② Jacques Marchais Museum of Tibetan Art, 338 Lighthouse Ave. An excellent collection of Tibetan art, courtesy of a former New York art dealer.

③ Historic Richmondtown. 441 Clark Ave. A 30-acre complex of historic buildings on the site of an early Dutch settlement-the oldest building is from 1695.

④ Alice Austen House. 2 Hylan Blvd. Alice Austen was an early 20th century amateur photographer and contemporary of Jacob Riis. Some of her 8,000 images are always on view at her house, which also has a great view of lower New York Harbor.

Nature

⑤ The Staten Island Greenbelt. Although this 2,500 swath of land (comprised of several different parks) in the center of the island houses a golf course, a hospital, a scout camp, and several graveyards, there is still plenty of real forest to explore on many different trails. Excellent views and nature-walking. A good starting point is High Rock Park, accessible from Nevada Ave.

⑥ Blue Heron Park. Accessible from Poillon Avenue in Southwestern Staten Island, this quiet 147-acre park has a unique serenity to it. Good ponds, bird-watching, wetlands, streams, etc.

⑦ Great Kills Park. This is part of the Gateway National Recreation Area and houses some excellent beaches, a marina, and a nature preserve. It's right off Hylan Boulevard.

⑧ Wagner College. Wagner sits atop a hill and commands beautiful views and has very serene, pleasant surroundings. Worth the winding drive up the hill. Accessible from Howard Ave.

"Other"

⑨ 110/120 Longfellow Road. The estate owned by the Corleone family in The Godfather. You might have to wait a while for Johnny Fontaine to show up and sing, though.

⑩ The Fresh Kills Landfill. Right off Route 440. Excellent hiking, backcountry camping, and scavenging. Bring the whole family.

⑪ Ship Graveyard, off of Richmond Terrace just west of the Bayonne Bridge. Excellent views of rotting ships, the Bayonne Bridge, and other industrial wonders. Recommended.

Driving In/Through Staten Island

At certain times, it can be a very quick trip from Brooklyn to New Jersey via Staten Island. You take the Verrazano to the Staten Island Expressway (Rt. 278) to Rt. 440 to the Outerbridge Crossing, and you're almost halfway to Princeton or the Jersey shore. However...the Staten Island Expressway can many times be jammed. Two scenic, though not really quicker, alternatives: one, you can take Hylan Blvd. all the way south to almost the southwest tip of Staten Island, and then cut up to the Outerbridge Crossing; two, you can take Richmond Terrace around the north shore and cross to New Jersey at the Goethals Bridge. Remember, neither is really faster, but at least you'll be moving.

Battery Park Parks Conservancy: 212-267-9700

To some, Battery Park City is Manhattan's worst nightmare, a planned, controlled, and safe community devoid of any amount of character or soul. But as the saying goes, it's come a long way, baby. While Battery Park City may not be replacing the Lower East Side as a hipster paradise any time soon, attractions such as the Winter Garden, the Museum of Jewish Heritage (designed by Kevin Roche), the new Mercantile Exchange, and several acres' worth of beautiful waterfront parks (with sculptures by Louise Bourgeois, Tom Otterness, Martin Puryear, and Jim Dine) are now making many New Yorkers grudgingly admit that while they still wouldn't want to live there, it is an okay place to visit.

Battery Park City is a 92-acre landfill on Manhattan's southwest tip. It has gone through many stages of urban planning over the course of its history, but the latest plan—42% residential, 30% open space, 19% streets, and 9% commercial—does seem to include something for everyone. A total of 14,000 living units are planned, with a potential occupancy of 25,000 residents. Its network of parks—Robert F. Wagner, Jr., South Cove, Rector, North Cove, the Esplanade, and Governor Nelson A. Rockefeller—are swiftly becoming known for beautiful views, excellent outdoor sculptures, and as great places to just chill out. And the presence of Stuyvesant High School, Siah Armajani's Tribeca Bridge, Kevin Roche's Museum of Jewish Heritage, and Caesar Pelli's Winter Garden and World Financial Center make the architecture of Battery Park City nothing to sneeze at.

BPC has taken several strides forward in the last year with regard to providing its residents and visitors with more services and diversions. New stores, restaurants, bars, and a 16-screen googol-plex have gone a long way to make BPC less dull at night. For more information, you can check out www.batteryparkcity.org (currently not working...is it gone forever?), www.batteryparkcityonline.com, www.bpcparks.org (under construction), www.bpcdogs.org, and www.northcovemarina.com. And if you're wondering how much it would be to dock your 30-foot boat at the marina, it's $3,375/month.

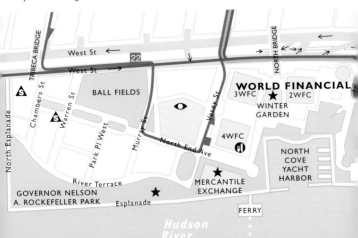

$ ATM
- Chase Manhattan • 331-337 South End Ave. (plus many in the World Financial Center)

★ Landmarks
- Museum of Jewish Heritage
- Winter Garden
- Mercantile Exchange
- Otterness Sculpture

S Schools
- PS/IS 89 School • 201 Warren St.
- Stuyvesant High School • 345 Chambers St.

Gyms
- Battery Park Gym • 375 South End Ave.
- Plus One Fitness • 1 WFC

Restaurants
- Hudson River Club • 4 World Financial Center
- Steamer's Landing • 375 South End Ave.
- Trattorio Gigino • Wagner Park

Liquor Store
- Bulls & Bears Winery • 309 South End Ave.

Movie Theater
- Regal Battery Park City 16 • 102 North End Ave.

Video Store
- Video Room • 300 Rector Pl.

Bus Lines

9	Avenue B/East Broadway
10	7th & 8th Aves/Douglass Blvd.
22	Madison/Chambers Sts.

⦿ Car Rental
- Avis Rent-A-Car • 345 South End Ave.

P Parking
- 333 Rector Pl.
- 350 Albany St.
- 339 South End Ave.
- 2 South End Ave.

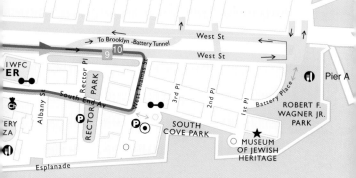

Central Park

Central Park Conservancy: 310-6600
Shakespeare in the Park: 539-8750

Central Park, designed by Frederick Law Olmsted (with help from Calvert Vaux) in the 1850s, is an 843-acre haven to many New Yorkers. On a summer Saturday, one can walk through the park and see jugglers, magicians, disco roller-skater-bladers, Hungarian folk dancing, skateboarders, joggers, operas, rock concerts, ball players, Troilus and Cressida, boaters, art, turtles, frogs, birds and...oh, yes, billions of people. However, the park is big enough so that there are many, many quiet spots (including official "quiet zones" such as the Shakespeare Gardens ⑰) for reading, picnicking, and napping.

Practicalities
Central Park is easily accessible by subway, since the A, C, B, D, N, R, 1, 2, 3, 9 trains all ring the park (odd, though, that there are no stations within the park). Parking along Central Park West is usually pretty good. And if you go in the mornings, for instance, you'll have an even easier time of it since most New Yorkers are "late to bed, late to rise" types. Unless you're there for a big concert, a softball game, or for Shakespeare in the Park, walking around Central Park (especially alone!) at night is not recommended.

Attractions
Like the city itself, Central Park is an eclectic mix of many different types of attractions. Just when you think that Central Park is nothing more than an overcrowded noisy place crawling with roller bladers banging into each other, you'll stumble upon a quiet glade that houses a small sculpture and three people reading books.

Nature
Ironically, perhaps the attributes of Central Park least thought about by New Yorkers are its flora and fauna. There are an amazing number of both plant and animal species that inhabit the park (separate from the creatures housed in its two zoos ④ & ⑧). A good source of information on all the flora and fauna is schoolteacher Leslie Day's web site, at http://www.nysite.com/nature/index.htm.

Architecture & Sculpture
Architecturally, Central Park is known for several structures. Calvert Vaux designed the beautiful Bethesda Fountain and Terrace ⑪ that has become the "center" of the park for many people. The view of Turtle Pond from Belvedere Castle ⑯ (home of the Central Park Learning Center) is also not to be missed. The Arsenal - ⑤ is a wonderful ivy-clad building that houses several Parks Department offices. There are tons of sculptures in the park, although two of the most notable are perhaps Alice in Wonderland ⑮ and the Obelisk ⑲. Oh...The Metropolitan Museum of Art also happens to be in the park.

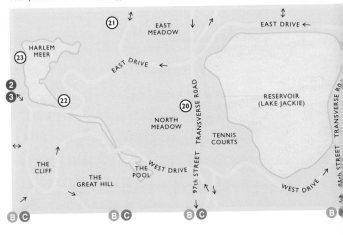

Central Park

Open Spaces

Perhaps the attractions most loved by New Yorkers are Central Park's "spaces." Space being at a premium in the average New Yorker's apartment probably has a lot to do with this, but nonetheless, places such as Strawberry Fields ⑩, The Great Lawn, The Ramble, and Sheep Meadow are prime hang-outs for many New Yorkers.

Performance

Central Park is a microcosm of the great cultural attractions New York has to offer. The Delacorte Theater ⑱ is the home of Shakespeare in the Park, a New York tradition begun by famous director Joseph Papp. Summerstage - ⑨ is now an extremely popular summer concert venue for all types of music, including the occasional killer rock concert. Opera companies and classical philharmonics also show up in the park frequently, as does the odd mega-star (Garth Brooks, Diana Ross, etc.).

Sports

There are so many types of sport occurring in Central Park at any one time that it's pretty dizzying to contemplate. Roller blading is very popular (not just at the Roller Skating Rink ⑦), as is jogging, especially around the Reservoir. The Great Lawn, since its reconstruction, has beautiful softball fields. There are also softball fields at Heckscher Playground. There are 30 tennis courts in Central Park (usually with a long waiting list). There is also volleyball, basketball, skateboarding, bicycling, and an infinite number of pick-up soccer, frisbee, football and kill-the-carrier games being played. Finally, Central Park is where the NYC Marathon ends each year, in case you're still not tired.

Landmarks of Central Park

1. Wollman Rink
2. Carousel
3. The Dairy
4. The Zoo
5. The Arsenal
6. Tavern on the Green
7. Roller Skating Rink
8. Children's Zoo
9. Summerstage

10. Strawberry Fields
11. Bethesda Fountain
12. Bow Bridge
13. Loeb Boathouse
14. Model Boat Racing
15. Alice in Wonderland
16. Belvedere Castle
17. Shakespeare Gardens
18. Delacorte Theater

19. The Obelisk
20. North Meadow Rec. Center
21. Conservatory Garden
22. Lasker Rink
23. Dana Discovery Center
24. Metropolitan Museum of Art

Police Precinct
86th St. & Transverse Rd.

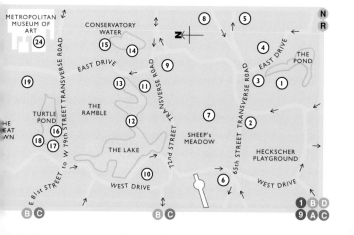

East River Park

Popular to residents of the East Village and the Lower East Side, East River Park is a long, thin slice of land sandwiched between the FDR Drive and the East River that runs from Jackson St. up to 14th St. East River Park was built in the early 40s as part of the FDR Drive (a.k.a. another Robert Moses) project.

How to Get There
Three FDR Drive exits will get you very close to East River Park – the 15th St. exit, the Houston St. exit, and the Grand St. exit. Technically, however, there are no cars allowed in the park. There is some parking available at the extreme south end of the park by Jackson Street off the access road, but it's hard to get to, and not really marked. Plan to find street parking just west of the FDR and cross over on a footbridge.

If you are taking the subway, you better have your hiking boots on – the fact that the closest subway (the F train) is so far away (at least 4 avenue blocks) is one of the reasons East River Park has stayed mainly a neighborhood park. Fortunately, if you're into buses, the 14 and the 8 get you pretty close. Regardless of the bus or subway lines, you will have to cross one of the 5 pedestrian bridges that traverse the FDR Drive. Of course, the most scenic way of getting to the park is by using the East River Esplanade that runs from Battery Park (these paths are still being worked on, so they aren't perfect yet) up to the Upper East Side.

Attractions
The usually quiet park comes alive in the summer and on weekends. Hundreds of families barbeque in the areas between the athletic fields, blaring music and eating to their hearts' content. Others take leisurely strolls or jogs along the East River Esplanade, which offers some of the most dramatic and pretty views of the East River and Brooklyn. Many have turned unused areas of the park into unofficial dog runs, places for pick-up games of ultimate frisbee or soccer, and places to simply sunbathe. It's common to see fishermen along the water trying to catch fish – believe it or not, people actually catch fish – bluefish and striped bass even. Unsurprisingly, nothing caught in the East River should be eaten — while the water quality has improved dramatically, it's still full of pollutants.

Sports

Many different sports leagues use the facilities of East River Park, from young children to over-30 teams. While most of the softball fields are in fairly good condition, the soccer field (the one with the track around it) is appalling. It's more like a quarry than a field. Given the amount of use the field gets, it's shocking that the parks department would allow a field to become so unsafe. And that's just what it is—soccer players sometimes go to the emergency room to be treated for cuts from broken glass on the field. Tennis players, with twelve well-kept courts, are a little more fortunate in East River Park – they only battle the distracting noise of the Williamsburg Bridge renovations.

Facilities

There are three bathroom facilities located in the park; one at the tennis courts, one at the soccer/track field, and one up in the northern part of the park by a children's playground. Aside from the occasional guy with a gro-cery cart full of cold drinks or pushcart with flavored ice, there aren't any food or drink facilities close by. Your best bet is to arrive to the park with any supplies you might need – if that's too difficult, try a bodega on Ave. D.

Safety

The park is relatively safe, especially during the daytime, but we would not recommend hanging out after dark, even if you are just passing through (this is coming from a person whose soccer game was delayed one morning due to the fact that there was a corpse on the field).

Esoterica

Anyone who has explored East River Park has noticed the sad looking, abandoned, graffiti-covered, crumbling band-shell like building in the south part of the park. Built in 1941, and closed since 1971, this amphitheater was actually the original home of Joseph Papp's "Shakespeare in the Park". A fancy $3.5 million, 3,000-seat, privately funded replacement amphitheater and restaurant was scheduled to be built and opened in 1999 – we guess they're behind schedule.

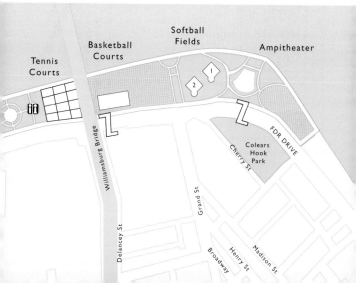

Lincoln Center

Lincoln Center

Lincoln Center is easily one of Manhattan's most vibrant and romantic spots. It's almost obscene how much culture is packed into this four-square-block area—Lincoln Center has one of the world's most famous opera houses, three beautiful theaters, an acoustically-designed music hall, an outdoor bandshell, a movie theater, a performing arts library, a ballet school, and an association with one of the best music schools in the country. Not bad for what was once a terrible, poverty-ridden section of New York. Even Robert Moses got some things right.

Lincoln Center, besides all its performance spaces, also boasts some of the city's signature art and architectural gems. Henry Moore's Reclining Figure is the centerpiece of the reflecting pool, and Mark Chagall's murals grace the foyer of the Metropolitan Opera House. Philip Johnson's plaza fountain holds the entire center together, creating an intimate space where New Yorkers can go to forget about their appallingly high rents and their unpaid parking tickets.

Who Lives Where

Lincoln Center is home to so many different companies, groups, and troupes that we figured we'd provide a chart on who is where. Perhaps the most confusing thing about Lincoln Center is that the "Lincoln Center Theater" is actually two theaters—the Vivian Beaumont and the Mitzi E. Newhouse Theaters. The newest building at Lincoln Center, the Samuel B. and David Rose Building, contains the Stanley Kaplan penthouse performance space, the School of American Ballet, the administrative offices of the Film Society and the Chamber Music Society, the Walter Reade Theater, dorms for the Juliard School, the Riverside Branch of the New York Public Library, and a fire house.

Company/Event/Space	Location
New York City Ballet	New York State Theater
New York City Opera	New York State Theater
Metropolitan Opera Company	Metropolitan Opera House
American Ballet Theater	Metropolitan Opera House
New York Philharmonic	Avery Fisher Hall
Mostly Mozart Festival	Avery Fisher Hall
Jazz at Lincoln Center	Avery Fisher Hall
Vivian Beaumont Theater	Lincoln Center Theater
Mitzi E. Newhouse Theater	Lincoln Center Theater
Chamber Music Society	Alice Tully Hall
Juliard Orchestra	Alice Tully Hall
Juliard Symphony	Alice Tully Hall
Film Society of Lincoln Center	Samuel B. and David Rose Building
School of American Ballet	Samuel B. and David Rose Building

Practical Information

Lincoln Center is right off Broadway and only a few blocks north of Columbus Circle, so getting there is pretty easy. The closest subway is the 66th St. 1 and 9 train, which has an exit right on the edge of the center. It's also only a five-minute walk from the plethora of trains that roll into Columbus Circle (1, 9, A, C, B, and D lines). There is a parking lot underneath Lincoln Center.

Phone Numbers

General Information:	546-2656
Alice Tully Hall:	875-5050
Avery Fisher Hall:	875-5030
The Chamber Music Society:	875-5788
Guided Tours:	875-5350
Jazz at Lincoln Center:	258-9822
The Juliard School:	769-7406
Lincoln Center Theater:	362-7600
The Metropolitan Opera House:	362-6000
New York Philharmonic:	875-5709
New York State Theater:	870-5570
Walter Reade Theater:	875-5601

Website

www.lincolncenter.org

Ticket Purchase Phone Numbers

Center Charge, Alice Tully and Avery Fisher Halls:	721-6500
MovieFone, Walter Reade Theater:	777-FILM
TeleCharge, Lincoln Center Theater:	239-6200
Ticketmaster, New York State Theater:	307-4100
Ticketmaster, Met & Ballet:	307-4100

Randalls & Wards Island

Bronx

Randalls Island Park

Bronx Kill

Triborough

I 27B

Sanitation

Triborough

NYPD

Manhattan

Sanitation

Amtrak

Soccer Fields

East River

M35

HellGate Bridge

Queens

103rd St. Footbridge
4/1–4/30 Open 6am–5pm
5/1–9/30 Open 6am–8pm
10/1–10/29 Open 6am–5pm
10/30–3/31 Closed

Parking

Soccer Fields

103 St.

Triborough

Wards Island Park

Hell Gate

Randalls Island Sports Foundation • 212-830-7714
www.risf.citysearch.com

Most New Yorkers associate Randalls Island solely with the Triborough Bridge, not realizing the island (Randalls & Wards Islands were connected together by landfill) has 440 acres of parkland for public use. In fact, Randalls & Wards Island is host to some of the best athletic fields and parkland in Manhattan. Originally conceived of and built by the infamous Robert Moses, Randalls & Wards Island Park is now administered by the Randalls Island Sports Foundation—the same way The Central Park Conservancy works. Their mission is to continue to improve and upgrade the park for the families of New York City. Phase I of their very big plan includes replacing Downing Stadium with a state-of-the-art track and field center and amphitheater for concerts. They are improving all the bike and pedestrian trails and renovating the soccer and softball fields. Future phases include adding a cricket field and ferry service—there's even talk of a water park. Hopefully part of their plan will include some food facilities. As it is, the only food available is the snack bar in the golf center, and the lunch trucks scattered around Downing Stadium and the Fire Training Center.

Getting there:

By Car — Take the Triborough bridge, exit Randalls Island.
There's a $3.50 toll ($3.00 with EZPass) to get on the island with your car. It's free to leave!

By Bus — From Manhattan: M35 bus from 125th St. to Randalls Island. There's a bus about every 40 minutes during the day. From Queens: Q53 from 61st St.-Woodside.

By Foot — A pedestrian footbridge at 103rd street was built by Robert Moses in the 50s to provide Harlem residents access to the recreational facilities of the parks after the then-city council president Newbold Morris criticized the lack of facilities in Harlem. Its hours are seasonal and limited. Please see the chart on the map.

---

1. Family Golf Center @ Randalls Island • 212-427-5689 • www.familygolfnyc.com
   Family Golf Center is a national chain of 92 golf centers. The golf center on Randall's Island was opened in 1994 by American Golf Center, and was taken over 3 years ago by Family Golf Center.
   The Driving Range is open year-round and has 80 heated stalls. There is a snack bar, bathrooms, 36-hole Mini-Golf, and 9 batting cages. A Shuttle service is available from Manhattan (86th and 3rd Ave.) with an $8 round-trip fee.
   Summer hours are 8am-1pm Tues - Fri, 7am - 10pm Sat & Sun, and 1pm - 11pm on Mondays.

2. Downing Stadium
   The 64-year-old Downing Stadium, used for sports competitions and outdoor concerts such as Lollapalooza and the HORDE tour, will be replaced by a state-of-the-art track and field center in the summer of 2002.

3. New York City Rodeo & Riding Academy • 212-860-2986

4. Manhattan Psychiatric Center • 212-369-0500

5. Project H.E.L.P. Employment Center • 212-534-3866

6. Keener Men's Shelter —Volunteers of America - Greater New York • 212-369-8900 • http://www.voa-gny.org/

7. Odyssey House Drug Rehab Center • 212-426-6677

8. DEP Water Pollution Control Plant • 718-595-6600 • http://www.ci.nyc.ny.us/html/dep/html/drainage.html

9. Fire Department Training Center • http://www.ci.nyc.ny.us/html/fdny/html/fire_academy/fa_index.html
   The NYC Fire Academy is located on 27 acres of parkland on the east side of Randall's Island. In an effort to keep the city's "bravest" in shape, the academy utilizes the easily accessible 68 acres of parkland for physical fitness programs. The ultra-cool training facility includes small Universal Studios-like buildings for simulations training, a 200,000 gallon water supply tank, gasoline and diesel fuel pumps and a 300-car parking lot. In addition, the New York Transit Authority installed tracks and subway cars for learning and developing techniques to battle subway fires and other emergencies. It's really too bad they don't sell tickets and offer tours!

10. Tennis Courts and Bathrooms • 212-534-4845. 11 outdoor courts. Indoor courts heated for winter use.

Roosevelt Island

Roosevelt Island could be one of the coolest places in New York—imagine, a 147-acre island in the middle of the East River, connected to Manhattan by tramway and subway, and connected to Queens by roadway and subway. Unfortunately, though, it's not one of the coolest places in New York. "Bland residential community" is Sidewalk.com's assessment, and we're forced to agree. All services are conveniently located on "Main St." (wherever did they come up with that name?!?), which makes the rest of the island feel deserted. Two hospitals, several abandoned buildings, and the lack of comforting city sights such as taxis, hot dog vendors, and crazy people make Roosevelt Island feel, well…creepy.

However, Roosevelt Island's creepiness is part of its charm. The ivy-covered remains of the Smallpox Hospital, the looming Octagon Tower (formerly the site of a 19th-century mental hospital), and the solitary house and church on West Rd. make a jaunt to Roosevelt Island interesting, to say the least. A trip to the island is best done on the Tramway (costing $1.50 and forever immortalized in the movie "Nighthawks"). Other attractions include the Chapel of the Good Shepherd, the Blackwell House, the western and eastern promenades, and the island's several parks. Perhaps the residential renovation of an abandoned factory near the subway station will add some grit and charm to this bland and creepy island. We certainly hope so.

Practical Information

Roosevelt Island can be reached via the B and Q subway lines, and by the extremely quick but not totally reliable tramway at 60th St. and Second Ave. in Manhattan. To get there by car, take the Queensboro Bridge and follow signs for the "21st St.-North" exit. Go north on 21st St. and make a left on 36th Ave. Go west on 36th Ave. and cross over the red Roosevelt Island Bridge. The only legal parking is at Motorgate Plaza at the end of the bridge, but it's more fun to drive around and harass the Roosevelt Island police by parking illegally and stopping in front of all the really creepy stuff. For more information, the Roosevelt Island Operating Corporation has a very informative website at www.rioc.com. This site discusses several interesting proposals for further development of the island, as well as providing practical information and demographics on the Roosevelt Island community.

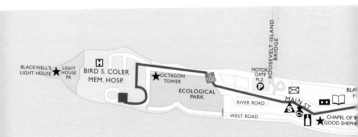

ATM
• Chase • 691 Main St.

Hospitals
• Bird S. Coler Memorial Hospital
• Goldwater Memorial Hospital

★ Landmarks
• Blackwell House
• Blackwell's Lighthouse
• Chapel of the Good Shepherd
• Octagon Tower
• Smallpox Hospital
• Tramway

Library
• Roosevelt Island Library • 524 Main St.

✉ Post Office
• Roosevelt Island Post Office • 694 Main St.

School
• PS-IS 217 • 645 Main St.

Gym
• Sportspark • Main St.

Liquor Store
• Grog Shop • 605 Main St.

Video Rentals
• KIO Enterprise • 544 Main St.

Subway
Q ....Roosevelt Island

Bus Line
12, 102 ....Main St./East and West Rds.

Parking
• Motorgate Plaza

General Information

Height of the Twin Towers:	1377 feet above street level, tallest buildings in Manhattan
Observation Deck:	9:30 a.m.-9:30 p.m. (Sept.-May), 9:30 a.m.-11:30 p.m. (June-August)
107th Floor, 2 WTC	Adult $13.50, Child $6.75, Student $11, Senior $10.50
Mall hours:	8:00 a.m.-7 p.m. Monday-Friday
(individual stores may vary)	10:00 a.m.-6 p.m. Saturday, Noon - 5 p.m. Sunday

Website:	www.panynj.gov/wtc/wtcfram.HTM
General Information:	212-435-4170
Lost and Found:	212-435-3540

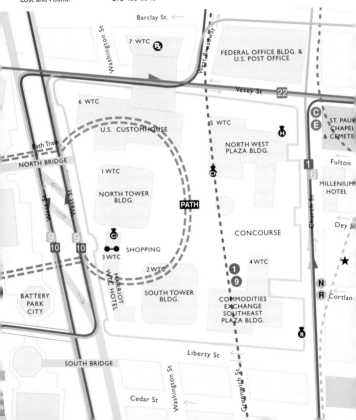

The World Trade Center, which consists of seven buildings including the 110 story twin office towers, is one of Manhattan's best-known landmarks, but, as a famous architectural historian once said, would have been a complete monstrosity if the architects (Minoru Yamasaki and Emery Roth & Sons) had only built one tower instead of two. Apparently, the overkill of the twin towers is what makes it bearable. That's New York logic for you; if we're going to be ridiculous, then let's be really ridiculous.

The WTC has ten million square feet of office space (seven times more than the Empire State Building!), a shopping mall with more than eighty shops and restaurants, an observation deck, a newly-reconstructed outdoor plaza, a summer concert series, access to the 1, 9, C, E, N, R and PATH trains, and tourists galore. It also has a daily working population of 40,000 people (we're really not making these numbers up, we promise). The dirt from the excavation was used to create Battery Park City. Our favorite place in the complex is, of course, Krispy Kreme.

💰 ATMs

Ch • Chase • 2 WTC
Ci • Citibank • 3 WTC
M • Marine Midland (HBSC) • 5 WTC
R • Republic Bank • 5 WTC Concourse

Concourse ATMs
HSBC - between J.Crew and Godiva
Chase - next to Coach
Chase - next to Golden Nugget

★ Landmark

• Century 21 • Church and Cortlandt Sts.

●━● Gym

• Executive Fitness Center • 3 WTC

🅡 24-Hour Pharmacy

• Duane Reade • 7 WTC

Subways

1 **9** ....Cortland St. / WTC
A **C** **E** ....Chambers St./WTC
N **R** ....Cortland St. / WTC

Bus Lines

22 ....Vesey St.
1 **6** ....Church St.
9 **10** ....West St. /Vesey St.

New Jersey PATH Trains

WTC Shops:

APPAREL
Ann Taylor Loft
August Max
Banana Republic
Barami
Casual Corner
The Children's Place
Coach
Cole Haan
Express
Gap
J.Crew
Johnston and Murphy
New Balance
Nine West
Strawberry
Structure
Thomas Pink
Tie Rack
Victoria's Secret

BANKS/FINANCE
Charles Schwab
Chase
Citibank
HSCB
New York State Finance
Republic Bank

ITEMS & SERVICES
Airline Tickets
Bath and Body Works
The Body Shop
Borders Books
Broadway New York
Choice Courier
Claire's
Cosmetics Plus
Crabtree & Evelyn
Duane Reade
Flowers of the World
Golden Nugget

Hallmark
Innovation Luggage
Kelly Film
Lechter's
LensCrafters
Minas Shoe Repair
Natisse Hair Salon
Papyrus
Daniel Pehr Locksmith
Perfumeria Milano
Radio Shack
Sam Goody
Sephora
Sunglass Hut
Thirteen/WNET
TKTS
Torneau Watches
Warner Bros. Studio
    Store
Watch World
Verizon Wireless

FOOD
America's Coffee
Au Bon Pain
Ben and Jerry's
Cornucopia
Devon and Blakely
Ecce Panis
Everything Yogurt and
    Salad
Fine and Schapiro
Gemelli
Godiva Chocolatier
Greenhouse Cafe
Hale and Hearty Soups
Krispy Kreme
Menchanko-Tei
Mrs Fields
Pastabreak
Pretzel Time
Sbarro
Tall Ships Bar & Grill
Windows on the World

The Empire State Building

The Empire State Building, designed by the firm of Schreve, Lamb & Harmon, was built in about 14 months by a lot of very determined individuals. Its framework was constructed in an unprecedented two-month span. Much of the building was prefabricated, and assembly took place at an average rate of four-and-a-half stories per week. It's no wonder, then, that the mayor gets frustrated when it takes four years to re-do a mile-long stretch of the FDR Drive.

The ESB is a natural lightning conductor and is struck up to 500 times a year. On Valentine's Day, the chapel on the 80th floor houses a giant group wedding for all who show up. The NYC Roadrunners Club hosts an annual Run-Up, where the fastest runners have to bound up all 1,860 steps in under 11 minutes. The Mezzanine is now the scene of "New York Skyride," a giant "thrill ride" simulation of a rooftop helicopter flight, complete with a crash over Wall Street and James Doohan (Star Trek's "Scottie") as the tour guide. There are two observation areas-the open terrace on the 86th floor and the glass-enclosed 102nd floor. Unfortunately, due to limited capacity and long waiting lines, the 102nd floor has been closed to the general public.

The ESB also has an excellent, info-packed website (www.esbnyc.com) that includes history, trivia, and a complete schedule of events.

The Lights
The top 30 floors of the ESB have automated color fluorescent lighting that is lit for holidays and other days of recognition, celebration, and memoriam. Between holidays and events, white lighting is used. The following semi-official lighting schedule lists colors from bottom to top as they appear from the street.

2002 Lighting Schedule (for updates/changes, check www.esbnyc.com)

- ■ ■ ■ January 21 • Martin Luther King, Jr. Day
- ■ January 16 • March of Dimes
- ■ February 14 • Valentine's Day
- ■ □ ■ February 18 • President's Day
- ■ March 17 • St. Patrick's Day
- □ ■ □ March 25 • Greek Independence Day
- ■ April • Rain Forest Day
- □ March 29–April 1 • Spring/Easter Week
- ■ □ ■ April 28 • Israel Independence Day
- ■ ■ ■ May 18 • Armed Forces Day
- ■ ■ May 27 • Memorial Day
- ■ May • Police Memorial Day
- ■ June 14 • Flag Day
- ■ ■ June 10 • Portugal Day
- □ □ June 21-23 • Stonewall Anniversary/Gay Pride
- ■ ■ ■ July 4 • Independence Day
- ■ ■ ■ August 13–15 • India Independence Day
- ■ ■ □ August 24–26 • Pakistan Independence Day

- ■ □ ■ September 1–3 • Labor Day
- ■ September 7 • Brazil Independence Day
- □ ■ September • Pulaski Day
- □ □ September • Breast Cancer Awareness
- ■ ■ ■ October 3 • German Reunification Day
- ■ □ ■ October 6–8 • Columbus Day
- ■ ■ ■ October 24 • United Nations Day
- ■ ■ October 31 until Nov 10 • Autumn
- ■ ■ ■ November 10–11 • Veterans' Day
- ■ ■ ■ November30–December 17 • Hannukah
- ■ ■ ■ December 1 • "Day Without Art/ Night Without Lights"/AIDS Awareness
- ■ ■ December 1 to Jan 7 (with interruptions) • Holiday Season
- □ ■ Pennant/World Series win for the Yankees
- ■ ■ Pennant/World Series win for the Mets

General Information
- Location: 5th Avenue at 34th Street (Grid 9)
- General Information: 212-736-3100 or info@esbnyc.com • Website: www.esbnyc.com
- Observatory Hours: 9:30 a.m. to midnight, last elevator to top is at 11:25 p.m.
- Observatory Admission: $9 for adults, $7 for military and seniors, and $4 for children aged 5-11. Add $2 for each ticoket ordered online.

New York City is a great, big, wonderful mess. Trying to provide a terse set of "facts" about our fair city is a very difficult job, but at least we'll give you what we think are the absolute basics. Here goes:

	NYC	Manhattan	Bronx	Brooklyn	Queens	Staten Island
Area (sq. miles)	307	24	43	72	109	59
Population (2000)	8,008,278	1,537,195	1,332,650	2,465,326	2,229,379	443,728
White	2,801,267	703,873	193,651	854,532	732,895	316,316
Black	1,962,154	234,698	416,338	703,873	422,831	39,704
Hispanic	2,160,554	417,816	664,704	487,878	556,605	53,550
Asian	780,229	143,291	38,558	184,291	389,303	24,786
American Indian	17,321	389,303	3,488	4,494	6,275	599
Pacific Islander	2,829	572	474	803	861	119
Two or more races	225,149	28,944	27,209	68,688	92,511	7,797
Other	58,775	5,536	8,227	16,057	28,098	857
Family Income	$34,460	$27,852	$25,479	$30,033	$40,426	$50,664

Bibliography/Reference

We have run across many, many great books, pamphlets, magazines, websites, etc. while researching NFT. The following list is by no means complete, but if you're at all interested in New York, each of these selections will provide you with at least one piece of information you didn't know before.

Books
The Curious New Yorker, Andrea Kannapell, Jesse McKinley, Daniel B. Schneider, Kathryn Shattuck, and Jennifer Steinhauer; Times Books, New York, NY, 1999.
The Encyclopedia of New York City, Kenneth T. Jackson, Editor; Yale University Press, New Haven, CT, 1995.
Eyewitness Travel Guides: New York, Elanor Berman, DK Publishing, New York, NY, 1997.
The Green Book 1996-97: Official Directory of the City of New York, E.C. Robbins, Editor; City Publishing Center, New York, NY, 1997.
Marden's Guide to Manhattan Booksellers, William Marden; City & Company, New York, NY, 1997.
Wild New York, Margaret Mittelbach and Michael Crewdson; Crown Publishers, New York, NY, 1997.
Zagat Survey: 1997 New York City Restaurants; Zagat Survey, LLC, New York, NY 1997.

Magazines
Time Out New York—Easily the most comprehensive weekly listings magazine for New York.
New York Magazine—A great source for keeping up with all things New York
Gallery Guide—Excellent listings for Art Galleries

Websites
www.newyork.citysearch.com - Provides excellent overview to almost every business, landmark and attraction in Manhattan
www.allny.com - The most detailed and varied site on just about anything you can imagine that relates to New York City.
www.nytoday.com - Mega-website run by the New York Times with information about almost every facet of New York City life from restaurants to fitness, from neighborhoods to weddings, with a great up-to-date classifieds section.
www.weather.yahoo.com/forecast/New_York_NY_US_f.html - Yahoo's very clear and concise guide to NYC weather.
www.fieldtrip.com/ny/index_ny.htm - Fieldtrip has hundreds of practical suggestions of places to visit in and around New York City with destination information, hour, admission and even helpful directions.

Bookstores

Gone but not forgotten: A Different Light, Academy, A Photographer's Place, Rizzoli Soho, and Tower Books. Still going strong: St. Mark's Books, The Strand, Gotham, Labyrinth, Books of Wonder, Housing Works Used Book Cafe. Our favorite B&N? 33E. 17th at Union Square.

	Address	Phone	Grid
12th Street Books & Records	11 E. 12th St.	645-4340	6
Acanthus Books	54 W. 21st St.	463-0750	9
Action Comics	337 E. 81st St.	639-1976	15
Alabaster Bookshop	122 Fourth Ave.	982-3550	6
Alba House Media Center	16 Barclay St.	732-4140	2, 3
AMA Management Bookstore	1604 Broadway	903-8286	12
American Museum of Natural History Museum Shop	79th St. & Central Park West	769-5150	14
Aperture Book Center	20 E. 23rd St.	505-5555	9
Applause Theater Books Inc.	211 W. 71st St.	496-7511	14
Archivia: The Art Book Shop	944 Madison Ave.	439-9194	15
Argosy Book Store, Inc.	116 E. 59th St..	753-4455	13, 15
Arka Gift Shop	26 First Ave.	473-3550	6, 7
Asahiya Bookstores New York Inc.	52 Vanderbilt Ave.	883-0011	13
Asia Society Bookstore	502 Park Ave.	288-6400	13, 15
Asian American Bookseller	37 St. Mark's Place	228-6718	7
Audiobook Store	125 Maiden La.	248-7800	1
Bank Street College Bookstore	610 W. 112th St.	678-1654	18
Barnes & Noble Bookstore	240 E. 86th St..	794-1962	17
Barnes & Noble Bookstore	600 Fifth Ave.	765-0590	12
Barnes & Noble Bookstore	1 Penn Plz.	695-1677	9
Barnes & Noble Bookstore	750 Third Ave.	697-2251	13
Barnes & Noble Bookstore	385 Fifth Ave.	779-7677	9
Barnes & Noble Bookstore	901 Sixth Ave.	268-2505	9
Barnes & Noble Bookstore	1280 Lexington Ave.	423-9900	17
Barnes & Noble Bookstore	675 Sixth Ave.	727-1227	9
Barnes & Noble Bookstore	160 E. 54th St..	750-8033	13
Barnes & Noble Bookstore	4 Astor Place	420-1322	6
Barnes & Noble Bookstore	1972 Broadway	595-6859	14
Barnes & Noble Bookstore	33 E. 17th St..	253-0810	9
Barnes & Noble Bookstore	396 Sixth Ave.	674-8780	5, 6
Barnes & Noble Bookstore	2289 Broadway	362-8835	14
Barnes & Noble Bookstore	105 Fifth Ave.	675-5500	9
Baruch College Bookstore	360 Park Ave. S.	889-4327	9, 10
Benjamin Cardozo School of Law Bookstore	55 Fifth Ave	790-0339/0200	6
Bilingual Publications	270 Lafayette St.	431-3500	6
Biography Book Shop	400 Bleecker St.	807-8655	5
Black Orchid Bookshop, The	303 E. 81st St.	734-5908	15
Blackout Books	50 Ave. B	777-1967	7
Bluestockings Womens Bookstore	172 Allen St.	777-6028	4, 6
Book Ark, The	173 W. 81st St.	787-3914	14
Book Smart	27 W. 20th St.	675-8677	9
Bookberries	983 Lexington Ave	794-9400	15
Bookleaves	304 W. 4th St.	924-5638	5, 6
Bookoff	12 E. 41st St.	685-1410	12
Books of Wonder	16 W. 18th St.	989-3270	9
Bookstore of The NY Psychoanalytic Institution	247 E. 82nd St.	772-8282	15
Borders Books, Music, & Cafe	461 Park Ave	980-6785	13
Borders Books, Music, & Cafe	5 World Trade Center	839-8049	1
Borders Books, Music, & Cafe	550 Second Ave.	685-3938	10
Borders Books, Music, & Cafe	551 Fifth Ave.	490-6688	12
British Travel Shop	787 Seventh Ave.	554-4888	12
Brooklyn Museum	230 E. 83rd St.	780-9767	15
Canick Michael Booksellers	Battery Park	344-7220	7
Castle Clinton Monument Bookstore	28 W. 27th St., 3rd Fl.	481-0295	9
Center for Book Arts	55 E. 52nd St.	308-0643	13
Chartwell Booksellers	212 W. 3rd St.	721-1234	5, 6
Children's Museum of Manhattan	1 Centre St., Rm. 2223	669-8245x8247	3
City Books Store	W. 138th St. and Convent Ave.	491-5771	22
City College of New York Bookstore	89 Worth St.	226-9506	5
Civil Service Book Shop	2003 Broadway	875-0306	14
Civilized Traveler, The	864 Lexington Ave.	288-9190	15
Civilized Traveler, The	5 W. 29th St.	779-2511	9
Cokesbury Bookstore			

	Address	Phone	Grid
Cokesbury Bookstore	175 Ninth Ave.	645-1984	8
Coliseum Books	1771 Broadway	757-8381	11, 12
College of Insurance Bookstore	101 Murray St.	962-4111	2, B
Columbia- Presbyterian Medical Center Bookstore	3954 Broadway	923-2149	23
Columbia University Bookstore	2922 Broadway	854-4131	18
Come Again	353 E. 53rd St.	308-9394	13
Compleat Strategist	11 E. 33rd St.	685-3880	9
Complete Traveller Bookstore	199 Madison Ave	685-9007	9
Computer Book Works	78 Reade St.	385-1616	2, 3
Cooper-Hewitt Museum Shop —Book Department	E. 91st St.	860-6939	17
Cornell University Medical College Bookstore	424 E. 70th St.	988-0400	15
Corner Bookstore	1313 Madison Ave	831-3554	17
Corporate Book Express	173 W. 81st St., Lower Level	501-8926	14
Crawford Doyle Booksellers	1082 Madison Ave	288-6300	15
Creative Visions Bookstore	548 Hudson St.	645-7573	5
Dahesh Heritage Fine Books	304 W. 58th St.	265-0600	11
Dictionary Store, The [Rockefeller Center Promenade]	1775 Broadway, #501	581-8810	11, 12
Drama Book Shop	723 Seventh Ave., 2nd Fl.	944-0595	12
Drougas Books	34 Carmine St.	229-0079	5
East Village Books and Records	101 St. Mark's Place	477-8647	7
East West Books	78 Fifth Ave.	243-5994	6, 9
Eastern Mountain Sports	611 Broadway	505-9860	6
Eastern Mountain Sports	20 W. 61st St.	397-4860	14
El Museo Del Barrio	1230 Fifth Ave	831-7272	17
F.A.O. Schwarz Book Department	767 Fifth Ave., 2nd Fl.	644-9400	12, 15
Fashion Design Books	234 W. 27th St.	633-9646	9
Fashion Institute Of Technology Bookstore	227 W. 27th St.	564-4275	9
Fine Art In Print	159 Prince St.	952-2088	6
Forbidden Planet	840 Broadway	473-1576/ 475-6161	6
Fordham University Bookstore	113 W. 60th St.	636-6079/636-6080	11, 14
French & European Publications	Rockefeller Center Promenade 610 5th Ave.	581-8810	12
Funny Business Comics	660-B Amsterdam Ave.	799-9477	16
German Book Center	1841 Broadway	307-7733	14
Good Field Trading Co. Inc.	74 B Mott St.	966-3338	3
Gotham Bookmart and Gallery	41 W. 47th St.	719-4448	12
Granary Books Inc.	307 Seventh Ave.	337-9979	9
Gryphon Book Shop	2246 Broadway	362-0706	14
Hacker Art Books	45 W. 57th St., 5th Fl.	688-7600	12
Hagstrom Map and Travel Center	57 W. 43rd St.	398-1222	12
Hagstrom Map and Travel Center	125 Maiden Lane	785-5343	1
Hayden Planetarium Bookstore	W. 81st St. and Central Park West	769-5910	14
Holland & Holland Limited	50 E. 57th St.	752-7755	13
Housing Works Used Book Cafe	126 Crosby St.	334-3324	6
Hudson News Bookstore	1 World Trade Center	432-9146	1
Hudson News Bookstore	265 E. 66th St.	988-2683	15
Hudson News Bookstore	Grand Central Station 89 E. 42nd St.	687-4580	13
Hudson News Bookstore	Penn Station	971-6800	9
Hudson News Bookstore	Port Authority Building, North Wing	563-1030	16
Hudson News Bookstore	1 World Trade Center	432-9146	1
Hunter College Bookstore	695 Park Ave	650-3970	15
Imperial Fine Books	790 Madison Ave	861-6620	15
J P Medical Books Inc	53 E. 124th St.	410-0593	20
Jay Bee Magazine Stores	150 W. 28th St., Rm. 601	675-1600	9
Jewish Museum	1109 Fifth Ave	423-3200	17
Jim Hanley's Universe	4 W. 33rd St.	268-7088	9
Joanne Hendricks Cookbooks	488 Greenwich St.	226-5731	2
Juillard School Bookstore	60 Lincoln Center Plaza	799-5000	14
Julian's Books	133 W. 25th St.	929-3620	9
K & W Books & Stationery	131 Bowery	343-0780	3
K-Mei Inc.	81 Bayard St.	693-1989	3
Kinokuniya Bookstores	10 W. 49th St.	765-7766	12

	Address	Phone	Grid
Koryo Books	35 W. 32nd St.	564-1844	9
La Boheme Bookstore	3441 Broadway	862-5500	21
Labyrinth Books	536 W. 112th St.	865-1588	18
Laissez Faire Books	73 Spring St.	925-8992	6
Last Word Used Books	1181 Amsterdam Ave.	864-0013	18
Lenox Hill Bookstore	1018 Lexington Ave	472-7170	15
Levine J Co. Books & Judaica	5 W. 30th St.	695-6888	9
Liberation Bookstore, Inc.	421 Lenox Ave.	281-4615	19
Little Book Shop, The	230 E. 80th St.	717-4235	15
Logos Book Store	1575 York Ave.	517-7292	15
Lower East Side Tenement Museum	90 Orchard St.	431-0233	4
Macondo Books, Inc.	221 W. 14th St.	741-3108	5, 6
Macy's Department Store Book Department	151 W. 34th St., 7th Fl.	695-4400x2027	9
Madison Avenue Bookshop	833 Madison Ave	535-6130	15
Manhattan Books	150 Chambers St.	385-7395	2
Manhattan Comics and Cards	228 W. 23rd St.	243-9349	9
Markland Books	40 Waterside Plaza	725-2901	10
Matthew's Mount Sinai School of Medicine Bookstore	1425 Madison Ave.	659-5650	17
McGraw-Hill Bookstore	1221 Ave. of the Americas	512-4100/800-352-3566	12
Mercer Street Books and Records	206 Mercer St.	505-8615	6
Metropolis Comics and Collectibles	873 Broadway	627-9691	9
Metropolitan Museum of Art Bookshop	1000 Fifth Ave	650-2911	15
Metropolitan Museum of Art Bookshop at Rockefeller Center	15 W. 49th St.	332-1360	12
Metropolitan Museum of Art Bookshop —Cloisters Branch	Fort Tyron Park	923-3700	24
Metropolitan Opera Gift Shop	835 Madison Ave	734-8406	15
Metropolitan Opera Gift Shop	Lincoln Center 136 W. 65th St.	580-4090	14
Michelin Guides & Maps	Rockefeller Center Promenade 610 5th Ave.	581-8810	12
Military Bookman, The	29 E. 93rd St.	348-1280	17
Mount Sinai Medical Bookstore	1 Gustave Levy Place	241-2665	17
Murder Ink	2486 Broadway	362-8905/800-488-8123	16
Museum for African Art	593 Broadway	966-1313x115	6
Museum of American Folk Art Museum Shop	2 Lincoln Square	496-2966	14
Museum of Modern Art Bookstore	11 W. 53rd St.	708-9700	12
Museum of Modern Art Design Store	44 W. 53rd St.	767-1050	12
Museum of Television and Radio Gift Shop	25 W. 52nd St.	621-6880	12
Museum of the City of New York Museum Shop	1220 Fifth Ave	534-1672 x230 or 227	17
Mysterious Book Shop, The	129 W. 56th St.	765-0900	12
National Museum of the American Indian	1 Bowling Green	825-8093	1
New Museum of Contemporary Art Bookshop	583 Broadway	219-1222	6
New York Historical Society Museum Shop	170 Central Park West	873-3400	14
New York Institute of Technology Bookstore	1855 Broadway	261-1551	14
New York Open Center Bookstore	83 Spring St.	219-2527x109	6
New York Public Library Bookstore	Fifth Ave. and 42nd St.	930-0641	6
New York Transit Museum	Grand Central Station	682-7572	12
New York Transit Museum	Penn Station		9
New York University Book Center—Main Branch	18 Washington Place	998-4667	6
New York University Book Center —Professional Bookstore	530 LaGuardia Place	998-4680	6
New York University Book Store —Health Sciences Bookstore	333 E. 29th St.	998-9990	10
Nur Al-Haqq Book Store	1711 Third Ave.	996-7323	17
Oan-Oceanie Afrique Noire Books	15 W. 39th St.	840-8844	12
Oriental Books, Stationery, & Arts Co.	29 East Broadway	962-3634	3
Oscar Wilde Memorial Bookshop	15 Christopher St.	255-8097	5
Other Books	224 W. 20th St.	414-0747	9
Pace University Bookstore	1 Pace Plaza	349-8580	3
Papyrus Booksellers	2915 Broadway	222-3350	18
Partners & Crime Mystery Booksellers	44 Greenwich Ave.	243-0440	5
Penn Concessions Inc.	1 Penn Plz.	239-0311/239-7433	9
Penn Concessions Inc.	371 Seventh Ave.	868-0438	9

	Address	Phone	Grid
Penn Station Book Store	1 Penn Plaza, Seventh Ave. side	594-9572	9
Perimeter Books On Architecture	21 Cleveland Place	334-6559	6
Pierpont Morgan Library Book Shop	29 E. 36th St.	685-0008 x358	9
		800-861-0001	
Polish American Bookstore	333 W. 38th St. #1	594-2386	11
Pomander Books	321 W. 94th St.	749-5906	16
Posman Books	70 Fifth Ave.	633-2525	6, 9
Posman Books	9 Grand Central Terminal	983-1111	13
Posman Books at Barnard College	2955 Broadway	961-1527/961-9140	18
Posman Collegiate Bookstores at Manhattan Community College	199 Chambers St.	608-1023	2
Potter's House Christian Bookstore, The	306 E. 111th St.	831-8726	20
Printed Matter	77 Wooster St.	925-0325	6
Quadrant Press Inc.	19 W. 44th St.	819-0822	12
Quest Book Shop	240 E. 53rd St.	758-5521	13
Rand McNally Map & Travel Store	150 E. 52nd St.	758-7488	13
Reel Books Book Store	1998 Broadway	479-0011	14
Renaissance Book Store	2262 Seventh Ave.	283-7810	19
Revolution Books	9 W. 19th St.	691-3345	9
Rizzoli Bookstore	31 W. 57th St.	759-2424	12
Romain's Bookstore	79 Chambers St.	385-0637	2, 3
Ruby's Book Sale	119 Chambers St.	732-8676	2, 3
Rudolf Steiner Bookstore An.	138 W. 15th St.	242-8945	5, 9
Russian Book & Art Shop Inc.	799 Broadway	473-7480	6
Russian House Ltd.	253 Fifth Ave.	685-1010	9
Saint Francis Book Shop	135 W. 31st St.	736-8500	9
Saint Mark's Bookshop	31 Third Ave.	260-7853/260-0443	6
Saint Mark's Comics	150 Chambers St.	385-4108	2
Saint Mark's Comics	11 St. Mark's Place	598-9439	7
School of Visual Arts Bookstore	207 E. 23rd St.	685-7140	10
Science Fiction Shop	214 Sullivan St., Rm. 2D	473-3010	6
Shakespeare & Co.	716 Broadway	529-1330	6
Shakespeare & Co.	939 Lexington Ave	570-0201	15
Shakespeare & Co.	1 Whitehall St.	742-7023	1
Shakespeare & Co.	137 E. 23rd St.	220-5199	10
Sisters Uptown Bookstore	1942 Amsterdam Ave.	862-0731	21
Skyline Books & Records	13 W. 18th St.	759-5463	9
Solomon R. Guggenheim Museum Bookstore	1071 Fifth Ave	423-3615	17
Solomon R. Guggenheim Museum Soho Bookstore	575 Broadway	423-3876	6
South Street Seaport Museum Bookstore	14 Fulton St.	748-8600x663	1
Specialty Book Marketing	443 Park Ave. S.	685-5560	9, 10
Stamm's For Books	172 Fulton St.	267-6036	1
Strand Bookstore	828 Broadway	473-1452	6
Strand Bookstore	95 Fulton St.	732-6070	1
Studio Museum	First Ave. bet. 45th and 46th St.	864-4500 x237	6, 7
Sufi Books	225 W. Broadway	334-5212	2
Surma Book & Music Co.	11 E. 7th St.	477-0729	6
Teachers College Bookstore	1224 Amsterdam Ave.	678-3920	18
Technical Career Institute Bookstore	320 W. 31st St.	594-4000x213	8
Three Lives and Co.	154 W. 10th St.	741-2069	5
Tompkins Square Books	111 E. 7th St.	979-8958	7
Traveler's Choice Bookstore	2 Wooster St.	941-1535	2
Trinity Bookstore	74 Trinity Place	349-0376	1
Ukranian Bookstore	203 Second Ave., 5th Fl.	228-0110	6
United Nations Bookshop	General Assembly Building, Room 32	963-7680/800-553-3210	13
U.S. Government Printing Office Bookstore	26 Federal Plaza, Room 110	264-3825	3
Unity Book Center Div of 237 Books Inc.	237 W. 23rd St.	242-2934	9
Unity Works Inc.	207 E. 125th St.	426-0329	20
Urban Center Books	457 Madison Ave	935-3595	12, 13
Ursus Books Ltd.	981 Madison Ave	772-8787	15
Village Comics	214 Sullivan St.	777-2770	6
Virgin Megastore Book Department	1540 Broadway, Level B-2	921-1020x296	12
West Side Judaica & Bookstore	2412 Broadway	362-7846	16
Whitney Museum of American Art Bookstore	945 Madison Ave.	570-3614	15

Dog Runs

Useful websites: www.doglaw.com, www.nycparks.org, www.allny.com/pets.html, www.nyc.doglife.com

NYC is full of dog runs—both formal and informal—scattered throughout the city's parks and neighborhood community spaces. The city, while not actually administrating the runs, does provide space to community groups who then manage them. The runs are eager for help (volunteer time or financial contributions) and most post volunteer information on park bulletin boards. The formal runs are probably your safest bet, as most are enclosed and are maintained for cleanliness and order. When your dog is in a run, it is important to remove any choke or pronged collars, as they may get tangled with another dog's collar or a fence (both of which can severely injure your dog). Do leave your dog's flat collar and identification tag on. Most runs prohibit dogs in heat, aggressive dogs, and dogs without inoculations. Many do not allow toys, balls or Frisbees.

Grid	Name • Address • Comments
Battery Park City	Battery Park City (south end) • Third Place at Battery Place •This long, narrow, concrete-surfaced enclosed run is located along the West Side Highway and offers a pleasant view of the river and some shade.
Battery Park City	Battery Park City • Along River Terrace between Park Pl. W. and Murray St. • Concrete-surfaced run with a view of the river.
2	P.S. 234 300 • Greenwich St. at Chambers St. • Private run. $50/year membership.
3	Fish Bridge Park • Pearl and Dover Streets • Concrete-surfaced run. Features water hose, wading pool, and lock box with newspapers.
6	Washington Square Park • MacDougal St. at W. 4th St. • Located in the southwest corner of the park, this is a large, gravel-surfaced run with many spectators. This popular run gets very crowded but is well-maintained nonetheless.
6	LaGuardia Place • Mercer St. at Houston St. • This is a private run with a membership (and a waiting list.) The benefits to this run include running water and a plastic wading pool for your dog to splash in.
6	Union Square • Broadway at 16th St. • Crushed stone surface.
7	Tompkins Square Park • Ave. B at 10th St. • New York City's first dog run is quite large and has a wood chip surface. Toys, balls, frisbees, and dogs in heat are all prohibited. This community-centered run offers lots of shade, benches, and running water.
8	Thomas Smith Triangle • Eleventh Ave. at 23rd St. • Concrete-surfaced run.
10	Madison Square Park • Madison Ave. at 25th St. • Medium-sized run with gravel surface and plenty of trees.
11	DeWitt Clinton Park • Eleventh Ave. at 52nd & 54th Sts. • Two small concrete-surfaced runs.
13	E. 60th Street Pavilion • 60th St. at the East River • Concrete-surfaced run.
13	Peter Detmold Park • Beekman Pl. at 51st St. • Large well-maintained run with cement and dirt surfaces and many trees.
13	Robert Moses Park • First Ave. and 42nd St. • Concrete surface.
14	Theodore Roosevelt Park • Central Park West at W. 81st St. Gravel surface.
14	Riverside Park • Riverside Dr. at 72nd St.
15, 17	Carl Schurz Park • East End Ave. at 85/86th Sts. • Medium-sized enclosed run with pebbled surface with separate space for small dogs. This run has benches, shady trees, and running water is available in the bathrooms.
16	Riverside Park • Riverside Dr. at 87th St. • Medium-sized run with gravel surface.
16	Riverside Park • Riverside Dr. at 105/106th Sts. • Medium-sized run with gravel surface.
21	Harlem • Riverside Dr. at 140th St.
23	J. Hood Wright Park • Haven Ave. at W. 173rd St. • An enclosed dirt-surfaced run.
20	Thomas Jefferson Park • E. 112th St. at 1st Ave. • Woodchips surface.
25	Inwood Hill Dog Run • W. 207th St. • Gravel surface.
11	Hell's Kitchen/Clinton Dog Run • W. 39th St. at 10th Ave. • A private dog run (membership costs $15 a year) featuring chairs, umbrellas, fenced graden and woodchip surface.
5	West Village D.O.G. Run • Little W. 12th St. • Features benches, water hose and drink bowl. Membership costs $40 annually but there's a waiting list.

The latest FedEx dropoff is at 9:30 p.m. M–F at 130 Leroy (Grid 5) and 537 W. 33rd St. (Grid 8). However, many Manhattan FedEx delivery trucks have a drop-off slot on the side of the truck itself, in case you're on your way to Leroy St. at 9:15 p.m. and see one. This list has duplicate entries for locations that are in more than one grid.

Grid 1

	Address	Pick-Up Time
Drop box	1 Broadway	8:30 p.m.
Drop box	1 State St. Plaza	7:30 p.m.
Kinko's	100 Wall St.	8:00 p.m.
Service Center	100 William St.	9:00 p.m.
Drop box	11 Broadway	8:00 p.m.
Service Center	110 Wall St.	9:00 p.m.
Kinko's	110 William St.	7:30 p.m.
Drop box	125 Maiden Lane	8:00 p.m.
Drop box	14 Wall St.	8:30 p.m.
Drop box	150 Broadway	8:30 p.m.
Drop box	17 Battery Pl.	8:30 p.m.
Service Center	175 Water St.	7:30 p.m.
Staples	217 Broadway	6:00 p.m.
Drop box	26 Broadway	8:30 p.m.
Complete Mail Centers	28 Vesey St.	6:30 p.m.
Postnet	29 John St.	7:00 p.m.
Drop box	33 Liberty St.	7:00 p.m.
Service Center	40 Broad St.	9:15 p.m.
Drop box	40 Exchange Pl.	8:00 p.m.
Drop box	40 Rector St.	8:30 p.m.
Drop box	45 Wall St.	7:00 p.m.
Service Center	5 Trade Center	8:00 p.m.
Service Center	55 Broadway	9:00 p.m.
Service Center	55 Water St.	9:00 p.m.
Packaging Store	66 West St.	4:30 p.m.
Drop box	67 Wall St.	8:30 p.m.
Drop box	7 Hanover Sq.	8:30 p.m.
Drop box	88 Pine St.	8:30 p.m.
Drop box	90 Broad St.	8:30 p.m.

Grid 2

	Address	Pick-Up Time
Drop box	100 6th Ave.	8:00 p.m.
Kinko's	105 Duane St.	8:00 p.m.
Drop box	11 Park Pl.	8:30 p.m.
Drop box	145 Hudson St.	7:30 p.m.
Drop box	150 Broadway	8:30 p.m.
Staples	217 Broadway	6:00 p.m.
Complete Mail Centers	28 Vesey St.	6:30 p.m.
Mail Boxes Etc.	295 Greenwich St.	5:30 p.m.
Drop box	315 Hudson St.	7:30 p.m.
Drop box	361 Broadway	6:30 p.m.
Service Center	4 Barclay St.	9:00 p.m.
Drop box	401 Broadway	8:30 p.m.
Drop box	434 Broadway	8:00 p.m.
Staples	488 Broadway	6:00 p.m.
Drop box	75 Varick St.	8:30 p.m.
Drop box	86 Warren St.	8:30 p.m.

Grid 3

	Address	Pick-Up Time
Kinko's	105 Duane St.	8:00 p.m.
Drop box	11 Park Pl.	8:30 p.m.
Drop box	150 Broadway	8:30 p.m.
Speedy Shipping Services	150 Lafayette St. #E	6:30 p.m.
Service Center	175 Water St.	7:30 p.m.
Staples	217 Broadway	6:00 p.m.
Complete Mail Centers	28 Vesey St.	6:30 p.m.
Drop box	361 Broadway	6:30 p.m.
Service Center	4 Barclay St.	9:00 p.m.
Drop box	401 Broadway	8:30 p.m.
Drop box	434 Broadway	8:00 p.m.
Staples	488 Broadway	6:00 p.m.

Grid 5

	Address	Pick-Up Time
Drop box	100 6th Ave.	8:00 p.m.
Service Center	130 Leroy St.	9:30 p.m.
Drop box	201 Varick St.	8:00 p.m.
Service Center	229 W. 4th St.	9:00 p.m.
Mail Boxes Etc.	302 W. 12th St.	5:00 p.m.
Drop box	315 Hudson St.	7:30 p.m.
Your Neighborhood Office	332 Bleecker St.	7:00 p.m.
Drop box	350 Hudson St.	8:30 p.m.
The Packaging Depot	48 8th Ave.	4:00 p.m.
Mail Boxes Etc.	511 6th Ave.	6:00 p.m.

Drop box	80 8th Ave.	8:00 p.m.
Drop box	95 Morton St.	8:00 p.m.

Grid 6

	Address	Pick-Up Time
Drop box	100 6th Ave.	8:00 p.m.
Mail Boxes Etc.	111 E. 14th St.	5:00 p.m.
Little Village Postal	151 1st Ave.	6:00 p.m.
Mail Boxes Etc.	168 2nd Ave.	5:00 p.m.
Drop box	200 Park Ave. S.	8:15 p.m.
Kinko's	21 Astor Place	8:00 p.m.
Drop box	225 Lafayette St.	8:00 p.m.
Kinko's	24 E. 12th St.	8:00 p.m.
Drop box	252 Greene St.	7:00 p.m.
Readers Stationery	270 Lafayette St.	8:00 p.m.
Drop box	35 E. 10th St.	4:00 p.m.
Service Center	375 Lafayette St.	8:30 p.m.
Drop box	4 Union Sq. E.	9:00 p.m.
Staples	45 E. 7th St.	7:00 p.m.
Mail Boxes Etc.	511 6th Ave.	6:00 p.m.
Drop box	580 Broadway	8:00 p.m.
Staples	5–9 Union Sq. W.	7:00 p.m.
Drop box	65 Bleecker St.	6:30 p.m.
Service Center	70 Spring St.	8:00 p.m.
Drop box	74 5th Ave.	7:00 p.m.
Drop box	799 Broadway	8:00 p.m.
Drop box	9 E. 4th St.	8:00 p.m.

Grid 7

	Address	Pick-Up Time
Little Village Postal	151 1st Ave.	6:00 p.m.
Kinko's	250 E. Houston St.	8:30 p.m.

Grid 8

	Address	Pick-Up Time
Drop box	111 8th Ave.	8:00 p.m.
Drop box	143 8th Ave.	5:30 p.m.
Drop box	322 8th Ave.	8:00 p.m.
Drop box	450 W. 15th St.	7:30 p.m.
Drop box	505 8th Ave.	8:00 p.m.
Drop box	519 8th Ave.	8:00 p.m.
Drop box	520 8th Ave.	7:00 p.m.
Service Center	537 W. 33rd St.	9:30 p.m.
Drop box	538 W. 34th St.	8:00 p.m.
Drop box	547 W. 27th St.	7:00 p.m.
Mail Boxes Etc.	645 W. 34th St.	5:00 p.m.
Drop box	75 9th Ave.	8:00 p.m.
Drop box	80 8th Ave.	8:00 p.m.

Grid 9

	Address	Pick-Up Time
Service Center	1 Madison Ave.	8:00 p.m.
Service Center	1 Penn Plz.	9:00 p.m.
Drop box	100 W. 33rd St.	7:00 p.m.
Service Center	108 E. 28th St.	9:00 p.m.
Drop box	111 8th Ave.	8:00 p.m.
Drop box	1133 Broadway	8:00 p.m.
Drop box	121 W. 27th St.	7:30 p.m.
Drop box	1225 Broadway	8:00 p.m.
Service Center	125 5th Ave.	9:00 p.m.
Service Center	125 W. 33rd St.	9:00 p.m.
Drop box	1250 Broadway	7:00 p.m.
Service Center	1350 Broadway	9:00 p.m.
Drop box	143 8th Ave.	5:30 p.m.
Service Center	149 Madison Ave.	9:00 p.m.
Service Center	157 W. 35th St.	9:00 p.m.
Staples	16 E. 34th St.	6:00 p.m.
Kinko's	191 Madison Ave.	7:00 p.m.
Service Center	193 Madison Ave.	9:00 p.m.
Service Center	2 Park Ave.	9:00 p.m.
Drop box	2 Penn Plaza	7:30 p.m.
Service Center	20 E. 20th St.	9:00 p.m.
Drop box	200 Park Ave. S.	8:15 p.m.
Service Center	207 W. 25th St.	7:00 p.m.
Drop box	21 Penn Plaza	8:00 p.m.
Drop box	220 5th Ave.	8:00 p.m.
Drop box	220 W. 19th St.	5:00 p.m.
Drop box	225 W. 34th St.	8:00 p.m.

FedEx Locations

Type	Address	Pick-Up Time
Drop box	230 5th Ave.	8:00 p.m.
Drop box	233 W. 18th St.	5:00 p.m.
Kinko's	245 7th Ave.	8:00 p.m.
Staples	250 W. 34th St.	6:00 p.m.
Drop box	257 Park Ave. S.	8:00 p.m.
Drop box	28 E. 28th St.	7:00 p.m.
Drop box	3 Park Ave.	7:00 p.m.
Service Center	322 8th Ave.	8:00 p.m.
Drop box	326 7th Ave.	9:00 p.m.
Drop box	330 5th Ave.	8:00 p.m.
Staples/Drop box	345 Park Ave. S.	8:00 p.m.
Service Center	350 5th Ave.	9:00 p.m.
Drop box	365 5th Ave.	7:00 p.m.
Drop box	390 5th Ave.	8:00 p.m.
Service Center	390 7th Ave.	9:00 p.m.
Service Center	4 Union Sq. E.	9:00 p.m.
Drop box	41 Madison Ave.	8:00 p.m.
Drop box	444 Park Ave. S.	7:00 p.m.
Drop box	45 W.18th St.	7:30 p.m.
Drop box	450 7th Ave.	8:00 p.m.
Drop box	463 7th Ave.	8:00 p.m.
Drop box	469 7th Ave.	8:00 p.m.
Drop box	475 Park Ave. S.	8:00 p.m.
Drop box	485 7th Ave.	8:00 p.m.
Drop box	5 Penn Plaza	8:00 p.m.
Drop box	5 W. 37th St.	7:00 p.m.
Drop box	50 W. 34th St.	7:00 p.m.
Drop box	505 8th Ave.	8:00 p.m.
Mail Boxes Etc.	511 6th Ave.	6:00 p.m.
Drop box	519 8th Ave.	8:00 p.m.
Drop box	520 8th Ave.	7:00 p.m.
Drop box	60 Madison Ave.	7:00 p.m.
Staples	699 6th Ave.	7:00 p.m.
Drop box	74 5th Ave.	7:00 p.m.
Service Center	8 E. 23rd St.	9:00 p.m.
Drop box	80 8th Ave.	8:00 p.m.
Drop box	875 6th Ave.	8:00 p.m.

Grid 10

Type	Address	Pick-Up Time
Service Center	108 E. 28th St.	9:00 p.m.
Mail Boxes Etc.	111 E. 14th St.	5:00 p.m.
Mail Boxes Etc.	163 3rd Ave.	5:00 p.m.
Drop box	192 Lexington Ave.	7:00 p.m.
Service Center	2 Park Ave.	9:00 p.m.
Drop box	200 Lexington Ave.	8:00 p.m.
Drop box	200 Park Ave.	8:15 p.m.
Drop box	220 E. 23rd St.	8:00 p.m.
Drop box	257 Park Ave. S.	8:00 p.m.
Drop box	3 Park Ave.	7:00 p.m.
Drop box	30 Waterside Plz.	8:00 p.m.
Staples/Drop box	345 Park Ave. S.	8:00 p.m.
Emerald Too	346 1st Ave.	7:00 p.m.
Mail Boxes Etc.	350 3rd Ave.	6:00 p.m.
Service Center	4 Union Sq. E.	9:00 p.m.
Drop box	425 E. 25th St.	7:30 p.m.
Drop box	444 Park Ave. S.	7:00 p.m.
Drop box	45 E. 49th St.	5:00 p.m.
Drop box	475 Park Ave. S.	8:00 p.m.
Mail Boxes Etc.	527 3rd Ave.	5:30 p.m.
Drop box	530 1st Ave.	8:00 p.m.
Drop box	545 1st Ave.	8:00 p.m.
Staples	5-9 Union Sq. W.	7:00 p.m.
Drop box	660 1st Ave.	6:00 p.m.

Grid 11

Type	Address	Pick-Up Time
Mail Boxes Etc.	331 W. 57th St.	6:00 p.m.
Drop box	429 W. 53rd St.	8:00 p.m.
Drop box	432 W. 58th St.	6:00 p.m.
Drop box	545 8th Ave.	8:00 p.m.
Drop box	601 W. 50th St.	8:00 p.m.
Drop box	630 9th Ave.	8:00 p.m.
Mail Boxes Etc.	676 A 9th Ave.	7:00 p.m.
Kinko's	677 11th Ave.	8:00 p.m.
Drop box	825 8th Ave.	8:00 p.m.
Service Center	980 8th Ave.	9:00 p.m.

Grid 12

Type	Address	Pick-Up Time
Drop box	10 E. 40th St.	8:00 p.m.
Service Center	10 E. 53rd St.	9:00 p.m.
Staples	1075 6th Ave.	7:00 p.m.
Service Center	112 W. 39th St.	9:00 p.m.
Service Center	1120 6th Ave.	9:00 p.m.
Drop box	1177 6th Ave.	8:30 p.m.
Drop box	120 W. 45th St.	8:00 p.m.
Kinko's/Service Center	1211 6th Ave.	9:00 p.m.
Drop box	1221 6th Ave.	8:00 p.m.
Drop box	1230 6th Ave.	8:30 p.m.
Drop box	1285 6th Ave.	8:00 p.m.
Service Center	1290 6th Ave.	9:00 p.m.
Drop box	1325 6th Ave.	8:30 p.m.
Service Center	135 W. 50th St.	9:00 p.m.
Drop box	1350 6th Ave.	8:00 p.m.
Drop box	1370 6th Ave.	8:00 p.m.
Drop box	1370 Broadway	7:00 p.m.
Drop box	1385 Broadway	7:00 p.m.
Drop box	1407 6th Ave.	6:00 p.m.
Drop box	1466 Broadway	8:00 p.m.
Drop box	1500 Broadway	8:00 p.m.
Drop box	1501 Broadway	8:00 p.m.
Drop box	1515 Broadway	8:30 p.m.
Drop box	152 W. 57th St.	8:00 p.m.
Drop box	156 W. 56th St.	8:00 p.m.
Kinko's	16 E. 52nd St.	8:30 p.m.
Drop box	1700 Broadway	8:00 p.m.
Drop box	1775 Broadway	5:00 p.m.
Service Center	200 W. 57th St.	9:00 p.m.
Service Center	233 W. 54th St.	9:00 p.m.
Kinko's	240 Central Park S.	8:00 p.m.
Service Center	261 Madison Ave.	9:00 p.m.
Drop box	3 E. 54th St.	8:00 p.m.
Drop box	30 Rockefeller Plaza	8:15 p.m.
Service Center	335 Madison Ave.	8:00 p.m.
Drop box	405 Park Ave.	9:00 p.m.
Service Center	43 W. 42nd St.	9:00 p.m.
Service Center	437 Madison Ave.	9:00 p.m.
Service Center	444 Madison Ave.	8:30 p.m.
Drop box	477 Madison Ave.	8:00 p.m.
Drop box	485 7th Ave.	8:00 p.m.
Drop box	488 Madison Ave.	8:30 p.m.
Drop box	489 5th Ave.	8:00 p.m.
Drop box	5 W. 37th St.	7:00 p.m.
Drop box	500 5th Ave.	8:00 p.m.
Service Center	51 E. 44th St.	9:00 p.m.
Service Center	525 7th Ave.	9:00 p.m.
Drop box	545 8th Ave.	8:00 p.m.
Drop box	550 Madison Ave.	8:00 p.m.
Drop box	555 Madison Ave.	8:00 p.m.
Staples	57 W. 57th St.	7:00 p.m.
Drop box	575 Madison Ave.	8:30 p.m.
Drop box	58 W. 40th St.	7:00 p.m.
Drop box	590 Madison Ave.	7:30 p.m.
Drop box	6 E. 43rd St.	8:30 p.m.
Service Center	6 W. 48th St.	9:00 p.m.
Drop box	60 E. 42nd St.	8:30 p.m.
Drop box	600 5th Ave.	7:30 p.m.
Drop box	600 Madison Ave.	8:30 p.m.
Mail Boxes Etc.	666 5th Ave.	5:30 p.m.
Drop box	712 5th Ave.	8:00 p.m.
Drop box	745 5th Ave.	8:00 p.m.
Drop box	787 7th Ave.	7:45 p.m.
Drop box	825 8th Ave.	8:00 p.m.
Service Center	980 8th Ave.	9:00 p.m.

Grid 13

Type	Address	Pick-Up Time
Service Center	10 E. 53rd St.	9:00 p.m.
Drop box	100 Park Ave.	8:30 p.m.
Mail Boxes Etc.	1040 1st Ave.	4:00 p.m.
Drop box	110 E. 59th St.	8:30 p.m.
Drop box	115 E. 57th St.	7:30 p.m.
Drop box	150 E. 42nd St.	7:00 p.m.
Drop box	150 E. 58th St.	8:30 p.m.
Kinko's	153 E. 53rd St.	7:00 p.m.
Staples	205 E. 42nd St.	6:00 p.m.
Mail Boxes Etc.	208 E. 51st St.	6:00 p.m.
Drop box	211 E. 43rd St.	8:30 p.m.
Drop box	220 E. 42nd St.	7:30 p.m.

Service Center	230 Park Ave.	8:30 p.m.
Service Center	261 Madison Ave.	9:00 p.m.
Drop box	280 Park Ave.	8:30 p.m.
Drop box	299 Park Ave.	7:00 p.m.
Kinko's/Service Center	305 E. 46th St.	9:00 p.m.
Drop box	335 Madison Ave.	8:00 p.m.
Drop box	350 Park Ave.	7:30 p.m.
Drop box	353 Lexington Ave.	7:30 p.m.
Drop box	40 E. 52nd St.	6:00 p.m.
Service Center	405 Lexington Ave.	9:00 p.m.
Service Center	405 Park Ave.	9:00 p.m.
Drop box	420 Lexington Ave.	8:30 p.m.
Staples	425 Park Ave.	6:00 p.m.
Service Center	437 Madison Ave.	9:00 p.m.
Drop box	444 Madison Ave.	8:00 p.m.
Drop box	477 Madison Ave.	8:00 p.m.
Service Center	480 Lexington Ave.	9:00 p.m.
Drop box	488 Madison Ave.	8:30 p.m.
Drop box	500 Park Ave.	7:30 p.m.
Service Center	51 E. 44th St.	9:00 p.m.
Drop box	55 E. 59th St.	8:30 p.m.
Drop box	550 Madison Ave.	8:00 p.m.
Drop box	555 Madison Ave.	8:00 p.m.
Service Center	560 Lexington Ave.	9:00 p.m.
Drop box	575 Lexington Ave.	7:00 p.m.
Drop box	575 Madison Ave.	8:30 p.m.
Drop box	590 Madison Ave.	7:30 p.m.
Drop box	60 E. 42nd St.	8:30 p.m.
Kinko's/Service Center	600 3rd Ave.	9:00 p.m.
Drop box	600 Madison Ave.	8:30 p.m.
Drop box	630 3rd Ave.	8:00 p.m.
Drop box	633 3rd Ave.	8:00 p.m.
Kinko's/Service Center	641 Lexington Ave.	9:00 p.m.
Drop box	660 1st Ave.	6:00 p.m.
Kinko's/Service Center	747 3rd Ave.	9:00 p.m.
Service Center	750 3rd Ave.	9:00 p.m.
Drop box	780 3rd Ave.	8:00 p.m.
Drop box	805 3rd Ave.	7:00 p.m.
Service Center	820 2nd Ave.	9:00 p.m.
Mail Boxes Etc.	847A 2nd Ave.	5:00 p.m.
Drop box	866 U.N.Plaza	8:00 p.m.
Service Center	880 3rd Ave.	9:00 p.m.
Drop box	885 3rd Ave.	8:00 p.m.
Service Center	90 Park Ave.	9:00 p.m.
Service Center	938 3rd Ave.	9:00 p.m.
Drop box	979 3rd Ave.	8:00 p.m.
Drop box	99 Park Ave.	8:00 p.m.

Grid 14

	Address	Pick-Up Time
Drop box	101 W. End Ave.	6:00 p.m.
Service Center	156 W. 72 St.	9:00 p.m.
Mail Boxes Etc.	163 Amsterdam Ave.	7:00 p.m.
Kinko's	2081 Broadway	6:30 p.m.
Drop box	211 W. 61st St.	7:00 p.m.
Drop box	2112 Broadway	7:30 p.m.
Mail Boxes Etc.	2124 Broadway	5:30 p.m.
The Padded Wagon	215 W. 85th St.	5:00 p.m.
FedEx	2211 Broadway	9:00 p.m.
Staples	2248 Broadway	5:00 p.m.
Mail Boxes Etc.	459 Columbus Ave.	8:00 p.m.
Copy Usa	491 Amsterdam Ave.	8:00 p.m.
Drop box	517 Amsterdam Ave.	8:00 p.m.

Grid 15

	Address	Pick-Up Time
Drop box	110 E. 59th St.	8:30 p.m.
Drop box	1114 1st Ave.	5:30 p.m.
Kinko's	1122 Lexington Ave.	8:30 p.m.
Mail Boxes Etc.	1173 2nd Ave. # A	5:30 p.m.
Mail Boxes Etc.	1202 Lexington Ave.	6:00 p.m.
Mail Boxes Etc.	1275 1st Ave.	5:30 p.m.
Drop box	1275 York Ave.	8:30 p.m.
Drop box	1300 York Ave.	8:30 p.m.
Drop box	1343 2nd Ave.	8:30 p.m.
Postal Express Bus	1382 3rd Ave.	6:00 p.m.
The Padded Wagon	1431 York Ave.	6:00 p.m.
Mail Boxes Etc.	1461 1st Ave.	6:00 p.m.
Mail Boxes Etc.	1562 1st Ave.	6:00 p.m.
The Padded Wagon	1569 2nd Ave.	6:00 p.m.

Faster Image	415 E. 72nd St.	5:00 p.m.
Drop box	428 E. 72nd St.	6:00 p.m.
Drop box	445 E. 69th St.	5:00 p.m.
Drop box	500 Park Ave.	7:30 p.m.
Drop box	55 E. 59th St.	8:30 p.m.
Drop box	650 Madison Ave.	7:30 p.m.
Drop box	667 Madison Ave.	8:30 p.m.
Drop box	695 Park Ave.	7:30 p.m.
Mail Boxes Etc.	954 Lexington Ave.	5:00 p.m.
Drop box	968 Lexington Ave.	8:30 p.m.
Drop box	979 3rd Ave.	8:00 p.m.

Grid 16

	Address	Pick-Up Time
Foxy Graphic Services	211 W. 92nd St.	7:30 p.m.
The Padded Wagon	215 W. 85th St.	5:00 p.m.
Metro Copy	2372 Broadway	6:00 p.m.
Copy Experts	2440 Broadway	7:00 p.m.
Mail Boxes Etc.	2472 Broadway	6:30 p.m.
Mail Boxes Etc.	2565 Broadway	6:00 p.m.
Copy Usa	491 Amsterdam Ave.	8:00 p.m.
Drop box	517 Amsterdam Ave.	8:00 p.m.
Drop box	70 W. 86th St.	7:00 p.m.

Grid 17

	Address	Pick-Up Time
Drop box	1 E. 104th St.	6:30 p.m.
Staples	1280 Lexington Ave.	8:00 p.m.
Mail Boxes Etc.	1369 Madison Ave.	5:00 p.m.
Drop box	1476 Lexington Ave.	8:00 p.m.
Mail Boxes Etc.	1636 3rd Ave.	5:30 p.m.
Mail Boxes Etc.	1710 1st Ave.	6:00 p.m.
Service Center	208 E. 86th St.	9:00 p.m.
Mail Boxes Etc.	217 E. 86th St.	6:00 p.m.
Drop box	225 E. 95th St.	8:30 p.m.

Grid 18

	Address	Pick-Up Time
Mail Boxes Etc.	2840 Broadway	6:00 p.m.
Kinko's	2872 Broadway	8:00 p.m.
Drop box	3022 Broadway	8:00 p.m.
Drop box	435 W. 116th St.	8:00 p.m.
Drop box	475 Riverside Dr.	8:00 p.m.
Drop box	525 W. 120th St.	8:00 p.m.
Kinko's/Service Center	60 W. 40th St.	9:00 p.m.
Service Center	600 W. 116th St.	9:00 p.m.

Grid 19

	Address	Pick-Up Time
Drop box	163 W. 125th St.	7:00 p.m.
Drop box	2261 A.C. Powell Blvd.	7:00 p.m.
Drop box	355 Lenox Ave.	5:00 p.m.
Drop box	55 W. 125th St.	7:00 p.m.

Grid 20

	Address	Pick-Up Time
Drop box	1824 Madison Ave.	7:00 p.m.
Drop box	1879 Madison Ave.	7:00 p.m.

Grid 21

	Address	Pick-Up Time
Mail Boxes Etc.	3792 Broadway	6:00 p.m.

Grid 23

	Address	Pick-Up Time
Drop box	100 Haven Ave.	7:00 p.m.
Drop box	1051 Riverside Dr.	7:00 p.m.
Drop box	1150 St. Nicholas Ave.	6:00 p.m.
Drop box	161 Ft. Washington Ave.	7:00 p.m.
Drop box	177 Ft. Washington Ave.	7:00 p.m.
Drop box	3960 Broadway	7:00 p.m.
Drop box	60 Haven Ave.	7:00 p.m.
Drop box	622 W. 168th St.	7:00 p.m.
Drop box	630 W. 168th St.	7:00 p.m.
Drop box	701 W. 168th St.	5:30 p.m.
Drop box	710 W. 168th St.	7:00 p.m.
Drop box	722 W. 168th St.	7:00 p.m.

Grid 24

	Address	Pick-Up Time
Northeast Service Group	817 W. 187th St.	5:00 p.m.

Battery Park City

	Address	Pick-Up Time
Drop box	1 Battery Park Plaza	8:30 p.m.
Kinko's/Service Center	102 N. End Ave.	9:00 p.m.

Gay and Lesbian Info: Resources

Websites

Lesbian and Gay Community Services Center: www.gaycenter.org —
Information about center programs, meetings, publications and events.

GayNYC.com: www.gaynyc.com/new_york —
A comprehensive guide to gay and lesbian bars, clubs, dining, arts, events, services, spas, books, travel and Inns.

Gay New York: www.gay-newyork.com — Guide to restaurants, bars, guest houses and cafes.

NYC Gay and Lesbian Guide: www.woofbyte.com/newyorkcity —
Listings of businesses, organizations, churches, resources and comprehensive calendar of events.

Lesbian and Gay New York: www.lgny.com —
Online newspaper for lesbian and gay New Yorkers including current local and national news items.

Blade News: www.nyblade.com —
Online gay and lesbian newspaper featuring local and national news items, classifieds, personals and an up-to-date calendar listing of local events.

Out and About: www.outandabout.com —
Travel website for gays and lesbians including destination information, a gay travel calendar, health information and listings of gay tour operators.

Edwina.com: www.edwina.com —
A New York online meeting place for gays and lesbians looking for love, lust or just friendship.

Publications

Free at Gay and Lesbian venues and shops and available at some street corners.

HX — Weekly magazine featuring information about bars, clubs, restaurants, events, meetings and loads of personals.

HX for Her — Same as HX but with lesbian listings.

LGNY (Lesbian and Gay New York) — Local and national news coverage with a political focus.

NY Blade — Also focuses on gay and lesbian politics and news.

Bookshops

Oscar Wilde Memorial Bookshop, 15 Christopher St., btw 6th & 7th Ave. (225-8097) —
Gay and lesbian books and magazines.

Blue Stockings, 172 Allen St. (777-6028) — Lesbian bookstore with regular readings and book signings.

Health Centers and Support Organizations

Michael Callen-Audre Lorde Community Health Center, 356 W. 18th St. btw 8th & 9th Ave. (271-7200) —
Service for gay, lesbian, bisexual and transgender New Yorkers.

Gay Men's Health Crisis, 129 W. 24th St. btw 6th and 7th Ave. (367-1000),
AIDS advice hotline (807-6655)

Lesbian and Gay Community Services Center, 208 W. 13th St. btw 7th & 8th Ave. (620-7310)
www.gaycenter.org

Gay and Lesbian Switchboard, (620-7310) — Switchboard for referrals, advice, counseling.

Club and Bar Events—Lesbian

Monday:	Fourplay at **Parlay Lounge**, Ave A & 12th St. (591-1065) – Hip-hop and House Music ($5)
	Pleasure at **Bar d'O**, 29 Bedford St. (627-1580) — Ladies loung, Sexy dancers ($3)
Tuesday:	Xena Night at **Meow Mix**, 269 E. Houston St. (254-0688) —
	Screenings, skits and partying Amazonians ($3)
Wednesday:	Lipstick at **Miri**, 179 Essex St. (260-5690) — Ladies Lounge
Thursday:	Gloss at **Meow Mix**, 269 E. Houston St. (254-0688) — Dance event with go-go performers ($7)
	Throb at **Studio 253**, 253 E. Houston St. (788-5122) –
	Slings, bondage bed and a wet room ($20)
	G's Spot at **2i's**, 248 W. 14th St. (917-541-7176) —
	DJs play hip-hop, R&B, reggae, house and soca ($8)
Friday:	Clit Club at **219 Flamingo**, 219 Second Ave. (533-2860) — DJ, dancers and Clit Cam ($9)
	Her/She Bar at **Escuelita**, 301 W. 39th St. (631-1093) — Latin DJ and go-go dancers ($8)
	Sweat at **Crazy Nanny's**, 21 Seventh Ave S. (366-6312) – Dance Party, exotic dancers ($8)
Saturday:	Beautiful Girl at **Henrietta Hudson**, 438 Hudson St. (924-3347) — Dance night ($5)
	Mixer at **Crazy Nanny's**, 21 Seventh Ave S. (366-6312) — Music by DJ ($5)
Sunday:	JacMal HotTea (946-1624) — DJ, contests, beautiful girls ($10)
	Sexy on Sundays at **Bistro Latino**, 1711 Broadway, 54th (888-784-8538) — ($8)

Club and Bar Events—Gay

Monday:	Blue Mon-Daze at **Townhouse**, 236 E. 58th St. (754-4649) — Jazz and Blues
	Musical Mondays at **Splash**, 50 W 17th St. (691-0073) — Show tunes and campy video clips
Tuesday:	Beige at **B Bar**, 358 Bowery at 4th St. (475-2220) – Restaurant-lounge
	Flashback Tuesdays at **The Monster**, 80 Grove St. (924-3558) — Disco Classics
Wednesday:	Big Boy Wednesdays at **Stonewall**, 53 Christopher St. (463-0950) — Music by DJ
	Gay, Straight, Whatever at **Heaven**, 579 Sixth Ave. (243-6100) — Music by DJ ($5)
Thursday:	Broadcast at **13**, 35 E. 13th St. (979-6677) — Sounds of the 80s and alternative 90s
	Celebrity Lounge at The Tapioca Room @ **Centro-Fly**, 45 W 21st St. (592-3032) —
	Clubbing with DJ
Friday:	Cock-Flavored Fridays at **Fat Cock 29**, 29 Second Ave. (946-1871) —
	Rotating guest hostesses ($5)
	Do-It!! at **Joy**, 253 W 28th St. (592-3032) — Music by DJ ($15)
	Kitsch Inn at **True**, 28 E. 23rd St. (254-6117) — Retro DJ ($5)
	Sugar! at **The Slipper Room**, 167 Orchard St. — Rock 'n' Roll, weekly guest performers ($7)
Saturday:	Audio Nasty at **219 Flamingo**, 219 Second Ave. (533-2860) — Dance and House Music ($10)
	Living Legends at **The Now Bar**, 22 Seventh Ave S. (802-9502) —
	She-males and their admirers ($20)
	The Roxy at **Roxy**, 515 W. 18th St., btw 10th and 11th ave. (645-5156) —
	Muscle boys and dancing ($40)
Sunday:	East Infection at **219 Flamingo**, 219 Second Ave. (533-2860) —
	Dance Party and Musical Showcase ($5)
	Mandance at **Splash**, 50 W 17th St. (691-0073) — Music and video clips

Annual Events

Pride Week — Usually the last full week in June – www.nycpride.org (807-7433)

Wigstock — Drag festival held in September with 50% of profits going to the Gay Men's Health Crisis; www.wigstock.nu (439-5139)

New York Lesbian and Gay Film Festival — Showcase of International gay and lesbian films, May/June; www.newfestival.com (254-8504)

Boston-New York Aids Ride — 325 miles, 3,000 riders raising money for AIDS-related organizations; July; www.aidsride.org/new (866-648-0747)

Hospitals

The most infamous of NYC Hospitals, Bellevue, is the nation's oldest public hospital, and in 1869 it became the first hospital in the nation to have an ambulance service.

Hospitals	Address	Phone	Grid
American Association For Bikur Cholim Hospital	156 Fifth Ave.	989-2525	9
American Friends of Laniado Hospital	18 W. 45th St.	944-2690	12
Babies & Children's Hospital Of New York	3959 Broadway	800-245-5437	23
Bellevue Hospital Center	462 First Ave.	562-4141	10
Beth Israel Medical Center	281 First Ave.	420-2000	7
Beth Israel Medical Center: Phillips Ambulatory Center/Cancer Center	10 Union Sq. E.	844-8288	6, 9
Beth Israel Medical Center: Singer Division	170 East End Ave.	870-9000	17
Cabrini Medical Center	227 E. 19th St.	995-6000	10
Columbia-Presbyterian Allen Pavilion	5141 Broadway	932-4000	25
Columbia-Presbyterian Medical Center	622 W. 168th St.	305-2500	23
Gouverneur Hospital	227 Madison St.	238-7000	4
Gracie Square Hospital	420 E. 76th St.	988-4400	15
Harlem Hospital Center	506 Lenox Ave.	939-1000	22
Hospital For Joint Diseases	301 E. 17th St.	598-6000	10
Hospital For Special Surgery	535 E. 70th St.	606-1000	15
Lenox Hill Hospital	100 E. 77th St.	434-2000	15
Manhattan Eye, Ear & Throat Hospital	210 E. 64th St.	838-9200	15
Manhattan Eye, Ear & Throat Hospital	55 E. 124th St.	987-1360	20
Memorial Sloan-Kettering Cancer Center	1275 York Ave.	639-2000	15
Metropolitan Hospital	1901 First Ave.	423-6262	17
Mt. Sinai Medical Center	Fifth Ave. at 100th St.	241-6500	17
National Jewish Center For Immunology	450 Seventh Ave.	868-3062	9
National Jewish Center For Immunology & Respiratory Medicine	535 Fifth Ave.	297-0857	12
New York Eye & Ear Infirmary	310 E. 14th St.	979-4000	6, 10
New York Foundling Hospital	590 Ave. of the Americas	633-9300	9
New York Foundling Hospital	546 W. 153rd St.	862-7975	21
New York Hospital - Cornell Medical Center	525 E. 68th St.	746-5454	15
North General Hospital	1879 Madison Ave.	423-4000	20
NYU Downtown Hospital	170 William St.	312-5000	3
NYU Medical Center: Tisch Hospital	560 First Ave.	263-7300	10
Renaissance Health Care Network	215 W. 125th St.	932-6500	19
Roosevelt Hospital Center	1000 Tenth Ave.	523-4000	11
St. Clare's Family Health Center	350 W. 51st St.	265-8950	11, 12
St. Clare's Hospital & Health Center	415 W. 51st St.	586-1500	11
St. Luke's Hospital Center	1111 Amsterdam Ave.	523-4000	18
St. Vincent's AIDS Center	412 Ave. of the Americas	604-1576	5, 6
St. Vincent's Hospital & Medical Center	153 W. 11th St.	604-7000	5
St. Vincent's Senior Health at Penn South	275 Eighth Ave.	463-0101	8, 9
The Floating Hospital	Pier 11	514-7447	1
The Paul Robeson Family Medical Center	140 W. 125th St.	316-3800	19
V. A. Hospital	408 First Ave.	686-7500	10

In addition to the regular branch system of the New York Public Library, there are several specialized "research" libraries in Manhattan. The Schomburg Center for Research in Black Culture contains an incredible amount of material relating to the history of African-Americans. The Science, Industry, and Business Library is perhaps the newest and swankiest of all Manhattan's libraries. The Library for the Performing Arts contains a wonderful archive of New York City theater on film and tape.† The Early Childhood Resource and Information Center runs workshops for parenting, and reading programs for children. And, of course, the main branch of the New York Public Library (one of Manhattan's architectural treasures designed by Carrere and Hastings in 1897) has several special collections and services, such as the Humanities and Social Sciences Library, the Map Division, Exhibition galleries, and divisions dedicated to various ethnic groups. It contains 88 miles of shelves and has over 10,000 current periodicals from almost 150 countries. You can check out the full system on-line at www.nypl.org.

Libraries	Address	Phone	Grid
115th St.	203 W. 115th St.	666-9393	19
125th St.	224 E. 125th St.	534-5050	20
58th St.	127 E. 58th St.	759-7358	13
67th St.	328 E. 67th St.	734-1717	15
96th St.	112 E. 96th St.	289-0908	17
Aguilar	174 E. 110th St.	534-2930	17, 20
Andrew Heiskell Library for The Blind	40 W. 20th St.	206-5400	9
Bloomingdale	150 W. 100th St.	222-8030	16
Chatham Square	33 E. Broadway	964-6598	3
Columbia	514 W. 113th St.	864-2530	18
Columbus	742 10th Ave.	586-5098	11
Countee Cullen	104 W. 136th St.	491-2070	22
Donnell Library Center	20 W. 53rd St.	621-0618	12, 13
Early Childhood Resource and Information Center	66 Leroy St.	929-0815	5
Epiphany	228 E. 23rd St.	679-2645	10
Fort Washington	535 W. 179th St.	927-3533	23
George Bruce	518 W. 125th St.	662-9727	18
Hamilton Fish Park	415 E. Houston St.	673-2290	7
Hamilton Grange	503 W. 145th St.	926-2147	21
Harlem	9 W. 124th St.	348-5620	19
Hudson Park	66 Leroy St.	243-6876	5
Inwood	4790 Broadway at Academy	942-2445	25
Jefferson Market	425 Ave. of the Americas	243-4334	5, 6
Kips Bay	446 3rd Ave.	683-2520	10
Macomb's Bridge	2650 A. C. Powell Jr. Blvd.	281-4900	22
Mid-Manhattan Library	455 5th Ave.	340-0833	12
Muhlenberg	209 W. 23rd St.	924-1585	8, 9
New Amsterdam	9 Murray St.	732-8186	2, 3
† New York Public Library for the Performing Arts	40 Lincoln Center Plaza	870-1630	14
Ottendorfer	135 2nd Ave.	674-0947	6
Riverside	127 Amsterdam Ave.	870-1810	14
Schomburg Center for Research in Black Culture	515 Malcolm X Blvd.	491-2200	22
Science, Industry, and Business Library	188 Madison Ave.	592-7000	9
Seward Park	192 E. Broadway	477-6770	4
St. Agnes	444 Amsterdam Ave.	877-4380	14
Terence Cardinal Cooke-Cathedral	560 Lexington Ave.	752-3824	13
Tompkins Square	331 E. 10th St.	228-4747	7
Washington Heights	1000 St. Nicholas Ave.	923-6054	23
* Webster	1465 York Ave.	288-5049	15
Yorkville	222 E. 79th St.	744-5824	15

* Closed for renovation.
†Currently closed for renovation until (tentatively) October 2001. Its archive collection of theater on film and tape may be viewed at the library's annex at 521 W. 43rd St. (870-1639) between 10th and 11th Aves.

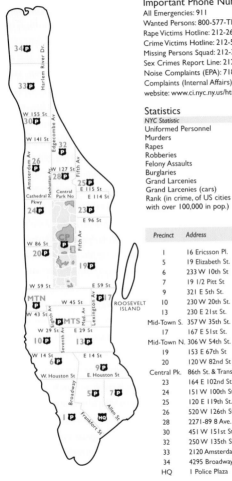

Important Phone Numbers:

All Emergencies: 911
Wanted Persons: 800-577-TIPS
Rape Victims Hotline: 212-267-7273
Crime Victims Hotline: 212-577-7777
Missing Persons Squad: 212-374-0501
Sex Crimes Report Line: 212-267-7273
Noise Complaints (EPA): 718-337-4357
Complaints (Internal Affairs): 212-741-8401
website: www.ci.nyc.ny.us/html/nypd/home.html

Statistics

NYC Statistic	2000	1999	1998
Uniformed Personnel	39,778	40,789	38,574
Murders	671	667	629
Rapes	2,067	2,088	2,479
Robberies	32,231	35,654	39,003
Felony Assaults	25,854	25,962	28,848
Burglaries	38,241	41,348	47,181
Grand Larcenies	49,381	50,138	51,461
Grand Larcenies (cars)	35,602	38,977	43,316
Rank (in crime, of US cities with over 100,000 in pop.)	160/217	165/217	166/217

Precinct	Address	Phone	Grid
1	16 Ericsson Pl.	334-0611	2
5	19 Elizabeth St.	334-0711	5
6	233 W 10th St	741-4811	5
7	19 1/2 Pitt St	477-7311	4, 7
9	321 E 5th St.	477-7811	7
10	230 W 20th St.	741-8211	9
13	230 E 21st St.	477-7411	9
Mid-Town S.	357 W 35th St.	239-9811	8
17	167 E 51st St.	826-3211	13
Mid-Town N.	306 W 54th St.	767-8400	11
19	153 E 67th St	452-0600	15
20	120 W 82nd St	580-6411	14
Central Pk.	86th St. & Transverse Rd	570-4820	C. Pk
23	164 E 102nd St.	860-6411	17
24	151 W 100th St.	678-1811	16
25	120 E 119th St.	860-6511	20
26	520 W 126th St.	678-1311	18
28	2271-89 8 Ave.	678-1611	18, 19
30	451 W 151st St.	690-8811	21
32	250 W 135th St.	690-6311	22
33	2120 Amsterdam Ave.	927-3200	23
34	4295 Broadway	927-9711	24
HQ	1 Police Plaza	374-5000	3

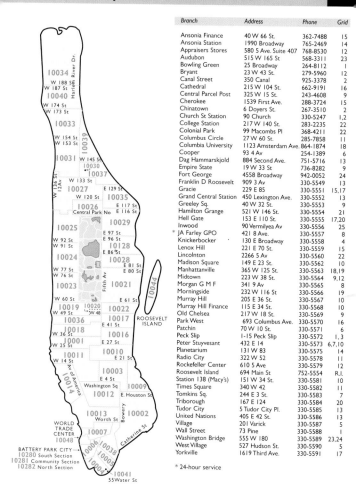

Branch	Address	Phone	Grid
Ansonia Finance	40 W 66 St.	362-7488	15
Ansonia Station	1990 Broadway	765-2469	14
Appraisers Stores	580 5 Ave. Suite 407	768-8530	12
Audubon	515 W 165 St.	568-3311	23
Bowling Green	25 Broadway	264-8112	1
Bryant	23 W 43 St.	279-5960	12
Canal Street	350 Canal	925-3378	2
Cathedral	215 W 104 St.	662-9191	16
Central Parcel Post	325 W 15 St.	243-4608	9
Cherokee	1539 First Ave.	288-3724	15
Chinatown	6 Doyers St.	267-3510	2
Church St Station	90 Church	330-5247	1,2
College Station	217 W 140 St.	283-2235	22
Colonial Park	99 Macombs Pl	368-4211	22
Columbus Circle	27 W 60 St.	285-7858	11
Columbia University	1123 Amsterdam Ave.	864-1874	18
Cooper	93 4 Av	254-1389	6
Dag Hammarskjold	884 Second Ave.	751-5716	13
Empire State	19 W 33 St	736-8282	9
Fort George	4558 Broadway	942-0052	24
Franklin D Roosevelt	909 3 Av	330-5549	13
Gracie	229 E 85	330-5551	15,17
Grand Central Station	450 Lexington Ave.	330-5552	13
Greeley Sq.	40 W 32 St.	330-5553	9
Hamilton Grange	521 W 146 St.	330-5554	21
Hell Gate	153 E 110 St.	330-5555	17,20
Inwood	90 Vermilyea Av	330-5556	25
* JA Farley GPO	421 8 Ave.	330-5557	8
Knickerbocker	130 E Broadway	330-5558	4
Lenox Hill	221 E 70 St.	330-5559	15
Lincolnton	2266 5 Av	330-5560	22
Madison Square	149 E 23 St.	330-5562	10
Manhattanville	365 W 125 St.	330-5563	18,19
Midtown	223 W 38 St.	330-5564	9,12
Morgan G M F	341 9 Av	330-5565	8
Morningside	232 W 116 St.	330-5566	19
Murray Hill	205 E 36 St.	330-5567	10
Murray Hill Finance	115 E 34 St.	330-5568	10
Old Chelsea	217 W 18 St.	330-5569	9
Park West	693 Columbus Ave.	330-5570	16
Patchin	70 W 10 St.	330-5571	6
Peck Slip	1-15 Peck Slip	330-5572	1,3
Peter Stuyvesant	432 E 14	330-5573	6,7,10
Planetarium	131 W 83	330-5575	14
Radio City	322 W 52	330-5578	11
Rockefeller Center	610 5 Ave	330-5579	12
Roosevelt Island	694 Main St	752-5554	R.I.
Station 138 (Macy's)	151 W 34 St.	330-5581	10
Times Square	340 W 42	330-5582	11
Tomkins Sq.	244 E 3 St.	330-5583	7
Triborough	167 E 124	330-5584	20
Tudor City	5 Tudor City Pl.	330-5585	13
United Nations	405 E 42 St.	330-5586	13
Village	201 Varick	330-5587	5
Wall Street	73 Pine	330-5588	1
Washington Bridge	555 W 180	330-5589	23,24
West Village	527 Hudson St.	330-5590	5
Yorkville	1619 Third Ave.	330-5591	17

* 24-hour service

Hotels	Address	Phone	Grid
Algonquin Hotel	59 W 44th St	840-6800	12
Allerton Hotel	302 W 22nd St	243-6017	8
Ameritania Hotel	1701 Broadway	247-5000	12
Amsterdam Court Hotel	226 W 50th St	459-1000	12
Amsterdam Inn	340 Amsterdam Ave	579-7500	14
Amsterdam Residence	207 W 85th St	873-9402	14, 16
Andrew's Hotel	197 Bowery	674-4938	6
Ansonia Hotel	2109 Broadway	724-2600	14
Arlington Hotel	18 W 25th St	645-3990	9
Barbizon Hotel	140 E 63rd St	838-5700	15
Beacon Hotel	2130 Broadway	787-1100	14
Bedford Hotel	118 E 40th St	697-4800	13
Beekman Tower Suite Hotel	3 Mitchell Pl	355-7300	13
Belvedere Hotel	319 W 48th St	245-7000	11
Benjamin Hotel	12 E 50th St	753-2700	12
Berkley	170 W 74th St	362-9800	14
Best Western Ambassador	132 W 45th St	921-7600	12
Best Western Inn	17 W 32nd St	736-1600	9
Best Western Inn	210 W 55th St	247-2000	12
Best Western Inn	234 W 48th St	246-8800	12
Best Western Inn	33 Peck Slip	766-6600	1, 3
Box Tree	250 E 49th St	593-9810	13
Bradford	210 W 70th St	787-5700	14
Brevoort East	20 E 9th St	254-1800	6
Bristol Plaza	210 E 65th St	753-7900	15
Broadmoor	235 W 102nd St	864-1300	16
Broadway Bed & Breakfast Inn	264 W 46th St	997-9200	12
Broadway Studio Hotel	230 W 101st St	865-7710	16
Bryant Park Hotel	40 W 40th St	869-0100	12
Cambridge Hotel	141 W 110th St	865-9110	16
Carlton	22 E 29th St	532-4100	9
Carlton Arms Hotel	160 E 25th St	679-0680	10
Carlyle Hotel	35 E 76th St	744-1600	15
Carnegie Hotel	229 W 58th St	245-4000	12
Central Park Hostel	19 W 103rd St	678-0491	16
Chalfonte Hotel	200 W 70th St	595-9400	14
Chelsea Hotel	222 W 23rd St	243-3700	9
Chelsea Inn	184 Eleventh Ave.	929-4096	8
Chelsea Lodge	318 W 20th St	243-4499	8
Chelsea Pines Inn	317 W 14th St	929-1023	5, 8
Chelsea Savoy Hotel	204 W 23rd St	929-9353	9
City Club Hotel	55 W 44th St	921-5500	12
Colonial House Hotel	611 W 112th St	662-1262	18
Comfort Inn	129 W 46th St	221-2600	12
Comfort Inn	42 W 35th St	947-0200	9
Cosmopolitan Hotel	125 Chambers St	566-1900	2, 3
Court Hotel	130 E 39th St	685-1100	13
Courtyard By Marriott	114 W 40th St	391-0088	12
Courtyard By Marriott	866 Third Ave.	644-9600	13
Crowne Plaza	1605 Broadway	977-4000	12
Crowne Plaza	304 E 42nd St	986-8800	13
Dawn Hotel	6 Saint Nicholas Pl	368-0300	5
Days Hotel	790 Eighth Ave.	581-7000	11, 12
Deauville Hotel	103 E 29th St	683-0990	10
Delmonico Hotel	502 Park Ave	355-2500	13, 15
Doral Park Avenue Hotel	70 Park Ave	687-7050	13
Doral Tuscany Hotel	120 E 39th St	686-1600	13
Doubletree Guest Suites	1568 Broadway	719-1600	12
Dumont Plaza	150 E 34th St	481-7600	10
Eastgate Tower Suite Hotel	222 E 39th St	687-8000	13
Eastside Inn	201 E 24th St	685-3854	10
Ellington Hotel	610 W 111th St	864-7500	18
Embassy Suites Hotel	102 N End Ave	945-0100	B
Empire Hotel	44 W 63rd St	265-7400	14
Essex House	160 Central Park S	247-0300	19

Hotels	Address	Phone	Grid
Euclid Hall	2345 Broadway	362-6400	14, 16
Excelsior Hotel	45 W 81st St	362-9200	14
Fitzpatrick Hotel	127 E 55th St	355-2755	13
Fitzpatrick Manhattan Hotel	687 Lexington Ave	355-0100	13
Flatotel International	135 W 52nd St	887-9400	12
Franklin Hotel	164 E 87th St	369-1000	17
Gershwin Hotel	7 E 27th St	545-8000	9
Gracie Inn	502 E 81st St	628-1700	15
Gramercy Park Hotel	2 Lexington Ave	475-4320	10
Grand Hyatt New York	109 E 42nd St	883-1234	13
Grant Hotel Europe	310 Fifth Ave.	279-1170	9
Greystone Hotel	212 W 91st St	724-1800	16
Hamilton Hotel	30 Hamilton Pl	368-5200	21
Hampshire Broadway Hotel	215 W 94th St	866-6400	16
Hampshire Hotel Suites	157 W 47th St	768-3700	12
Hayden Hall	117 W 79th St	787-4900	14
Helmsley Carlton House Hotel	680 Madison Ave	838-3000	15
Helmsley Middletowne Hotel	148 E 48th St	755-3000	13
Helmsley Windsor Hotel	100 W 58th St	265-2100	12
Herald Square Hotel	19 W 31st St	279-4017	9
Hilton	1335 Avenue Of The Americas	586-7000	3
Hilton	230 W 41st St	840-8222	12
Hilton	3 E 54th St	751-9022	12
Holiday Inn	1260 Broadway	736-3800	9
Holiday Inn	138 Lafayette St	966-8898	3
Holiday Inn	15 Gold St	232-7700	1
Holiday Inn	440 W 57th St	581-8100	11
Hotel Allerton Annex	350 W 23rd St	243-9129	8, 9
Hotel Avalon	16 E 32nd St	299-7000	9
Hotel Bryant	230 W 54th St	247-9700	12
Hotel Carter	250 W 43rd St	944-6000	12
Hotel Casablanca	147 W 43rd St	869-1212	12
Hotel Des Artistes	1 W. 67th St.	362-6700	14
Hotel Dexter House	345 W 86th St	873-9600	16
Hotel Edison	228 W 47th St	840-5000	12
Hotel Elk	360 W 42nd St	563-2864	11
Hotel Elysee	60 E 54th St	753-1066	13
Hotel Gorham	136 W 55th St	245-1800	12
Hotel Habitat	130 E 57th St	753-8841	13
Hotel Inter-Continental	111 E 48th St	755-5900	13
Hotel Inter-Continental	112 Central Park S	757-1900	19
Hotel Madison	21 E 27th St	532-7373	9
Hotel Marlton	5 W 8th St	473-5886	6
Hotel Metro	45 W 35th St	947-2500	9
Hotel Plaza Athenee	37 E 64th St	734-9100	15
Hotel Regina	202 E 13th St	982-2831	6
Hotel Riverside	350 W 88th St	724-6100	16
Hotel Riverside Studios	342 W 71st St	873-5999	14
Hotel Riverview	113 Jane St	929-0060	5
Hotel Salisbury	123 W 57th St	246-1300	12
Hotel Seventeen	225 E 17th St	475-2845	10
Hotel Shoreham	33 W 55th St	247-6700	12
Hotel St James Inc	109 W 45th St	221-3600	12
Hotel Stanford	43 W 32nd St	563-1500	9
Hotel Washington-Jefferson	318 W 51st St	246-7550	11, 12
Hotel Wellington	871 Seventh Ave.	247-3900	12
Hotel Windermere	666 W End Ave	724-8200	12
Howard Johnson	1551 Broadway	354-1445	12
Howard Johnson	215 W 34th St	947-5050	9
Howard Johnson	429 Park Ave S	532-4860	9, 10
Howard Johnson	851 Eighth Ave.	581-4100	11, 12
Hudson Hotel	353 W 57th St	554-6000	11, 12
Imperial Court Hotel	307 W 79th St	787-6600	14
Inn At Irving Place	56 Irving Pl	533-4600	10
Inn New York City	266 W 71st St	580-1900	14

Hotels	Address	Phone	Grid
Iroquois Hotel	49 W 44th St	977-2719	12
Jolly Madison Towers	22 E 38th St	802-0600	12, 13
Keller Hotel	150 Barrow St	924-3084	5
Kitano Hotel	66 Park Ave	885-7000	13
La Samanna Inn	25 W 24th St	255-5944	9
Larchmont Hotel	27 W 11th St	989-9333	6
Le Marquis Hotel	12 E 31st St	684-7480	9
Le Parker Meridien Hotel	118 W 57th St	245-5000	12
Liberty Inn	51 Tenth Ave.	741-2333	8
Lincoln Spencer Apartments	140 W 69th St	787-4700	14
Lincoln Square Hotel	166 W 75th St	873-3000	14
Loews Hotels	569 Lexington Ave	752-7000	13
Loews Regency Hotel	540 Park Ave	759-4100	15
Lombardy Hotel	111 E 56th St	753-8600	13
Lowell Hotel	28 E 63rd St	838-1400	15
Lyden Gardens Hotel	215 E 64th St	355-1230	15
Lyden House Suite Hotel	320 E 53rd St	888-6070	13
Malibu Studios Hotel	2688 Broadway	222-2954	16
Manhattan Club	200 W 56th St	707-5000	12
Manhattan East Suite Hotels	500 W 37th St	465-3690	8
Manhattan Inn	303 W 30th St	629-4064	8
Mansfield Hotel	12 W 44th St	944-6050	12
Mark Hotel	25 E 77th St	744-4300	15
Marriott Hotel	3 World Trade Ctr	938-9100	1
Marriott Hotels & Resorts	1535 Broadway	398-1900	12
Marriott Hotels & Resorts	525 Lexington Ave	755-4000	13
Marriott Hotels & Resorts	85 West St	385-4900	1
Master Apartments	310 Riverside Dr	864-1700	16
Mayfair New York Hotel	242 W 49th St	586-0300	12
Mayflower Hotel	15 Central Park W	265-0060	12
Mercer	149 Mercer St	478-7878	6
Michelangelo	152 W 51st St	765-1900	12
Milburn Hotel	242 W 76th St	362-1006	14
Milford Plaza Hotel	270 W 45th St	869-3600	11
Millenium Hilton Hotel	55 Church St	693-2001	1
Millennium Broadway	145 W 44th St	768-4400	12
Moderne Hotel	243 W 55th St	397-6767	12
Morgan's Hotel	237 Madison Ave	686-0300	9, 12
Murray Hill East Suites	149 E 39th St	661-2100	13
Murray Hill Inn	143 E 30th St	545-0879	10
New Holland Hotel	305 W 10th St	243-9730	, 6
New York Helmsley Hotel	212 E 42nd St	490-8900	13
New York Inn	765 Eighth Ave.	247-5400	11, 12
New York Renaissance Hotel	714 Seventh Ave.	765-7676	12
New York's Hotel Pennsylvania	401 Seventh Ave.	736-5000	9
New Yorker Hotel	481 Eighth Ave.	971-0101	8, 9
Newton Hotel Corp	2528 Broadway	678-6500	16
Novotel New York Hotel	226 W 52nd St	315-0100	12
Off Soho Suites Hotel	11 Rivington St	353-0860	6
Olcott Hotel	27 W 72nd St	877-4200	14
Omni Berkshire	16 E 52nd St	888-4705	12
Orleans	100 W 80th St	362-5500	14
Paramount Hotel	235 W 46th St	764-5500	12
Park Central Hotel	870 Seventh Ave.	247-8000	12
Park Lane Helmsley Hotel	36 Central Park S	371-4000	19
Park Royal Hotel	23 W 73rd St	496-5000	14
Park South Hotel	124 E 28th St	448-0888	10
Park West Studios	465 Central Park W	866-1880	12
Parkview Studio Hotel	55 W 110th St	369-3340	16
Peninsula New York Hotel	700 Fifth Ave.	956-2888	12
Pennington Hotel	316 W 95th St	222-9191	16
Phillips Club	155 W 66th St	835-8800	14

Hotels	Address	Phone	Grid
Pickwick Arms Hotel	230 E 51st St	355-0300	13
Pierre Hotel	2 E 61st St	838-8000	15
Pioneer Hotel	341 Broome St	226-1482	3, 6
Plaza Fifty Suite Hotel	155 E 50th St	751-5710	13
Plaza Hotel	19 W 58th St	546-5456	12
Portland Square Hotel	132 W 47th St	382-0600	12
Prince Hotel	220 Bowery	226-6564	6
Quality Hotel	3 E 40th St	447-1500	12
Quality Inn	161 Lexington Ave	545-1800	10
Radisson Hotel	511 Lexington Ave	755-4400	13
Ramada Inn	700 Eighth Ave.	536-2200	11, 12
Regent Wall Street Hotel	55 Wall St	845-8600	1
Rihga Royal Hotel	151 W 54th St	468-8888	12
Riverside Inn	319 W 94th St	316-0656	16
Riverside Tower Hotel	80 Riverside Dr	877-5200	14
Roger Smith Hotel	501 Lexington Ave	755-1400	13
Roger Williams Hotel	131 Madison Ave	448-7000	9
Roosevelt Hotel	45 E 45th St	661-9600	12
Royalton Hotel	44 W 44th St	869-4400	12
San Carlos Hotel	150 E 50th St	755-1800	13
Senton Hotel	39 W 27th St	684-5800	9
Seton Hotel	144 E 40th St	889-5301	13
Shelburne	303 Lexington Ave	689-5200	13
Sheraton	45 Park Ave	685-7676	9, 10
Sheraton	790 Seventh Ave.	621-8500	12
Sheraton	811 Seventh Ave.	581-1000	12
Sherry Netherland Hotel	781 Fifth Ave.	355-2800	12, 15
Skyline Hotel	725 Tenth Ave.	586-3400	11
Sleep Inn	69 W 38th St	840-2019	12
Sofitel	45 W 44th St	354-8844	12
Soho Grand Hotel	310 W Broadway	965-3000	2
Southgate Tower Suite Hotel	371 Seventh Ave.	563-1800	9
St Marks Hotel	2 Saint Marks Pl	674-2192	5
St Regis	2 E 55th St	753-4500	12
Stanhope	995 Fifth Ave.	774-1234	15
Star Hotel	302 W 30th St	695-1616	8
Starwood Hotel & Resorts	650 Fifth Ave.	977-5720	12
Stratford Arms Hotel	117 W 70th St	877-9400	14
Sunshine Hotel	241 Bowery	674-3445	6
Surrey Suite Hotel	20 E 76th St	288-3700	15
Sutton Hotel	330 E 56th St	752-8888	13
Swissotel	440 Park Ave	421-0900	13
Time Hotel	224 W 49th St	768-3700	12
Times Square	255 W 43rd St	354-7900	12
Travelers Hotel	274 W 40th St	382-1789	12
Tribeca Grand Hotel	25 Walker St	519-6600	2, 3
Trump International	1 Central Park W	299-1000	12
U N Plaza Hotel	1 United Nations Plz	758-1234	13
W New York	541 Lexington Ave.	755-1200	13
W Union Square	201 Park Ave. South	253-9119	9, 10
Waldorf Astoria Hotel	301 Park Ave	872-4534	13
Waldorf Towers	100 E 50th St	355-3100	13
Wales Hotel	1295 Madison Ave	876-6000	17
Wall Street Inn	9 S William St	747-1500	1
Warwick Hotel	65 W 54th St	247-2700	12
Washington Square Hotel	103 Waverly Pl	777-9515	5, 6
West End Studios	850 W End Ave	749-7104	12
West Side Branch Ymca	5 W 63rd St	875-4100	14
Westin Central Park South	112 Central Park S	757-1900	19
Woodstock House	127 W 43rd St	730-1642	12
Wyndham Hotels & Resorts	42 W 58th St	753-3500	12
Yale Hotel	316 W 97th St	666-7500	16

Selected Restaurants

Key: ❀ : Ethnic / ▲ : Top end / ❖ : Neighborhood / ☺ :Vegetarian / ✔ : Greasy / ➡ : Street food / ✪ : Late-night/24-hour
$: Under $10 / $$: $10–$20 / $$$: $20–$30 / $$$$: $30+
* : Does not accept credit cards. / † : Accepts only American Express.

Grid 1

Burritoville	20 John St.	➡	766-2020	$	Takeout Mexican.
Burritoville	36 Water St.	➡	747-1100	$	Takeout Mexican.
Cosi Sandwich Bar	54 Pine St.	➡		$*	
Cosi Sandwich Bar	55 Broad St.	➡		$*	
Daily Soup	2 Rector St.	➡		$*	
Daily Soup	55 Broad St.	➡		$*	
Daily Soup	41 John St.	➡		$*	
Le Marais	15 John St.	▲	285-8585	$$$$	Kosher.
Lemongrass Grill	110 Liberty St.	❖	962-1370	$$	Serviceable Thai.
Quartino	21 Peck Slip	❖	349-4433	$$†	Good, clean pizza & pasta.
Red	14 Fulton St.	❀	571-5900	$$	Acceptable Mexican.
St. Maggie's Cafe	120 Wall St.	❀	943-9050	$$$	

Grid 2

Alison on Dominick Street	38 Dominick St.	▲	727-1188	$$$$	Extremely intimate & romantic.
Bouley Bakery	120 W. Broadway	▲	964-2525	$$	Excellent breads & such.
Bubby's	120 Hudson St.	❖	219-0666	$$	Great atmosphere.
Burritoville	144 Chambers St.	➡	571-1144	$	Takeout Mexican.
Cafe Noir	32 Grand St.	❀	431-7910	$$$	Tapas. Open 'till 4.
Chanterelle	2 Harrison St.	▲	966-6960	$$$$	One of the greats.
Danube	30 Hudson St.	▲	791-3771	$$$$	That Bouley guy.
Il Giglio	81 Warren St.	▲	571-5555	$$$$	Stellar Italian.
Kitchenette	80 W. Broadway	❖	267-6740	$$	Great breakfast. Try the bacon.
Kori	253 Church St.	❀	334-4598	$$$	Korean.
Le Pain Quotidien	100 Grand St.	➡	625-9009	$$*	Excellent breads.
Nobu	105 Hudson St.	▲	219-0500	$$$$	Designer Japanese.
Tiffin	18 Murray St.	☺	791-3510	$$	Indian.
Yaffa's	353 Greenwich St.	✪	274-9403	$$	Cooly eclectic. Food 'till 1 a.m.

Grid 3

Ba Ba Malaysian	53 Bayard St.		766-1318	$$*	Excellent Malaysian.
Bridge Cafe	279 Water St.	❖	227-3344	$$$	Consistently good.
Cafe Noir	32 Grand St.	❀	431-7910	$$$	Tapas. Open 'till 4.
Joe's Shanghai	9 Pell St.	❀	233-8888	$$*	Great crab soup dumplings.
Kori	253 Church St.	❀	334-4598	$$$	Korean.
Le Pain Quotidien	100 Grand St.	➡	625-9009	$$*	Excellent breads.
Mandarin Court	61 Mott St.	❀	608-3838	$*	Consistent dim sum.
New York Noodle Town	28 1/2 Bowery			$*	Cheap Chinese.
Pho Viet Huong	73 Mulberry St.	❀	233-8988	$$	Very good Vietnamese.
Ping's Seafood	20 East Broadway	❀	965-0808	$$	Extremely eclectic Chinese.
Quartino	21 Peck Slip	❖	349-4433	$$†	Good, clean pizza & pasta.
Thailand Restaurant	106 Bayard St.	❀	349-3132	$$	Great, spicy Thai.
Tiffin	18 Murray St.	☺	791-3510	$$	Indian.
Vegetarian Paradise	33 Mott St.	☺	406-6988	$	A paradise indeed.
Vietnam	11-13 Doyers St.	❀	693-0725	$*	Dirt(y) cheap Vietnamese.

Grid 4

Canton	45 Division St.	▲	226-4441	$$$*	Top-shelf Chinese.
Cup & Saucer	89 Canal St.	✔	925-3298	$*	Good greasy burgers.
El Castillo de Jaqua	113 Rivington St.	❀	982-6412	$*	Great cheap Dominican.
Essex Restaurant	120 Essex St.	▲	533-9616	$$$	Great space, OK food.
Good World Bar & Grill	3 Orchard St.	❖	925-9975	$$	Friendly finger food.
Great Shanghai	27 Division St.	❀	966-7663	$$	Try the duck.
Ratners	138 Delancey St.	❖	677-5588	$$	Mostly kosher.

Grid 5

Aquagrill	210 Spring St.	▲	274-0505	$$$$	Excellent seafood.
Babbo	110 Waverly Place	▲	777-0303	$$$$	Super Mario.
Benny's Burritos	113 Greenwich Ave.	❀	727-3560	$$	A NYC Mexican institution.
Corner Bistro	331 W. 4th St.	✔	242-9502	$*	Top NYC burgers. Open 'till 4.
Cowgirl Hall of Fame	519 Hudson St.	❖	633-5133	$$	Good chicken fried steak.

Selected Restaurants

El Cid	322 W. 15th St.	✴	929-9332	$$$	Spanish/tapas.
Florent	Gansevoort St.	✿▲	989-5779	$$*	Great, great 24-hour joint.
French Roast	78 W. 11th St.	✿	533-2233	$$	Open 24 hours. Comfort food.
Home	20 Cornelia St.	✜	243-9579	$$$	There's no place like it.
Les Deux Gamins	170 Waverly Place	✴	807-7357	$$	The best french toast, period.
Lupe's East L.A. Kitchen	110 Sixth Ave.	✴	966-1326	$$*	Great cheap Cal-Mex.
Moustache	90 Bedford St.	✴	229-2220	$$*	Above-average Middle Eastern.
One If By Land, TIBS	17 Barrow St.	▲	228-0822	$$$	Exudes romance.
Po	31 Cornelia St.	▲	645-2189	$$$$	Creative Italian.
Rio Mar	7 Ninth Ave.	▲	242-1623	$$	Classic Spanish.
Taste of India	181 Bleecker St.	✴	982-0810	$$	Better Indian than anything on 6th St.
Two Boots	201 W. 11th St.	➡	633-9096	$	Cajun pizza.
Yama	38-40 Carmine St.	✴	989-9330	$$$	Sushi deluxe.

Grid 6

Aquagrill	210 Spring St.	▲	274-0505	$$$$	Excellent seafood.
Around The Clock	8 Stuyvesant St.	✿	598-0402	$$	Open 24 hours. NYU hangout.
Arturo's	106 W. Houston St.	✜	677-3820	$$	Great pizza and vibe.
Balthazar	80 Spring St.	▲	965-1414	$$$$	Simultaneously pretentious and amazing.
Baluchi's	104 Second Ave.	✴	780-6000	$$	Servicable Indian.
Ben's Pizza	177 Spring St.	✴	966-4494	$*	Decent pizza.
Blue Ribbon	97 Sullivan St.	✴	274-0404	$$$	Open 'till 4. Everything's great.
Blue Ribbon Sushi	119 Sullivan St.	✴	343-0404	$$$	Great sushi.
Boca Chica	13 First Ave.	✴	473-0108	$$	Excellent, fun South American.
Coffee Shop	Union Sq. W.	✿		$$	Open 24 hours. Diner.
Corner Bistro	331 W. 4th St.	✔	242-9502	$*	Top NYC burgers. Open 'till 4.
Dojo	14 W. 4th St.	✴	505-8934	$	Two words: soy burger.
Dok Suni's	119 First Ave.	✴	477-9506	$$$*	Excellent Korean fusion.
First	87 First Ave.	✿	674-3823	$$	The best BLT on the planet.
French Roast	78 W. 11th St.	✿	533-2233	$$	Open 24 hours. Comfort food.
Ghenet	284 Mulberry St.	✴	343-1888	$$$	Excellent, unpretentious Ethiopian.
Iso	175 Second Ave.	✴	777-0361	$$$$	Crowded Japanese.
John's of 12th Street	302 E. 12th St.	✜	475-9531	$$*	Classic Italian. Get the rollatini.
Lupe's East L.A. Kitchen	110 Sixth Ave.	✴	966-1326	$$*	Great cheap Cal-Mex.
M & R Bar	264 Elizabeth St.	✜	226-0559	$$	Pleasant neighborhood bar & grill.
Penang	109 Spring St.	✴	274-8883	$$$	Snooty but good Malaysian.
Sammy's Roumanian	157 Chrystie St.	✔	673-0330	$$$$	An experience not to be missed.
Shabu-Tatsu	216 E. 10th St.	✴	472-3322	$$	Affordable, homey sushi joint.
Taste of India	181 Bleecker St.	✴	982-0810	$$	Better Indian than anything on 6th St.
Zen Palate	34 Union Sq. E.	✴	614-9291	$$$	

Grid 7

7A	7th St. & Ave. A	✿	475-9001	$$	Open 24 hours. Great burgers.
Benny's Burritos	93 Ave. A	✴	254-2054	$	A NYC Mexican institution.
Boca Chica	13 First Ave.	✴	473-0108	$$	Excellent, fun South American.
Cafe Margaux	175 Ave. B	▲	260-7960	$$$$	Quiet, romantic French.
Dojo	24-26 St. Mark's Pl.	✴	674-9821	$$*	Two words: soy burger.
Dok Suni's	119 First Ave.	✴	477-9506	$$$*	Excellent Korean fusion.
El Castillo de Jaqua	113 Rivington St.	✴	982-6412	$*	Great cheap Dominican.
Essex Restaurant	120 Essex St.	▲	533-9616	$$$	Great space, OK food.
First	87 First Ave.	✿	674-3823	$$	The best BLT on the planet.
Il Bagatto	192 E. 2nd St.	▲	228-0977	$$$*	Packed Italian.
Katz's Delicatessen	205 E. Houston St.	✔	254-2246	$$	Great corned beef and fries.
Khyber Pass	34 St. Mark's Place	✴	473-0989	$$	Good Afghani.
Mama's Food Shop	200 E. 3rd St.	✴	777-4425	$*	Great home-cookin' take-out.
Moustache	265 E. 10th St.	✴	228-2022	$*	Excellent Middle Eastern.
Odessa	119 Ave. A	✿	253-1470	$$	Open 24 hours. Diner.
Old Devil Moon	511 E. 12th St.	✜	475-4357	$$	Good southern food. Great biscuits.
Ratners	138 Delancey St.	✜	677-5588	$$	Mostly kosher.
Takahachi	85 Ave. A	✴	505-6524	$$$	Excellent mid-range Japanese.
The Hat (Sombrero)	108 Stanton St.	✴	254-4188	$$*	Cheap margaritas.
Two Boots	42 Ave. A	➡	505-2276	$	Cajun Pizza.

Selected Restaurants

Key: ⊛ : Ethnic / ▲ : Top end / ❖ : Neighborhood / ☕ : Vegetarian / ✔ : Greasy / ➡ : Street food / ✪ : Late-night/24-hour
$: Under $10 / $$: $10–$20 / $$$: $20–$30 / $$$$: $30+
* : Does not accept credit cards. / † : Accepts only American Express.

Grid 8

Bendix Diner	219 Eighth Ave.	❖	366-0560	$$	Eclectic diner.
Bottino	246 Tenth Ave.	❖	206-6766	$$$	Good, clean Italian.
Chelsea Bistro & Bar	358 W. 23rd St.	▲	727-2026	$$$	Charming French.
El Cid	322 W. 15th St.	⊛	929-9332	$$$	Spanish/tapas.
Empire Diner	210 Tenth Ave.	✪	243-2736	$$	A Chelsea institution. 24 Hours.
Frank's Restaurant	85 Tenth Ave.	▲	243-1349	$$$$	Noisy beef-fest.
Grand Sichuan Int'l	229 Ninth Ave.	⊛	620-5200	$$	Some of the best Chinese in NYC.
Havana Chelsea	190 Eighth Ave.	➡	243-9421	$$*	Great Cuban sandwiches.
La Lunchonette	130 Tenth Ave.	▲	675-0342	$$$$	A truly great restaurant.
Moonstruck Diner	400 W. 23rd St.	✪	924-3709	$$	24-hours on weekends only.
Pacific East	318 W. 23rd St.	⊛	243-0777	$$	Chinese.
Skylight Diner	402 W. 34th St.	✪	244-0395	$	24-hour diner.
Tick Tock Diner	481 Eighth Ave.	✪	268-8444	$	24-hour diner.
Woo Chon	8-10 W. 36th St.	✪	695-0676	$$$	All-night Korean.

Grid 9

Basta Pasta	37 W. 17th St.	⊛	366-0888	$$$	Pac-rim Italian.
Bendix Diner	219 Eighth Ave.	❖	366-0560	$$	Eclectic diner.
Burritoville	264 W. 23rd St.	➡	367-9844	$	Takeout Mexican.
Cafeteria	119 Seventh Ave.	✪	414-1717	$$$	Apres-club.
Coffee Shop	Union Sq. W.	✪		$$	Open 24 hours. Diner.
Cosi Sandwich Bar	3 E. 17th St.	➡		$*	
Francisco's Centro Vasco	159 W. 23rd St.	⊛	645-6224	$$$	Fun Spanish.
Hangawi	12 E. 32nd St.	☕	213-0077	$$$$	Serene Korean.
Havana Chelsea	190 Eighth Ave.	➡	243-9421	$$*	Great Cuban sandwiches.
Kang Suh	1250 Broadway	✪	564-6645	$$$	All-night Korean. Bliss.
Kum Gang San	49 W. 32nd St.	✪	967-0909	$$$	Another late Korean paradise.
L'Express	249 Park Ave. S.	✪	254-5858	$$	Always open French bistro.
Le Madri	168 W. 18th St.	▲	727-8022	$$$$	Chelsea Tuscan Class.
Mesa Grill	102 Fifth Ave.	▲	807-7400	$$$$	Southwest heaven.
Old Town Bar	45 E. 18th St.	❖	529-6732	$$	Good, cheap burgers.
Pacific East	318 W. 23rd St.	⊛	243-0777	$$	Chinese.
Park Avenue Country Club	381 Park Ave. S	v	685-3636	$$	Somewhat bearable sports bar.
Patria	250 Park Ave. S	▲	777-6211	$$$$	
Periyali	35 W. 20th St.	▲	463-7890	$$$	Upscale Greek.
Tick Tock Diner	481 Eighth Ave.	✪	268-8444	$	24-hour diner.
Toledo	6 E. 36th St.	▲	696-5036	$$$$	Classy Spanish.
Union Square Cafe	21 E. 16th St.	▲	243-4020	$$$$	
Zen Palate	34 Union Sq. E.	☕	614-9291	$$$	Tasty tofu.

Grid 10

El Parador Cafe	325 E. 34th St.	⊛	679-6812	$$$	Friendly Spanish.
Gramercy Restaurant	184 Third Ave.	✪	982-2121	$$	Open 24 hours. Diner.
I Trulli	122 E. 27th St.	▲	481-7372	$$$	Italian. Great garden.
Jackson Hole	521 Third Ave.	✔	679-3264	$$	Extremely large burgers.
Jai Ya Thai	396 Third Ave.	⊛	889-1330	$$	Inventive, spicy Thai.
L'Express	249 Park Ave. S.	✪	254-5858	$$	Always open French bistro.
Old San Juan	462 Second Ave.		779-9360	$$	Good, cheap Puerto Rican.
Park Avenue Country Club	381 Park Ave. S	❖	685-3636	$$	Somewhat bearable sports bar.
Patria	250 Park Ave. S	▲	777-6211	$$$$	
Pete's Tavern	129 E. 18th St.	❖	473-7676	$$	Classic tavern.
Pongal	110 Lexington Ave.	☕	696-9458	$$	Possibly NY's best Indian.
Pongsri Thai	311 Second Ave.	⊛	477-4100	$$	Great, spicy Thai.
Sarge's Deli	548 Third Ave.	✪	679-0442	$$	Open 24 hours. Jewish deli.
Sonia Rose	150 E. 34th St.	▲	545-1777	$$$$	
Tatany	380 Third Ave.	⊛	686-1871	$$$	Japanese.
Union Pacific	111 E. 22nd St.	▲	995-8500	$$$$	
Verbena	54 Irving Place	▲	260-5454	$$$$	
Water Club	500 E. 30th St.	▲	683-3333	$$$$	Romantic, good brunch.
Yama	122 E. 17th St.	⊛	475-0969	$$$	Sushi deluxe.
Zen Palate	34 Union Sq. E.	☕	614-9291	$$$	Tasty tofu.

Grid 11

Afghan Kebab House	764 Ninth Ave.	✺	307-1612	$$	Great kebabs.
Baluchi's	240 W. 56th St.	✺	397-0707	$$	Slightly above-average Indian.
Burritoville	625 Ninth Ave.	➡	333-5352	$	Takeout Mexican.
Burritoville	352 W. 39th St.	✺	563-9088	$	Takeout Mexican.
Churruscaria Plataforma	316 W. 49th St.	✺	245-0505	$$$$	Popular but uneven Brazilian.
Hallo Berlin	402 W. 51st St.	✺	541-6248	$$	Indeed the best wurst.
Island Burgers & Shakes	766 Ninth Ave.	✔	307-7934	$$*	Aptly named.
Jezebel	630 Ninth Ave.	❖	582-1045	$$$	Southern charm.
Joe Allen	326 W. 46th St.	❖	581-6464	$$$	
Les Sans Culottes	347 W. 46th St.	❖	247-4284	$$$	Friendly French.
Meskerem	468 W. 47th St.	✺	664-0520	$$	Standard Ethiopian.
Old San Juan	765 Ninth Ave.	✺	262-6761	$$	Good, cheap Puerto Rican.
Orso	322 W. 46th St.	▲	489-7212	$$$$	
Pongsri Thai	244 W. 48th St.	▲	582-3392	$$	Great, spicy Thai.
Sandwich Planet	534 Ninth Ave.	➡	273-9768	$*	
Soul Cafe	444 W. 42nd St.	✺	244-7685	$$$	
Zen Palate	663 Ninth Ave.	✺	582-1669	$$$	Tasty tofu.

Grid 12

'21' Club	21 W. 52nd St.	▲	582-7200	$$$$	Old, clubby New York.
Aquavit	13 W. 54th St.	▲	307-7311	$$$$	Top-drawer Scandinavian.
Baluchi's	240 W. 56th St.	✺	397-0707	$$	Slightly above-average Indian.
Carnegie Deli	854 Seventh Ave.		757-2245	$$$*	Still good.
Cosi Sandwich Bar	38 E. 45th St.	➡		$*	
Cosi Sandwich Bar	1633 Broadway	➡		$*	
Cosi Sandwich Bar	61 W. 48th St.	➡		$*	
Cosi Sandwich Bar	11 W. 42nd St.	➡		$*	
Joe Allen	326 W. 46th St.	❖	581-6464	$$$	
Les Sans Culottes	347 W. 46th St.	❖	247-4284	$$$	Friendly French.
Nation Restaurant & Bar	12 W. 45th St.	▲	391-8053	$$$$	Loud, pretentious, good.
Orso	322 W. 46th St.	▲	489-7212	$$$$	
Pongsri Thai	244 W. 48th St.	▲	582-3392	$$	Great, spicy Thai.
Redeye Grill	890 Seventh Ave.	❖	541-9000	$$$	Sprawling and diverse.
Virgil's Real BBQ	152 W. 44th St.	▲	921-9494	$$$	It's real.

Grid 13

An American Place	565 Lexington Ave.		888-5650	$$$$	
Chianti	1043 Second Ave.	▲	980-8686	$$$	Nice, relaxed Italian.
Clarke's P.J.	915 Third Ave.	❖	759-1650	$$$	Pub grub.
Cosi Sandwich Bar	60 E. 56th St.	➡		$*	
Cosi Sandwich Bar	165 E. 52nd St.	➡		$*	
Dawat	210 E. 58th St.	✺	355-7555	$$$$	Top-end Indian.
Docks Oyster Bar	633 Third Ave.	❖	986-8080	$$$	Consistently good seafood.
Felidia	243 E. 58th St.	▲	758-1479	$$$$	Top Northern Italian.
Four Seasons	99 E. 52nd St.	▲	754-9494	$$$$	Designer everything.
Lutece	249 E. 50th St.	▲	752-2225	$$$$	$32 prix fixe lunch.
March	405 E. 58th St.	▲	754-6272	$$$$	Lovely.
Menchanko-tei	131 E. 45th St.	❖	986-6805	$$	Japanese noodle shop.
Oyster Bar	Lower Level	▲	490-6650	$$$	Sit at the counter.
Palm	837 Second Ave.	▲	687-2953	$$$$	Steak.
Rosa Mexicano	1063 First Ave.	▲	977-7700	$$$$	Inventive Mexican. Great guac.
Sarge's Deli	548 Third Ave.	✪	679-0442	$$	Open 24 hours. Jewish deli.
Shun Lee Palace	155 E. 55th St.	▲	371-8844	$$$$	
Smith & Wollensky	797 Third Ave.	▲	753-1530	$$$$	Don't order the fish.
Sono	106 E. 57th St.	▲	752-4411	$$$$	French-Japanese fusion.
Sparks Steak House	210 E. 46th St.	▲	687-4855	$$$	If you can't get to Lugers.
Vong	200 E. 54th St.	▲	486-9592	$$$$	$38 pre-theater menu.

Selected Restaurants

Key: ⚛ : Ethnic / ▲ : Top end / ❖ : Neighborhood / 🍲 : Vegetarian / ✔ : Greasy / ➡ : Street food / ✪ : Late-night/24-hour
$: Under $10 / $$: $10–$20 / $$$: $20–$30 / $$$$: $30+
* : Does not accept credit cards. / † : Accepts only American Express.

Grid 14

All State Cafe	250 W. 72nd St.	❖	874-1883	$$	Very comfy and friendly joint.
Balducci's	155 W. 66th St.	➡	653-8320	$$	Satisfying takeout.
Baluchi's	283 Columbus Ave.	❖	579-3900	$$	Slightly above-average Indian.
Big Nick's	2175 Broadway	✔	362-9238	$$	Death by burger.
Cafe Des Artistes	1 W. 67th St.	▲	877-3500	$$$$	A fine romance.
Caprice	199 Columbus Ave.	❖	580-6948	$$$	
China Fun	246 Columbus Ave.	⚛	580-1516	$$	Cheap Chinese.
Citarella	2135 Broadway	➡	874-0383	$$	Useful takeout.
D & S Place	169 Amsterdam Ave.	➡	769-2995	$$	Excellent takeout.
EJ'S Luncheonette	447 Amsterdam Ave.	❖	873-3444	$$*	Homey diner.
Fairway Cafe	2127 Broadway	❖	595-1888	$$	When it's all too much.
French Roast	2340 Broadway	✪	799-1533	$$	Open 24 hours. Good C.
					Monsieur.
Gray's Papaya	2090 Broadway	➡	799-0243	$*	Open 24 hours. An institution.
Harry's Burrito Junction	241 Columbus Ave.	❖	580-9494	$$	
Jean Georges	1 Central Park West	▲	299-3900	$$$$	$20 prix fixe summer lunch!
John's Pizzeria	48 W. 65th St.	⚛	721-7001	$$	Quintessential NY pizza.
Josie's	300 Amsterdam Ave.	🍲	769-1212	$$	Eclectic and organic.
La Caridad 78	2197 Broadway	⚛	874-2780	$$*	Cheap Cuban paradise.
La Fenice	2014 Broadway	⚛	989-3071	$$$	Good Italian.
Lenge	200 Columbus Ave.	⚛	799-9188	$$	Serviceable Japanese.
Manhattan Diner	2180 Broadway	✪	877-7252	$	Diner.
Penang	240 Columbus Ave.	⚛	769-3988	$$$	Snooty but good Malaysian.
Picholine	35 W. 64th St.	▲	724-8585	$$$$	Go for the cheese.
Rosa Mexicano	51 Columbus Ave.	⚛	753-7407	$$$	Inventive Mexican. Great guac.
Saloon, The	1920 Broadway	❖	874-1500	$$$	Standard.
Santa Fe	72 W. 69th St.	❖	724-0822	$$	Southwestern.
Sarabeth's	423 Amsterdam Ave.	❖	496-6280	$$	Go for brunch.
Taco Grill	146 W. 72nd St.	➡		$$	Top-end Chinese.
Van West	247 W. 72nd St.	⚛	579-6828	$$	Viet-Chinese.
Vince and Eddie's	70 W. 68th St.	❖	721-0068	$$$	Cosy comfort food.
Vinnie's Pizza	285 Amsterdam Ave.	➡	874-4382	$*	Good slice pizza.

Grid 15

Afghan Kebab House	1345 Second Ave.	⚛	517-2776	$$	Great kebabs.
Atlantic Grill	1341 Third Ave.	▲	988-9200	$$$$	Seafood galore.
Aureole	34 E. 61st St.	▲	319-1660	$$$$	Beautiful and great.
Baluchi's	1565 Second Ave.	❖	288-4810	$$	Slightly above-average Indian.
Baluchi's	1149 First Ave.	❖	371-3535	$$	Slightly above-average Indian.
Brunelli's	1409 York Ave.	❖	744-8899	$$	Italian.
Canyon Road	1470 First Ave.	❖	734-1600	$$$	Southwest haven.
Daniel	60 E. 65th St.	▲	288-0033	$$$$	Great $100+ meal.
EJ'S Luncheonette	1271 Third Ave.	❖	472-0600	$$*	Homey diner.
Haru	1329 Third Ave.	❖	452-2230	$$	Sushi. Takeout recommended.
J.G. Melon	1291 Third Ave.	❖	744-0585	$$*	Burgers. Open 'till 2:30 a.m.
Jackson Hole	232 E. 64th St.	✔	371-7187	$$	Extremely large burgers. Cozy.
Jo Jo	160 E. 64th St.	▲	223-5656	$$$$	Charming.
John's Pizzeria	408 E. 64th St.	⚛	935-2895	$$	Quintessential NY pizza.
Mary Ann's	1503 Second Ave.	⚛	249-6165	$$	Good Mex, order margaritas.
Maya	1191 First Ave.	⚛	585-1818	$$$$	Top-drawer Mexican.
Our Place	1444 Third Ave.	⚛	288-4888	$$	Next level Chinese.
Park Avenue Cafe	100 E. 63rd St.	▲	644-1900	$$$$	
Penang	1596 Second Ave.	⚛	585-3838	$$$	Snooty but good Malaysian.
Post House	28 E. 63rd St.	▲	935-2888	$$$$	Good bet: steak.
Rain	1059 Third Ave.	⚛	223-3669	$$$	Pan-Asian.
Rughetta	347 E. 85th St.	❖	517-3118	$$$	Small, quiet Italian.
Serafina Fabulous Grill	29 E. 61st St.	❖	702-9898	$$	Good pizza and pasta.
Totonno Pizzeria Napolitano	1544 Second Ave.	v	327-2800	$$	Quality pizza.
Viand	1011 Madison Ave.	❖	249-8250	$$	This one closes at 10 p.m.
Viand	673 Madison Ave.	❖	751-6622	$$*	This one closes at 10 p.m.

Grid 16

Cafe Con Leche	726 Amsterdam Ave. ✸	678-7000	$$	Cuban-Dominican haven.
Carmine's	2450 Broadway	362-2200	$$$	Large-portion Italian.
Docks Oyster Bar	2427 Broadway	724-5588	$$$	Consistently good seafood.
Flor de Mayo	2651 Broadway	595-2525	$$	Cuban-Chinese-Chicken-Chow.
Gabriela's	685 Amsterdam Ave. ✸	961-0574	$$	Cheery Mexican.
Gennaro	665 Amsterdam Ave. ✸	665-5348	$$*	Crowded Italian.
Jackson Hole	517 Columbus Ave. ✔	362-5177	$$	Extremely large burgers.
Lemongrass Grill	2534 Broadway	666-0888	$$	Serviceable Thai.
Mary Ann's	2452 Broadway	877-0132	$$	Good Mex, order margaritas.
Pampa	768 Amsterdam Ave. ✸	865-2929	$$$*	Good Argentinian.
Saigon Grill	2381 Broadway	875-9072	$$	Vietnamese.

Grid 17

Barking Dog Luncheonette	1678 Third Ave.	831-1800	$$*	
Burritoville	1606 Third Ave. ▬	410-2255	$	Takeout Mexican.
Elaine's	1703 Second Ave.	534-8103	$$$$	It's still there.
Jackson Hole	1270 Madison Ave. ✔	427-2820	$$	Extremely large burgers.
Rughetta	347 E. 85th St.	517-3118	$$$	Small, quiet Italian.
Saigon Grill	1700 Second Ave.	996-4600	$$	Vietnamese.
Viand	300 E. 86th St.		$$	Open all night.

Grid 18

Le Monde	2885 Broadway	531-3939	$$	Student brasserie.
M & G Soul Food Diner	383 W. 125th St.	864-7326	$$*	
Massawa	1239 Amsterdam Ave. ✸	663-0505	$$	
Ollie's	2957 Broadway	932-3300	$$	Only if you must.
Terrace in the Sky	400 W. 119th St. ▲	666-9490	$$$$	Rooftop French.
Zula	1260 Amsterdam Ave. ✸	663-1670	$$$	Designer African.

Grid 19

Amy Ruth's	113 W. 116th St.	280-8779	$$	
Emily's	1325 Fifth Ave.	996-1212	$$	Southern heaven.
M & G Soul Food Diner	383 W. 125th St.	864-7326	$$*	
Sylvia's	328 Lenox Ave.	996-0660	$$$	Soul food heaven.

Grid 20

Andy's Colonial	2257 First Ave.	410-9175	$$	
Emily's	1325 Fifth Ave.	996-1212	$$	Southern heaven.
Patsys Pizza	2287-91 First Ave.	534-9783	$$*	The original thin-crust pizza.
Rao's	455 E. 114th St. ▲	722-6709	$$$$*	

Grid 21

Copeland's	547 W. 145th St.	234-2357	$$$	

Grid 22

Charles's Southern-Style Chicken	2841 Eighth Ave.	926-4313	$$*	
Londel's Supper Club Douglass Blvd.	2620 Frederick	234-6114	$$$	Good Southern.

Grid 23

Empire Szechuan	4041 Broadway	568-1600	$$	
Kismat	187 Fort Washington Ave. ✸	795-8633	$$ Indian.	

Grid 24

Bleu Evolution	808 W. 187th St.	928-6006	$$	Uptown bohemian. Calm.

24-Hour Services

Newsstands

	Grid
49th St. and 8th Ave.	11, 12
42nd St. and 7th Ave.	12
23rd St. and 3rd Ave.	10
3rd Ave. (34/35th Sts.)	10
6th Ave. (South of 8th St.)	5, 6
St. Marks Pl.(8th St.)/Bowery (3rd Ave.)	6
6th Ave. and 3rd St.	5, 6
2nd Ave. and St. Marks Pl.	6
Delancey and Essex Sts.	4, 7
1st Ave. and 57th St.	13
Broadway and 50th St.	11, 12
59th St. and 3rd Ave.	13, 15
2nd Ave. (60/61st Sts.)	13, 15
72nd St. and Broadway	14
76th St. and Broadway	14
79th St. and York (1st Ave.)	15
86th St. and Lexington Ave.	15, 17
1st Ave. and 63rd St.	15
Columbus Ave. and 81st St.	14
Broadway and 116th St.	18

Pharmacies

	Address	Phone	Grid
CVS	342 E. 23rd St.	473-5750	10
CVS	1400 2nd Ave.	249-5062	15
CVS	1 Columbus Pl.	245-0611	11
CVS	1223 Second Ave.	752-7703	15
Duane Reade	224 W. 57th St.	541-9708	11, 12
Duane Reade	2465 Broadway	799-3172	16
Duane Reade (*9:00 pm)	378 6th Ave.	674-5357	5, 6
Duane Reade	1279 3rd Ave.	744-2668	15
Duane Reade	485 Lexington Ave.	682-5338	13
Duane Reade (*9:00 pm)	5 WTC	912-0998	1
Duane Reade (*9:00 pm)	866 Third Ave.	759-9412	13
Duane Reade (*10:00 pm)	155 E. 34th St.	683-3042	10
Duane Reade (*9:30 pm)	401 E. 86th St.	917-492-8801	17
Duane Reade (*9:00 pm)	1231 Madison Ave.	360-6586	17
Duane Reade (*8:45 pm)	2025 Broadway	579-9955	14
Duane Reade (*10:00 pm)	24 E. 14th St.	989-3632	6, 10
Eckerd (*11:00 pm)	1299 Second Ave.	772-0104	15
Rite Aid	2833 Broadway	663-3135	16, 18
Rite Aid	408 Grand St.	529-7115	4
Rite Aid	144 E. 86th St.	876-0600	15, 17
Rite Aid (*9:00 pm)	210 Amsterdam Ave.	787-2903	14
Rite Aid (*10:00 pm)	542 Second Ave.	213-9887	10
Rite Aid	303 W. 50th St.	247-8384	11, 12

* These *stores* are open 24 hours, but the pharmacy in the store closes at this time.

Gas Stations

	Address	Grid
Amoco	Broadway and Houston	6
Amoco	8th Ave. and 110th St.	16, 18, 19
Amoco	Amsterdam Ave. and 165th St.	23
Amoco	10th Ave. and 207th St.	25
Citgo	Bowery and 3rd St.	6
Exxon	110th St. & CPW	18, 19
Gaseteria	Houston and Lafayette Sts.	6
Gaseteria	West End Ave. and 59th St.	11
Gaseteria	Broadway and 193rd St.	24
Getty	8th Ave. and 13th St.	5
Getty	10th Ave. and 20th St.	8
Gulf	10th Ave. and 23rd St.	8
Jerusalem	10th Ave. and 201st St.	25
Merit	7th Ave. and 145th St.	22
Mobil	Allen and Division Sts.	4
Mobil	6th Ave. and Spring St.	5, 6
Mobil	Houston St. and Ave. C	7
Mobil	11th Ave. and 51st St.	11
Mobil	11th Ave. and 57th St.	11
Mobil	7th Ave. and 145th St.	22
Shell	Amsterdam Ave. and 167th St.	23
Shell	Amsterdam Ave. and 181st St.	23, 24

Veterinarian

	Address	Phone	Grid
Animal Medical Center	510 East 62nd St.	838-8100	15

Car Washes

	Address	Phone	Grid
Broadway Car Wash	614 Broadway (Houston St.)	673-5115	6
Eastside Car Wash	1770 1st Ave. (92nd St.)	722-2222	17
Westside Highway Car Wash	638 W. 47th St.	757-1141	11

Car Rental

	Address	Phone	Grid
Avis	217 E. 43rd St.	593-8378	13

Garages/Repair

	Address	Phone	Grid
Yellow Box of Tin	300 Lafayette St.	925-0228	6

Delivery & Messengers

	Address	Phone	Grid
Moonlite Courier	125 E. 23rd St.	473-2246	9
City Sprint	65 W. 36th St.	687-5515	9

Gyms

	Address	Phone	Grid
Crunch (Mon. - Fri. only)	Lafayette and 4th St.	614-0120	6

Locksmiths

	Address	Phone	Grid
A Alpha Locksmith	45 Ave. A	228-1070	6, 7
A&M Locksmith	215 1st Ave.	242-4733	6, 7, 10
Aaron-Hotz Locksmith	Multiple locations	243-7166	N/A
Abbey Locksmiths	1558 2nd Ave.	535-2289	15
American Locksmiths	247 E. 50th St.	888-8888	13
ATB Locksmith & Hardware	1603 York Ave.	(800) 774-4364	15, 17
Big A Locksmith	Multiple locations	860-2400	N/A
Big John Locksmith	N/A	333-3740	N/A
CBS Locksmith	Multiple locations	410-0090	N/A
Champion Locksmiths	Multiple locations	362-7000	N/A
Citi Security Locksmiths	Multiple locations	483-9494	N/A
Eagle Master Locksmiths	43 E. 28th St.	532-1075	9, 10
East Manhattan Locksmith	160 E. 88th St.	369-9063	17
Emergency Locksmith 24 Hours	Multiple locations	369-4107	N/A
Lockmasters Locksmith	532 W. 145th St.	690-4018	21
Locksmith, Inc.	Multiple locations	319-7657	N/A
Major Locksmith	Multiple locations	799-8808	N/A
Manhattan Budget Locksmiths	Multiple locations	831-8500	N/A
Manhattan Locksmiths	2449-A Broadway	877-7787	16
Master Locksmith	Multiple locations	579-2050	N/A
Mobile Locksmith	Multiple locations	315-2020	N/A
Night and Day Locksmith	1335 Lexington Ave.	722-1017	17
Presto Lockout Service	Multiple locations	831-9667	N/A
S&L Locksmith	Multiple locations	799-9490	N/A
West Side Locksmiths	Multiple locations	564-7070	N/A

Plumbers

	Address	Phone	Grid
New York Plumbing & Heating Service	244 5th Ave.	496-9191	9
RR Plumbing (Roto-Rooter)	N/A	687-1661	N/A
Sanitary Plumbing & Heating	211 E. 117th St.	734-5000	20
Pipeline of New York	2014 2nd Ave.	267-4241	17
Express Plumbing, Heating & Gas	183 E. 104th St.	427-9000	17

Copying

	Address	Phone	Grid
ADS Copying	29 W. 38th St	398-6166	12
Copycats (Mon.–Fri. only)	216 E. 45 St.	557-2110	13
Kinko's	2872 Broadway	316-3390	18
Kinko's	16 E. 52nd St.	308-2679	12
Kinko's	191 Madison Ave.	685-3449	9
Kinko's	24 E. 12th St.	924-0802	6
Kinko's	245 7th Ave.	929-2679	9
Kinko's	13-25 Astor Pl.	228-9511	6
Kinko's	105 Duane St.	406-1220	2
Kinko's	1211 Ave. of Americas	391-2679	12
Kinko's	233 W. 54th St.	977-2679	12
Kinko's	305 E. 46th St.	319-6600	13
Kinko's	600 3rd Ave.	599-2679	13
Kinko's	100 Wall St.	269-0024	1
Metro Copying & Duplicating	222 E. 45th St.	687-6699	13
National Reproductions	130 Cedar St.	619-3800	1
National Reproductions	25 W. 45th St.	840-3091	12
On-Site Sourcing, Inc.	443 Park Ave. S.	252-9700	9
The Village Copier	420 Lexington Ave.	599-3344	13
The Village Copier	25 W. 43rd St.	869-9665	12

Post Office

	Address	Phone	Grid
JA Farley GPO	421 8th Ave.	330-5557	8, 9

Art Galleries

Some favorites: The Broken Kilometer (permanent), The Earth Room (permanent), HERE art, Edward Carter (photography), Exit Art, Broadway Windows, etc.

	Address	Phone	Grid
113 Greene Street Gallery	113 Greene St.	966-4864	6
123 Watts Gallery	123 Watts St.	219-1482	2
14 Sculptors	332 Bleecker St., Ste. K35	966-5790	5
303 Gallery	525 W. 22nd St.	255-1121	8
@304.art	526 W. 26th St.	414-1715	8
450 Broadway Gallery	450 Broadway	941-5952	2, 3
494 Gallery	494 Broadway	925-9841	6
55 Mercer Gallery	55 Mercer St.	226-8513	6
80 Washington Square East	80 Washington Sq. E.	998-5747	6
A/D	560 Broadway	966-5154	6
Abraham Lubelski Gallery	473 Broadway	274-8993	2, 3
AC Project Room	453 W. 17th St.	645-4970	8
ACA	41 E. 57th St.	644-8300	13
	2nd Floor	516-877-4460	2
Adelphi University	529 W. 20th St.	463-0164	8
Admit One Gallery	416 E. 59th St.	754-2600	13, 15
Agama	560 Broadway	226-4406	6
Agora Gallery	377 Broome St.	343-3950	3, 6
Ahra Lee Gallery	40 Wooster St.	966-0799	2
AIR Gallery	17 Cornelia St., #1C	366-5778	5
Akira Ikeda	132 Tenth Ave.	367-7474	8
Alexander and Bonin	135 W. 24th St.	989-9919	9
Allen Sheppard Gallery	291 Seventh Ave.	206-9108	9
Alp Galleries	114 Spring St.	431-9431	6
Ambassador Galleries	22 Wooster St.	941-0401	2
American Fine Arts Co.	594 Broadway	966-1530	6
American Primitive Gallery	41 E. 57th St.	935-1110	13
Ameringer/Howard Fine Art	59 Franklin St.	226-5342	2
Amos Eno	515 W. 20th St.	255-0202	8
Andre Zarre Gallery	525 W. 24th St.	627-6000	8
Andrea Rosen Gallery	516 W. 20th St.	741-8849	8
Andrew Kreps Gallery	474 Broome St.	226-7374	3, 6
Animazing Art	530 W. 22nd St.	741-8695	8
Annina Nosei	442 Sixth Ave.	942-6218	5, 6
Ansonia Window Show	558 Broadway	965-1706	6
Anton Kern Gallery	291 Church St.	431-5270	2, 3
Apex Art	51 Greene St.	965-1387	2
Arcadia Gallery	580 Broadway, Ste 1203	625-3434	6
Ariel Meyerowitz Gallery	98 Greene St.	274-1704	6
Art Alliance	50 Wooster St.	941-7995	2
Art At Format	52 Thompson St.	966-6800	2, 6
Art et Industrie	79 Walker St.	210-0473	3
Art in General	26 Grand St.	625-0490	2, 3
Art of Beauty by Linda Mason	210 Eleventh Ave.	691-5956	8
Art Resources Transfer	215 W. 57th St., 2nd Fl.	247-4510	12
Art Students League of NY	38 Greene St.	226-3970	2
Artists Space	155 Ave. of the Americas, 5th Fl.	255-9900	5, 6
Artlife	24 W. 57th St.	333-5952	12
Artsforum	547 W. 27th St.	594-1372	8
Asyl Gallery	323 W. 22nd St.	620-8103	8
Atelier A/E	40 Wooster St.	219-3183	2
Atlantic Gallery	81 Greene St.	343-9115	6
Atmosphere Gallery	526 W. 26th St.	675-9082	8
Audiello Fine Art, Inc.	787 Seventh Ave.	554-4818	12
AXA Gallery	123 W. Broadway	766-4793	2
Axel Raben Gallery	148 Spring St.	226-2262	6
Axelle Fine Arts Ltd.	453 W. 17th St.	741-2582	8
Axis Gallery	724 Fifth Ave.	767-1852	12
Babcock	453 W. 17th St., 3rd Fl.	645-7810	8
Barbara Ann Levy Gallery	515 W. 24th St.	206-9300	8
Barbara Gladstone Gallery	525 W. 22nd St., Unit 3E	462-4123	8
Barbara Greene Fine Art	41 E. 57th St.	752-5135	13
Barbara Mathes	50 W. 57th St.	581-9191	12
Baron/Boisante			

	Address	Phone	Grid
Baruch College/Sidney Mishkin Gallery	135 E. 22nd St.	802-2690	10
Baumgartner Gallery	418 W. 15th St.	633-2276	8
Beadleston	724 Fifth Ave.	581-7544	12
Beatrice Conde Gallery	529 W. 20th St.	691-9866	8
Belenky Gallery	151 Wooster St.	674-4242	6
Benedetti	52 Prince St.	226-2238	6
Bernarducci - Meisel	37 W. 57th St., 6th Fl.	593-3757	12
Bill Maynes Gallery	529 W. 20th St.	741-3318	8
Blue Heron Arts Center	123 E. 24th St.	979-5000	10, 10
Blue Mountain Gallery	530 W. 25th St.	941-9753	8
Bose Pacia Modern Gallery	508 W. 26th St.	966-3224	8
Bound & Unbound	601 W. 26th St.	463-7348	8
Bowery Gallery	530 W. 25th St.	226-9543	8
Brent Sikkema	530 W. 22nd St.	929-2262	8
Bridgewater/Lustberg & Blumenfeld	560 Broadway	941-6355	6
Broadway Windows	Broadway & E. 10th St.		6
Broken Kilometer, The	393 W. Broadway	925-9397	6
Bronwyn Keenan Gallery	3 Crosby St.	431-5083	3
Brooke Alexander Gallery	59 Wooster St.	925-4338	6
Broome Street Gallery	498 Broome St.	226-6085	3, 6
Bruce R. Lewin Gallery	136 Prince St.	431-4750	6
Bruce Silverstein	504 W. 22nd St.	627-3930	8
Caelum Gallery	526 W. 26th St.	924-4161	8
Caldwell Snyder Gallery	451 W. Broadway	387-0208	6
Camhy Studio Gallery	526 W. 26th St.	741-9183	8
Canada	359 Broadway, Basement	925-4631	2, 3
Capeluto Arts	443 Greenwich St. Studio 6F	219-8287	2
Caren Golden Fine Art	526 W. 26th St.	727-8304	8
Carlo Alessi Unpublished	157 W. 26th St.	336-9869	9
Casey M. Kaplan	416 W. 14th St.	645-7835	5, 8
Cast Iron Gallery	159 Mercer St.	274-8624	6
Cavin-Morris Gallery	560 Broadway	226-3768	6
Cecilia De Torres	140 Greene St.	431-5869	6
Center for Figurative Painting	115 W. 30th St.	736-1520	9
Ceres	584 Broadway	226-4725	6
CFM	112 Greene St.	966-3864	6
Chambers Fine Art	210 Eleventh Ave., 2nd Fl.	414-1169	8
Chappell Gallery	526 W. 26th St., #904	414-2673	8
Charles Cowles Gallery	537 W. 24th St.	925-3500	8
Chashama Gallery	135 W. 42nd St.	340-1952	12
Cheim & Read	521 W. 23rd St.	242-7727	8
Chelsea Ceramic Guild	233 W. 19th St.	243-2430	9
Chelsea Studio Gallery	515 W. 19th St.	243-6778	8
Cheryl Hazan Arts	35 North Moore St.	343-8964	2
Cheryl Pelavin Fine Art	13 Jay St.	431-3037	2
China 2000 Fine Art	5 E. 57th St.	588-1198	12
Christine Burgin	243 W. 18th St.	462-2668	9
Clementine Gallery	526 W. 26th St.	243-5937	8
Coda Gallery	472 Broome St.	334-0407	3, 6
Cornell DeWitt Gallery	547 W. 27th St.	529-8659	8
Corporate Art Associates, Ltd.	578 Broadway	941-9685	6
CRG Gallery	535 W. 22nd St.	966-4360	8, 3
Cricket Hill Gallery	416 W. 13th St., Suite 316	727-8078	5
Cristinerose Gallery	529 W. 20th St.	206-0297	8
Culture	415 W. Broadway, 5th Fl.	226-8921	6
Curt Marcus Gallery	578 Broadway	226-3200	6
Curt Marcus Gallery	578 Broadway	226-3200	6
Cynthia Broan Gallery	423 W. 14th St.	633-6525	5, 8
D-Amelio Terras Gallery	525 W. 22nd St.	352-9460	8
Dactyl	64 Grand St.	219-2344	2, 3
Dai Ichi Arts, Ltd.	24 W. 57th St.	262-0239	12
Danese	41 E. 57th St.	223-2227	13
David Beitzel Gallery	102 Prince St.	219-2863	6
David Findlay Jr. Fine Art	41 E. 57th St.	980-2650	13
David Zwirner Gallery	43 Greene St.	966-9074	2

	Address	Phone	Grid
DC Moore	8th Floor	247-2111	12
DCA Gallery	525 W. 22nd St.	255-5511	8
De Chiara Stewart	521 W. 26th St.	967-6007	8
Debra Force Fine Art, Inc.	14 E. 73rd St.	734-3636	15
Debs & Co.	525 W. 26th St.	643-2070	8
Dee/Glasoe	529 W. 20th St.	924-7545	8
Deep Dale Gallery	248 1/2 Broome St.	505-6250	5, 6
Deitch Project	76 Grand St.	343-7300	2, 3
Denise Bibro Fine Art	529 W. 20th St.	647-7030	8
Derek Eller	526 W. 25th St.	206-6411	8
DFN Gallery	176 Franklin St.	334-3400	3
Dialectica Gallery	415 W. Broadway	226-8968	6
Diane Upright Fine Arts	188 E. 76th St.	734-3072	15
Diane Villani Editions	271 Mulberry St., #3D	925-1075	8
Dieu Donne Papermill and Gallery	433 Broome St.	226-0573	3, 6
Dorfman Projects	529 W. 20th St.	352-2272	8
Dorsky Gallery	379 W. Broadway	966-6170	6
Dranoff Fine art	591 Broadway	966-0153	6
Drawing Center, The	35 Wooster St.	219-2166	2
Earth Room, The	141 Wooster St.	989-5566	6
Edelman Fine Arts	141 W. 20th St.	226-1198	9
Edition Schellmann	50 Greene St.	219-1821	2
Edlin Fine Art@Seiren Studios	601 W. 26th St., 2nd Mezz.	242-8244	8
Edward Carter Gallery	560 Broadway	966-1933	6
Edward Thorp	210 Eleventh Ave.	691-6565	8
Edwynn Houk Gallery	4th Floor	750-7070	12
Egizio's Project	596 Broadway	226-4561	6
Eleanor Ettinger	119 Spring St.	925-7474	6
Elizabeth Foundation for the Arts	323 W. 39th St., 2nd Fl.	675-1616	11
Elizabeth Harris	529 W. 20th St.	463-9666	8
Emily Harvey Gallery	537 Broadway	925-7651	6
Entree Libree	110 Wooster St.	431-5279	6
Ernst Neizvestny Studio	81 Grand St.	226-2677	2, 3
Esso Gallery	211 W. 28th St.	714-8192	9
Ethan Cohen Fine Arts	37 Walker St.	625-1250	2, 3
Exhibit A Gallery	160 Mercer St.	343-0230	6
Exit Art: The First World	548 W. Broadway, 2nd Floor	966-7745	6
Feature Inc.	530 W. 25th St.	675-7772	8
Feigen Contemporary	535 W. 20th St.	929-0500	8
Fischbach	24 W. 57th St.	759-2345	12
Fitch-Febvrel	5 E. 57th St.	688-8522	12
Florence Lynch Gallery	147 W. 29th St.	967-7584	9
Folin/Riva Gallery	529 W. 20th St.	242-3434	8
Forum	745 Fifth Ave.	355-4545	12
Foster Goldstrom, Inc.	560 Broadway	941-9175	6
Fountain Gallery	702 Ninth Ave.	262-2756	11
Franklin Bowles Galleries	431 W. Broadway	228-4200	6
Franklin Parrasch, Inc.	20 W. 57th St.	246-5360	12
Frederick Schultz Ancient Art	41 E. 57th St.	832-0448	13
Fredericks Freiser Gallery	504 W. 22nd St.	633-6555	8
Fredericks-Freiser Gallery	504 W. 22nd St.	633-6555	8
Frederieke Taylor Gallery	535 W. 22nd St., 6th Fl.	646-230-0992	8
Friedrich Petzel Gallery	535 W. 22nd St.	334-9466	8
Gagosian	980 Madison Ave.	744-2313	15
Gagosian	555 W. 24th St.	741-1111	8
Galeria Ramis Barquet	41 E. 57th St., 5th Floor	644-9090	13
Galerie Lelong	20 W. 57th St.	315-0470	12
Gallerie St. Etienne	24 W. 57th St.	245-6734	12
Gallery 24	552 W. 24th St.	414-0370	8
Gallery 292	120 Wooster St.	431-0292	6
Gallery @49	3 W. 49th St.	767-0855	12
Gallery 5	131 Spring St.	925-6200	6
Gallery 91	91 Grand St.	966-3722	2, 3
Gallery Alexie	529 W. 20th St.	741-7957	8
Gallery: Gertrude Stein	56 W. 57th St.	535-0600	12

	Address	Phone	Grid
Gallery Henoch	555 W. 25th St.	966-6360	8
Gallery Juno	568 Broadway	431-1515	6
Gallery Korea	460 Park Ave., 6th Fl.	759-9550	13
Gallery Onetwentyeight	128 Rivington St.	674-0244	4, 7
Gallery Revel	96 Spring St.	925-0600	6
Gallery Stendhal	386 W. Broadway	334-4649	6
Garth Clark	24 W. 57th St.	246-2205	12
Gary Snyder Fine Art	601 W. 29th St.	871-1077	8
Gary Tatintsian	526 W. 26th St.	633-0110	8
Gavin Brown's Enterprise	436 W. 15th St.	627-5258	8
Generous Miracles Gallery	529 W. 20th St.	352-2858	8
George Adams	41 W. 57th St.	644-5665	12
George Billis Gallery	508 W. 26th St.	645-2621	8
Geri Obler	153 E. 57th St.	917-913-4244	13
German House Gallery	871 United Nations Plaza	610-9719	13
Get Real Art	156 Fifth Ave.	741-2278	9
Gorney Bravin & Lee	534 W. 26th St.	352-8372	8
Gracie Mansion Gallery	504 W. 22nd St.	505-7055	8
Grant Gallery	484 Broome St.	343-2919	3, 6
Grant Selwyn Fine Art	37 W. 57th St.	755-0434	12
Greene Naftali	526 W. 26th St., 8th Floor	463-7770	8
Greer Gallery	81 Wooster St.	431-6025	6
Gregory Gallery	41 E. 57th St.	754-2760	13
Grey Art Gallery	100 Washington Sq.	998-6780	6
Haim Chanin Fine Arts	210 Eleventh Ave., Ste. 201	230-7200	8
Hammer	33 W. 57th St.	644-4400	12
Heller	420 W. 14th St.	414-4014	5, 8
Henry Urbach Architecture	526 W. 26th St.	627-0974	8
Herbert Arnot, Inc.	250 W. 57th St.	245-8287	11
Herbert Lust Gallery	61 Sullivan St.	925-5355	6
HEREArt	145 Sixth Ave.	647-0202	5, 6
Hirschl & Adler Galleries	21 E. 70th St.	535-8810	15
Holly Solomon Gallery	222 W. 23rd St.	941-5777	8
Howard Greenberg & 292 Gallery	120 Wooster St., 2nd Floor	334-0010	6
Howard Scott	529 W. 20th St., 7th Fl.	646-486-7004	8
I-20 Gallery	529 W. 20th St.	645-1100	8
Illustration House, Inc.	96 Spring St.	966-9444	6
Inframundo	106 Spring St.	431-7276	6
International Poster Center	601 W. 26th St.	787-4000	8
International Print Center New York	526 W. 26th St., Rm. 824	989-5090	8
Isack Kousnsky	111 Mercer St.	226-3798	6
ISE Art Foundation	555 Broadway	925-1649	6
J. Cacciola Galleries	501 W. 23rd St.	462-4646	8
Jack Shainman Gallery	513 W. 20th St.	645-8316	8
Jack Tilton Gallery	49 Greene St.	941-1775	2
Jadite	413 W. 50th St.	315-2740	11
Jain Marunouchi	24 W. 57th St.	969-9660	12
James Cohan	41 W. 57th St.	755-7171	12
James Goodman	41 E. 57th St.	593-3737	13
Jan Krugier	41 E. 57th St.	755-7288	13
Jan Van Der Donk Rare Books	601 W. 26th St.	691-5973	8
Jane Hartsook Gallery	16 Jones St.	242-4106	6
Janet Borden	560 Broadway	431-0166	6
Jason McCoy Inc.	525 W. 22nd St.	255-5959	8
Jay Grimm	505 W. 28th St.	564-7662	8
Jeffrey Coploff	526 W. 26th St.	741-1149	8
Jeffrey Ruesch Fine Art	134 Spring St.	925-1137	6
Jim Kempner Fine Art	501 W. 23rd St.	206-6872	8
Joan Prats Gallery	568 Broadway	219-0510	6
Joan T. Washburn	20 W. 57th St.	397-6780	12
Joan Whalen Fine Art	24 W. 57th St.	397-9700	12
John Elder Gallery	529 W. 20th St.	462-2600	8
John Gibson Gallery	568 Broadway	925-1192	6
John Michlin Gallery	449 W. Broadway	475-6603	6
John Stevenson Gallery	338 W. 23rd St.	5352-0070	8, 9

	Address	Phone	Grid
John Szoke Editions	591 Broadway	219-8300	6
Joseph Helman	20 W. 57th St.	245-2888	12
Julie Saul Gallery	535 W. 22nd St.	431-0747	8
June Kelly Gallery, Inc.	591 Broadway	226-1660	6
Kagan Martos Gallery	515 Broadway, Suite 5BF	343-4293	6
Katharina Rich Perlow	41 E. 57th St.	644-7171	13
Katherine Markel Fine Arts	560 Broadway	226-3608	6
Kavehaz	123 Mercer St.	343-0612	6
Kennedy	730 Fifth Ave.	541-9600	12
Kent Gallery, Inc.	67 Prince St.	966-4500	6
Kew Gallery	1010 First Ave.	813-0333	13
Kim Foster	529 W. 20th St.	229-0044	8
Kimcherova	532 W. 25th St.	929-9720	8
Kitchen Art Gallery, The	512 W. 19th St.	255-5793	8
Klemens Gasser & Tanja Grunert, Inc.	524 W. 19th St.	807-9494	8
Knickerbocker Gallery	121 1/2 Division St.	406-0187	4
Koho Gallery	64 MacDougal St.	673-5190	6
Kraushaar	724 Fifth Ave.	307-5730	12
Kravets/Wehby Gallery	529 W. 20th St.	352-2238	8
La Mama La Galeria	6 E. 1st St.	505-2746	6
Lance Fung Gallery	537 Broadway	334-6242	6
Latin Collector Art Center	153 Hudson St.	334-7813	2
Laurence Miller	20 W. 57th St.	397-3730	12
Lawrence Rubin Greenberg Van Doren Fine Art	730 Fifth Ave., 7th Floor	445-0444	12
Le Page	72 Thompson St.	966-2646	2
Lehmann-Maupin	39 Greene St.	965-0753	2
Lennon, Weinberg, Inc.	560 Broadway	941-0012	6
Leo Castelli	59 E. 79th St.	249-4470	15
Leo Kaplan Modern	41 E. 57th St.	872-1616	13
Leo Koenig	359 Broadway	334-9255	2, 3
Leonard Hutton	41 E. 57th St.	751-7373	13
Leslie Tonkonow Artworks	535 W. 22nd St.	255-8450	8
Leslie-Lohman Gay Art Foundation	127B Prince St.	673-7007	6
LFL Gallery	531 W. 26th St., 4th Fl.	631-7700	8
LiebmanMagnan	552 W. 24th St.	255-3225	8
Limner	870 Sixth Ave.	725-0999	9
Lin Weinberg	84 Wooster St.	219-3022	6
Littlejohn Contemporary	41 E. 57th St.	980-2323	13
Lo Spazio	179 Stanton St.	677-5234	7
Locus Media	594 Broadway	334-6424	6
Lombard-Freid Fine Arts	531 W. 26th St.	967-8040	8
Long Fine Art	427 W. 14th St.	337-1940	5, 8
Louis K. Meisel Gallery	141 Prince St.	677-1340	6
Lucas Schoormans	508 W. 26th St.	243-3159	8
Luhring Augustine	531 W. 24th St.	206-9100	8
Luise Ross	568 Broadway	343-2161	6
Lyonswier Packer Gallery	526 W. 26th St., #702	242-2660	8
M B Modern	41 E. 57th St.	371-2340	13
M.Y Art Prospects	135 W. 29th St.	268-7132	9
Mandes Kish	27 Greene St.	925-7850	2
Marcello Marvelli Fine Art	526 W. 26th St., #603	627-3363	8
Margaret Thatcher Projects	529 W. 20th St.	675-0222	8
Margarete Roeder Gallery	545 Broadway	925-6098	6
Marian Goodman	24 W. 57th St.	977-7160	12
Marianne Boesky Gallery	535 W. 22nd St.	941-9888	8
Mark Miller	1200 Madison Ave.	253-9479	17
Marlborough	40 W. 57th St.	541-4900	12
Marlborough Chelsea	211 W. 19th St.	463-8634	9
Martin Lawrence	457 W. Broadway	995-8865	6
Mary Boone	541 W. 24th St.	752-2929	8
Mary Delahoyd Gallery	426 Broome St.	219-2111	3, 6
Mary Ryan	24 W. 57th St.	397-0669	12
Matthew Marks Gallery	523 W. 24th St.	243-0200	8
Matthew Marks Gallery	522 W. 22nd St.	243-0200	8
Max Protech Gallery	511 W. 22nd St.	633-6999	8

	Address	Phone	Grid
Maxwell Davidson	41 E. 57th St.	759-7555	13
McKee	745 Fifth Ave.	688-5951	12
Medialia	335 W. 38th St., 4th Fl.	971-0953	11
Mela Foundation	275 Church St., 3rd Fl.	925-8270	2, 3
Mendez Masks & Sculpture	421 W. Broadway	334-4956	6
Meridian Fine Art- Max Lang, Rita Krauss	41 E. 57th St., 8th Fl.	980-2400	13
Merton D. Simpson Gallery	38 W. 28th St., 5th Fl.	686-6735	9
Messineo Wyman Projects	525 W. 22nd St.	414-0827	8
Metro Pictures	519 W. 24th St.	206-7100	8
Michael Gold Gallery	474 Broadway	625-1723	2, 3
Michael Ingbar Gallery	568 Broadway	334-1100	6
Michael Rosenfeld	24 W. 57th St.	247-0082	12
Michaelian &Kohlberg	578 Broadway	431-9009	6
Mimi Ferzt Gallery	114 Prince St.	343-9377	6
Mitchell Algus Gallery	25 Thompson St.	966-1758	2
Modern Culture at the Gershwin Hotel	3 E. 27th St.	213-8289	9
Monique Goldstrom Gallery	560 Broadway	274-8650	6
Montserrat Gallery	584 Broadway	941-8899	6
Multiple Impressions	128 Spring St.	925-1313	6
Murray Guy	453 W. 17th St.	463-7372	8
Nancy Hoffman Gallery	429 W. Broadway	966-6676	6
Nancy Margolis Gallery	560 Broadway	343-9523	6
Nathalie Karg Gallery	100 Greene St.	334-0436	6
National Sculpture Society	Park Ave. Atrium, 237 Park Ave.	764-5645	13
Neuhoff	41 E. 57th St.	838-1122	13
New Century Artists	168 Mercer St.	431-5353	6
New York Studio School	8 W. 8th St.	673-6466	6
Nexus Gallery	345 E. 19th St.	982-4712	6
Nicholas Davies Gallery	23 Commerce St.	243-6842	5
Nicole Klagsbrun	526 W. 26th St.	243-3335	8
Nikolai Fine Art	505 W. 22nd St.	414-8511	8
Nippon	145 W. 57th St.	581-2223	12
NoHo Gallery in SoHo	168 Mercer St.	219-2210	6
Nohra Haime	41 E. 57th St.	888-3550	13
Nolan/Eckman Gallery	560 Broadway	925-6190	6
O.J. Gallery	121 Spring St.	343-2706	6
O.K. Harris Works of Art	383 W. Broadway	431-3600	6
O'Hara	41 E. 57th St.	355-3330	13
One Great Jones	1 Great Jones St.	460-8640	6
Opera Gallery	115 Spring St.	966-6675	6
Orange Chicken, The	146 Reade St.	431-0337	2, 3
Organization of Independent Artists	19 Hudson St.	219-9213	2
P.P.O.W. Inc.	476 Broome St.	941-8642	3, 6
Pace Wildenstein	32 E. 57th St.	421-3292	13
Pacifico Fine Art	546 Hudson St.	462-2709	5
Painting Center, The	52 Greene St.	343-1060	2
Pamela Auchincloss	601 W. 26th St.	727-2845	8
Papp Gallery	529 W. 20th St., 4E	741-7957	8
Paris NY Studio	187 Lafayette St., 7th Fl.	334-9449	3
Parkett Editions	155 Sixth Ave., 2nd Fl.	673-2660	5, 6
Pat Hearn Gallery	530 W. 22nd St.	727-7366	8
Paul Kasmin Gallery	293 Tenth Ave.	563-4474	8
Paul Morris Gallery	465 W. 23rd St.	727-2752	8
Paul Rodgers/9W	529 W. 20th St., 9th Fl.	414-9810	8
Paula Barr New York	508/526 W. 26th St., 12th Fl.	691-9482	8
Paula Cooper Gallery	534 W. 21st St.	255-1105	8
Peder Bonnier, Inc.	420 W. Broadway	431-1939	6
Pen & Brush, Inc.	16 E. 10th St.	475-3669	6
Perimeter Gallery	526 W. 26th St., Ste. 701	675-1585	8
Perry Art Gallery	481 Washington St.	925-6796	5, 6
Perry Rubenstein	521 W. 23rd St.	206-7348	8
Pescepalla Docks	345 Greenwich St.	625-0957	2
Peter Blum Gallery	99 Wooster St.	343-0441	6
Peter Findlay	41 E. 57th St.	644-4433	13
Phoenix Gallery	568 Broadway	226-8711	6

Art Galleries

	Address	Phone	Grid
Phyllis Kind Gallery	136 Greene St.	925-1200	6
Pleiades Gallery	530 W. 25th St.	274-8825	8
Plum Blossoms Gallery	555 W. 25th St.	719-7008	8
pop international galleries	473 W. Broadway	533-0162	6
Portraits & Paintings	203 Lafayette St.	334-9626	3, 6
Postmasters Gallery	459 W. 19th St.	727-3323	8
Prince St. Gallery	530 W. 25th St.	226-9402	8
Puffin Room, The	435 Broome St.	343-2881	3, 6
R 20th Century	82 Franklin St.	343-7979	3
Rachel Adler Fine Art	1200 Broadway	308-0516	9
Radio House Gallery	601 W. 26th St.	620-7630	8
Rare	435 W. 14th St.	645-5594	5, 8
Reece	24 W. 57th St.	333-7366	12
Rehs Galleries, Inc.	5 E. 57th St.	355-5710	12
Rennie Johnson Art & Urban Architecture	210 Eleventh Ave., #401	924-1688	8
Rhonda Schaller Studio	57 Franklin St.	226-0166	2
Ricco/Maresca Gallery	529 W. 20th St.	627-4819	8
Robert Mann Gallery	210 Eleventh Ave.	989-7600	8
Robert Miller	526 W. 26th St.	980-5454	8
Robert Pardo	210 Eleventh Ave.	242-8523	8
Robert Steele Gallery	547 W. 27th St.	736-5565	8
Roger Smith Gallery	501 Lexington Ave.	319-9130	13
Ronald Feldman Fine Arts	31 Mercer St.	226-3232	2
Rosenberg + Kaufman Fine Art	115 Wooster St.	431-4838	6
Rosenberg + Kaufman Fine Art	30 W. 57th St.	431-4838	12
Rupert Goldsworthy Gallery	453 W. 17th St.	414-4560	8
Rush Arts Gallery	526 W. 26th St.	691-9552	8
S. E. Feinman Fine Arts Ltd.	448 Broome St.	431-6820	3, 6
Sacred Tattoo	365 Canal St.	226-4286	2, 3
Salander- O'Reilly	20 E. 79th St.	879-6606	15
Sally Hawkins Gallery	448 W. Broadway	477-5699	6
Salmagundi Club	47 Fifth Ave.	255-7740	6
Sandra Gering Gallery	534 W. 22nd St.	226-8195	8, 6
Sara Meltzer's	516 W. 20th St.	343-8256	8
Sarah Morthland Gallery	225 Tenth Ave.	242-7767	8
Scalo	560 Broadway	334-9393	6
Schmidt Bingham	41 E. 57th St.	888-1122	13
Scott Pfaffman Gallery	35 E. 1st St.	353-8415	6
Sculptors Guild Inc.	110 Greene St.	431-5669	6
Sean Kelly Gallery	528 W. 29th St.	343-2405	8
Sears-Peyton	210 Eleventh Ave.	966-7469	8
Senior & Shopmaker	21 E. 26th St.	213-6767	9
Sepia International	148 W. 24th St.	645-9444	9
Shakespeare's Fvlcrvm	480 Broome St.	966-6848	3, 6
Sherry French Gallery	601 W. 26th St.	647-8867	8
Silas Seandel Studio	551 W. 22nd St.	645-5286	8
Silverstein Gallery	520 W. 21st St.	929-4300	8
Skoto Gallery	529 W. 20th St.	352-8058	8
SoHo 20	545 Broadway	226-4167	6
Soho Center for the Arts	55 Mercer St.	925-0258	6
SoHo Triad Fine Arts	107 Grand St.	965-9500	2, 3
Sonnabend Gallery	536 W. 22nd St.	966-6160	8
Sono Art Gallery	639 Tenth Ave., 4S	245-1768	11
Spanierman Gallery	45 E. 58th St.	832-0208	13
Spencer Brownstone Gallery	39 Wooster St.	334-3455	2
Sperone Westwater Gallery	121 Greene St.	431-3685	6
Sragow Gallery	73 Spring St.	219-1793	6
St. Mark's Church in the Bowery	131 E. 10th St.	674-6377 x 12	6
St. Mark's Church In-The-Bowery	10th St. at 2nd Ave.	673-7603	6
Staley-Wise Gallery	560 Broadway	966-6223	6
Stark Gallery	555 W. 25th St., 2nd Floor	807-1051	8
Stefan Stux Gallery	529 W. 20th St.	352-1600	8
Steltman Gallery	41 E. 57th St., 2nd Floor	317-9200	13
Stephen Gang Gallery	529 W. 20th St.	741-7832	8
Stephen Haller Gallery	560 Broadway	219-2500	6

	Address	Phone	Grid
Stream	69 Mercer St.	226-2328	6
Stricoff Fine Art, Ltd.	118 Greene St.	219-3977	6
Stuart Parr Gallery	532 W. 20th St.	606-6644	8
Studio 18 Gallery	18 Warren St.	385-6734	2, 3
Subculture Gallery	376 Broome St.	965-9613	3, 6
Susan Inglett	100 Wooster St.	998-1938	6
Susan Sheehan	20 W. 57th St.	489-3331	12
Susan Teller Gallery	568 Broadway	941-7335	6
Swiss Institute	495 Broadway	925-2035	6
Synagogue for the Arts	49 White St.	966-7141	2, 3
Synchronicity Fine Arts	106 W. 13th St.	646-230-8199	5
Taipei Gallery	1221 Ave. of the Americas	373-1854	12
Talwar Gallery	108 E. 16th St.	673-3096	10
Tanya Bonakdar	521 W. 21st St., 2nd Fl.	414-4144	8
Tanya Bonakdar Gallery	521 W. 21st St.	414-4144	8
Tatistcheff & Co. Inc.	529 W. 20th St.	664-0907	8
Tawa Africa Art	594 Broadway	219-1313	6
Team Gallery	527 W. 26th St.	279-9219	8
Ten in One Gallery	526 W. 26th St.	604-9660	8
Terrain Gallery	141 Greene St.	777-4490	6
Thomas Korzelius Fine Art	529 W. 20th St.	206-9723	8
Thread Waxing Space	476 Broadway	966-9520	2, 3
Throckmorton Fine Art	153 E. 61st St.	223-1059	15
Tibor de Nagy	724 Fifth Ave.	262-5050	12
Tim Gleason Gallery	191 Elizabeth St.	966-5777	6
Time Is Always Now, The	476 Broome St.	343-2424	3, 6
Tobey Fine Arts	580 Broadway	431-7878	6
Tony Shafrazi Gallery	119 Wooster St.	274-9300	6
Trans Hudson Gallery	416 W. 13th St.	242-3232	5
Tribeca Fine Arts	53 Beach St.	925-2434	2
Tribeca Hall at the NY Academy of Art	111 Franklin St.	966-0300	3
Tribes Gallery	285 E. 3rd St.	674-3778	7
UFA Gallery	508-526 W. 26th St., #317	633-2735	8
Universal Concepts Unlimited	507 W. 24th St.	727-7575	8
Urban Architecture	210 Eleventh Ave.	924-1688	8
Venetia Kapernekas	526 W. 26th St.	462-4150	8
Vera Engelhorn Gallery	470 Broome St.	966-6882	3, 6
Viridian	24 W. 57th St.	245-2882	12
Visionaire	11 Mercer St.	274-8959	2
Visual Arts Gallery	137 Wooster St.	598-0221	6
Von Lintel and Nusser	555 W. 25th St.	242-0599	8
Vorpal Gallery	459 W. Broadway	777-3939	6
Walter Wickiser Gallery	568 Broadway	941-1817	6
Ward-Nasse Gallery	178 Prince St.	925-6951	6
Washington Square Windows	80 Washington Sq. E.	998-5752	6
Water Street Gallery	241 Water St.	349-9090	1
Wessel + O'Connor	242 W. 26th St.	242-8811	9
Westbeth Gallery	155 Bank St.	989-4650	5
Westwood Gallery	578 Broadway	925-5700	6
White Columns	320 W. 13th St.	924-4212	5
WhiteBox	525 W. 26th St.	727-0767	8
William Secord	52 E. 76th St.	249-0075	15
Woodward Gallery	476 Broome St.	966-3411	3, 6
Wooster Gallery	86 Wooster St.	219-2190	6
Work Space Gallery, The	96 Spring St.	219-2790	6
World Financial Center Courtyard Gallery	220 Vesey St.	945-3392	B
World Fine Art	210 Eleventh Ave.	941-8602	8, 3
Wright	41 E. 57th St.	702-0132	13
Yancey Richardson Gallery	535 W. 22nd St.	343-1255	8
York's Shona Gallery	99 Spring St.	431-7444	6
Zabriskie	41 E. 57th St., 4th Floor	752-1223	13
Zwirner & Wirth	32 E. 69th St.	517-8677	15

Clubs & Cabarets

This list of clubs and cabarets is current as of July 2001. We know it won't be by July 2002, so make sure to check your Time Out, Village Voice, New York Press, etc. for changes. We haven't separated out music clubs from dance clubs, since some places are both. Other places listed here are mainly bars, with occasional, er, "happenings."

	Address	Phone	Grid
101	101 Seventh Ave. S.	620-4000	5
1050 Lounge	735 Tenth Ave.	445-0149	11
107 West Restaurant	2787 Broadway	864-1555	16
203 Spring St.	203 Spring St.	334-3855	5, 6
219 Flamingo	219 Second Ave.	533-2860	6, 10
2i's	248 W. 14th St.	807-1775	9, 5
55 Bar	55 Christopher St.	929-9883	5
55 Grove St.	55 Grove St.	366-5438	5
667 Bar Gallery Lounge	667 Fulton St.	718-855-8558	Brooklyn
85A	85 Ave. A	673-1775	7
9C	700 E. 9th St.	358-0048	7
ABC No Rio	156 Rivington St.	254-3697	4, 7
Acme Underground	9 Great Jones St.	677-6963	6
Alchymy	12 Ave. A	477-9050	7
Alphabet Lounge	104 Ave. C	780-0202	7
Angel Bar	174 Orchard St.	780-0313	7
Anyway Cafe	34 E. 2nd St.	533-3412	6
Apollo Theatre	253 W. 125th St.	749-5838	19, 18
APT	419 W. 13th St.	414-4245	5
Aria	539 W. 21st St.	229-1618	8
Arlene Grocery	95 Stanton St.	358-1633	7
Arts at St. Ann's	157 Montague St.	718-858-2424	4
Astor Lounge	316 Bowery	253-8644	6
Aubette	119 E. 27th St.	686-5500	10
Avenue A Sushi	103 Ave. A	982-8109	7
B.B. King Blues Club	243 W. 42nd St.	997-4144	12
B Bar	358 Bowery	475-2220	6
B3	33 Ave. B	614-9755	7
Back Fence	155 Bleecker St.	475-9221	6
Baggot Inn	82 W. 3rd St.	477-0622	6
Baktun	418 W. 14th St.	206-1590	5, 8
BAMcafe	30 Lafayette Ave.	718-636-4139	Brooklyn
Bar 169	169 East Broadway	473-8866	4
Bar Code	1540 Broadway	869-9397	12
Bar d'O	29 Bedford St.	627-1580	5
Bar-B	188 Allen St.	982-5336	6, 7
Baraza	133 Ave. C	539-0811	7
Barmacy	538 E. 14th St.	228-2240	7, 10
Beard Cafe	125 Elizabeth St.	334-5120	3
Beauty Bar	231 E. 14th St.	539-1389	6, 10
Belmont Lounge	117 E. 15th St.	533-0009	10
Birdland	315 W. 44th St.	581-3080	11
Bitter End, The	147 Bleecker St.	673-7030	6
Black Betty	366 Metropolitan Ave.	718-599-0243	Brooklyn
Black Star Lounge	92 Second Ave.	254-4747	6
Blah Blah Lounge	501 11th St.	718-369-2524	Brooklyn
Blarney Star	43 Murray St.	732-2873	2, 3
Blue Angel	323 W. 44th St.	262-3333	11
Blue Note	131 W. 3rd St.	475-8592	5, 6
bOb	235 Eldridge St.	777-0588	6
Botanica	47 E. Houston St.	343-7251	6
Bottom Line	15 W. 4th St.	228-7880	6
Bouche Bar	540 E. 5th St.	475-1673	7
Bowery Ballroom	6 Delancey St.	533-2111	6
Bowlmor Lanes	110 University Pl.	255-8188	6
Brandy's Piano Bar	235 E. 84th St.	650-1944	15
Brownies	169 Ave. A	420-8392	7
Bubble Lounge	228 W. Broadway	431-3433	2
C-Note	157 Ave. C	677-8142	7
Cachette	14 Ave. B	260-7100	7
Cafe Novecento	343 W. Broadway	925-4706	2
Cafe Wha?	115 MacDougal St.	254-3706	6
Cajun	129 8th Ave.	691-6174	8, 9
Casa Mexicana	133 Ludlow St.	473-0443	7
Caviar Studios	46 Washington Ave.	718-222-9456	Brooklyn

	Address	Phone	Grid
CB's 313 Gallery	313 Bowery	254-0983	6
CBGB and OMFUG	315 Bowery	982-4052	6
Centro-Fly	45 W. 21st St.	627-7770	9
Chaos	225 E. Houston St.	475-3200	7
Charleston Bar & Grill	174 Bedford Ave.	718-782-8717	
Cheetah	12 W. 21st St.	206-7770	9
Chicago Blues	73 Eighth Ave.	924-9755	5, 9
China Club	268 W. 47th St.	398-3800	11, 12
China White	143 Madison Ave.	684-0004	9
Club New York	252 W. 43rd St.	997-9510	12
Club Privilege	565 W. 23rd St.	243-6888	8
Cock, The	188 Ave. A	777-6254	7
Connolly's Pub and Restaurant	14 E. 47th St.	867-3767	12
Context Studios	28 Ave. A	505-2702	7
Continental	25 Third Ave.	529-6924	6
Cooler, The	416 W. 14th St.	645-5189	5, 8
Copacabana	617 W. 57th St.	582-2672	11
Cornelia Street Cafe	29 Cornelia St.	989-9318	5
Cotton Club	656 W. 125th St.	663-7980	18
Coup	509 E. 6th St.	979-2815	7
Coz	511 E. 6th St.	995-8889	7
Crazy Nanny's	21 Seventh Ave.	366-6312	5
Cream	246 Columbus Ave.	712-1666	14
Cutting Room, The	19 W. 24th St.	691-1900	9
David Copperfield's	1394 York Ave.	734-6152	15
Decade	1117 First Ave.	835-5979	15
Demerara	215 W. 28th St.	643-1199	9
Dempsey's Pub	61 Second Ave.	388-0662	6
Den at Two Boots, The	44 Ave. A	254-3300	7
Denial	46 Grand St.	925-9449	2, 3
Dinerbar	1569 Lexington Ave.	348-0200	17
Don Hill's	511 Greenwich St.	334-1390	5
Double Happiness	173 Mott St.	941-1282	3, 6
Downtime	251 W. 30th St.	695-2747	9
Drinkland	339 E. 10th St.	228-2435	7
Duplex, The	61 Christopher St.	255-5438	5
Eamonn Doran	136 W. 33rd St.	967-7676	9
Eat Here Cafe Bar	145 Sixth Ave.	414-8821	5, 6
Eau	913 Broadway	673-6333	9
El Flamingo	547 W. 21st St.	243-2121	8
Elbow Room	144 Bleecker St.		6
Exit	605 W. 55th St.	582-8282	11
Exit Art	548 Broadway	966-7745	6
Experimental Intermedia	224 Centre St.	431-5127	3, 6
Fez	380 Lafayette St.	533-2680	6
Filter 14	432 W. 14th St.	366-5680	5, 8
Finally Fred's	765 Washington St.	255-5101	5
Frank's Lounge	660 Fulton St.		Brooklyn
Freddy's Bar	485 Dean St.	718-622-7035	12
Fun	130 Madison St.	964-0303	4
Galapagos	70 N. 6th St.	718-782-5188	
Garage	99 Seventh Ave.	645-0600	9
Gemini Lounge	221 Second Ave.	254-5260	6, 10
Gonzalez y Gonzalez	625 Broadway	473-8787	6
Good World	3 Orchard St.	925-9975	4
Gravity Lounge	8612 Third Ave.	718-748-5200	Brooklyn
Greatest Bar on Earth	1 World Trade Center	524-7000	1
Groove	125 MacDougal St.	254-9393	6
Guernica	25 Ave. B	674-0984	7
Halcyon	227 Smith St.	718-260-9299	
Hammerstein Ballroom	311 W. 34th St.	564-4882	8
Hannah's Lava Lounge	923 Eighth Ave.	974-9087	11, 12
Hard Rock Cafe	221 W. 57th St.	459-9320	12
Helena's	432 Lafayette St.	677-5151	6
Hi Life Bar & Grill	1340 First Ave.	249-3600	15
Hi Life Bar & Grill	277 Amsterdam Ave.	787-7199	14
Hogs & Heifers Uptown	1843 First Ave.	722-8635	17
Hush	17 W. 19th St.	989-HUSH	9
Ideya	349 W. Broadway	625-1441	2
Idlewild	145 E. Houston St.	477-5005	6
Iridium	44 W. 63rd St.	582-2121	14

Clubs & Cabarets

	Address	Phone	Grid
Irving Plaza	17 Irving Pl.	777-5005	10
Izzy Bar	166 First Ave.	228-0444	6, 7
Jack Rose	771 Eighth Ave.	247-7518	11, 12
Jack's Joint	771 Eighth Ave.	247-7518	11, 12
Jazz Gallery	290 Hudson St.	242-1063	5
Jazz Standard, The	116 E. 27th St.	576-2232	10
Jet Lounge	286 Spring St.	625-9121	5
Joe's Pub	425 Lafayette St.	539-8776	6
Kate Kearney's	251 E. 50th St.	935-2045	13
Kavehaz	123 Mercer St.	343-0612	6
Kenny's Castaways	157 Bleecker St.	473-9870	6
Kiko's	279 Church St.	219-0225	2, 3
Knitting Factory	74 Leonard St.	219-3055	2, 3
L'Amour	1546 63rd St.	718-837-9506	Brooklyn
La Belle Epoque	827 Broadway	254-6436	6
La Dolce Vita	54 W. 13th St.	807-0580	6
La Linea	15 First Ave.	592-3138	6, 7
La Nouvelle Justine	24 First Ave.	673-8908	6, 7
Lady Luci's Cocktail Lounge	2306 Frederick Douglass Blvd.	864-8760	19
Lakeside Lounge	162 Ave. B		7
Lansky Lounge	104 Norfolk St.	677-9489	7
Latin Quarter	2551 Broadway	864-7600	16
Lava	28 W. 20th St.	627-7867	9
Le Bar Bat	311 W. 57th St.	307-7228	11, 12
Le Madeleine	403 W. 43rd St.	246-2993	11
Lei Bar	139 E. 7th St.	420-9517	7
Lenox Lounge	288 Lenox Ave.	427-0253	19
Leopard Lounge	248 E. 5th St.	253-2222	6
Level X	107 N. 6th St.	718-302-3313	Brooklyn
Lion's Den	214 Sullivan St.	477-2782	6
Liquids	266 E. 10th St.	677-1717	7
Living Room, The	84 Stanton St.	533-7235	7
Lotus Music	109 W. 27th St.	627-1076	9
Lu Lu's Cafe Lounge	499 Tenth Ave.	244-4521	11
Luahn	59 Fifth Ave.	242-9709	6
Lucky Cheng's	24 First Ave.	473-0516	6, 7
Ludlow Bar	165 Ludlow St.	353-0536	7
Luna Lounge	171 Ludlow St.	260-2323	7
Lush	110 Duane St.	766-1295	2
M & R	264 Elizabeth St.	226-0559	6
Madame X	94 W. Houston St.	539-0808	6
Makor	35 W. 67th St.	601-1000	14
Manitoba's	99 Ave. B	982-2511	7
Marion's Continental	354 Bowery	475-7621	6
Maxwell's	1039 Washington St.	201-798-0406	Hoboken
Meow Mix	269 Houston St.	254-0688	5
Mercury Lounge	217 E. Houston St.	260-4700	7
Metronome	915 Broadway	505-7400	9
Michael's Pub	118 W. 57th St.	758-2222	12
Mother	432 W. 14th St.	366-5680	5, 8
Muses Cafe	8320 Third Ave.	718-745-2721	Brooklyn
Naked Lunch	17 Thompson St.	343-0828	2
Nativa	5 E. 19th St.	420-8636	9, 10
Nell's	246 W. 14th St.	675-1567	5, 6
Nicholson	323 E. 58th St.	355-6769	13
Nightingale Bar	213 Second Ave.	473-9398	6
No Moore	234 W. Broadway	925-2595	2
Nowbar	22 Seventh Ave.	293-0323	5
NV	289 Spring St.	929-NVNV	5
O'Connor's	39 Fifth Ave.	718-783-9721	Brooklyn
Octagon	555 W. 33rd St.	947-0400	8
Ohm	16 W. 22nd St.	229-2000	9
Openair	121 St. Mark's Pl.	979-1459	7
Opium Den	29 E. 3rd St.	505-7344	6
Orange Bear	47 Murray St.	566-3705	2, 3
Orchard Bar	200 Orchard St.	673-5350	7
Ozone Bar & Lounge	1720 Second Ave.	860-8950	17
Paddy Reilly's	519 Second Ave.	686-1210	10
Parkside Lounge	317 E. Houston St.	473-9257	7
Passerby	439 W. 15th St.	228-2435	8
Pete's Candy Store	709 Lorimer St.	718-302-3770	Brooklyn

	Address	Phone	Grid
Plant Bar	217 E. 3rd St.	375-9066	7
Polly Esther's	186 W. 4th St.	924-5707	5, 6
Potion	370 Columbus Ave.	721-4386	14
Pressure	110 University Pl.	255-8188	6
Pyramid	101 Avenue A	473-7184	7
Rasputin	2670 Coney Island Ave.	718-332-8111	Brooklyn
Raven Cafe, The	194 Ave. A	529-4712	7
Recess	310 Spring St.		5
Red Lion, The	151 Bleecker St.	260-9797	6
Rising, The	186 Fifth Ave.		Brooklyn
Rivertown Lounge	187 Orchard St.	388-1288	7
Rocky Sullivan's	129 Lexington Ave.	725-3871	10
Rodeo Bar & Grill	375 Third Ave.	683-6500	10
Roseland	239 W. 52nd St.	247-0200	12
Roulette	228 W. Broadway	219-8242	2
Roxy	515 E. 18th St.	645-5156	10
Rubber Monkey	279 Church St.	625-8220	2, 3
Rue-B	188 Ave. B	358-1700	7
S.O.B.'S	200 Varick St.	243-4940	5
Saci	135 W. 41st St.		12
Sala	344 Bowery	979-6606	6
Sapphire	249 Eldridge St.	777-5153	6
Serena	222 W. 23rd St.	255-4646	9
Shampu	9 Ave. A	602-2590	7
Shine	285 W. Broadway	941-0900	2
Sidewalk	94 Ave. A	473-7373	7
Siren	12 St. Mark's Pl.	995-9100	6
Slipper Room, The	167 Orchard St.	253-7246	7
Small's	183 W. 10th St.	929-7565	5
Smoke	2751 Broadway	864-6662	16
Soho Grand Hotel	310 W. Broadway	965-3499	2
Sound Factory	618 W. 46th St.	643-0728	11
Spa	76 E. 13th St.	388-1062	6
Speeed	20 W. 39th St.	719-9867	12
Splash	50 W. 17th St.	691-0073	9
St. Nick's Pub	773 St. Nicholas Ave.	769-8275	21, 22
Standard	158 First Ave.	387-0239	6, 7
Stinger Club	241 Grand St.	718-218-6662	Brooklyn
Street	14 Ave. B	260-7100	7
Supper Club	240 W. 47th St.	921-1940	12
Swim	146 Orchard St.	673-0799	4, 7
Swing 46	349 W. 46th St.	262-9554	11, 12
Tavaru	192 Third Ave.	471-9807	10
Terra Blues	149 Bleecker St.	777-7776	6
Thirteen	35 E. 13th St.	979-6677	6
Tir na nOg	5 Penn. Plz.	630-0249	9
Tonic	107 Norfolk St.	219-3006	7
Top of the Tower	Beekman Tower, 3 Mitchell Pl.	355-7300	13
Triad	158 W. 72nd St.	362-2590	14
Tribe	132 First Ave.	979-8965	6, 7
Tribeca Blues	16 Warren St.	766-1070	2, 3
True	28 E. 23rd St.	254-6117	9
Tunnel	220 Twelfth Ave.	695-4682	8
Twilo	530 W. 27th St.	268-1600	8
Twirl	208 W. 23rd St.	691-7685	9
Union Pool	484 Union Ave.	718-609-0484	Brooklyn
Up Over Jazz Cafe	351 Flatbush Ave.	718-398-5413	Brooklyn
Velvet Lounge	223 Mulberry St.	965-0439	6
Venue	505 Columbus Ave.	579-9463	16
Village Underground	130 W. 3rd St.	777-7745	5, 6
Village Vanguard	178 7th Ave. S.	255-4037	5
Vinyl	6 Hubert St.	343-1379	2
Void	16 Mercer St.	941-6492	2
Vudu	1487 First Ave.	249-9540	15
Warehouse, The	141 E. 140th St.	718-992-5974	Bronx
Webster Hall	125 E. 11th St.	353-1600	6
Westbeth Theatre Center	151 Bank St.	741-0391	5
Wetlands	161 Hudson St.	966-4225	2
Wonderbar	505 E. 6th St.	777-9105	7
Yabby	265 Bedford St.	718-384-1664	Brooklyn
Zinc Bar	90 W. Houston St.	477-8337	6

Movie Theaters

New York's movie scene has improved greatly over the past few years—new revival houses such as Cinema Classics, the Cine-Noir Film Society, and Tonic compete with outdoor venus at Bryant Park and De Salvo Park, foreign films at the French Institute and the Goethe Institute, and the latest mega-plexes at Union Square and Kips Bay. It still ain't Paris, but it's close. You can get showtimes and buy tickets for most of these theaters using 777-FILM.

	Address	Grid
92nd St. Y	Lexington Ave. at 92nd St.	17
Aaron Davis Hall	W. 135th St. and Convent Ave.	21, 18
Africa Arts Theatre Co. Inc	660 Riverside Dr.	21
AMC Empire 25	234 W. 42nd St.	12
American Museum of Natural History	Central Park West at 79th St.	14
Angelika Film Center	18 W. Houston St.	6
Anthology Film Archives	32 Second Ave.	6
Asia Society	725 Park Ave.	15
Astor Place Theatre	434 Lafayette St.	6
Bryant Park Summer Film Festival (outdoors)	Bryant Park, between 40th and 42nd Sts.	12
Cine One & Two	711 7th Ave.	12
Cinema Classics	332 E. 11th St.	6
Cinema Village	22 E. 12th St.	6
Cineplex Odeon: Beekman	1254 Second Ave.	15
Cineplex Odeon: Coronet Cinemas	993 Third Ave.	13, 15
Cineplex Odeon: Encore Worldwide	340 W. 50th St.	11, 12
Clearview's Ziegfeld	141 W. 54th St.	12
City Cinemas 1, 2, 3	1001 Third Ave.	13, 15
City Cinemas: East 86th St.	210 E. 86th St.	17
City Cinemas: Eastside Playhouse	919 Third Ave.	13
City Cinemas: Murray Hill	160 E. 34th St.	10
City Cinemas: Sutton 1 & 2	205 E. 57th St.	13
City Cinemas: Village East Cinemas	189 Second Ave.	6
Clearview's 59th St. East	239 E. 59th St.	13, 15
Clearview's 62nd & Broadway	1871 Broadway	14
Clearview's Chelsea	260 W. 23rd St.	9
Clearview's Chelsea West	333 W. 23rd St.	8, 9
Clearview's First & 62nd St.	400 E. 62nd St.	15
Clearview's Metro Twin	2626 Broadway	16
Clearview's Olympia Twin	2770 Broadway	16
Clearview's Park & 86th St. Twin	125 E. 86th St.	17
Clearview's Waverly Twin	323 Sixth Ave.	5, 6
Coliseum Theatre	Broadway at 181st St.	23, 24
Common Basis Theater	750 Eighth Ave.	11, 12
Crown Gotham Cinema	969 Third Ave.	13
Crown Theatres	712 Fifth Ave.	12
Crown Theatres	375 Park Ave.	13
Czech Center	1109 Madison Ave.	15
Fez	380 Lafayette St.	6
Film Forum	209 W. Houston St.	5
French Institute	Florence Gould Hall, 55 E. 59th St.	13, 15
Gavin Brown's Enterprise	436 W. 15th St.	8
Goethe Institute	1014 Fifth Ave.	15
Guggenheim Museum	1071 Fifth Ave.	17
Hudson Park Conservancy	Pier 54 at 13th St.	5
Hudson River Park Conservancy	Pier 25 at North Moore St.	2
Instituto Cervantes	122 E. 42nd St.	13

	Address	Grid
Japan Society	333 E. 47th St.	13
Lincoln Plaza Cinemas	30 Lincoln Plaza at Broadway & 62nd St.	14
Loew's 84th St.	2310 Broadway	14
Loews 19th St. East	890 Broadway	9
Loews 42nd Street E. Walk	42nd St. and 8th Ave. in Times Square	12
Loews Astor Plaza	44th St. between Broadway & Eighth Ave.	12
Loews Kips Bay	Second Ave. & 32nd St.	10
Loews New York Twin	1271 Second Ave.	15
Loews Orpheum	1538 Third Ave.	17
Loews State	1540 Broadway	12
Loews Tower East	1230 Third Ave.	15
Loews Village	66 Third Ave.	6
Magic Johnson Harlem USA	124th St. & Frederick Douglass Blvd.	18, 19
Makor	35 W. 67th St.	14
Manhattan Ensemble Theatre Inc.	55 Mercer	6
Manhattan Twin	220 E. 59th St.	13
Metropolitan Museum of Art	1000 Fifth Ave.	15
Millennium	66 E. 4th St.	6
Morgan Library	29 E. 36th St.	9
Museum of Modern Art	11 W. 53rd St.	12
Museum of TV and Radio	25 W. 52nd St.	12
New Federal Theatre	292 Henry	4
New Heritage Theatre Group	646 Lenox Ave.	22
New Manhattan Repertory, Inc.	1650 Broadway	12
New School	66 W. 12th St.	6
New York Public Library-Donnell Library Center	20 W. 53rd St.	12
New York Youth Theater	593 Park Ave.	15
Nova Cinema	3589 Broadway	21
NYU Cantor Film Center	36 E. 8th St.	6
Nyurican Poets Café	236 E. 3rd St.	7
Paris Theatre	4 W. 58th St.	12
Quad Cinema	34 W. 13th St.	6
Reading Entertainment	950 Third Ave.	13
Regal Battery Park City 16	102 North End Ave.	BPC
Reel Diner	357 West Street	5
Schomburg Center for Research in Black Culture	515 Malcolm X Blvd.	22
Screening Room	54 Varick St.	2
Show World	675 Eighth Ave.	11, 12
Sony Lincoln Square & IMAX Theatre	1992 Broadway	14
St. Mark's-in-the-Bowery Archives	131 E. 10th St.	6
Symphony Space	2537 Broadway	16
The Kitchen	512 W. 19th St.	8
Tonic	107 Norfolk St.	7
Tribeca Performing Arts Center	199 Chambers St.	2
Two Boots Pioneer Theater	155 E. 3rd St.	7
United Artists: 64th and 2nd Ave.	1210 Second Ave.	15
United Artists: E. 85th St.	1629 First Ave.	17, 15
United Artists: Union Square	850 Broadway at 13th St.	6
Void	16 Mercer St.	2
Walter Reade Theater	70 Lincoln Center Plaza	14
Whitney Museum	945 Madison Ave.	15
YWCA	610 Lexington Ave.	13

Museums

	Address	Phone	Grid
Abigail Adams Smith Museum	421 E. 61st St.	838-6878	15
African American Institute	833 UN Plaza	949-5666	18
African American Wax Museum	316 W. 115th St.	678-7818	19
Alternative Museum	594 Broadway	966-4444	6
American Academy of Arts & Letters	633 W. 155th St.	368-5900	21
American Bible Society Gallery and Archives	1865 Broadway	408-1236	14
American Craft Museum	40 W. 53rd St.	956-6047	12
American Geographical Society	120 Wall St.	422-5456	1
American Museum of Natural History	175-208 Central Park West at 79th St.	769-5100	14
American Numismatic Society	617 155th St. and Broadway	234-3130	21
Americas Society	680 Park Ave.	249-8950	15
Asia Society	725 Park Ave.	288-6400	15
Asian American Art Centre	26 Bowery	233-2154	3
Black Fashion Museum	155 W. 126th St.	666-1320	19
Carnegie Hall Museum	881 Seventh Ave.	903-9629	12
Chaim Gross Studio Museum	526 LaGuardia Pl.	529-4906	6
Children's Museum of Manhattan	212 W. 83rd St.	721-1234	14
Children's Museum of the Arts	182 Lafayette St.	941-9198	3
Children's Museum of the Native Americans	550 W. 155th St.	283-1122	21
China Institute	125 E. 65th St.	744-8181	15
Cooper-Hewitt National Design Museum	2 E. 91st St.	849-8300	17
Czech Center	1109 Madison Ave.	288-0830	15
Dahesh Museum	601 Fifth Ave.	759-0606	12
Dia Center for the Arts	548 W. 22nd St.	989-5566	24
Drawing Center	35 Wooster St.	219-2166	2
Dyckman Farmhouse Museum	4881 Broadway	304-9422	25
El Museo del Barrio	1230 Fifth Ave.	831-7272	17
Ellis Island Immigration Museum	Ellis Island, via ferry at Battery Park	363-7620	1
Exit Art / The First World	548 Broadway	966-7745	6
Federal Hall	33 Liberty St.	825-6870	1
Fraunces Tavern Museum	54 Pearl St.	425-1778	1
French Institute	22 E. 60th St.	355-6100	15
Frick Collection	1 E. 70th St.	288-0700	15
Goethe House	1014 Fifth Ave.	439-8700	15
Gracie Mansion	East End Ave. at 88th St.	570-4751	17
Guggenheim Museum	1071 Fifth Ave.	423-3500	17
Guggenheim Museum Soho	575 Broadway	423-3500	6
Guiness World Records Exhibit Hall	350 Fifth Ave.	947-2335	9
Hispanic Society of America	617 155th St. and Broadway	926-2234	21
ICP Midtown	1133 Sixth Ave.	860-1777	12
International Center of Photography (ICP)	1130 Fifth Ave.	860-1777	17
Intrepid Sea-Air-Space Museum	Pier 86, W. 46th St. at the Hudson River	245-0072	11
Japan Society	333 E. 47th St.	752-3015	13
Jewish Museum	1109 Fifth Ave.	423-3200	17
Lower East Side Tenement Museum	90 Orchard St.	431-0233	4
Merchant's House Museum	29 E. 4th St.	777-1089	6
Metropolitan Museum of Art	1000 5th Ave. at 82nd St.	535-7710	15

	Address	Phone	Grid
Morris-Jumel Mansion	65 Jumel Ter.	923-8008	23
Museum at the Fashion Institute of Technology	227 27th St. at 7th Ave.	217-5800	9
Museum for African Art	593 Broadway	966-1313	6
Museum of African American History and Arts	352 W. 71st St.	873-5040	14
Museum of American Financial History	28 Broadway	908-4110	1
Museum of American Folk Art	2 Lincoln Sq. (Columbus Ave. between 65th & 66th St.)	595-9533	14
Museum of American Illustration	128 E. 63rd St.	838-2560	15
Museum of Chinese in the Americas	70 Mulberry St.	619-4785	3
Museum of Jewish Heritage	Battery Park City	968-1800	BPC
Museum of Modern Art (MOMA)	11 W. 53rd St.	708-9400	12
Museum of Television and Radio	25 W. 52nd St.	621-6800	12
Museum of the American Piano	211 W. 58th St.	246-4823	12
Museum of the City of New York	1220 Fifth Ave.	534-1672	17
National Academy of Design	1083 Fifth Ave.	369-4880	17
National Museum of Catholic Art & History	30 Rockefeller Plaza	957-8866	12
National Museum of the American Indian	1 Bowling Green	668-6624	1
New Museum of Contemporary Art	583 Broadway	219-1222	6
New York City Fire Museum	278 Spring St.	691-1303	5
New-York Historical Society	2 W. 77th St.	873-3400	14
Newseum New York	580 Madison Ave.	317-7596	12, 13
Nicholas Roerich Museum	319 W. 107th St.	864-7752	16
Ocean Liner Museum	1158 Fifth Ave.	369-6076	17
Pierpont Morgan Library	29 E. 36th St.	685-0008	9
Police Academy Museum	235 E. 20th St., 2nd Floor	477-9753	10
Rose Museum	154 W. 57th St.	247-7800	12
School of Visual Arts Museum	209 E. 23rd St.	592-2144	10
Skyscraper Museum	16 Wall St.	766-1324	1
Sony Wonder Technology Lab	550 Madison Ave.	833-8100	12, 13
South Street Seaport Museum	12 Fulton St.	748-8600	1
Statue of Liberty Museum	Liberty Island, via ferry at Battery Park	363-3200	1
Studio Museum in Harlem	144 W. 125th St.	864-4500	19
The Cloisters	Ft. Tryon Park	923-3700	1
Ukrainian Museum	203 Second Ave.	228-0110	6
Whitney Museum of American Art	945 Madison Ave.	570-3676	15
Whitney Museum of American Art at Philip Morris	120 Park Ave.	878-2550	13
Yeshiva University Museum	2520 Amsterdam Ave.	960-5390	24

Theaters

Here is, as best we can figure out, all the theaters in Manhattan. The difference between "Off" and "Off-Off", you ask? Size, of course. "Off-Off" is under 100 seats, "Off" is 100-500 seats. Some favorites, though: Pearl Theater, Kraine Theater, HERE, Context, The Kitchen, P.S. 122, and, of course, the Delacorte.

Broadway	Address	Phone	Grid
Ambassador Theatre	219 W. 49th St.	239-6200	12
Apollo Theater	253 W. 125th St.	749-5838	19
Beacon Theater	2124 Broadway	496-7070	14
Belasco Theatre	111 W. 44th St.	239-6200	12
Booth Theatre	222 W. 45th St.	239-6200	12
Broadhurst Theatre	235 W. 44th St.	239-6200	12
Broadway Theater	1681 Broadway	239-6200	12
Brooks Atkinson Theatre	256 W. 47th St.	307-4100	12
Circle in the Square Theatre	1633 Broadway	239-6200	12
City Center Stage II	131 W. 55th St.	581-1212	12
Cort Theatre	138 W. 48th St.	239-6200	12
Criterion Center	1530 Broadway	764-7903	12
Ethel Barrymore Theatre	243 W. 47th St.	239-6200	12
Eugene O'Neill Theatre	230 W. 49th St.	239-6200	12
Ford Center for the Performing Arts	214 W. 43rd St.	307-4100	12
Gershwin Theatre	222 W. 51st St.	307-4100	12
Helen Hayes Theatre	240 W. 44th St.	239-6200	12
Imperial Theater	249 W. 45th St.	239-6200	12
John Golden Theatre	252 W. 45th St.	239-6200	12
Judith Anderson Theatre	412 W. 42nd St.	564-7853	11
Kit Kat Club	124 W. 43rd St.	819-0377	12
Lincoln Center's Vivian Beaumont Theatre	Broadway & 64th St.	239-6200	14
Longacre Theatre	220 W. 48th St.	239-6200	12
Lunt-Fontanne Theatre	205 W. 46th St.	307-4747	12
Lyceum Theatre	149 W. 45th St.	239-6200	12
Majestic Theater	245 W. 44th St.	239-6200	12
Marquis Theatre	211 W. 45th St.	307-4100	12
Martin Beck Theatre	302 W. 45th St.	239-6200	11
Minskoff Theatre	200 W. 45th St.	869-0550	12
Music Box Theatre	239 W. 45th St.	239-6200	12
Nat Horne Theatre	9th Ave. & 42nd St.	279-4200	11
Nederlander Theatre	208 W. 41st St.	307-4100	12
Neil Simon Theatre	250 W. 52nd St.	307-4100	12
New Amsterdam Theatre	214 W. 42nd St.	307-4100	12
New Victory Theatre	209 W. 42nd St.	239-6200	12
Palace Theatre	1564 Broadway	307-4747	12
Plymouth Theatre	236 W. 45th St.	239-6200	12
Radio City Music Hall	1260 6th Ave.	247-4777	12
Richard Rogers Theatre	226 W. 46th St.	221-1211	12
Royale Theatre	242 W. 45th St.	239-6200	12
Shubert Alley	West of Broadway, b/t 44th & 45th Sts.	302-4111	12
Shubert Theatre	225 W. 44th St.	239-6200	12
St. James Theater	246 W. 44th St.	239-6200	12
Studio 54	524 W. 54th St.	239-6200	11
The Theater at Madison Square Garden	2 Pennsylvania Plz.	307-4111	9
Virginia Theatre	245 W. 52nd St.	239-6200	12
Vivian Beaumont Theatre	Lincoln Center, 150 W. 65th St.	362-7600	14
Walter Kerr Theatre	219 W. 48th St.	239-6200	12
Winter Garden Theater	1634 Broadway	239-6200	12

Off-Broadway & Off-Off Broadway	Address	Phone	Grid
13th Street Theatre	50 W. 13th St.	675-6677	6
28th Street Theater	120 W. 28th St., 2nd Fl.	727-7765	9
29th Street Repertory Theatre	212 W. 29th St.	465-0575	9
47th Street Theater	304 W. 47th St.	265-1086	12
74A	E. 4th St. b/t Bowery & Second Ave.	475-7710	6
78th Street Theatre Lab	236 W. 78th St.	414-7717	14
Access Theater, Inc.	380 Broadway, 4th Fl.	501-3909	2, 3
Actor's Playhouse	100 7th Ave. South	239-6200	5
Actors Studio Theater	432 W. 44th St.	757-0870	11
All Souls Unitarian Church	1157 Lexington Ave.	642-5068	15
American Jewish Theatre	307 W. 26th St.	633-9797	8
American Place Theatre	111 W. 46th St.	239-6200	12
American Theatre of Actors	314 W. 54th St.	239-6200	11
Angel Orensanz Foundation Center for the Arts	172 Norfolk St.	780-0175	7
ArcLight Theatre	152 W. 71st St.	595-0355	14

	Address	Phone	Grid
Arno Ristorante	141 W. 38th St.	800-687-3374	12
Astor Place Theatre	434 Lafayette St.	254-4370	6
Atlantic Theater	336 W. 20th St.	239-6200	8
Axis Theater	1 Sheridan Sq.	807-9300	5
Bank Street Theater	155 Bank St.	633-6533	5
Barter Theatre	62 Perry St.	741-9466	5
Blue Heron Arts Center	123 E. 24th St.	358-3903	10
Blue Light Theater Co.	136 E. 13th St.	279-4200	7
Bouwerie Lane Theatre	330 Bowery	677-0060	6
Cap 21 Theatre	15 W. 28th St.	581-8896	9
Castillo Theatre	500 Greenwich St.	941-1234	5
CBGB's 313 Gallery	313 Bowery	677-0455	6
Center Stage NY	48 W. 21st St., 4th Fl.	841-0326	9
Centerfold Theater/West End Theatre	263 W. 86th St.	866-4454	16
Century Center Theatre	111 E. 15th St.	982-6782	10
Chashama	111 W. 42nd St.	981-9391	12
Chelsea Playhouse	125 W. 22nd St.	924-7415	9
Chicago City Limits Theatre	1105 1st Ave.	239-6200	15
Circle in the Square-Downtown	159 Bleecker St.	254-6330	6
Classic Stage Company (CSC Rep)	136 E. 13th St.	677-4210	6
Clemente Solo Velez Cultural Center	107 Suffolk St.	260-4080	7
Clockworks Theatre	508 E. 12th St.	614-0001	7
Club El Flamingo	547 W. 21st St.	307-4100	8
Collective Unconscious	145 Ludlow St.	254-5277	7
Community Service Council of Greater Harlem	207 W. 133rd St.	368-9314	19
Connelly Theatre	220 E. 4th St.	982-2287	7
Context	28 Avenue A	505-2702	7
Currican Theatre	154 W. 29th St., 2nd Fl.	414-8181	9
Daryl Roth Theatre	20 Union Square East at 15th St.	239-6200	9
Delacorte Theater	Central Park, 81st St.	539-8750	6
Dominion Theatre	428 Lafayette St.	674-4066	6
Douglas Fairbanks Theatre	432 W. 42nd St.	239-6200	11
Duffy Theater	1553 Broadway	695-3401	12
Duke on 42nd Street	229 W. 42nd St.	239-6200	12
Duo Theatre	62 E. 4th St.	598-4320	6
Duplex Cabaret Theatre	61 Christopher St.	255-5438	5
Educational Alliance-Mazer Theater	197 E. Broadway	780-2300	4
Ensemble Studio Theatre	549 W. 52nd St.	247-4982	11
Expanded Arts	85 Ludlow St.	253-1813	4
Flatiron Theater	119 W. 23rd St.	330-7144	9
Flea Theatre	41 White St.	226-0051	2
Fools Company Space	356 W. 44th St.	307-6000	11
Fourth Street Theatre	83 E. 4th St.	726-1561	6
Franklin Furnace	112 Franklin St.	925-4671	2
Gramercy Theatre	127 E. 23rd St.	307-4100	10
Grammery Arts Theatre	138 E. 27th St.	889-2850	10
Greenwich House Theater	27 Barrow St.	541-8441	5
Greenwich Street Theatre	547 Greenwich St.	255-3940	5
Grove Street Playhouse	39 Grove St.	741-6436	5
Hamlet of Bank St.	155 Bank St.	989-6445	5
Harold Clurman Theatre	412 W. 42nd St.	594-2370	11
Harry DeJur Playhouse	466 Grand St.	353-1176	4
HERE	145 Sixth Ave.	647-0202	6
House of Candies	99 Stanton Street	420-1466	7
Hudson Guild	441 W. 26th St.	760-9800	8
Ibis Supper Club	321 W. 44th St.	239-6200	11
Impact Theatre Company	612-614 Eighth Ave.	592-3172	11, 12
Independent Art Here	145 Spring St.	647-0202	6
Intar Theatre	420 W. 42nd St.	279-4200	11
Interlude Theatre	45 W. 21st St.	388-2260	9
Irish Arts Center	553 W. 51st St.	581-6125	11
Irish Repertory Theatre	133 W. 22nd St.	727-2737	9
J.E.T. Theatre	134 W. 26th St., 7th Fl.	647-8949	9
Jane Street Theatre at the Hotel Riverview Ballroom	113 Jane St.	239-6200	5
Jean Cocteau Repertory	330 Bowery	677-0060	5
John Houseman Theater	450 W. 42nd St.	239-6200	11
John Montgomery Theater	134 W. 26th St., Studio 1202	627-7076	9
Joseph Papp Public Theater	425 Lafayette St.	539-8500	6
Kaufman 92nd YMCA	1395 Lexington Ave.	996-1100	17

Theaters

	Address	Phone	Grid
KGB	85 E. 4th St.	505-3360	7
Knitting Factory-Alterknit Theater	74 Leonard St.	219-3055	3
La MaMa ETC.	74A E. 4th St.	475-7710	6, 7
Lambs Theater	130 W. 44th St.	997-1780	13
Lark Theatre Studio	939 8th Ave., 2nd Fl.	246-2676	16
Lillie Blake Auditorium at P.S. 6	45 E. 81st St.	737-9774	15
Lucille Lortel Theatre	121 Christopher St.	239-6200	6
Manhattan Class Co.	120 W. 28th St.	727-7722	9
Manhattan Theatre Club	311 W. 43rd St.	399-3000	11
Manhattan Theatre Club Stage I	131 W. 55th St.	581-1212	12
Manhattan Theatre Club Stage II	131 W. 55th St.	581-1212	12
Manhattan Theatre Source	177 MacDougal St.	501-4751	6
Mark Goodson Theatre	2 Columbus Circle, A Level	841-4100	11, 12
Martin R. Kaufman Theater	534 W. 42nd St.	279-4200	11
Maverick Theatre	307 W. 26th St.	239-6200	8
McGinn/Cazale Theatre	2162 Broadway	279-4200	14
Medicine Show Theatre	552 W. 53rd St.	279-4200	11
Metropolitan Playhouse	220a E. 4th St., 2nd Fl.	995-5302	7
Milagro Theatre	107 Suffolk St.	886-4551	7
Miller Theater-Columbia University	200 Dodge Hall, Broadway & 116th St.	854-7799	19
Minetta Lane Theatre	18 Minetta Lane	307-4100	6
Miranda Theatre	259 W. 30th St.	268-9829	8, 9
Mitzi E. Newhouse Theater	Lincoln Center, Broadway at 64th St.	239-6200	14
Musical Theatre Works	440 Lafayette St., Space 3-D	677-0040	6
Nada	167 Ludlow St.	420-1466	4
Nada 45	445 W. 45th St.	712-6571	11
National Arts Club	15 Gramercy Park South	362-2560	10
National Black Theatre	2031-33 5th Ave.	722-3800	19, 20
Neighborhood Playhouse	340 E. 54th St.	688-3770	13
New 42nd St. Theatre	348 W. 42nd St.	712-6675	11
New York Performance Works	85 W. Broadway	566-1500	2
New York Theatre Workshop	79 E. 4th St.	239-6200	6, 7
New York Youth Theater	422 W. 57th St.	315-1737	11
Nuyorican Poets Cafe	236 E. 3rd St.	505-8183	7
Oasis Theatre	230 E. 9th St.	673-3706	7
Ohio Theater	66 Wooster St.	800-965-4827	6
One Dream	232 W. Broadway	274-1450	2
Orpheum Theater	126 2nd Ave.	477-2477	6
P.S. 122	150 1st Ave.	477-5288	6, 7
Paradise Theater	64 E. 4th St.	253-8107	5
Partners & Crime	44 Greenwich Ave.	462-3027	5
Pearl Theatre Co., Inc.	80 St. Marks Pl.	598-9802	6
Pelican Studio Theatre	750 8th Ave., Suite 601	730-2030	11
Performing Garage	33 Wooster St.	966-3651	6
Players Theatre	115 MacDougal St.	239-6200	6
Playhouse 46 at St. Clement's	423 W. 46th St.	279-4200	11
Playhouse 91	316 E. 91st St.	307-4100	17
Playwrights Horizons Theater	416 W. 42nd St.	279-4200	11
Primary Stages	354 W. 45th St.	333-4052	11
Producers Club Times Square Theatre	300 W. 43rd St.	262-2309	12
Promenade Theatre	2162 Broadway	239-6200	14
Provincetown Playhouse	133 MacDougal St.	777-2571	6
Puerto Rican Traveling Theatre	304 W. 47th St.	354-1293	11
Raw Space	529 W. 42nd St.	643-6399	11
Raymond J. Greenwald Theatre	307 W. 26th St.	633-9797	8
Repertorio Español	138 E. 27th St.	889-2850	10
Riant Theatre	161 Hudson St.	925-8353	2
Rio's Supper Club	393 Eighth Ave.	800-MURDER-INC	8, 9
Roundabout/Laura Pels Theatre	1530 Broadway	719-9300	12
Saint Clement's Church	423 W. 46th St.	246-7277	11
Saint John's Lutheran Church	81 Christopher St.	666-0176	5
Samuel Beckett Theatre	412 W. 42nd St.	307-4100	11
Sanford Meisner Theatre	164 11th Ave.	206-1764	8
Second Stage Theatre	307 W. 43rd St.	246-4422	11
Shooting Star Theatre	40 Peck Slip	791-7827	1
Signature Theatre	555 W. 42nd St.	244-7529	11
Soho Playhouse	15 Vandam St.	239-6200	2
Soho Repertory Theatre/Walker Street Theater	46 Walker St.	334-0962	2
Solo Arts Group	36 W. 17th St.	463-8732	9
St. Lukes Church	308 W. 46th St.	239-6200	11
Stand-Upstairs Theatre	236 W. 78th St.	873-9050	14

	Address	Phone	Grid
Stardust Theatre	1650 Broadway	239-6200	12
Stella Adler Theatre	419 Lafayette St.	260-0525	6
Studio Theater	416 W. 42nd St.	279-4200	11
Sullivan Street Lounge	189 Sullivan St.	420-1999	6
Sullivan Street Playhouse	181 Sullivan St.	674-3838	6
Surf Reality	172 Allen St., 2nd Fl.	673-4182	4
Sylvia and Danny Kaye Playhouse	695 Park Ave.	772-5207	15
Symphony Space	2537 Broadway	864-5400	16
Synchronicity Space	55 Mercer St.	925-8645	6
T. Schreiber Studio	151 W. 26th St.	741-0209	9
TADA!	120 W. 28th St.	627-1732	9
Tenement Theater	97 Orchard St.	431-0233	4
The Actors Studio Free Theater at Raw Space	529 W. 42nd St.	279-4200	11
The Creative Place Theatre	750 8th Ave., Suite 602	332-9833	11, 12
The Kitchen	512 W. 19th St.	255-5793	8
The Kraine Theater	85 E. 4th St.	539-7686	6
The Melting Pot Theatre at Theater 3	311 W. 43rd St.	279-4200	11
The Next Stage	145 W. 46th St.	354-6121	12
The Ontological Theater at St. Mark's Church	131 E. 10th St.	533-4650	6
The Piano Store	158 Ludlow St.	420-1466	4
The Present Company Theatorium	198 Stanton St.	946-5537	7
The Producers Club II	358 W. 44th St.	315-4743	11
The Red Room	85 E. 4th St.	539-7686	6
The Studio	145 W. 46th St.	354-6121	12
Theater for the New City	155 First Ave.	254-1109	6, 7
Theatorium	196 Stanton St.	246-7277	7
Theatre 80	80 St. Marks Pl.	598-9802	6
Theatre East	211 E. 60th St.	838-9090	11, 14
Theatre Four	424 W. 55th St.	239-6200	11
Theatre of St. Peter's Church	Citicorp Center, 619 Lexington Ave.	935-2200	13
Theatre Off Park	224 Waverly Pl.	627-2556	6
Triad Theater	158 W. 72nd St.	239-6200	14
Trilogy Theatre	341 W. 44th St.	316-0400	11
UBU Rep	15 W. 28th St.	679-7562	9
Union Square Theater	100 E. 17th St.	307-4100	10
Upright Citizens Brigade Theatre	161 W. 22nd St.	366-9176	9
Upstairs at Barrio	99 Stanton St.	229-8319	7
Urban Stages	259 W. 30th St.	268-9829	8, 9
Variety Arts Center	110 3rd Ave.	239-6200	6
Victoria Five Theater	310 W. 125th St.	828-7991	20
Village Theater	158 Bleecker St.	307-4100	6
Vineyard Theatre	108 E. 15th St.	353-0303	10
Waterloo Bridge Theatre	203 W. 38th St.	330-8879	9, 12
West Park Auditorium	165 W. 86th St.	946-5321	14, 16
Westbeth Theatre Center	151 Bank St.	741-0391	5
Westside Theatre	407 W. 43rd St.	239-6200	11
Wings Theater	154 Christopher St.	606-4088	5
Workhouse	41 White St.	431-9220	2
Worth Street Theater	33 Worth St.	226-1043	2
WOW Cafe	59 E. 4th St.	777-4280	6
York Theatre	619 Lexington Ave.	935-5820	13

Performing Arts

	Address	Phone	Grid
Amato Opera	319 Bowery	228-8200	6
CAMI Hall	165 W. 57th St.	841-9650	12
Carnegie Hall	154 W. 57th St.	247-7800	12
City Center	131 W. 55th St.	581-7907	12
Dance Theatre Workshop	219 W. 19th St.	924-0077	9
Grace Rainey Rogers Auditorium	Met. Museum, 1000 5th Ave.	570-3949	15
Joyce Theater	175 8th Ave.	242-0800	8, 9
Julliard School	60 Lincoln Center Plz.	799-5000	14
Manhattan School of Music	120 Claremont Ave.	749-2802	18
Merkin Concert Hall	129 W. 67th St.	362-8719	14
Music Room	Frick Museum, 1 E. 70th St.	288-0700	15
New Museum of Contemporary Art	583 Broadway	219-1222	6
Riverside Church	490 Riverside Dr.	870-6700	18
St. Mark's Church-in-the-Bowery	131 E. 10th St.	674-6377	6
Town Hall	123 W. 43rd St.	840-2824	12
Warren St. Performance Loft	46 Warren St.	732-3149	2
Washington Square Church	135 W. 4th St.	777-2528	6

Swimming & Bowling

Pools

	Address	Phone	Type	Fees	Grid
All Star Fitness Club	75 W End Ave.	265-8200	Indoor	$25 per day	14
Asphalt Green	555 E 90th St.	369-8890	Indoor	$900 per year	17
Asser Levy	E 23rd & Asser Levy Pl.	447-2020	Indoor	$25 per day	10
			Outdoor	Free	
Battery Park Swim & Fitness Center	375 South End Ave.	321-1117	Indoor/Outdoor	$26 per day	BPC
Carmine Recreation Center	1 Clarkson St.	242-5228	Indoor	$25 per day	5
			Outdoor	Free	
Chelsea Piers Sports Center	Pier 60	336-6000	Indoor	$50 per day	8
Club La Raquette	119 W 56th St.	245-1144	Indoor	$50 per day	12
Crowne Plaza	1601 Broadway	977-4000	Indoor	$25 per day	12
Downtown Athletic Club	19 West St.	425-7000	Indoor	$2340 per year	1
East 54th Street	348 E 54th St.	397-3154	Indoor	$25 per year	13
Excelsior Athletic Club	301 E 57th St.	688-5280	Indoor	$25 per day	13
New York Sports Club	1637 3rd Ave.	987-7200	Indoor	$25 per day	23
Hamilton Fish Recreation Center	128 Pitt St.	387-7687	Outdoor	Free	7
Hansborough Recreation Center	35 W 134th St.	234-9603	Indoor	$25 per year	19
Highbridge	173rd St. & Amsterdam	927-2400	Outdoor	Free	23
Holiday Inn	440 W 57th St.	581-8100	Indoor	$17 per day	11
Jackie Robinson Pool	146 st & Bradhurst Ave.	234-9606	Outdoor	Free	21,22
John Jay	E77th St. & Cherokee Pl.	794-6566	Outdoor	Free	15
Lasker Pool	110 Lenox Ave.	534-7639	Outdoor	Free	19
Lenox Hill Neighborhood House	331 E 70th St.	744-5022	Indoor	$10 per day	15
Major Robert F. Wagner	E. 124th St. bet 1st & 2nd	534-4238	Outdoor	Free	20
Manhattan Plaza Health Club	482 W 43rd St.	563-7001	Indoor	$25 per day	11
Marcus Garvey Swimming Pool	13 E 124th St.	410-2818	Outdoor	Free	20
Marriott Hotel	3 World Trade Center	466-9266	Indoor	$20 per day	1
Marymount Manhattan College	221 E 71st St.	517-0564	Indoor	$235 per semester	15
Monterey Sports Club	175 E 96th St.	996-8200	Indoor	$695 per year	17
Paris Health Club	752 W End Ave.	749-3500	Indoor	$836 per year	16
Reebok Sports Club	160 Columbus Ave.	362-6800	Indoor	$1200 membership, +$188 per month	14
Riverbank State Park	679 Riverside Dr.	694-3600	Indoor/Outdoor	$2 per day	21
Sheltering Arms Park W	129th & Amsterdam Av.	662-6191	Outdoor	Free	18
Sheraton New York Health Club	811 7th Ave.	841-6714	Indoor	$20 per day	12
Szold Place	E 10th St. and Szold Pl.	677-4481	Outdoor	Free	7
Thomas Jefferson Swimming Pool	2180 1st Ave.	860-1372	Outdoor	Free	20
UN Plaza Health Club	1 UN Plaza	702-5016	Indoor	$35 per day	13
West 59th Street Swimming Pool	533 W 59th St.	397-3159	Indoor	$25 per year	11
YM-YWHA Alliance	344 E 14th St.	780-0800	Indoor	$515 per year	6,10
YMCA	180 W 135th St.	281-4100	Indoor	$12 per day	19,22
YMCA	1395 Lexington Ave.	415-5700	Indoor	$30 per day	17
YMCA	224 E 47th Street	756-9600	Indoor	$25 per day	13
YWCA	610 Lexington Ave.	755-4500	Indoor	$15 per day	13

Bowling Alleys

	Address	Phone	Fees	Grid
Bowlmor	110 University Pl.	255-8188	$6-7 per person per game $4 for shoes	6
AMF Chelsea Bowl	Pier 60	835-2695	$8 per person per game $4.50 for shoes	8
Leisure Time	625 Eighth Ave. (Port Authority)	268-6909	$5-6 per person per game $3.50 for shoes	12

Chelsea Piers

www.chelseapiers.com
F, Path to Sixth Ave.
1,9 to Seventh Ave.
C, E to Eighth Ave.
M23 bus

First opened in 1910 as a very popular port for trans-Atlantic ships, Chelsea Piers found itself abandoned, neglected and deteriorating by the 60s. In 1992, Roland W. Betts began the plan to renovate and refurbish the piers as a shiny, huge 30-acre sports and entertainment center. In 1995, Chelsea Piers re-opened its doors to the public. The cost of renovating the piers was an estimated $120 million when all was said and done – all private money. The only help from the state was a very generous 49-year lease. In 1998, Chelsea Piers was the third-most-visited attraction in New York City.

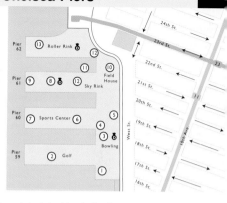

Chelsea Piers is amazing. It's got swimming pools, ice skating rinks, a bowling alley, spa, restaurants, shops, batting cages… you name it. So, what's the catch? Well, it's gonna cost ya. Like Manhattan rents, only investment bankers can afford this place. And, unless you live in Chelsea, it's a real pain to get to. BTW, parking is free if you're there for less than 20 minutes, otherwise it starts at $8 for the first hour. Street parking in the west 20s is an excellent alternative in the evenings after 6pm. To drive there, take 23rd St. to 10th Ave., make a right, then a left on 24th St. Go completely across the West Side Highway and make a left past the concrete barriers down to the parking attendant booth.

1. Chelsea Brewing Company
212- 336-6440
Microbrewery and restaurant.

2. Golf Club
212-336-6400
Aside from potentially long wait times, the 200-yard driving range with 52 heated stalls is pretty awesome. There is an automated ball-feed—no buckets or bending over.

3. AMF Chelsea Piers
212-835-BOWL
A very schmancy 40-lane bowling alley equipped with video games and bar.

4. Miss Rita's Burgers and Barbecue
212-604-6060
Mediocre burgers, but nice atmosphere.

5. New York Presbyterian Sports Medicine Center
212-366-5100

6. Origins Spa
212-336-6780
It's not Canyon Ranch.

7. The Sports Center
212-336-6144
A very expensive, monster health club with a 10,000 sq. ft. climbing wall, a quarter-mile track, swimming pool, and enough fitness equipment for a small army in training.

8. Sky Rink
212-336-6100
Two 24/7 ice rinks.

9. The Lighthouse
212-336-6060
10,000 Sq. ft. event space for private gatherings.

10. The Field House
212-336-6500
The Field House is an 80,000 sq. ft building that has a 30ft climbing wall, a gymnastics training center, 4 batting cages, 2 basketball courts, and 2 indoor soccer fields.

11. Spirit Cruise
212-727-2789

12. Blades Board & Skate
212-336-6299 @roller rinks
212-336-6199 @sky rink
A cool, hip supplier of skating gear.

13. Roller Rink
212-336-6200
Two regulation-size outdoor skating rinks and skate park.

Golf

Unfortunately, but not surprisingly, there are no golf courses on the island of Manhattan. Thankfully, there are two driving ranges where you can at least smack the ball around until you can get to a real course. NYC has a number of private and public courses throughout the outer boroughs and Westchester; however, they by no means satisfy the area's huge demand for courses.

Golf Courses	Borough	Address	Par	Phone
Mosholu Golf Course	Bronx	3700 Jerome Ave	70	(718) 655-9164
Pelham/Split Rock Golf Course	Bronx	870 Shore Rd(in Pelham Bay Park)	71	(718) 885-1258
Van Cortlandt Golf Course	Bronx	Van Cortlandt Pk S & Bailey Ave	70	(718) 543-4595
Dyker Beach Golf Course	Brooklyn	86th St at 7th Ave.	71	(718) 836-9722
Marine Park Golf Club	Brooklyn	2880 Flatbush Ave.	72	(718) 338-7113
Breezy Point Pitch & Putt	Queens	155th St. & Boardwalk	55	(718) 474-1623
Clearview Golf Course	Queens	202 - 12 Willets Point Blvd.	70	(718) 225-GOLF
Douglaston Golf Course	Queens	6320 Marathon Pkwy.	67	(718) 428-1617
Flushing Meadows Pitch & Putt	Queens	Flushing Meadows–Corona Park	54	(718) 277-8182
Forest Park Golf Course	Queens	101 Forest Park Dr.	67	(718) 296-0999
Kissena Park Golf Course	Queens	164 - 15 Booth Memorial Ave.	64	(718) 939-4594
LaTourette Golf Course	Staten Island	1001 Richmond Hill Rd.	72	(718) 351-1889
Silver Lake Golf Course	Staten Island	915 Victory Blvd.	69	(718) 447-5686
South Shore Golf Course	Staten Island	200 Huguenot Ave.	72	(718) 984-0101

Fees are generally as follows (Reservations are a must, so call ahead):

Weekdays before 1pm-$21.00
Weekdays after 1pm-$19.00
Weekends before 1pm-$23.50
Weekends after 1pm-$21.50

Manhattan Driving Ranges	Address	Fees	Phone
Chelsea Piers: Pier 59	59, Chelsea Piers (at 23rd Street) Golf Club Pier	$25.00/100 balls	(212) 336-6400
Randalls Island Golf Center	1 Randalls Rd.	$6.00/small bucket $10.00/large bucket	(212) 427-5689

There are more tennis courts on the island of Manhattan than you might think, although getting to them may be a bit more than you've bargained for. Most of the public courts in Manhattan (listed in the "Parks" section of the chart below) are either smack in the middle of Central Park, or are on the edges of the city—East River Park, for instance, and Riverside Park. These courts in particular can make for some pretty windy playing conditions.

Public Courts	Address	# of Cts.	Type	Phone
Battery Park	I World Financial Center	2	Hard	(212) 374-0973
Central Park Tennis Center	93rd St. & Central Park West	30	Clay/Hard	(212) 280-0205
East River Park Tennis Courts	FDR Dr. No. of Delancey St.	12	Hard	(212) 529-7185
Fort Washington Park	H. Hudson Pkwy. & 172nd St.	10	Hard	(212) 234-9609
F. Johnson Playground	51st Street at Seventh Ave.	8	Hard	(212) 234-9609
Inwood Hill Park	207th St. & Seaman Ave.	9	Hard	(212) 234-9609
Octagon Park	Main St., Roosevelt Island	4	Hard	(212) 304-2381
Randall's Island Sunken Meadow	Randall's Island	11	Hard	N/A
Riverbank State Park	W. 145th & Riverbank Dr.	4	Hard	(212) 860-1827
Riverside Park	96th St. & Riverside Dr.	10	Clay	(212) 694-3600
Riverside Park	119th-122nd St. & Riverside Dr.	10	Hard	(212) 496-2006
				(212) 496-2103

Private Clubs	Address	# of Cts.	Type	Phone
Columbus Tennis Club	795 Columbus Ave.	9	Clay	(212) 662-8367
Crosstown Tennis	14 W. 31st St.	4	Hard	(212) 947-5780
EHCCI/Pasarell YTC	E. 120th Avenue & First Ave.	4	Hard	N/A
Harlem Tennis Center	40 W. 143rd St.	4	Rubber	(212) 283-4028
HRC Tennis	South Street, Piers 13 and 14	8	Clay	(212) 422-9300
Manhattan Plz. Racquet Club	450 W. 43rd St.	8	Hard	(212) 594-0554
Midtown Tennis Club	341 8th Ave.	8	Clay	(212) 989-8572
River Club	447 E. 57th St.	2	Clay	(212) 751-0100
Roosevelt Island Racquet Club	281 Main St.	11	Clay	(212) 935-0250
Sutton East Tennis Club	488 E. 60th St.	8	Clay	(212) 751-3452
The Tennis Club	15 Vanderbilt Ave.	2	Hard	(212) 687-3841
The Vertical Club	330 E. 61st St.	8	Hard	(212) 355-2052
Town Tennis	430 E. 56th St.	3	Hard	(212) 752-4059
UN Plz./Park Hyatt Hotel	I United Nations Plaza	1	Hard	(212) 702-5016
Village Tennis Court	110 University Place	2	Hard	(212) 989-2300

Schools	Address	# of Cts.	Type	Phone No.
Coles Center, NYU	181 Mercer St.	10	Clay	(212) 998-2020
Columbia U. Tennis Center	575 W. 218th St.	7	Hard	(212) 942-7100
JHS 167 YTC	E. 75th St. (bet. 2nd & 3rd)	4	Hard	(212) 879-7562
PS 125	425 W. 123rd St.	3	Hard	N/A
PS 137	327 Cherry St.	5	Hard	N/A
PS 144	134 W. 122nd St.	4	Hard	N/A
PS 146	421 E. 106th St.	3	Hard	N/A
PS 187	349 Cabrini Blvd.	4	Hard	N/A
Rockefeller University	1230 York Ave.	1	Hard	(212) 327-8000

Getting a Permit

The tennis season, according to the NYC Parks Department, lasts from April 7 to November 30. Permits are good for use until the end of the season at all public courts, and are good for one hour of singles or two hours of doubles play. Fees are:

Juniors (17 yrs and under) $10
Adults (18-61yrs) $50
Senior Citizen (62 yrs and over) $20
Single-play tickets $5

General Information

Manhattan Parks Dept.: (212) 360-8131
website: http://nycparks.completeinet.net
Permit Locations: The Arsenal, 830 5th Ave. @ 64th St., Paragon Sporting Goods, Broadway @ 18th St.

Giants Stadium

Giants Stadium, located in the scenic and smelly Meadowlands Sports Complex of New Jersey, is the home of both the New York Giants and New York Jets football teams. They play here on alternating Sundays throughout the fall and the only way to get regular-priced tickets is to inherit them, since both teams are sold out through the next ice age. Giants Stadium also houses Major League Soccer's Metrostars (for which many, many tickets are available) and is the site of several concerts and other sporting and religious events throughout the year.

How to Get There—Driving
Giants Stadium is only 5 miles from the Lincoln Tunnel (closer to mid-town than Shea Stadium, even) but leave early if you want to get to the game on time—remember that the Giants and the Jets are a) sold out for every game and b) have tons of fans from both Long Island and the five boroughs. You can take the Lincoln Tunnel to Route 3 West to Route 120 North to get there, or you can try either the Holland Tunnel to the New Jersey Turnpike (North) to exit 16W, or the George Washington Bridge to the New Jersey Turnpike (South) to exit 16W. Accessing the stadium from exit 16W allows direct access to the parking areas.

How to Get There—Mass Transit
A less stressful way to get to Giants Stadium than driving is to take a bus from the Port Authority Bus Terminal directly to the stadium. It costs $3.25 each way, and buses usually start running two hours before kickoff.

How to Get Tickets
For the Jets and the Giants, scalpers and friends are the only options. For the MetroStars and for concerts, you can call Ticketmaster or visit Ticketmaster's website.

Practical Information
Giants Stadium Information: 201-935-3900
Ticketmaster: 212-307-3131
Website: www.giantsstadium.com

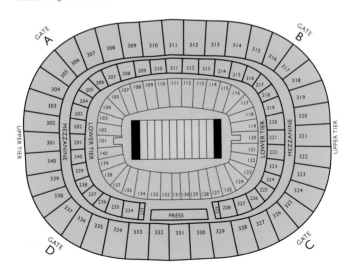

Madison Square Garden

Madison Square Garden is home to the Knicks, the Rangers, and the Liberty. If you don't know which sports these teams play, then we can't help you. Either way, we probably can't help you get tickets for the Knicks or the Rangers. Don't worry, though—the Liberty games are the most fun, anyway. MSG also hosts a ton of other events throughout the year, including rock concerts, tennis tournaments, political conventions, and, for those of you with 2+ years of graduate school, monster truck rallies and "professional" wrestling. Check out MSG's website for the full calendar of events.

How to Get There—Mass Transit
MSG is right next to Penn Station, so it's extremely convenient to get there. You can take the A-C-E and 1-2-3-9 lines to 34th St. and Penn Station, or the N-R, B-D-F-Q, and PATH lines to 34th St. and 6th Ave.

How to Get Tickets
You can try Ticketmaster for single seats for the Knicks and the Rangers, but a better bet would be to try the "standby" line for these teams (show up a half-hour before game time). There are also the ubiquitous ticket scalpers ringing the Garden for when your rich out-of-town friends breeze in to see a game. You can usually get Liberty tickets (and tickets for other events) through Ticketmaster.

Practical Information
General Information: 212-465-6741
Knicks Hotline: 212-NYK-DUNK
Liberty Hotline: 212-564-WNBA
Rangers Hotline: 212-308-NYRS
Ticketmaster: 212-307-7171
Website: www.thegarden.com

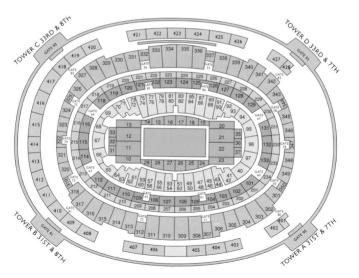

Shea Stadium

Shea Stadium is the home of the New York Mets. It's painted in those lovely clashing colors of Dodger Blue and Giant Orange (homage to the two baseball teams that deserted New York City for the west coast), and is located in Flushing Meadows in Queens. Although the Mets had one of the most abysmal starts in baseball history in 1962 (going 40-120), since that time, they've won two World Series (in 1969 and 1986), appeared in two others, and have been competitive in at least some portion of every decade.

How To Get There—Driving

Driving to Shea Stadium is easy, although commuter traffic during the week can cause tie-ups. You can take the Triborough Bridge to the Grand Central Parkway; the Mid-Town Tunnel to the Long Island Expressway to the Grand Central; or the Brooklyn-Queens Expressway to the LIE to the Grand Central.

How To Get There—Mass Transit

The good news is that the 7 train runs straight to Shea Stadium. The bad news is: 1) it's the 7 train, usually rated the worst among all train lines; and 2) it's the only train that goes there. However, it will get you there and back (eventually), and the 7 is accessible from almost all the other train lines in Manhattan. Alternately, you can take the E to Roosevelt Ave. and pick up the 7 there, saving about 30 minutes. Also New York Waterway runs a ferry service (the "Mets Express") to Shea from the South Street Seaport, E. 34th St, and E. 94th St. The other option is the Port Washingotn LIRR from Penn Station, which stops at Shea on game days.

How To Get Tickets

You can order Mets tickets by phone through the Mets box office, on the internet through the Mets' website, or at the Mets Clubhouse Shop.

Practical Information

• Mets Clubhouse Shop: 143 E. 54th St., Manhattan
• Shea Stadium Box Office: 718-507-METS (6387)
• Website: www.mets.com
• Location: 126th St. and Roosevelt Ave., Flushing, Queens
• Ferry: 800-53-FERRY

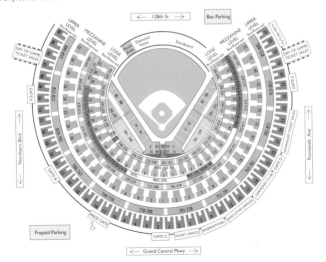

Yankee Stadium

Yankee Stadium, or "The House That Ruth Built", has been The Bronx's most famous landmark since the 1920s. Since moving in, the Yankees have won more than a quarter of the World Series that have been played (26 of 98), making them one of the most successful sports franchises in history. And with four championships in the last five years, even Mr. Steinbrenner has mellowed somewhat.

How To Get There—Driving

Driving to Yankee Stadium from Manhattan usually isn't that bad. Games don't generally start on weeknights until 7:30, so leaving at around 6:45 from midtown will get you close, if not in your seats, by game time. It's best to take the Willis Ave. Bridge from either 1st Ave. or the FDR Drive and get on the Major Deegan for about one mile until you see the stadium exit. From the upper west side, you can try taking Broadway up to 155th St. and using the Macombs Dam Bridge to cross over to the stadium (avoiding lots of crosstown traffic). Parking (as compared to ticket prices) is usually pretty cheap, especially at those lots that are a few blocks from the stadium.

How To Get There—Mass Transit

Getting to the stadium by subway is easy. The 4 and the D both run express to the stadium, and you can easily hook up with either train at several junctions in Manhattan. It should take you about half an hour from any point in Manhattan. Also, New York Waterway runs a wonderful ferry (the "Yankee Clipper") from South Street Seaport, E. 34th St., and E. 94th St.

How To Get Tickets

You can order tickets by phone through Ticketmaster, buy tickets at the box office or at the Yankee store, or buy tickets over the web through either Ticketmaster or the Yankee web site.

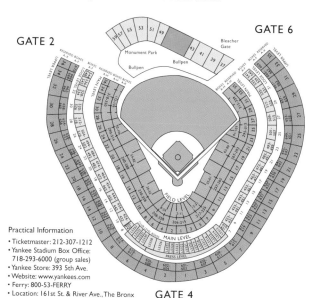

Practical Information
- Ticketmaster: 212-307-1212
- Yankee Stadium Box Office:
  718-293-6000 (group sales)
- Yankee Store: 393 5th Ave.
- Website: www.yankees.com
- Ferry: 800-53-FERRY
- Location: 161st St. & River Ave., The Bronx

Airlines

Airline	Phone	JFK	Nwk	LGA
Aer Lingus	888-474-7424	■	■	
Aeroflot	800-340-6400	■		
Aerolineas Argentinas	800-333-0276	■		
Aeromexico	800-237-6639	■		
Air Afrique	800-456-9192	■		
Air Canada	888-247-2262	■	■	■
Air China-CAAC	800-982-8802	■		
Air Europa	888-238-7672	■		
Air France	800-237-2747	■	■	
Air India	212-751-6200	■		
Air Jamaica	800-523-5585	■	■	
Air Malta	800-756-2582			
Air Nova	800-776-3000		■	
Air Plus Comet	877-999-7587	■		
Air Tran Airlines	800-247-8726		■	■
Air Ukraine	212-230-1001	■		
Alaska Airlines	800-426-0333		■	
Alitalia	800-223-5730	■	■	
All Nippon	800-235-9262	■		
Allegro Airlines	800-903-2779	■		
America West	800-235-9292	■	■	■
American	800-433-7300	■	■	■
American Eagle	800-433-7300	■	■	■
Asiana	800-227-4262	■		
ATA (Domestic)	800-435-9282	■	■	■
ATA (International)	800-435-9282	■		
Austrian Airlines	800-843-0002	■		
Avianca	800-284-2622	■		
Balkan Bulgarian	800-822-1106	■		
British Airways	800-538-2942	■	■	
BWIA	800-538-2942	■		
Canada 3000	877-658-3000			■
Cathay Pacific	800-233-2742	■		
China Airlines	800-227-5118	■		
Colgan	800-428-4322		■	■
Comair	800-354-9822			■
Continental (Domestic)	800-525-0280	■		
	800-523-3273		■	■
Continental (Int'l)	800-231-0856	■		
Corsair	800-677-0720	■		
Czech Airlines	212-765-6022	■		
Delta (Domestic)	800-221-1212	■	■	■
Delta Express	800-325-5205	■	■	■
Delta (International)	800-241-4141	■	■	
Ecuatoriana	877-328-2367	■		
Egyptair	212-315-0900	■		
El Al	800-223-6700	■	■	
Ethiopian Airlines	212-867-0095	■		
Eva Airways	800-695-1188	■		
Finnair	800-950-5000	■		
Frontier Airlines	800-432-1359			■
Ghana Airways	800-404-4262	■		
Guyana	800-242-4210	■		
Iberia	800-772-4642	■		
Icelandair	800-223-5500	■		
Japan Airlines	800-525-3663	■		
Jet Blue	800-538-2583	■		
KLM	800-374-7747	■	■	

Airline	Phone	JFK	Nwk	LGA
Korean Air	800-438-5000	■	■	
Kuwait Airways	800-458-9248	■		
Lacsa	800-225-2272	■		
Lan Chile	800-735-5526	■		
Lan Peru	800-735-5590	■		
Lot Polish	800-528-7208	■	■	
LTU	800-888-0200	■	■	
Lufthansa	800-645-3880	■	■	
Malaysia	800-552-9264			■
Malev Hungarian	800-223-6884	■		
Martinair (Seasonal)	800-627-8462		■	
Mexicana	800-531-7921	■		
Miami Air	305-871-3300	■	■	■
Midway	800-446-4392	■		■
Midwest Express	800-452-2022	■		■
National Airlines	888-757-5387	■	■	
North American	718-656-2650	■	■	
Northwest (Domestic)	800-225-2525	■	■	■
Olympic	212-838-3600	■		
Pakistan	212-370-9157	■		
Qantas	800-227-4500	■	■	
Royal Air (Seasonal)	800-344-6726		■	
Royal Air Maroc	800-344-6726	■		
Royal Jordanian	212-949-0050	■		
Sabena	800-955-2000	■	■	
Saeta Ecuador	800-827-2382	■		
SAS	800-221-2350		■	
Saudi Arabian Airlines	800-472-8342	■		
Servivensa	305-381-8001	■		
Shuttle America	888-999-3213			■
Singapore Airlines	800-742-3333	■	■	
Skyway Airlines	800-452-2022			■
South African Airways	800-722-9675	■		
Spirit	800-772-7117	■		■
Sun Country	800-359-5786	■		
Sunjet International	800-386-2786	■		
Swissair	800-221-4750	■	■	
TACA	800-535-8780	■		
TAM	888-235-9826	■		
Tap Air Portugal	800-221-7370	■	■	
Tarom Romanian	212-687-6013	■		
Thai Airways	800-560-0840			
Tie Aviation	888-244-8922	■		
Trade Winds	847-446-2644	■		
Trans Meridian	770-732-6900	■		
Turkish	800-874-8875	■		
TWA (Domestic)	800-221-2000	■	■	■
TWA (International)	800-892-4141	■		
United Airlines (Dom.)	800-241-6522	■	■	■
United Airlines (Int'l)	800-241-6522	■		
US Airways	800-428-4322	■		■
Uzbekistan	212-245-1005	■		
Vanguard	800-826-4827			■
Varig	800-468-2744	■		
VASP	800-732-8277		■	
Virgin Atlantic	800-862-8621	■	■	
World Airways	703-834-9400	■		

JFK Airport

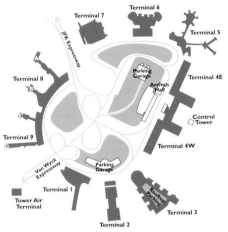

AIRLINE	TERMINAL	
	dep.	arr.
Lan Chile	4	4
Lan Peru	4	4
Lot Polish	8	8
Lufthansa	1	1
Malev Hungarian	2	2
Miami Air	4	4
National Airlines	4	4
North American	4	4
Northwest	4	4
Olympic	1	1
Pakistan	4	4
Qantas	7	7
Royal Air Maroc	1	1
Royal Jordanian	5	5
Sabena	4	4
Saeta Ecuador	2	3
Saudi Arabian Airlines	2	3
Servivensa	4	4
Singapore Airlines	1	1
South African Airways	3	3
Sun Country	4	4
Sunjet International	7	7
Swissair	4	4
TACA	2	3
TAM	8	8
Tap Air Portugal	4	4
Tarom Romanian	4	4
Thai Airways	7	7
Tie Aviation	4	4
Trans Meridian	4	4
Trade Winds	4	4
Turkish	1	1
TWA (Domestic)	5	5
TWA (International)	5	5
TW Express	5	5
United Airlines	7	7
United Express	7	7
United Airlines—		
SFO/LAX Flights	6	6
US Airways	7	7
Uzbekistan	4	4
Varig	4	4
Virgin Atlantic	1	1
World Airways	4	4

AIRLINE	TERMINAL	
	dep.	arr.
Aer Lingus	4	4
Aeroflot	3	3
Aerolineas Argentinas	4	4
Aeromexico	3	3
Air Afrique	1	1
Air Canada	7	7
Air China-CAAC	3	3
Air Europa	4	4
Air France	1	1
Air India	4	4
Air Jamaica	2	3
Air Malta	4	4
Air Plus Comet	4	4
Air Ukraine	4	4
Alitalia	1	1
Allegro Airlines	4	4
All Nippon	3	3
America West	6	6
American (Domestic)	9	9
American (International)	8	8
American Eagle	9	9
Asiana	8	8
ATA	4	4
Austrian Airlines	1	1

AIRLINE	TERMINAL	
	dep.	arr.
Avianca	3	3
Biman Bangladesh	4	4
British Airways	7	7
BWIA	4	4
Cathay Pacific	7	7
China Airlines	3	3
Continental	4	4
Corsair	4	4
Delta	3	3
Delta Connection	3	3
Ecuatoriana	4	4
Egyptair	4	4
El Al	4	4
Finnair	8	8
Ghana Airways	4	4
Guyana	4	4
Iberia	8	8
Icelandair	7	7
Japan Airlines	1	1
JetBlue	6	6
KLM	4	4
Korean Air	1	1
Kuwait Airways	4	4
Lacsa	2	3

Ah, JFK. It's long been a nemesis to New Yorkers (and others) due to the fact that it's so far away from Manhattan. Nonetheless, it's expected that 35 million people will annually use JFK by the year 2000. Expansion and modernization plans are moving forward, but all we can say is: If you've got the choice, go to Newark.

How to Get There–Driving

You can take the lovely and scenic Belt Parkway straight to JFK as long as it's not rush hour. This is about a 30-mile trip, even though JFK is only 15 or so miles from Manhattan. You can access the Belt by taking the Brooklyn-Battery Tunnel to the Gowanus (the best route), or by taking the Brooklyn, Manhattan, or Williamsburg Bridges to the Brooklyn-Queens Expressway to the Gowanus. We of course do not recommend this, because the idea of driving 30 miles to go 15 miles makes us nuts. Instead, get to Atlantic Avenue in Brooklyn and drive east until you hit Conduit Ave. You can take this straight to JFK. It's direct and fairly simple. You can get to Atlantic Ave. from any of the three downtown bridges (look at a map first, though!) From midtown, you can take the Queens Midtown Tunnel to the Long Island Expressway to the Van Wyck Expressway South (there's never much traffic on the LIE, of course...). From uptown, you can take the Triboro Bridge to the Grand Central Parkway to the Van Wyck Expressway South.

How to Get There–Mass Transit

This is your chance to finish "War and Peace." Take the A train going to Far Rockaway. When you arrive at the Howard Beach/JFK Airport stop 17 hours later, you can take the free JFK shuttle bus (which does run pretty often). If you want to give your Metrocard a workout, take the Turnpike/Kew Gardens stop, and transfer to the Q10. Another possibility is the 3 train to New Lots Avenue, where you transfer tot he B15 to JFK. The easiest option is to take a bus from either Grand Central or the Port Authority on either Olympia or New York Airport Service buses ($11–13). Taxis from the airport to Mahnattan are a flat $30 + tolls. Fares tot he airport are metered + tolls.

Parking

Public parking rates are similar to LaGuardia's and actually cheaper for long-term parking. Rates are $2 for the first half-hour, $4 for up to 2 hours, $2 for every hour after that, and $24 per day. Long-term parking is $8 per day.

Rental Cars (on-Airport)

1. Avis, 718-244-5406 or 800-230-4898
2. Budget, 718-656-6010 or 800-527-0700
3. Dollar, 718-656-2400 or 800-800-4000
4. Hertz, 718-656-7600 or 800-654-3131
5. National, 718-632-8300 or 800-227-7368

Phone Numbers

Recorded Information: 718-244-4444
Police/ Lost and Found: 718-244-4225/6
Medical Services: 718-656-5344
Radio Station: 530 AM (traffic updates near airport)
Website: www.panynj.gov/aviation/jfkmain.htm

Hotels

Four Points Sheraton • 151-20 Baisley Blvd. • 718-489-1000
Hilton JFK Airport • 138-10 135th Ave. • 718-322-8700
Holiday Inn JFK Airport • 144-02 135th Ave. • 718-659-0200
Pan American Hotel • 79-00 Queens Blvd • 718-446-7676
Radisson Hotel at JFK • 135-40 140th St. • 718-322-2300
Sheraton JFK Hotel • 151-20 Baisley Blvd. • 718-489-1000
Ramada Plaza Hotel • Van Wyck Expressway • 718-995-9000

Car Services

Airport Limousine Service	1-973-961-3220
Classic Limousine	1-631-567-5100
Precept Transportation Service	1-800-910-5466
	or 1-201-997-7268
Super Saver by Carmel	1-800-924-9954 or 1-212-666-6666
Tel Aviv Limo Service	1-800-222-9888 or 1-212-777-7777

La Guardia Airport

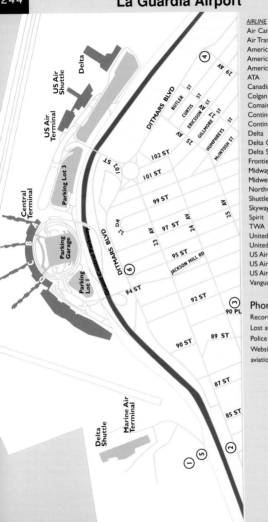

AIRLINE	TERMINAL
Air Canada	A
Air Tran Airlines	C
America West	B
American	D
American Eagle	C
ATA	C
Canadian Airlines	D
Colgan	B/USAirways
Comair	Delta
Continental	A
Continental Express	A
Delta	Delta
Delta Connection	Delta
Delta Shuttle	Marine
Frontier Airlines	C
Midway	D
Midwest Express	C
Northwest	Delta
Shuttle America	
Skyway Airlines	
Spirit	C
TWA	
United	
United Express	
US Airways	USAirways
US Airways Express	USAirways
US Airways Shuttle	USAir Shuttle
Vanguard	

Phone Numbers

Recorded Info: 718-533-3400
Lost and Found: 718-533-3935
Police Emergency: 718-533-3900
Website: http://www.panynj.gov/
aviation/lgaframe.HTM

The best thing we can say about LaGuardia Airport is that it is named for a most excellent (and, unfortunately, dead) New York City mayor, Fiorello LaGuardia. Although LaGuardia has improved over recent years, there is still a ways to go before it catches up to the nation's other airports. However, a number of new food and beverage stands and retail stores have opened up, particularly in the Central Terminal and US Airways Terminal. There are also two bookstores in the airport: Barbara's Bestsellers in Central Terminal and Benjamin Books in US Airways Terminal. LaGuardia is inconvenient to public transportation, since the nearest subway station is miles away. But if you're driving, the best thing about LaGuardia remains its easy access to a major highway, the Grand Central Parkway. It's many miles closer to the city than either Kennedy or Newark, especially from the Upper West or Upper East Sides.

How to Get There—Driving
LaGuardia is mere inches away from the Grand Central Parkway, which can be reached from both the Brooklyn-Queens Expressway (BQE) or from the Triboro Bridge. From lower Manhattan, take the Brooklyn, Manhattan, or Williamsburg bridge to the BQE to the Grand Central Parkway East. From midtown Manhattan, take the FDR Drive to the Triboro to the Grand Central. A potential alternate route (and money-saver) would be to take the 59th Street Bridge to 21st Street North in Queens. Once you're heading north on 21st Street, you can make a right on Astoria Boulevard and follow it all the way to 94th Street, where you can make a left and go straight into LaGuardia. This can be used if the FDR and/or the BQE is jammed, though that probably means that the 59th Street Bridge won't be much better.

How to Get There—Mass Transit
Alas, no subway line goes to LaGuardia (although there should be one that runs across 96th Street in Manhattan, through Astoria, and ending at LaGuardia—but that's another story). The closest the subway gets is the 7/E/F/G/R Jackson Heights/Roosevelt Ave/74th Street stop in Queens, where you can then transfer to the Q33 bus that goes to LaGuardia. Sound exciting? It stinks, actually. The better bus to take is the 60, which runs across 125th St. and goes right to the airport. A better bet would be to pay the extra few bucks and take the New York Airport Service Express Bus ($10) from Grand Central Station. It runs every 15-30 minutes, only takes half an hour, and doesn't stop anywhere else. You can get it on Park Avenue between 41st and 42nd streets. It also runs from Penn Station and the Port Authority Bus Terminal. A taxi will cost you at least $20.

How to Get There—Really
Two words: car service. Call them, they'll pick you up at your door, drop you at the terminal, and you're done. Some car services are: Allstate Car and Limousine: 212-333-3333 (20 + tolls from Union Square; SABRA: 212-777-7171 ($20 + tolls from Union Square; best to call in the morning); Tel Aviv: 212-777-7777 ($20 +tolls from Union Square after 6 p.m.; $25 + tolls before 6 p.m.).

Parking
Typically usurious, parking rates at LaGuardia are $2 for the first half-hour, $4 for up to 2 hours, $2 for every hour after that, and $24 per day. Long-term parking is $24 maximum for the first day and then $10 per day thereafter.

Rental Cars
① Avis • LGA • 800-230-4898 or 718-507-3600
② Budget • 83-34 23rd Ave. •
   800-527-0700 or 718-639-6400
③ Dollar • 90-05 25th Ave. •
   718-779-5600 or 800-800-4000
⑤ Hertz • LGA • 800-654-3131 or 718-478-5300
⑥ National • Ditmars Blvd. & 95th St. • 800-227-7368
   or 718-429-5893

Hotels
Airway Motor Inn • 82-80 Astoria Blvd. •
   718-565-5100
Clarion Hotel • 94-00 Ditmars Blvd. • 718-335-1200
Crowne Plaza • 104-04 Ditmars Blvd. •
   718-457-6300 or 800-692-5429
Marriott Hotel • 102-05 Ditmars Blvd. • 718-565-8900
Skyway Motel • 102-10 Ditmars Blvd. • 718-899-6900
Westway • 71-11 Astoria Blvd. • 718-274-2800

Newark Airport

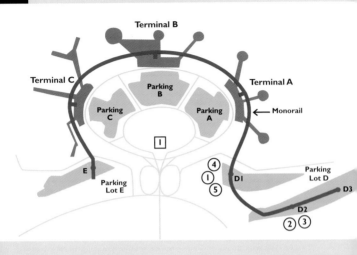

AIRLINE	TERMINAL			AIRLINE	TERMINAL	
	dep.	arr.			dep.	arr.
Aer Lingus	B	B		Lot Polish	B	B
Air Canada	A	A		Lufthansa	B	B
Air France	C	B		Malaysia	B	B
Air Jamaica	B	B		Martinair (Seasonal)	B	B
Alitalia	B	B		Mexicana	B	B
America West	A	A		Miami Air	B	B
American (Domestic)	A	A		Midway	A	A
American (International)	A	B		Midwest Express	B	B
ATA	B	B		North American	B	B
British Airways	B	B		Northwest/KLM	B	B
Canada 3000	B	B		Qantas	A	A
Canadian	A	A		SAS	B	B
Continental (London)	B	B		Sabena	B	B
Continental (Domestic)	C	C		Singapore Airlines	B	B
Continental O'Hare/Atlanta/Dallas	A	A		Spirit	A	A
Continental Express	C	C		Swissair	B	B
Continental (International)	C	C		Tap Air Portugal	B	B
Czech Airlines	B	B		TWA	A	A
Delta	B	B		United (Domestic)	A	A
Delta Express	B	B		United (International)	A	B
El Al	B	B		United Express	A	A
Ethiopian Airlines	B	B		US Airways	A	A
Eva Airways	B	B		US Airways Express	A	A
KLM	B	B		VASP	C	B
Korean Air	B	B		Virgin Atlantic	B	B

Newark Airport is easily the nicest of the three major metropolitan airports. A new monorail (unfortunely, closed for $25 million worth of repairs at least until Christmas 2000) and the availability of actual human food in its food court makes a layover in Newark much more palatable than one in La Guardia or Kennedy. And Newark's burgeoning international connections are increasing its popularity. It's also miles closer to Manhattan than Kennedy Airport is (if you're taking the Belt Parkway to get to Kennedy, that is)—although you might be languishing in the Holland Tunnel trying to get there long after your plane has left the ground.

How to Get There–Driving

By car, the route to Newark Airport is easy—just take either the Holland Tunnel or the Lincoln Tunnel to the New Jersey Turnpike South. You can use either Exit 14 or Exit 13A. If possible, check a traffic report before leaving Manhattan—sometimes there are viciously long tie-ups, especially at the Holland Tunnel. It's always worth it to see which outbound tunnel has the shortest wait.

How to Get There–Mass Transit

If you're allergic to traffic, try taking New Jersey Transit trains which go right into Newark's Penn Station from Penn Station in New York. However, if you're leaving from downtown Manhattan, a clever alternative is to take the PATH train from the World Trade Center to Newark's Penn Station. Once there, frequent buses and cheap taxis will get you to the airport within twenty minutes.

You can also take direct buses from Port Authority Bus Terminal (which has the advantage of a bus-only lane running right out of it into the Lincoln Tunnel), Grand Central Terminal, and Penn Station (the New York version) on Olympia (for $10). A taxi will cost you close to $50.

How to Get There–Car Services

Car services are always the simplest option, although they're a bit more expensive for Newark Airport than they are for La Guardia. Some car services are: Allstate Car and Limousine: 212-333-3333 ($32 + tolls from Union Square); SABRA: 212-777-7171 ($30 + tolls from Union Square; best to call in the morning); Tel Aviv: 212-777-7777 ($30 + tolls from Union Square between 6 p.m. and 3 p.m.; $35 + tolls between 3 p.m. and 6 p.m.).

Parking

Regular parking rates are $2 for the first half-hour, $4 for up to 2 hours, $2 for every hour after that, and $24 per day. Long-term parking $12 per day for monorail–serviced lots (recommended if they're not full). Parking lots G and H are a lot farther away, are only serviced by a shuttle bus and are $8 per day.

Rental Cars (on-Airport)

① Avis • 800-230-4898
② Budget • 800-527-0700
③ Dollar • 973-824-2002
⑤ Hertz • 800-654-3131
⑥ National • 800-227-7368

Rental Cars (off-Airport)

Alamo • 800-327-9633
Enterprise • 800-325-8007

Hotel (on-Airport)

Ⅰ Marriott Hotel, 973-623-0006

Phone Numbers

Recorded Information: 973-961-6000
Police/Lost and Found : 201-961-6230
Transportation Info: 800-AIR-RIDE (247-7533)
Parking Info: 888-397-4636 ext. 22
Medical Services : 201-961-2525
Radio Station: 530 AM (traffic reports near airport)
Website: www.panynj.gov/aviation/ewrframe.HTM

Bridges & Tunnels

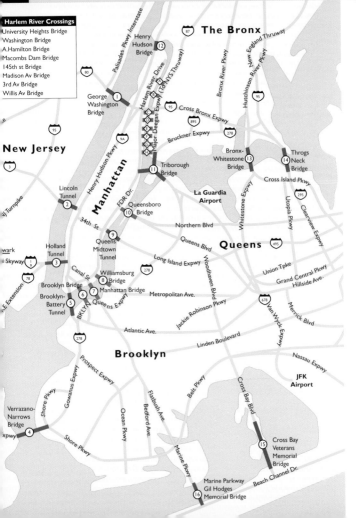

Harlem River Crossings

University Heights Bridge
Washington Bridge
A.Hamilton Bridge
Macombs Dam Bridge
145th st Bridge
Madison Av Bridge
3rd Av Bridge
Willis Av Bridge

The Bronx

Palisades Pkwy Interstate

Henry Hudson Bridge

New England Thruway

Bronx River Pkwy

Hutchinson River Pkwy

George Washington Bridge

Harlem River Drive (To NYS Thruway)

Cross Bronx Expwy

Major Deegan Expwy (To NYS Thruway)

Bruckner Expwy

New Jersey

Henry Hudson Pkwy

Manhattan

Triborough Bridge

Bronx-Whitestone Bridge

Throgs Neck Bridge

Cross Island Pkwy

Whitestone Expwy

Utopia Pkwy

Clearview Expwy

Lincoln Tunnel

FDR Dr.

Queensboro Bridge

La Guardia Airport

Northern Blvd

Turnpike

34th St

Queens

Queens Blvd

Union Tpke

Grand Central Pkwy

Hillside Ave.

newark

Skyway

Holland Tunnel

Queens Midtown Tunnel

Long Island Expwy

Woodhaven Blvd

Canal St.

N.E. Extension

Williamsburg Bridge

Brooklyn Bridge

Manhattan Bridge

Metropolitan Ave.

Van Wyck Expwy

Merrick Blvd

Brooklyn-Battery Tunnel

BKLYN

Queens Expwy

Jackie Robinson Pkwy

Atlantic Ave.

Linden Boulevard

Brooklyn

Nassau Expwy

Prospect Expwy

Gowanus Expwy

Shore Pkwy

Flatbush Ave.

Bedford Ave.

Belt Pkwy

Cross Bay Blvd

JFK Airport

Verrazano-Narrows Bridge

Ocean Pkwy

xpwy

Shore Pkwy

Cross Bay Veterans Memorial Bridge

Marine Pkwy

Marine Parkway Gil Hodges Memorial Bridge

Beach Channel Dr.

Since NYC is an archipelago, it's no wonder that there are so many bridges and 5 major tunnels. Most of the bridges listed in the chart below have broken records or are considered landmarks. The world's first vehicular tunnel ever built was the Holland Tunnel in 1927. New York City's first bridge, King's Bridge, built between Manhattan and the Bronx, was built in 1693, but, sadly, demolished in 1917. Highbridge, the oldest existing bridge in NYC, was built in 1843 but is not open to vehicles or pedestrians. Brooklyn Bridge, built in 1883, is the oldest NYC bridge open to vehicles and pedestrians and is still considered one of the most beautiful bridges ever built. Unfortunately, there was severe neglect in the maintenance of many of the bridges during the 70s. Inspections in the 80s and huge maintenance and refurbishment plans in the 90s/00s will make the bridges stronger and safer than before.

Websites

Port Authority of NY and NJ: www.panynj.gov
DOT: www.ci.nyc.ny.us/html/dot/home.html • 212 or 718/CALLDOT
MTA: http://www.mta.nyc.ny.us/
EZPass: www.e-zpassny.com • 1-800-333-TOLL
Transportation Alternatives: www.transalt.org
Best overall site: www.nycroads.com

#		Toll/EZPass Peak/EZPass off-peak	# of lanes	Pedestrians/Bicyclists?	# of Vehicles/Day (in thousands)	Original Cost (in millions)	Engineer	Main Span/Length	Operated by	Opened to Traffic
1	Geo. Washington Bridge	6.00/5.00/4.00 (inbound only)	14	YES	300	59	Othmar H. Ammann	3,500'	PANYNJ	10/25/31
2	Lincoln Tunnel	6.00/5.00/4.00 (inbound only)	6	NO	120	75	Othmar H. Ammann Ole Singstad	8,216'	PANYNJ	12/22/37
3	Holland Tunnel	6.00/5.00/4.00 (inbound only)	4	NO	100	48	Clifford Holland/ Ole Singstad	8,558'	PANYNJ	11/13/27
4	Verrazano-Narrows Bridge	*	12	NO	190	320	Othmar H. Ammann	4,260'	MTA	11/21/64
5	Brooklyn-Battery Tunnel	3.50/3.00	4	NO	60	90	Ole Singstad	9,117'	MTA	5/25/50
6	Brooklyn Bridge	Free	6	YES	140	15	John Roebling/ Washington Roebling	1,595.5'	DOT	5/4/1883
7	Manhattan Bridge	Free	7	NO	150	25	Gustav Lindenthal/ Rudolph Modjeski	1,470'	DOT	12/31/09
8	Williamsburg Bridge	Free	8	YES	140	30	Leffert L. Buck	1,600'	DOT	12/19/03
9	Queens-Midtown Tunnel	3.50/3.00	4	NO	80	52	Ole Singstad	6,414'	MTA	11/15/40
10	Queensboro Bridge	Free	10	YES	155	20	Gustav Lindenthal	1,182'	DOT	3/30/09
11	Triborough Bridge	3.50/3.00	8/ 6/8	YES	200	60	Othmar H. Ammann	1,380'/ 310'/383'	MTA	7/11/36
12	Henry Hudson Bridge	1.75/1.25	7	YES	75	5	David Steinman	800'	MTA	12/12/36
13	Whitestone Bridge	3.50/3.00	6	NO	110	20	Othmar H. Ammann	2300'	MTA	4/29/39
14	Throgs Neck Bridge	3.50/3.00	6	NO	100	92	Othmar H. Ammann	1800'	MTA	1/11/61
15	Cross Bay Veterans Memorial Bridge	1.75/1.25	6	YES	20	29	N/A	3000'	MTA	5/28/70
16	Marine Parkway Gil Hodges Memorial Bridge	1.75/1.25	4	NO	25	12	Madigan and Hyland	540'	MTA	7/3/37

* $7.00/$6.00 with EZPass to Staten Island ($3.20 for registered Staten Island residents with EZPass). Free to Brooklyn.

Driving in Manhattan

Driving in Manhattan

Hardware requirements: Small, durable car with big, wide tires. New York plates. Plenty of dents and scratches. Loud, obnoxious horn. Stick shift. Semi-automatic tripod-mounted tommy gun.

Software requirements: NFT. Hagstrom 5-Borough Atlas. EZ-Pass. Sweet 'n Low. Fix-a-flat can.

Basic rules: Never look in your rear-view mirror.
  Always assume that the cab that looks like it's about to cut you off, will.
  Always assume that the bus that looks like it's about to cut you off, will.
  Never, ever pull into an intersection unless you're SURE you can make it all the
  way through before the light turns red.
  Never let them see the whites of your eyes.

But seriously, driving in Manhattan is not for the timid, clueless, or otherwise emotionally fragile. Following are some tips that we've encountered over the years:

Hudson River Crossings

The George Washington Bridge is by far the best Hudson River crossing. It's got more lanes and better access than the two crappy tunnels. If you're going anywhere in the country that's north of central New Jersey, take it. The Lincoln Tunnel is pretty good inbound, but check 1010 AM (WINS) if you have the chance—even though they can be horribly inaccurate and frustrating. If you have to take the Holland Tunnel, try the Broome Street approach.

East River Crossings

Brooklyn

Pearl Street to the Brooklyn Bridge is the least-known approach to the Brooklyn Bridge. Only the Williamsburg Bridge has direct access (i.e. no traffic lights) to the northbound BQE in Brooklyn, and only the Brooklyn Bridge has direct access to the FDR Drive in Manhattan. Again, listen to the radio if you can but all three bridges can suck hard simultaneously, especially since all are perpetually being worked on. The Williamsburg Bridge's reconstruction, when complete, may become the best route into Brooklyn, and is usually better than the Manhattan Bridge back into Manhattan. Your best option to go anywhere in Brooklyn is usually the Brooklyn-Battery Tunnel, which can be reached from the FDR. It's not free ($3.50) but you've got EZ-Pass anyway (if you're not a schmuck).

Queens

There are three options for crossing into Queens by car. The Queens Midtown Tunnel is under construction and is usually miserable, since it feeds directly onto the always-busy Long Island Expressway The 59th Street bridge is the only free crossing to Queens. The best approach to it is First Avenue to 57th Street. If you're in Queens and want to go downtown in Manhattan, you can take the lower level of the 59th Street Bridge since it will feed directly onto 2nd Avenue, which of course goes downtown. The Triborough Bridge is usually the best option (especially if you're going to LaGuardia, Shea, or Astoria for Greek food). The FDR to the Triborough is good except for rush hour—then try 3rd Avenue to 124th Street.

Harlem River Crossings

The Triborough ($3.50) will get you to The Bronx in pretty good shape, especially if you are heading east on the Bruckner towards 95 or the Hutchinson (which will take you to eastern Westchester and Connecticut). To get to Yankee Stadium, take the Willis or the Macomb's Dam (which are both free). The Henry Hudson Bridge will take you up to western Westchester along the Hudson, and, except for the antiquated and completely unnecessary toll plaza, is pretty good. Always attempt to avoid the Cross Bronx Expressway.

Manhattan's "Highways"

There are two so-called highways in Manhattan, the Harlem River Drive/FDR Drive (which prohibits commercial vehicles), and the Henry Hudson Parkway/West Side Highway. The main advantage of the FDR is that it has no traffic lights, while the West Side Highway has lights from Battery Park up through 57th Street. If there's been a lot of rain, both highways will flood so you're out of luck. We also think that FDR Drive drivers are one percent better than West Side Highway drivers.

Driving Uptown

The 96th Street transverse across Central Park is usually the best one. If you're driving on the West Side, Riverside Drive is the best route, followed next by West End Avenue. People drive like morons on Broadway, and Columbus jams up Columbus Circle. Amsterdam is a good uptown route if you can get to it. For the East Side, you can take Fifth Avenue downtown to about 65th Street, whereupon you should bail out and cut over to Park Avenue for the rest of the trip. The 96th Street entrance to the FDR screws up First and Third Avenues going north and the 59th Street Bridge screws up Lexington and Second Avenues going downtown. Getting stuck in 59th Street Bridge traffic is one of the most frustrating things in the universe because there is absolutely no way out of it.

Driving in Midtown

Good luck! Sometimes, Broadway is best because everyone's trying to get out of Manhattan, jamming up the West Side (via the Lincoln Tunnel) and the East Side (via the 59th Street Bridge and the Queens Midtown Tunnel). The "interior" city is the last place to get jammed up—it's surprisingly quiet at 8 a.m. At 10 a.m., however, it's a parking lot.

Driving in the Village

If you're coming into the Village from the northwest, 14th Street is the safest crosstown route heading east. However, going west, take 13th Street. Houston Street is usually okay in both directions and has the great benefit of having direct access to the FDR Drive, both getting onto it and coming off of it. If you want to get to Houston Street from the Holland Tunnel, take Hudson Street to King Street to the Avenue of the Americas to Houston Street (this is the ONLY efficient way to get to the Village from the Holland Tunnel). First Avenue is good going north and 5th Avenue is good going south. Washington Street is the only way to make any headway in the West Village.

Driving Downtown

Don't do it unless you have to. Western Tribeca is okay and so is the Lower East Side—try not to "turn in" to Soho, Chinatown, or City Center. Canal Street is a complete mess during the day (avoid it at all costs), since on its western end everyone is trying to get to the Holland Tunnel, and on its eastern end everyone is mistakenly driving over the Manhattan Bridge (your only other option when heading east on Canal is to turn RIGHT on the Bowery!)

General Information

EZ-PASS Information: 800-333-TOLL
Radio Station Traffic Updates: 1010 WINS
DOT Website: http://www.ci.nyc.ny.us/html/dot/html/travroad/travroad.html
Real-Time Web Traffic Information: www.metrocommute.com

Parking in Manhattan

Information:
Department of Transportation: (DOT): (212) 225-5368 (24 hours)
TTY Deaf or Hearing-Impaired: (212) 442-9488
Website:www.ci.nyc.ny.us/calldot
Parking Violations Help Line: (718) 422-7800
TTY Automated Information for the Hearing Impaired: (718) 802-3555
Website: www.ci.nyc.ny.us/finance

Parking Meter Zones
All No Parking signs in meter zones are suspended on ASP and MLH days; however, coins must be deposited during posted hours.

Meters
At a broken meter, parking is allowed ONLY up to one hour (60 minutes). Where a meter is missing, parking is still allowed for the maximum time on the posted sign. (An hour for a one-hour meter, 2 hours for a two-hour meter, etc.).

Signs
New York City Traffic Rules state that one sign per block is sufficient. Check the entire block and read all signs carefully before you park. Then read them again.

If there is more than one sign posted for the same area, the more restrictive one is the one in effect (of course). If a sign is missing on a block, the remaining posted regulations are the ones that are in effect.

The Blue Zone
The Blue Zone is a "No Parking" (Mon-Fri 7am - 7pm) area in lower Manhattan. Its perimeter has been designated with blue paint; however, there are no individual "Blue Zone" signs posted. Any other signs posted in that area supersede Blue Zone regulations. Confused yet??

General
- All of NYC was designated a Tow Away Zone under the State's Vehicle & Traffic Law and the NYC Traffic Rules. This means that any vehicle parked or operated illegally, or with missing or expired registration or inspection stickers, may and probably will be towed.

- On major legal holidays stopping, standing and parking are permitted except in areas where stopping, standing and parking rules are in effect seven days a week (for example, "No Standing Anytime").

- Double parking of passenger vehicles is illegal at all times, including street cleaning days, regardless of location, purpose or duration. Everyone of course does this anyway.

- It is illegal to park within 15 feet of either side of a fire hydrant. The painted curbs at hydrant locations do not indicate where you can park. Isn't New York great?

- If you think you're parked legally in Manhattan, you're probably not, so go and read the signs again.

Alternate Side Parking Suspension Calendar 2002 (estimated*)

Holiday	Date	Day	Rules
NEW YEAR'S DAY	January 1	Tuesday	MHL
Martin Luther King Jr.'s Birthday	January 21	Monday	ASP
Lincoln's Birthday	February 12	Tuesday	ASP
President's Day	February 18	Monday	ASP
Washington's Birthday	February 22	Friday	ASP
Idul Adha	February 22-24	Friday-Sunday	ASP
Passover, 1st/2nd Day	March 28-29	Thursday-Friday	ASP
Holy Thursday	March 28	Thursday	ASP
Good Friday	March 29	Friday	ASP
Passover, 7th/8th Day	April 3-4	Wednesday-Thursday	ASP
Solemnity of Ascension	May 12	Sunday	ASP
MEMORIAL DAY	May 27	Monday	MHL
Shavout, 1st/2nd Day	June 6-7	Thursday-Friday	ASP
INDEPENDENCE DAY	July 4	Thursday	MHL
Assumption of the Blessed Virgin	August 15	Thursday	ASP
LABOR DAY	September 2	Monday	MHL
Rosh Hashanah, 1st/2nd Day	September 7-8	Saturday-Sunday	ASP
Yom Kippur	September 16	Monday	ASP
Succoth, 1st/2nd Day	September 21-22	Saturday-Sunday	ASP
Shemini Atzereth	September 28	Saturday	ASP
Simchas torah	September 29	Sunday	ASP
Columbus Day	October 14	Monday	ASP
All Saints Day	November 1	Friday	ASP
Election Day	November 5	Tuesday	ASP
Veterans Day	November 11	Monday	ASP
THANKSGIVING DAY	November 28	Thursday	MHL
Idul-Fitr, 1st/2nd/3rd Day	December 6-8	Friday-Sunday	ASP
Immaculate Conception	December 9	Monday	ASP
CHIRSTMAS DAY	December 25	Wednesday	MHL

*Note: We go to press before the DOT issues its official calendar. However, using various techniques, among them a Ouija Board, a chainsaw, and repeated phone calls to said DOT, we think it's pretty accurate. Nonetheless, caveat emptor.

- Street Cleaning Rules (SCR)
  Most SCR signs are clearly marked with the " P " symbol with the broom through it. Some SCR signs are the traditional 3-hour ones ("8am to 11am" etc.) but many others vary considerably. Check the times before you park. Then check them again.

- Alternate Side Parking Suspended (ASP)
  No Parking signs in effect one day a week or on alternate days are suspended on days designated ASP; however, all No Stopping and No Standing signs remain in effect.

- Major Legal Holiday Rules in Effect (MLH)
  No Parking and No Standing signs that are in effect fewer than 7 days a week are suspended on days designated MLH in the above calendar.

General Information on the Bus System

Phone Number: 718-330-1234

website: www.mta.nyc.ny.us

Fare: $1.50 per trip, but there are Metrocard discounts available

Times: 24/7, just like we like it

Ridership: 1.2 million people per day
600 million people per year

1 — 5 & Madison Avs

2 — 5 & Madison Avs/Powell Blvd

2 — 5 & Madison Avs/Powell Blvd

3 — 5 & Madison Avs/St Nicholas Av

4 — 5 & Madison Avs/Broadway

5 — 5 Av/Av of Americas/Riverside Dr

5 — 5 Av/Av of Americas/Riverside Dr

6 — 7 Av/Broadway/Av of Americas

7 — Columbus/Amsterdam/Lenox/6/7Avs/B'way

8 — 8/9 Sts Crosstown

9 — Av B/E Broadway

10 — 7/8 Avs(Cent Pk w)/.Douglass Blvd

11 — 9(Columbus)& 10 (Amsterdam) Avs

14 — 14 St Crosstown

14 — 14 St Crosstown

15 — 1/2 Avs

15 — 1/2 Avs

16 — 34 St Crosstown

18 — Convent Av

21 — Houston St/Av C

22 — Madison/Chambers Sts

23 — 23 St Crosstown

27 — 49/50 Sts Crosstown

30 — 52/72 Sts Crosstown

31 — 57 St/York Av

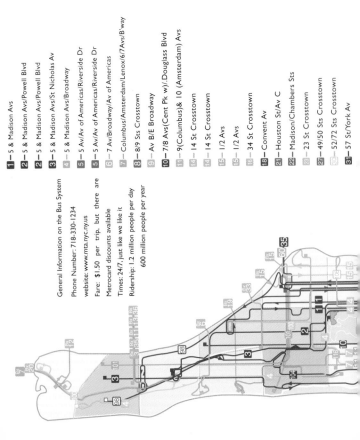

New York's bus system is pretty good and gets better every year, as more new buses are added–some with clean air technology, even. However, you're likely to only get nauseous (as opposed to riding the bus very far during rush hour. The MTA's website publishes a constantly updated list of all temporary and permanent route changes, which occur quite frequently.

M34 — 34 St Crosstown
M35 — Randall's/Ward's Island
M42 — 42 St Crosstown
M50 — 49/50 Sts Crosstown
M57 — 57 St Crosstown
M60 — Laguardia Airport via 125 St
M66 — 66/67 Sts Crosstown
M72 — 72 St Crosstown
M79 — 79 St Crosstown
M86 — 86 St Crosstown
M96 — 96 St Crosstown
M98 — Washington Heights/Midtown
M100 — Amsterdam Av/Broadway/125 St
M101 — 3/Lexington/Amsterdam Avs
M102 — 3/Lexington/Amsterdam Avs
M103 — 3/Lexington Avs/Malcolm X Blvd
M104 — 3/Lexington Avs
M104 — Broadway/42 St
M106 — 96/106 St Crosstown
M116 — 116 St Crosstown
M161 — E 161/E 163 Sts
M100 — Riverdale Av/Broadway
M125 — 125 St Crosstown
M145 — 145 St Crosstown
M — Penn Station-Jackson Heights

PATH & Light Rail

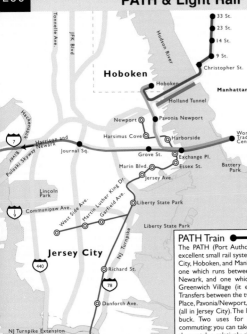

Hudson River

33 St.
23 St.
14 St.
9 St.
Christopher St.

Hoboken

Hoboken

Manhattan

Holland Tunnel

Newport
Pavonia Newport

Harsimus Cove
Harborside

World Trade Center

Harrison and Newark

Journal Sq.

Grove St.
Exchange Pl.

Marin Blvd.
Essex St.

Battery Park

Jersey Ave.

Lincoln Park

Communipaw Ave.
West Side Ave.
Martin Luther King Dr.
Garfield Ave.
Liberty State Park

Liberty State Park

Jersey City

NJ Turnpike

Richard St.

Danforth Ave.

NJ Turnpike Extension

Stephen R. Gregg Bayonne County Park

E. 45th St.

JFK Blvd.

E. 34th St.

Newark Bay

Bayonne

City Park

Kill Van Kull

Bayonne Bridge

Staten Island

PATH Train

The PATH (Port Authority Trans-Hudson Corp.) is an excellent small rail system which services Newark, Jersey City, Hoboken, and Manhattan. There are two basic lines: one which runs between the World Trade Center and Newark, and one which runs between Hoboken and Greenwich Village (it ends at 33rd St. in Manhattan). Transfers between the two lines are available at Exchange Place, Pavonia/Newport, Grove Street, and Journal Square (all in Jersey City). The PATH runs 24/7 and only costs a buck. Two uses for the PATH other than basic commuting: you can take it to Newark's train station and then catch a relatively cheap cab to Newark Airport; and you can take it back to the Village late at night when you've finished seeing a show at Maxwell's in Hoboken (enjoy the wait!). The night schedule for the PATH is a bit confusing, so make sure to look at the map while you're waiting.

Hudson-Bergen Light Rail

The Hudson-Bergen Light Rail system (brought to you by NJ Transit) is the newest rail line in the New York area, and may bring about some exciting changes (a.k.a. "gentrification") in Jersey City and Bayonne, NJ. Currently there are 15 stops in the system, 2 in Bayonne and 10 in Jersey City, ending at Newport. You can then take the PATH from Exchange Place into Manhattan. The Light Rail is $1.50 per trip, and the second phase of the system-running up to Hoboken from Newport (parallel to the PATH) is underway. Future plans take it up to Weehawken , southern Bergen County, and further south into Bayonne, for a total of 32 stations. We're psyched.

Amtrak is the United States version of a national train system, and while it's not very good, it can at least get you to many major northeastern cities in half a day or less. Prices aren't very good either, sometimes making it almost as attractive to fly to cities such as Boston or Washington, DC. However, since air fares have been increasing, you might want to at least shop Amtrak's fares.

General Information
Amtrak was created by the federal government in 1971. Currently, Amtrak runs to 500+ stations in 45 states (no service in Alaska, Hawaii, South Dakota, Wyoming, and Maine). Amtrak serves over 21 million passengers a year, employs 25,000 people, and provides "contract-commuter services" for several state and regional rail lines. Amtrak has 278 diesel locomotives and 65 electric locomotives, 1400 passenger cars, and 1500 freight cars in its fleet. Amtrak's phone number is 800-USA-RAIL.

Amtrak in New York
In New York City, Amtrak runs out of Pennsylvania Station, which is currently located in a basement underneath Madison Square Garden at 7th Avenue and 33rd Street. However, don't despair—chances are, the city you'll wind up in will have a very nice station, and, if all goes well, so will we, once the front half of the Farley Post Office is converted to a "new" Penn Station.

Popular Destinations
While you can (eventually) wind up anywhere Amtrak goes starting at Penn Station, many New Yorkers use Amtrak to get to Boston, Philadelphia, or Washington, DC. Amtrak also runs a line up to Montreal, and another one which goes through most of the major cities in western New York state (Buffalo, Rochester, Albany, etc.) You can get a complete listing of all stations on Amtrak's web site, www.amtrak.com.

Going to Boston
Amtrak usually runs 13 trains daily to Boston, Massachusetts. The one-way fare is either $52 or $58 depending on which train you take; it takes about five hours to get to South Station in downtown Boston. For $111 one-way you can take the express train and complete the journey in just over three-and-a-half hours.

Going to Philadelphia
You can get on 40 or so different Amtrak trains on any given day that will pass through Philadelphia. It will cost you about $43 on a regular Amtrak train; if you're really in a hurry, you can take the special "Metroliner" service for $79 which will get you there in an hour and fifteen minutes. The cheapest rail option to Philly is actually to take NJ Transit to Trenton and then hook up with Eastern Pennsylvania's excellent SEPTA service—this will take longer, but will cost you under $20.

Going to Washington, DC (subtitle: How Much is Your Time Worth?)
Amtrak runs over 30 trains daily to DC and the prices vary dramatically. The cheapest trains cost $67 and take a bit less than 4 hours. However, the Metroliner service costs almost double at $115 one-way, and delivers you there in 3 hours. The Express takes just over two-and-a-half hours at $134 one-way. Worth it? It's your call.

A Note About Fares
While the prices quoted above for Boston, Philly, and DC destinations tend to stay fairly consistent, fare rates to other destinations such as Cleveland, Chicago, etc. can vary depending on how far in advance you book your seat. For instance, if you want to take a train to Chicago tomorrow, you might pay $150 one way; booking 2 months in advance will cut that almost in half to $82. Again, check www.amtrak.com's database for particulars.

Baggage Check (Amtrak Passengers)
A maximum of three items may be checked up to thirty minutes prior to departure. Up to three additional bags may be checked for a fee of $10. (Two carry on items allowed). No electronic equipment, plastic bags, or paper bags may be checked.

LIRR Railroad

General Information   New York City (718) 217-LIRR
Nassau County (516) 822-LIRR
Suffolk County (631) 231-LIRR
TDD (Hearing Impaired) (718) 558-3022

Public Affairs & Cyc-n-Ride(Weekdays 9AM-5PM): (718) 558-8228
Group Travel and Tours (M-F 8AM-4PM): (718) 558-7498
Mail and Ride (Toll Free): (800) 649-NYNY
Public Affairs (Weekdays 9AM-5PM): (718) 558-8228
MTA Police Eastern Region: (718) 558-3300 or (516) 733-3900
Lost & Found (Weekdays 7:20AM - 7:20PM): (212) 643-5228
Ticket Refunds: (718) 558- 488
Ticket Vending Machine Assistance: (800) 325-LIRR
Hamptons Reserve Service: (718) 558-8070
Website: http://www.lirr.org/lirr/

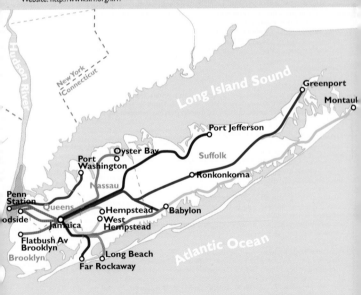

The Long Island Rail Road is the busiest railroad in North America. It has nine lines with 124 stations stretching from Penn Station in midtown Manhattan, to the eastern tip of Long Island Montauk Point. An estimated 82.1 million people rode the LIRR in 1999. If you enjoy traveling on overcrowded, smelly trains with intermittent air conditioning, then the LIRR is for you. For further information, check out www.ihatethelirr.com or the somewhat tamer site, www.geocities.com/RodeoDrive/Mall/4322.

Fares and Schedules

Fares and schedules can be obtained by calling one of the general information lines, depending on your area. They can also be found on the LIRR website. Make sure to buy your ticket before you get on the train, if the ticket window is open. Otherwise it costs an extra two dollars. As it is a commuter rail road, the LIRR offers weekly and monthly passes, as well as ten-trip packages for on or off-peak hours. If you are a fancy pants and need a parlor car reservation, call Public Affairs at (718) 558-8228.

Pets on the LIRR

Trained service animals accompanying passengers with disabilities are permitted on LIRR trains. Other small pets are allowed on trains but they must be confined to closed, ventilated containers.

The Port Jefferson Branch
- Port Jefferson
- Stony Brook
- St. James
- Smithtown
- Kings Park
- Northport
- Greenlawn
- Huntington
- Cold Spring Harbor
- Syosset
- Hicksville
- Westbury
- Carle Place
- Mineola
- Merillon Avenue
- New Hyde Park
- Jamaica
- Penn Station (New York)/
- Flatbush Avenue (Brooklyn)

The Ronkonkoma Branch
- Greenport
- Southold
- Mattituck
- Riverhead
- Yaphank
- Medford
- Ronkonkoma
- Central Islip
- Brentwood
- Deer Park
- Wyandanch
- Pinelawn
- Farmingdale
- Bethpage
- Hicksville
- Jamaica
- Penn Station (New York)/
- Flatbush Avenue (Brooklyn)

The Babylon Branch
- Babylon
- Lindenhurst
- Copiague
- Amityville
- Massapequa
- Seaford
- Wantagh
- Bellmore
- Merrick
- Freeport
- Baldwin
- Rockville Centre
- Jamaica
- Penn Station (New York)/
- Flatbush Avenue (Brooklyn)

The Montauk Branch
- Montauk
- Amagansett
- East Hampton
- Bridgehampton
- Southampton
- Hampton Bays
- Westhampton
- Speonk
- Mastic-Shirley
- Bellport
- Patchogue
- Sayville
- Oakdale
- Great River
- Islip
- Bay Shore
- Jamaica
- Penn Station (New York)/
- Flatbush Avenue (Brooklyn)

The Far Rockaway Branch
- Far Rockaway
- Inwood
- Lawrence
- Cedarhurst
- Woodmere
- Hewlet
- Gibson
- Valley Stream
- Rosedale
- Laurelton
- Locust Manor
- Jamaica
- Penn Station (New York)/
- Flatbush Avenue (Brooklyn)

The Port Washington Branch
- Port Washington
- Plandome
- Manhasset
- Great Neck
- Little Neck
- Douglaston
- Bayside
- Auburndale
- Broadway
- Murray Hill
- Flushing Main Street
- Woodside
- Penn Station (New York)

The Oyster Bay Branch
- Oyster Bay
- Locust Valley
- Glen Cove
- Glen Street
- Sea Cliff
- Glen Head
- Greenvale
- Roslyn
- Albertson
- East Williston
- Jamaica
- Penn Station (New York)/
- Flatbush Avenue (Brooklyn)

The Hempstead Branch
- Hempstead
- Country Life Press
- Garden City
- Nassau Boulevard
- Stewart Manor
- Floral Park
- Bellerose
- Queens Village
- Hollis
- Jamaica
- Penn Station (New York)/
- Flatbush Avenue (Brooklyn)

The West Hempstead Branch
- West Hempstead
- Hempstead Gardens
- Lakeview
- Malverne
- Westwood
- St. Albans
- Jamaica
- Penn Station (New York)/
- Flatbush Avenue (Brooklyn)

The Long Beach Branch
- Long Beach
- Island Park
- Oceanside
- East Rockaway
- Centre Avenue
- Lynbrook
- Valley Stream
- Rosedale
- Laurelton
- Locust Manor
- Jamaica
- Penn Station (New York)/
- Flatbush Avenue (Brooklyn)

Metro North Railroad

General Information (NYC): 212-532-4900
General Information (All other areas): 800-METRO-INFO
Lost and Found (Grand Central Terminal): 212-340-2555
MTA Inspector General Hotline: 800-MTA-IG4U
Website: http://www.mta.nyc.ny.us/mnr/

Metro North Railroad

Metro North is an extremely accessible and efficient railroad that originates from Grand Central Station in Manhattan. Its three main lines (Hudson, Harlem, and New Haven) form one of the largest commuter railroads in the U.S. There are over 100 stations in its system, and each of the main lines travels more than 70 miles from New York City.

Fares and Schedules

Fares and schedules can be easily obtained at Grand Central Station or on Metro North's website. If you wait to pay until you are on the train, you will pay an extra two bucks, but since Metro-North is a commuter rail line, there are monthly and weekly rail passes available. For more information, use Metro-North's extraordinarily detailed website, which offers in-depth information on each station, full time tables, and excellent maps.

The Harlem Line
- Wassaic
- Tenmile River
- Dover Plains
- Harlem Valley-Wingdale
- Appalachian Trail
- Pawling
- Patterson
- Brewster North
- Brewster
- Croton Falls
- Purdy's
- Golden's Bridge
- Katonah
- Bedford Hills
- Mt. Kisco
- Chappaqua
- Pleasantville
- Hawthorne
- Mt. Pleasant
- Valhalla
- North White Plains
- White Plains
- Hartsdale
- Scarsdale
- Crestwood
- Tuckahoe
- Bronxville
- Fleetwood
- Mount Vernon West
- Wakefield
- Woodlawn
- Williams Bridge
- Botanical Garden
- Fordham
- Tremont
- Melrose
- 125th Street
- Grand Central Station

The Hudson Line
- Poughkeepsie
- New Hamburg
- Beacon
- Breakneck Ridge
- Cold Spring
- Garrison
- Manitou
- Peekskill
- Cortlandt
- Croton-Harmon
- Ossining
- Scarborough
- Philipse Manor
- Tarrytown
- Irvington
- Ardsley
- Dobbs Ferry
- Hastings
- Greystone
- Glenwood
- Yonkers
- Ludlow
- Riverdale
- Spuyten Duyvil
- Marble Hill
- University Heights
- Morris Heights
- 125th Street
- Grand Central Station

The New Haven Line
- New Haven
- Milford
- Stratford
- Bridgeport
  - Derby Shelton
  - Ansonia
  - Seymour
  - Beacon Falls
  - Naugatuck
  - Waterbury
- Fairfield
- Southport
- Green's Farms
- Westport
- East Norwalk
- South Norwalk
  - Merritt 7
  - Wilton
  - Cannondale
  - Branchville
  - Redding
  - Bethel
  - Danbury
- Rowayton
- Darien
- Noroton Heights
- Stamford
  - Glenbrook
  - Springdale
  - Talmadge Hill
  - New Canaan
- Old Greenwich
- Riverside
- Cos Cob
- Greenwich
- Port Chester
- Rye
- Harrison
- Mamaroneck
- Larchmont
- New Rochelle
- Pelham
- Mount Vernon
- Fordham
- 125th Street
- Grand Central Station

NJ Transit

NJ Transit carries hundreds of thousands of New Jersey commuters to New York every morning—well, almost. The main problem is that some lines don't run directly into Penn Station—you have to transfer at Hoboken to another train. Also, while the trains are usually clean (and immune to the weirdness that plagues the LIRR), some lines (such as the Pascack Valley Line) just seem to creep along—and then you have to transfer. However, more "through" lines are in the works, as well as several other projects such as a light rail system which will service the Jersey side of the Hudson River. And while NJ Transit isn't going to compete with Japanese rail systems any time soon, it still beats waiting in traffic at the three measly Hudson River automobile crossings.

General Information: 973-762-5100 or 800-772-3606
Mail Tik (monthly passes): 973-491-8491
Emergency Hotline: 973-491-7400
Newark Lost and Found: 973-491-8792
Hoboken Lost and Found: 201-714-2739
New York Lost and Found: 212-630-7389
Website: www.njtransit.com

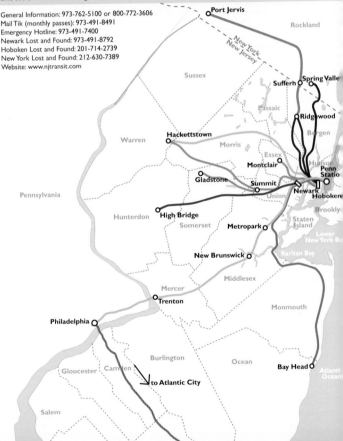

NJ Transit

Fares and Schedules

Fares and schedules can be obtained at Hoboken, Newark, and Penn Station, or on NJ Transit's website. If you wait to pay until you're on the train, you'll pay extra for the privilege. However, NJ Transit does have monthly, weekly, weekend, and ten-trip tickets available

The Pascack Valley Line
- Spring Valley
- Nanuet
- Pearl River
- Montvale
- Park Ridge
- Woodcliff Lake
- Hillsdale
- Westwood
- Emerson
- Oradell
- River Edge
- North Hackensack
- Hackensack (Anderson Street)
- Hackensack (Essex Street)
- Teterboro
- Wood-Ridge
- Hoboken

The Port Jervis Line
- Port Jervis
- Otisville
- Middletown
- Campbell Hall
- Salisbury Mills/ Cornwall
- Harriman
- Tuxedo
- Sloatsburg
- Suffern

The Atlantic City Line
- Atlantic City
- Absecon
- Egg Harbor City
- Hammonton
- Atco
- Lindenwold
- Cherry Hill
- Philadelphia

The Northeast Corridor Line
- Philadelphia
- Trenton
- Princeton Junction
  - Princeton
- Jersey Avenue
- New Brunswick
- Edison
- Metuchen
- Metropark
- Rahway
- Linden
- Elizabeth
- North Elizabeth
- Newark
- Penn Station (New York)/ Hoboken

The Main and Bergen Lines
- Suffern
- Mahwah
- Ramsey
- Allendale
- Waldwick
- Ho-Ho-Kus
- Ridgewood
- Glen Rock
- Radburn (Fairlawn)
- Broadway (Fairlawn)
- Plauderville
- Garfield
- Rutherford
- Harmon Cove
- Hoboken
  - Glen Rock
  - Hawthorne
  - Paterson
  - Clifton
  - Passaic
  - Delawanna
  - Lyndhurst
  - Kingsland

The Boonton Line
- Hackettstown
- Mount Olive
- Netcong
- Lake Hopatcong
- Dover
- Denville
- Mountain Lakes
- Boonton
- Towaco
- Lincoln Park
- Mountain View (Wayne)
- Little Falls
- Great Notch
- Montclair Heights
- Mountain Ave. (Montclair)
- Upper Montclair
- Watchung Ave. (Montclair)
- Walnut St. (Montclair)
- Benson St. (Glen Ridge)
- Rowe St. (Bloomfield)
- Arlington(Kearny)
- Hoboke

The Raritan Valley Line
- High Bridge
- Annandale
- Lebanon
- White House
- North Branch
- Raritan
- Somerville
- Finderne
- Bridgewater
- Bound Brook
- Dunellen
- Plainfield
- Netherwood
- Fanwood
- Westfield
- Garwood
- Cranford
- Roselle Park
- Newark
- Penn Station (New York)/ Hoboken

The North Jersey Coast Line
- Bay Head
- Point Pleasant Beach
- Manasquan
- Spring Lake
- Belmar
- Bradley Beach
- Asbury Park
- Allenhurst
- Elberon
- Long Branch
- Monmouth Racetrack
- Little Silver
- Red Bank
- Middletown
- Hazlet
- Matawan
- South Amboy
- Perth Amboy
- Woodbridge
- Avenel
- Rahway
- Linden
- Elizabeth
- North Elizabeth
- Newark
- Penn Station (New York)/ Hoboken

The Morris and Essex Lines
- Hackettstown
- Mount Olive
- Netcong
- Lake Hopatcong
- Dover
- Denville
- Mt. Tabor
- Morris Plains
- Morristown
- Convent Station
- Madison
- Chatham
- Summit
- Short Hills
- Millburn
- Maplewood
- South Orange
- Mountain Station
- Highland Avenue
- Orange
- Brick Church
- East Orange
- Newark
- Penn Station (New York)/ Hoboken
  - Gladstone
  - Peapack
  - Far Hills
  - Bernardsville
  - Basking Ridge
  - Lyons
  - Millington
  - Stirling
  - Gillette
  - Berkeley Heights
  - 986 Murray Hill
  - New Providence
  - Montclair(Bay St.)
  - Glen Ridge
  - Bloomfield
  - Watsessing

Grand Central Station

Grand Central Terminal, designed in the Beaux Arts style by Warren & Wetmore, is by far the most beautiful of Manhattan's major terminals; indeed, it ranks as one of the most beautiful terminals in the world. What's also nice about it is that it's convenient (located right in the heart of Midtown), newly refurbished, and utterly cool. The only bad thing is that it only services Metro North-you have to go to Penn Station for LIRR and NJ Transit trains.

The refurbishment of Grand Central has been taking place over the last few years and it seems to be going quite nicely. The star ceiling has been cleaned and modernized, a second grand staircase has been constructed, and a mall on the lower level is moving towards completion. These improvements, along with Grand Central's existing attractions (the central clock, the Oyster Bar, the catwalks) make it one of New York's most impressive buildings. It's no surprise, then, that there are THREE separate tours of Grand Central; the hour-long LaSalle Tour (212-340-3404), the Municipal Arts Society Tour (212-935-3960), and the Grand Central Partnership Tour (212-697-1245).

General Information:

NFT Grid Number: 13
Address: 42nd Street and Park Ave.
General Information: 212-935-3560 • Lost and Found: 212-340-2555
Website: www.grandcentralterminal.com
MTA Subway Stops: 4, 5, 6, 7, S • MTA Bus Lines: 1, 2, 3, 4, 42, 98, 101, 102, 103, 104
Other Rail Lines: Metro North
Newark Airport Bus Service: Olympia (212-964-6233, $10)
LaGuardia Airport Bus Service: NY Airport Service (718-706-9658, $13)
JFK Airport Bus Service: NY Airport Service (718-706-9658, $10)
Year Opened: 1913

Terminal Shops:

APPAREL
Banana Republic
Central Watch Band Stand
Kenneth Cole
LaCrasia Gloves
Leeper Kids
Matt Hunter and Company
Pink Slip
Super Runners Shop

BANKS/FINANCE
Avis Currency Exchange
Chase Bank

ITEMS & SERVICES
Children's General Store
Cobbler and Shine
Dahlia
Discovery Channel Store
Douglas Cosmetics
Eastern News
Eddie's Shoe Repair
Flowers on Lexington
General Nutrition Center
Grand Central Optical
Hudson News
Joon Stationery
L'Occitane
Michael Eigen Jewelers
Neuhaus Boutique
New York Transit Museum

Gallery and Store
Grand Central Racquet
O'Henry's Film Works
Oliviers & Co.
Origins
Our Name Is Mud
Papyrus
Posman Books
Rite Aid
TOTO
trainTUNES
Tumi
Watch Station

FOOD
America's Coffee
Godiva Chocolatier
Grande Harvest Wines
Hot and Crusty Bakery
Park Avenue Sweets
Starbucks

RESTAURANTS & DINING
CONCOURSE
Cafe Spice
Central Market
Christer's
Custard Beach
Dim Sum
Junior's
Knodel

Little Pie Company
Masa Sushi
Mendy's Kosher Delicatessen
Métrazur
Michael Jordan's The Steak
House NYC
Mike's Take-Away
Nem
New York Pretzel
Oyster Bar and Restaurant
Shoebox Cafe
The Campbell Apartment
Two Boots
Zócalo Bar and Restaurant

GRAND CENTRAL MARKET
Adriana's Caravan
Ceriello Fine Foods
Corrado Bread and Pastry
Greenwich Produce
Kashkaval
Koglin German Hams
Li-Lac Chocolates
Ninth Avenue Cheese
Oren's Daily Roast
Perigord
Pescatore Seafood Company
Ronnybrook Farm Dairy
Wild Edibles
Zaro's Bread Basket

Penn Station, designed by McKim, Mead & White (New York's greatest architects), is a Beaux Arts treasure, filled with light and...oh, that's the one they tore down. Penn Station today is essentially a basement, only without the bowling trophies and the Johnny Walker Black.

BUT...good news seems to be coming from around the corner, in the form of a proposal to convert the eastern half of the Farley Post Office (also designed by McKim, Mead, & White) to a new, above-ground (a novel concept), light-filled station. We can't wait. Until then, Penn Station will just go on being an ugly, crappy underground terminal (citysearch.com says it has "all the charm of a salt mine") under Madison Square Garden, a terminal which services over 600,000 people per day-making it the busiest railway station in the United States.

Penn Station services Amtrak, the LIRR, and NJ Transit trains, which is admittedly a lot of responsibility. Amtrak (800-872-7245), which is surely the worst national train system of any country above the poverty line, administers the station. Although we're hoping the new station proposal will go through, we still won't be able to afford the ridiculously high fares that Amtrak charges to go to places like D.C., Philly, and Boston.

General Information:

NFT Grid Number: 8
Address: 7th Avenue and 33rd Street
MTA Subway Stops: 1, 2, 3, 9, A, C, E
Train Lines: LIRR, Amtrak, NJ Transit
Newark Airport Bus Service: Olympia (212-964-6233, $10)
LaGuardia Airport Bus Service: NY Airport Service (718-706-9658, $13)
JFK Airport Bus Service: NY Airport Service (718-706-9658, $10)
Passengers per day: 600,000

General Information (Amtrak): 800-872-7245
MTA Bus Lines: 4, 10, 16, 34, Q32

Year Opened: 1968

Terminal Shops:

On the LIRR Level

Food & Drink
Auntie Anne's Pretzels
Caruso's Pizza
Central Market
Charley O's Sports
    Bar and Grill
Dunkin' Donut's
Haagan Daaz
Hot and Crusty
Java Shop
Knot Just Pretzels
Le Bon Café
McDonalds
NY City's Famous
    5 Star Grill
Riese Restaurants

Rosa's Pizza and Pasta
Seattle Coffee Roasters
Smoothie King

Other
Carlton Cards
Dreyfus Financial Center
Hallmark
Hudson News
K-Mart
Paula's Designer
    Fragrances
Penn Books
Perfumania
Soleman-shoe repair,
    locksmith
The Petal Pusher
Voice Stream Wireless

On Amtrak Level

Food & Drink
Baskin Robbin's
Dipsy Dog
Don Pepi Pizza
Don Pepi's Delicatessen
Houlihan's Restaurant and
    Bar
Kabooz's Bar and Grille
Krispy Kreme Doughnuts
Primo Cappuccino
Zaro's Breadbasket

Other
Book Corner
Duane Reade
Elegance

Gifts and Electronics
New York New York
Shoetrician-Shoe
    repair and shine
Tiecoon
Tourist Information
    Center
TSR Wireless

On Both Levels
Nathan's
Pizza Hut
Roy Rogers

There is a Chase 24 hour ATM located on the Amtrak level and Fleet 24 hour ATM located on the LIRR level in addition to a generic (money thieving) ATM located in the Smoothie King store.

Temporary Parcel/Baggage Check
The only facility for storing parcels and baggage in Penn Station is at the Baggage Check on the Amtrak level (to the left of the ticket counter). There are no locker facilities at Penn Station. The Baggage Check is open from 5am until midnight and costs $1.50 per item for each 24 hour period.

Port Authority Bus Terminal

In 1939, eight separate bus terminals scattered through the city were increasing traffic congestion. Although a consolidated, larger central terminal seemed like the obvious solution, many of the smaller terminals refused to merge. At that point Mayor Fiorello La Guardia asked The Port Authority of New York and New Jersey to take over the project and develop one central terminal. On January 27, 1949, construction began at the site bordered by Eighth Ave., 40th St., Ninth Ave., and 41st St. On December 15, 1950, after an investment of $24 million, the Port Authority Bus Terminal was opened.

That investment has now grown to $422 million, and although the terminal is located in perhaps the last genuinely seedy neighborhood in Manhttan, the dozens of terminal shops and amenities (including a post office, bank, refurbished bathrooms, a blood bank, subway access, and even a bowling alley) make Port Authority a convenient departure and arrival point. The last remaining grungy area of the terminal is the lower bus level, which is a dirty, exhaust-filled space, best visited just a few minutes before you need to board you bus. The chart on the right shows which bus companies run out of the Port Authority and a basic description of their destinations.

On Easter Sunday, Christmas Eve, or Thanksgiving, one can see all the angst-ridden sons and daughters of suburban New Jersey parents joyfully waiting in cramped, disgusting corridors for that nauseating bus ride back to Leonia or Morristown or Plainfield or wherever. A fascinating sight.

General Information:
NFT Grid Number: 11 • Address: 41st Street and 8th Avenue
General Information: 212-564-8484 • Kinney System P.A. Garage: 212-502-2341
Lost and Found: are you kidding?
Website: www.panynj.gov/tbt/pabframe.HTM
MTA Subway Stops: Ⓐ Ⓒ Ⓔ ❼ (Port Authority);
❶ ❷ ❸ ❼ ❾ Ⓝ Ⓡ Ⓢ (Times Square)
MTA Bus Lines: 10 11 16 27 42 104
Other Bus Lines: see right-hand page
Newark Airport Bus Service: Olympia (212-964-6233, $10)
LaGuardia Airport Bus Service: NY Airport Express (718-706-9658, $13)
JFK Airport Bus Service: NY Airport Express (718-706-9658, $10)
Passengers per day: 200,000 • Passengers since opening: 3 billion
Year Opened: 1950

Terminal Shops:
South Wing–Main Concourse
Au Bon Pain
California Burrito
Cosmetics Plus
Deli Plus
Duane Reade
General Nutrition Center
Krispy Kreme
Marrella Hair Stylists
NY Blood Center
Radio Shack
Ruthie's Hallmark
Timothy's
Villa Pizza
World's Fare Restaurant Bar
Zaro's Bake Shop

South Wing–Second Floor
Bonini 1 Watch Shop
BT Books
Café Metro
Drago Shoe Repair
Fleet Bank
Kelly Film Express
Hudson News
Leisure Time Bowling Center
   and Cocktail Lounge
Mrs. Fields Bakery Café
NY Lottery
McAnn's
Munchie's
Saks Florist
Sweet Factory

North Wing–Second Floor
Fleet Bank (ATMs)
Jay's Hallmark Bookstore
Tropica Juice Bar
USO
U.S. Postal Service

North Wing–Third Floor
Hudson News
Tropica Juice Bar

Port Authority Bus Terminal

Bus Company	Phone	Area Served
Academy Bus Transportation	800-242-1339	Serves New York City, including Staten Island, Wall St. and Port Authority and New Jersey, including Hoboken.
Adirondack Trailways	800-858-8555	Serves all of New York State with coach connections throughout the U.S.
Atlantic Express Service	212-962-1122	Service between New York and New Jersey, including Atlantic City, Mammoth & Ocean Counties, South Jersey, and local service in Hudson County. Also offers service between Staten Island and Manhattan.
Bonanza Bus	800-556-3815	Serves many points between New York and New England, including Cape Cod and the Berkshires.
Capitol Trailways	800-333-8444/ 800-444-2877	Service between Pennsylvania, Virginia, New York State, and New York City.
Carl Bieber Bus	800-243-2374	Service to and from Port Authority and Wall Street in New York and Redding, Cookston, Wescosville, Hellertown, and Easton in Pennsylvania.
Community Coach	800-522-4514	Service between New York City and W. Orange, Livingston, Morristown, E.Hanover, Whippany, and Floram Park, New Jersey.
DeCamp Bus	800-631-1281	Service between New York City and New Jersey, including the Meadowlands.
Greyhound Bus	800-231-2222	Services most of the U.S. and Canada.
Gray Line Bus	212-397-2620	Service offered throughout the U.S. and Canada. Also offers international trips.
Hudson Bus	201-653-2220	Serves 48 states.
Lakeland Bus	201-366-0600	Service between New York and New Jersey.
Leisure Lines	800-524-027	Services Atlantic City to and from the Bronx/Queens/ Washington Heights. Also services Rockland County, Fort Lee, and Spring Valley into Manhattan city streets, including midtown and Wall St. and Bergen County into Port Authority.
Martz Coach	800-233-8604	Service between New York and Pennsylvania.
New Jersey Transit	800-772-2222(NJ)/ 973-762-5100 (all other)	Serves New York, New Jersey, and Philadelphia.
NY Airport Service	212-964-6233	Service between Port Authority and Kennedy and LaGuardia Airports.
Olympia Trails	212-964-6233	Provides express bus service between Manhattan and Newark Airport. Makes stops all over New York City, including World Trade Center, Grand Central, and many connections with hotel shuttles.
Peter Pan Lines	800-343-9999	Serves the East, including N.H., Maine, Philly, DC. Also goes to Canada.
Pine Hill-Kingston	800-858-8555	Services New York state area.
RocklandCoaches/ Red and Tan Services	201-384-2400	Services New York's Port Authority, GW bridge, and 44th and 8th streets to and from most of Bergen County and upstate New York.
ShortLine Bus	800-631-8405	Serves the New York City airports, Atlantic City, and the Hudson Valley.
Suburban Trails	732-249-1100	Offers commuter service from Central New Jersey to and from Port Authority and Wall Street. Also services between the Route 9 Corridor and New York City.
Susquehanna	800-692-6314	Service to and from New York City and Newark (Greyhound Terminal) and Summerville, New Jersey and many stops in Central Pennsylvania, ending in Williamsport and Lock Haven.
Trans-Bridge Lines	610-868-6001 800-962-9135	Offers service between New York, Pennsylvania, and New Jersey, including Newark and Kennedy airports.
Trans-Hudson Express	800-772-3689	

Ferries, Heliports, & Marinas

Ferries/Boat Tours, Rentals, & Charters

Name	Contact Info	Grid
Staten Island Ferry	Phone: 718-815-2628 • www.ci.nyc.ny.us/html/dot/html/get_around/ferry/statfery.html This free ferry goes from Battery Park to Staten Island. On weekdays it leaves every 15-20 minutes from 6:30am-9:00am and 4:00-7:00pm. All other times it's every half hour. On weekends, it leaves every hour from 9:30pm-7:30am. All other times it's every half hour.	I
NY Waterway	Phone: 800-53-FERRY • www.nywaterway.com This is the largest ferry service in NY. They offer many commuter routes (mostly from New Jersey), sightseeing tours, and very popular shuttles to Yankees and Mets games.	I, 10, 15
Sea Streak	Phone: 1-800-BOAT-RIDE • www.seastreakusa.com Catamarans that go pretty fast from the highlands in NJ to Wall Street, East 34th St. and the Brooklyn Army Terminal.	I, 10
NY Fast Ferry	Phone: 1-800-NYF-NYFF • www.nyff.com This ferry goes between Highlands, NJ and Pier 11 (Wall St.) or E. 34th St., Manhattan	I, 10
Circle Line	Phone: 212-563-3200 • http://www.circleline.com Circle Line offers many sightseeing tours including the full island cruise (departs from pier 83 at 42nd St. — $24, no reservations needed), and the visit to Ellis Island (departs from pier 16 at South St. Seaport —$12—212-630-8888)	I, 11
Spirit of New York	Phone: 212-727-2789 • www.spiritcruises.com Offers lunch and dinner cruises everyday. Prices start at $29.95. Leaves from Pier 61 at Chelsea Piers. Make a reservation at least one week in advance, but the earlier the better.	8
Loeb Boathouse	Phone: 212-517-2233 • www.centralparknyc.org/vp-template.php?id=47 Central Park You can rent rowboats from April through October at The Lake, seven days a week weather permitting, in Central Park. It's $10 for the first hour and $2.50 each additional hour ($30 cash deposit). It's open 10-6, but the last boat goes out at 5:30. Up to five people per boat. No reservations needed.	
World Yacht Cruises	Phone: 212-630-8100 • www.worldyacht.com These very fancy dinner cruises start at $67 per person. They leave from Pier 81 (41st St.) and you need a reservation. The cruise boards at 6, sails at 7, and returns at 10. There's also a weekend brunch cruise March-December that is $41.90 per person.	11

Marinas/Passenger Ship Terminal

Name	Contact Info	Grid
Surfside III	Phone: 212-336-7873 • www.surfside3.com Dockage at Chelsea Piers. They have daily, weekly, and seasonal (there is a waiting list) per foot rates.	8
North Cove Yacht Harbor	Phone: 212-938-9000 • www.northcoveyachts.com A very, very fancy place to park your yacht in Battery Park City.	I
NY Skyports Inc.	Phone: 212-686-4547 Located on the East River at 23rd St. Transient Dockage is $3 per foot.	10
79th St. Marina	Phone: 212-496-2105 This dock has lots of long-term houseboat residents. It's located at 79th St. and the Hudson River.	14
Dyckman Marina	Phone: 212-567-5120 Transient dockage on the Hudson River at Dyckman St.	25
Passenger Ship Terminal	Phone: 212-246-5451 • www.pst.com If Love Boat re-runs aren't enough, and you decide to go on a cruise, you'll leave from the Passenger Ship Terminal. W. 55th St. at 12th Ave. Take the West Side Highway to Piers 88-92.	11

Helicopter Services

Name	Contact Info	Grid
Helicopter Flight Services	Phone: 212-355-0801 • www.heliny.com For a minimum of $100, you can hop on a helicopter at one of three locations—E. 34th St., W. 30th St., or the Downtown Manhattan Heliport at South St. Seaport. Make sure to call in advance.	3, 8, 10
Liberty Helicopter Tours	Phone: 212-967-6464 • www.libertyhelicopters.com Leaves from the heliport at W. 30th St. and 12th Ave. (9am-9pm) or the Downtown Manhattan Heliport at South St. Seaport (9am,-6:30pm). Prices start at $48 and you don't need a reservation. Flights depart every 5-10 mins once there is a full load of six passengers.	3, 8
Wall Street Helicopter	Phone: 212-943-5959 • www.wallstreetheli.qpg.com Leaves from the South St. Heliport (Pier 6). Executive/corporate helicopter and twin engine aircraft charters.	3

Bike & Skate Information

General Information

Department of City Planning website: www.ci.nyc.ny.us/html/dcp/html/bikenet.html
Transportation Alternatives website: www.transalt.org   Phone: 212-629-8080
New York Cycle Club: www.nycc.org   Empire Skate Club: www.empireskate.org

While not for the faint of heart, biking and skating around Manhattan can be one of the most efficient and exhilarating forms of transportation (insight into the abundance of bike messengers careening around town). The terrain of Manhattan is pretty flat (for the most part), and the fitness and environmental advantages of using people power are immense. However, there are also some downsides, including but not limited to: psychotic cab drivers, buses, traffic, pedestrians, pavement with potholes, glass, and debris, and poor air quality. In 1994 the Bicycle Network Development Program was created to increase bicycle usage in the NYC area. Since then, many bike lanes have been created on streets and in parks. These tend to be the safest places to ride (to get a listing, go to the web-sites listed above). Central Park is a great place to ride, as are the newly developed paths from Battery Park to Chelsea Piers that run along the Hudson River. You'll also find East River Park to be nice for recreational riding and skating – just not after dark! In addition to bicycle rentals, RB Bicycle (1306 2nd Ave. – 288-5592) offers recorded tours of Central Park, so you can learn about the park and exercise at the same time.

An advantage of skating is that you can easily put your skates in a bag and carry them with you anywhere – subways, indoors, on buses – which also eliminates the possibility of theft. Recreational skating venues in Manhattan include Wollmann Rink in Central Park, Chelsea Piers, The Roxy (515 W. 18th), Riverbank State park (Riverside Drive at 145th St.), and Rivergate Ice Rink (401 E. 34th St.). For more information about where to skate in the boroughs, check out www.skatecity.com. For organized events, see Empire Skate Club at www.empireskate.com.

Bikes are less convenient than skates, and are always at risk of being stolen (always lock them to immovable objects with the best lock you can afford), but can be a much faster, less demanding form of transport.

Bike Rentals (and Sales)

Metro Bicycle Stores:
• 88th St. at Lexington • 427-4450 • Grid 17
• 360 W 47th St. at 9th • 581-4500 • Grid 11
• 96th St. at Broadway • 663-7531 • Grid 16
• 14th St. between 1st & 2nd • 228-4344 • Grids 6, 10
• 6th Ave. at W 15th St. • 255-5100 • Grids 5, 6, 9
• 6th Ave. between Canal & Grand • 334-8000 • Grid 2
Anewgen Bicycles • 832 9th Ave. • 757-2418 • Grid 11
Toga Bikeshop • 110 West End Ave at 64th • 799-9625 • Grid 14
Gotham Bikes • 112 W Broadway between Duane & Reade • 732-2453 • Grid 2
Bicycle Habitat • 244 Lafayette between Spring & Prince • 431-3315 • Grid 6

Bike Works • 106 Ridge St. • 388-1077 • Grid 7
CNC Bicycle Works • 1101 1st Ave. between 60th & 61st • 230-1919 • Grid 15
City Bicycles Inc. • 508 9th Ave. • 563-3373 • Grid 11
Eddie's Bicycles Shop • 490 Amsterdam Ave. • 580-2011 • Grid 14
I Bike New York Rentals • 54 Greene St. • 274-1580 • Grid 2
Larry and Jeff's Bicycles Plus • 1690 2nd Ave. between 87th & 88th • 722-2201 • Grid 17
RB Bicycle • 1306 2nd Ave. • 288-5592 • Grid 15
Manhattan Bicycles • 791 9th Ave. • 262-0111 • Grid 11
New York Cyclist • 301 W 110th St. • 864-4449 • Grid 16

Bikes and Mass Transit

Surprisingly, you can take your bike on trains and some buses—just make sure it's not during rush hour and you are courteous to other passengers. The subway requires you to carry your bike down staircases, use the service gate instead of the turnstile, and board at the very front or back end of the train. The commuter railroads require you to purchase a bike permit. See transportation pages (248-260) for contact information.

Amtrak: Train with baggage car required.
LIRR: $5 permit required.
Metro-North: $5 permit required.
New Jersey Transit: Free permit required.

PATH: No permit required.
NY Waterway: $1 extra fee.
Staten Island Ferry: Enter at lower level.
Bus companies: Call individual companies.

Street Index

Street Index

Street Index

Street Index